MW00644057

No Guilty Bystander

No Guilty Bystander

The Extraordinary Life of
Bishop Thomas J. Gumbleton

Frank Fromherz and Suzanne Sattler, IHM

ORBIS BOOKS
Maryknoll, New York 10545

Founded in 1970, Orbis Books endeavors to publish works that enlighten the mind, nourish the spirit, and challenge the conscience. The publishing arm of the Maryknoll Fathers and Brothers, Orbis seeks to explore the global dimensions of the Christian faith and mission, to invite dialogue with diverse cultures and religious traditions, and to serve the cause of reconciliation and peace. The books published reflect the views of their authors and do not represent the official position of the Maryknoll Society. To learn more about Maryknoll and Orbis Books, please visit our website at www.orbis-books.com.

Copyright © 2023 by Frank Fromherz and Suzanne Sattler, IHM

Published by Orbis Books, Box 302, Maryknoll, NY 10545-0302.

All rights reserved.

No part of this publication may be reproduced or transmitted in any form or by any means, electronic or mechanical, including photocopying, recording, or any information storage or retrieval system, without prior permission in writing from the publisher.
Queries regarding rights and permissions should be addressed to: Orbis Books, P.O. Box 302, Maryknoll, NY 10545-0302.

Manufactured in the United States of America

Library of Congress Cataloging-in-Publication Data

Names: Fromherz, Frank, 1953– author. | Sattler, Suzanne, author.
Title: No guilty bystander : the extraordinary life of Bishop Thomas
    Gumbleton / Frank Fromherz and Suzanne Sattler, IHM.
Description: Maryknoll, NY : Orbis Books, [2023] | Includes bibliographical
    references and index. | Summary: "A biography of Thomas Gumbleton,
    auxiliary bishop of Detroit (retired), who has been a prophetic champion
    for peace, social justice, and church reform"— Provided by publisher.
Identifiers: LCCN 2022057390 (print) | LCCN 2022057391 (ebook) | ISBN
    9781626985230 (print) | ISBN 9781608339846 (ebook)
Subjects: LCSH: Gumbleton, Thomas J. | Catholic Church—United
    States—Bishops—Biography. | Catholic Church—United
    States—History—20th century. | Social justice—Religious
    aspects—Catholic Church. | Social justice—Developing countries.
Classification: LCC BX4705.G8433 F76 2023 (print) | LCC BX4705.G8433
    (ebook) | DDC 282.092 [B]—dc23/eng/20230315
LC record available at https://lccn.loc.gov/2022057390
LC ebook record available at https://lccn.loc.gov/2022057391

CONTENTS

CONTENTS

Part Three

PREFACE

Bishop Thomas J. Gumbleton

I am an introvert. This might seem a strange statement since I have from time to time been on the local, national or international platform. But I am at my happiest when I am sitting in a comfortable chair and reading a good book. That is why having someone write my biography has been a bit uncomfortable. I would much rather be reading the stories of others.

There have been some real blessings in this process, however. I have been able to reconnect with friends from the past. We have shared memories long forgotten but cherished nonetheless. I have been reminded once again of what blessings these friendships are for me; what life-lessons they have taught me, and how I have been inspired by them to "Keep on keeping on."

I thank God for all those in my life who have shown me by their example —Thomas Merton, Archbishop Oscar Romero, Franz Jägerstätter, Dorothy Day, Cardinal John Dearden, Archbishop Ray Hunthausen, and many others—what it means to live as followers of Jesus in the struggle for justice. They integrated their whole ways of being into the message of Jesus.

I would add to my "Grateful List" men and women from the parishes where I served who sought to live their Catholic faith in a family setting. I marvel at how parents with jobs, a mortgage, school tuition, managing a household and children, were able to create Catholic families of faith where a guiding principle was the Beatitudes.

I would also include those who did not even know they were an inspiration to me. I have encountered young people around the world and in the United States who received little encouragement from within their countries to build the reign of God. They didn't give up. They kept struggling to spread the message of peace and nonviolence. I continue to be deeply inspired by these young men and women.

I feel deep gratitude for a trip I took to the Holy Land during the time I was living in Rome. I went with two other priests, and on the way we visited

Cairo. In that city, we were looking for the place where tradition has it that Mary and Joseph took Jesus. Of course, it was in one of the oldest parts of Cairo. As we walked along, we began to come into a large area that was teeming with homeless people. These were people who were living on the streets all the time, without access to water, food, or any clean clothing. It was a situation of absolute poverty. I grew up in Michigan during the Depression. It was a struggle for my parents to pay their bills, and keep us dressed and fed. But our poverty was nothing like that which I experienced that day.

For all those who have allowed me to share in your lives through my priestly ministry and through friendship, thank you. It has been my privilege to celebrate your families' marriages, births, and deaths—and everything in between: family reunions, graduations, and baptisms. You have allowed me the chance to share in the joys and sorrows of your lives, and I am a better person because of your friendship.

By going back over my ninety-plus years in preparation for this book, I have been reminded of how history repeats itself. As followers of Jesus, we know our clarion call: to be doers of God's word and to build God's reign in the here-and-now. This call is one that has guided my life. The challenge has not changed over the years.

How do we respond to this call? Start with one thing: the defense of democracy, opposition to human trafficking, reform of the prison system, support for LGBTQ rights.... And be aware. Keep reading to find out what is going on in the world and let yourself be touched by the events around you. For example, a recent issue is climate change. We are at the point of bringing harm to our planet that will make it unlivable within the next twenty years. This issue needs to be faced, as Pope Francis spelled out for us in his encyclical *Laudato Si'*.

Lest all of this seem overwhelming, the important thing is to recognize that each of us has a small part to play in the whole picture. No one does it alone. We must join with others in common efforts to bring about the kind of societal changes that are necessary.

Finally, since our task is to build up the reign of God, we must have as our basis a deep and abiding relationship with Jesus. I remember that I was once told that we should act as though everything depended on us and pray as though everything depended on God. But more recently I've come to know that we must pray as though everything depends on us, but that the results depend on God. With that kind of spirit, we can constantly move forward with calmness and determination in our effort to transform our world into as close an image of the reign of God as possible. As Jesus put it in his call to each of us, "The reign of God is at hand. Change your lives."

INTRODUCTION

In *Conjectures of a Guilty Bystander*, the famous spiritual master and Trappist monk-poet Thomas Merton described himself as necessarily something of a "guilty bystander," living a monastic life in retreat from the swirl of social forces and conflicts "out there" in the world. It could be argued, however, that through his prolific writings about the spiritual life and its inescapable ties to wider social currents and concerns, in fact, Merton was no guilty bystander.

The same could be said of the subject of this book, Thomas Gumbleton. When it comes to many things that truly matter, he has not been a guilty bystander. *No Guilty Bystander* captures the broad range of social concerns, historical forces, and systemic injustices, both in society and in the church, that have engaged him. This book endeavors to be a worthy examination of a remarkable life, but it also aims to provide insight on the social forces, movements, and reactions surrounding his life story. The operative premise upon which this book relies is: "Neither the life of an individual nor the history of a society [and a church as well, in this case] can be understood without understanding both." (C. Wright Mills, *The Sociological Imagination*)

From war and peace to poverty and marginalization, from the primacy of conscience to the call to collective advocacy and activism, from pastoring neighborhood parishes to accompanying the vulnerable across the globe, *No Guilty Bystander* relates the story of an extraordinary life. In telling this story we have drawn on a treasure trove of archival sources as well as interviews and conversations with both its central subject and many of the people with whom he has journeyed.

Part One starts not at a chronological beginning but rather at a profound turning point (not the first, and certainly not the last), when Fr. Tom Gumbleton first became aware of what his nation was doing in Southeast Asia. The story then shifts back to the 1930s to his family home and childhood, his seminary years and the emergence of the highly "competitive Gump," then to the young priest who becomes, in 1968, a young bishop called to action on behalf of justice and Gospel-inspired nonviolence, a Christmas Eve presence to U.S. hostages in Tehran, a key role in the committee of bishops charged with writing a pastoral letter on the morality of nuclear weapons, and a tenacious commitment to various forms of peace work during the decades thereafter.

Part Two begins with another period of personal transformation, relating what happened in Tom Gumbleton's heart and ministry when his brother Dan came out as gay. It then traces Bishop Gumbleton's steps as he responded to the assassination of San Salvador's Archbishop Romero, and the brutal rape and murder of his friend Sr. Dorothy Kazel and three other missioners in El Salvador. We chronicle some of his many journeys of accompaniment and solidarity in Central America and follow with the story of his response to the cries of the Iraqi people, the victims of 9/11, and the people of Afghanistan. In the course of his ministry Gumbleton traveled to some thirty countries, some on multiple occasions. No single volume can begin to document the complete itinerary of his global reach; in fact, in the interests of space, we have had to omit numerous campaigns and commitments and greatly abbreviate some of these episodes. But this book includes two poignant and transformative experiences, first in Haiti, his work with Kay Lasante, the nonprofit health clinic he helped to found (the clinic will receive the royalties from sales of this book), and then in a small village in Austria, the home of war objector Franz Jägerstätter. Finally, no adequate account of Gumbleton's ministry could overlook the many years of pastoring and the bonds he made, beginning in 1983, with St. Leo's parish in Detroit, nor what happened in 2006 and 2007 when, on behalf of sex-abuse victims, he gave deeply personal testimony that upset some higher powers in the Catholic Church. This resulted in his removal from his beloved St. Leo's.

Part III offers a portrait of Tom Gumbleton's character, including what might seem to be some contradictions or paradoxes. The final chapter explores his significance, from the wellsprings that have fed his soul to the causes and energies that have propelled him to far corners of the planet.

This is a story filled with pathos and even anger over so many injustices, and yet it is no less a story filled with hope and inspiration, one capable of both probing and stimulating our consciences. *No Guilty Bystander* aims to bring to better light the inner and outer journeys of a man who became a transformational figure on the world stage and in his hometown of Detroit, and whose influence in the church and the wider world is yet to be fully measured or vindicated. May this story offer inspiration and courage in an unjust, conflicted, and anguished world.

PART ONE

1

Personal Turning Point

America's War in Vietnam

He had never thought seriously about the morality of war. Two older brothers had served during World War II, another during the Korean War, and in general his hometown Detroit family trusted the United States government when it came to such matters.[1] He was also a loyal son of the Catholic Church. Ordained to the priesthood at age twenty-six in 1956, he would rise to become a bishop in 1968. His boss, Archbishop John Dearden, one of the country's more powerful prelates by the close of the Second Vatican Council, would be named a cardinal in 1969. Both men would be strong advocates for church reforms in the spirit of Vatican II, yet both of them had been trained and socialized in a hierarchical-clerical culture.

Most people had paid little attention to America's involvement in Southeast Asia, but in 1965 President Lyndon Johnson ordered a dramatic increase in troops. Before long, tens of thousands of draftees found themselves fighting in a land thousands of miles from U.S. shores. Many had begun to sense that the war in Vietnam was not going to have a good ending. Television news from the jungle battlefront brought troubling images into American living rooms. In 1967, folksinger Pete Seeger put some unsettling lyrics to music: "We're waist deep in the Big Muddy and the Big Fool says to push on."[2]

Already by late 1965 there were priests, nuns, and lay Catholics joining protests in the streets. In the archdiocese of Detroit, many "God and country" parishioners were upset by the presence of activist clergy in some

3

of these protests. "People started to complain," now-retired Bishop Gumbleton recalls. "They wrote letters to the archbishop and the chancery: 'How do you let these priests go against the government?'" Fr. Gumbleton, who was then vice-chancellor of the archdiocese, received word from the chancellor, Msgr. Bernard Kearns: "We are getting all of these complaints about priests and protests and all, so why don't you go and talk with these fellows and urge them to pull back, give us a break, you know, talk them out of these public protests."

Gumbleton drove over to meet face to face with a handful of activist priests who had gathered at Detroit's Visitation Catholic Church. Although he could not recall everyone who was present, almost certainly among the clergy waiting for him were Maurice (Mo) Geary, one of the first to oppose the war, and Dennis Maloney, who had engaged in civil disobedience. He told the priests about the complaints. "I was operating out of my sense that you presume that if the government says go to war, then it is the right thing to do. I hadn't thought much about the war and really didn't know much about it." He let them make their case—for two and a half hours. They were both passionate and persuasive. "By listening to their arguments and the facts as they laid them out, it became clear to me that the war was wrong."[3]

That impassioned discussion at Visitation stimulated his determination to examine the morality of the war. Regretting not having done so back when first introduced to moral theology, he now pored over the writings of Augustine and Aquinas on just war theory. Only from a presumption in favor of peace could one begin to consider any exceptions that might possibly justify war. Among the conditions to be met were that a just war must be declared by a legitimate authority, as a last resort, with good intentions, allowing for the protection of the innocent, and producing more benefit than harm. "Back in seminary we were reasoning on the basis that the presumption is to go to war unless you can prove you should not. We were not even encouraged to prove that you should not. Just do what the government says." He began to listen to more critical voices and ask critical questions of his own. "What if the government hides facts? We were too easily cooperating with the government without due investigation."[4]

As the war escalated, anti-war sentiment reached a fervor. Colleges ran "teach-ins" on racism, classism, and militarism, among other issues. It was in the midst of this turmoil, in the spring of 1968, that Gumbleton became a bishop. But he kept on reading and thinking. One of his favorite writers was Thomas Merton. In the 1960s, the already famous Trappist monk was writing about many social issues including the roots of war. Gumbleton had read Merton's classic spiritual autobiography *Seven Storey Mountain*, when it was first published in the late 1940s, but now he read Merton with a keen eye on social questions. "I looked at what he wrote about nonviolence. I had never really noticed it before." And the witness of Catholic Worker founder Dorothy Day, with her bold pacifism and her solidarity with the poor, captured his imagination. He studied biblical scholarship on the nonviolence of Jesus and examined the writings of scholars such as Gordon Zahn, who researched the case of Franz Jägerstätter, the Austrian peasant who paid the ultimate cost of discipleship by refusing to serve in Hitler's army.[5]

As a new member of the National Conference of Catholic Bishops (NCCB) in 1968, Gumbleton hoped the conference would raise its collective voice against what he had come to view as an unjust war. The prior year or so, with Dearden in a leadership role, the NCCB had justified America's war in Southeast Asia, while urging the government to pursue every opportunity for a peaceful settlement. Rare were the prelates who raised alarms about the perils of escalation. Cardinal Lawrence Shehan of Baltimore spoke out against the war in a prophetic pastoral letter,[6] but Archbishop Patrick O'Boyle of Washington, DC, instructed the priests in his archdiocese not to preach on the issue. "Under no circumstances should they express the individual priest's views about the foreign policy of our government in conducting the war."[7] In early April 1967, in San Antonio, Texas, in the Catholic cathedral, President Johnson, sitting in the front row, listened as Archbishop Robert Lucey praised the war: "Such intervention is not merely allowed and lawful, it is a sad and heavy obligation imposed by the mandate of love." At almost the same time, another religious leader, of a very different worldview from Lucey's or O'Boyle's, climbed the pulpit at Riverside Church in New York City to deliver an eloquent history lesson on the follies of colonialism. Rev. Dr. Martin Luther King Jr. called on leaders of every faith to "to raise our voices and our lives if our nation persists in its perverse ways in Vietnam. We must be prepared to match actions with words by seeking out every creative means of protest possible."[8]

Conscientious Objection

Many Catholic bishops and priests were wary of questioning the government's foreign policies. However, when the NCCB, in a 1968 pastoral letter, *Human Life in Our Day*, spotlighted the primacy of conscience, Gumbleton advocated broadening the scope on life issues to include war as a matter of conscience. The focus on conscience resonated deeply with Gumbleton. Especially significant for him were encounters he began to have with young men who faced their own personal and existential questions of conscience: Would they go to war? Would they serve in a war they thought to be unjust? Could they kill in such a war?

"Sometimes these young people who were questioning the war were derided and disparaged as being 'cowards' or selfish. The ones I began to meet who were seeking conscientious objector's status were not that type at all." He could see in many of them a deep spirit. Local draft boards mostly assumed that a Catholic could not be a conscientious objector (CO). These young men needed letters to support their appeals.[9] Bishop Gumbleton read and responded to many personal declarations of conscience. Each person had to "write their life story, indicating how this kind of conviction had evolved within them, and how it was based on a religious spirit or motivation. Almost no other experience in my life was so moving as to read these deeply probing, and very honest statements of these young men as they searched their own life, their own feelings, their own history, to discover why they knew they could not ever kill anyone else, even in a war that some thought would be just." Their appeals gave the bishop "some of the deepest insights into the true meaning of the life of Jesus that I had ever received."[10]

Nancy Driscoll, Gumbleton's unflappable secretary for many years starting in 1970, has said that the letters started to pour in from young men asking the bishop if he would write to their draft board. "He met with many young men, and he would talk with them on the phone. They weren't all from Detroit, they were from all over the place. Some would come to the office; some would write out maybe three or four pages of what they believed. There were many cases where Tom went to the draft board with them and spoke on their behalf."[11] In one example, he wrote to the chairperson of the local draft board of Roseville, Michigan:

I am writing to you on behalf of Mr. John Dubosh in order to support his claim as a conscientious objector. As a bishop within the Catholic Church, Vicar General and Vicar for Parishes in the Archdiocese of Detroit, it is my responsibility to become involved in and minister to the people of Detroit. In the last few years I have become increasingly involved with many young people who are being faced with very serious questions, both mentally and morally, in regard to war.

I realize fully that one of the more difficult tasks facing a local draft board is the effort to determine the sincerity of an individual who is claiming to be a conscientious objector. Even as a bishop and spiritual leader I would find this a very difficult thing to do. However, it seems to me that the presumption should be in favor of the truthfulness of the person involved. I am convinced that John Dubosh's position as a conscientious objector has been adopted from very sincere motives.[12]

He learned from conscientious objectors something he would later say he ought to have learned long before, but he had never searched out the scriptures, never allowed the life, words, and actions of Jesus to influence him in this profound way. He dug deeper into the writings of Merton and other authors who pointed to what he now saw as "the genuine and true thrust of the Gospel message of Jesus." The COs he supported were deepening his conviction that "the kind of evil that was being done in Vietnam did truly surpass whatever good we had hoped to achieve in that war effort."[13]

Activist priests, like the group he had met at Visitation, continued to influence him. In 1969, Fr. Tom Lumpkin, a young assistant pastor at St. Louise Catholic Church in Warren, Michigan, engaged in conscientious war tax resistance/redirection. When the Internal Revenue Service informed him that he had to pay back taxes, he asked Gumbleton to write to the pastor on his behalf. It was May 1972 when Bishop Gumbleton wrote to Fr. Benedict Rembelski:

Dear Ben,

Recently I got a letter from Tom Lumpkin indicating that he was withholding part of his income tax on the basis of his conscientious opposition to our involvement in the war in Southeast Asia. The Internal Revenue Department has since notified him that he is in arrears. Evidently the next step will be for them to make an effort to obtain the money from his employer. Both St. Louise Parish and the Archdiocese of Detroit are considered to be his employers, and the Internal Revenue might come to you or to us in order to obtain the money. Tom has asked that we not give it to them. I recognize that this may seem unusual, but I believe we ought to honor Tom's request. The amount due is rather minimal actually, approximately $200, but I believe personally that the principle is quite important, and I would like to be sure that we support Tom's position.

He cc'd the chancery's business office, asking that no money be sent to the IRS from the archdiocese either, and wrote a note to Lumpkin, "You're right, things really are wild today. It seems unbelievable that we have to 'break' the law in order to act in a moral way. I appreciate your taking this kind of stand and I will give you whatever support I possibly can."[14]

Early on Bishop Gumbleton put himself in the public square as well. In November 1970, he entered the set of "The Advocates" for a televised debate carried by two hundred public broadcasting stations. Rep. Edward Koch of New York had introduced a congressional bill that would permit eligible men to claim conscientious objection to particular wars, and "Advocates" participants were asked: "Should those subject to military service and those who have evaded it now be eligible for selective conscientious objector status?" According to the law at that time, a draft eligible person had to hold a position opposed to all war in any form in order to qualify for CO status. Selective Service head Curtis Tarr debated with Bishop Gumbleton, asserting that the Koch bill would pose great challenges for draft boards trying to distinguish those "who have a problem of conscience from those who have a problem of politics." Matters of conscience are never merely political, Gumbleton countered. A person could judge a particular war to be unjust even if they were not pacifist. He argued that selective conscientious objection should not only be codified but made retroactive "to give a second chance to men who were denied a chance the first time."[15]

Moral Reasoning on the War

In early July 1971, the *New York Times* published Bishop Gumbleton's opinion essay, which spells out the features of his moral reasoning at that time:

> The military involvement of the United States in Southeast Asia is more than a hotly debated political issue. "Vietnam" is an urgent moral question demanding an examination by all thinking Americans. That war is always a moral matter should be clear enough. Political and military policies which provide soldiers and weapons for the purposes of death and destruction require a moral judgment of the individual citizens with whose tax money and, in some cases, [with whose] very lives those policies are implemented.

He noted that "A citizen is untrue to his human dignity as an intelligent, compassionate person if he surrenders his conscience to his government in time of war," and cited statements by the American Catholic bishops as well as the Vatican on the primacy of conscience, and the statement of Pope John XXIII, who wrote, "Therefore, in an age such as ours which prides itself on its atomic energy, it is contrary to reason to hold that war is now a suitable way to restore rights which have been violated." Gumbleton noted that many might suppose this was a new attitude toward war, yet he traced it back to the earliest Christian tradition.

> Obviously, for one who would follow the earliest Christian tradi-
> tion, supporting the Vietnam War is morally unthinkable. But even
> if one were to base his conscientious judgment of the Vietnam War
> on the "just war" doctrine, I believe his conclusion could only be
> that continuing American military involvement in Southeast Asia
> is gravely immoral.

He laid out the criteria for a just war and applied these in turn to an evaluation of the war in Vietnam.

> What is the cause for which American forces are fighting in South-
> east Asia? Millions of Americans can be excused for having no
> clear answer to that question. We have been given so many differ-
> ent reasons, even to the point where we are told it is simply to up-
> hold American prestige rather than accept the humiliation of de-
> feat. We may be excused for not knowing the reason of the war.
> We cannot be morally excused for participating without sure
> knowledge that the reason is *sufficient*.

Finally, he concluded:

> Whether we judge this war in the light of the earliest Christian tra-
> dition on war, or according to the "just war" doctrine, I can reach
> only one conclusion: our participation in it is gravely immoral.
> When Jesus faced his captors, He told Peter to put away his sword.
> It seems to me He is saying the same thing to the people of the
> United States in 1971.[16]

Gumbleton went on to play a leading role in November 1971 in the approval by the nation's Catholic bishops of a resolution calling for an end to the war. The resolution read, in part: "At this point in history it seems clear to us that whatever good we hope to achieve through continued involvement in this war is now outweighed by the destruction of human life and of moral values which it inflicts." He drew criticism when he pointed out that because a crucial just war criterion, proportionality, was not being met, any person who concurred with this Catholic position "may not participate in this war."[17] But Gumbleton was undaunted and resolute. If he were a young man, he said, he would seek draft status as a conscientious objector. "If refused, I wouldn't go. I'd go to jail, maybe, or leave the country. This is the dilemma that young people face."[18]

Such assertions provoked angry letters. One viewer wrote to him, "Having listened to you on TV a few weeks ago, I was shocked at your stupidity. Your attitude only incites violence, makes cowards, and plays right into the hands of the Communists." Gumbleton replied:

> I am sorry that some of my statements distressed you. I do not believe that we should harshly condemn those who have decided to participate in the war, even if we ourselves come to the conclusion that the war is immoral. . . . And using the same reasoning, I do not think we should harshly condemn those who refuse to participate in what they consider to be an immoral action. In fact, their refusal to participate might cause a number of us to reconsider whether or not the war is as we see it.[19]

Others applauded him. Douglas White of Detroit wrote:

> I am writing to tell you what a great job I thought you did in presenting both your personal position regarding the war in Vietnam and the implications of the Bishops' statement on participation in that war. I was especially impressed with the sensitive manner in which you responded to a radio call by a gentleman who presumably had lost a son in that war. You were able to sincerely empathize with his hurt and pain while at the same time maintaining a well-reasoned and compassionate position regarding the numbers of young people who are in Canada and Sweden and in other ways exiled from this country.[20]

But the attacks were unrelenting. A critic from New York wrote to him:

> What right do you have as a Bishop to urge America's youth to refuse to defend it? Why don't you come out and say what you are really trying to do—undermine the American Government as you have already done to the Catholic Church. Why don't you admit that you are probably lacking in what it takes to defend your coun-

try and are so scared that you are urging the long hairs to follow your suit?...Priests like you are driving Catholics like me out of the Church. Why don't you go first?

Gumbleton responded:

You ask in your letter why I do not leave as a result of my beliefs. However, I have chosen to remain in the active ministry for many reasons. My whole life has been based on the Gospel message of Jesus Christ, and it is for this reason mainly, that I as a priest and bishop have been impelled to speak out on moral issues such as the Vietnam War.[21]

Fr. Daniel Berrigan's Push

On May 13, 1968, nine anti-war activists including Fr. Dan Berrigan and his brother Fr. Phil Berrigan entered the Catonsville, Maryland draft office. They grabbed draft files, headed out to a parking lot, and set the files ablaze. Then they waited to be arrested. The trial of "the Catonsville Nine" drew national coverage. They were sentenced, but before serving prison time for their audacious act of civil disobedience, several of the nine went underground. Dan Berrigan proved the most elusive. In a candid and compelling story, Tom Gumbleton later recounted how Berrigan challenged him.

People all over the country kept up with his flight from the FBI. His spirit of playfulness and creativity served him well as he managed to make the FBI and the whole U.S. government look foolish as he found ways to show up at rallies, make a powerful call to end the killing and bring peace to Vietnam, and then slip away before federal agents could capture him.

Of course, not everyone who heard about Dan Berrigan's activities applauded what he was doing. Many people became angry. Dan was "un-American" or in the eyes of others a genuine traitor to the United States and all it stood for. Within the church his religious superiors and his fellow Jesuits had mixed reactions to him. He generated great controversy.

When he was finally captured and jailed, I confess that I was disappointed. Dan had forced me to do some serious thinking about the war and U.S. involvement in it. This was the effect he had on many people. But for most Catholics, there was a lot of discomfort with his activities against the war. Rallies and marches were bad enough but getting arrested and jailed really upset people.

In my own life I was struggling to determine what my response to the war should be....As my own convictions became more deeply rooted, I talked and wrote about the evil of the war. I began to be attacked as a communist and traitor to the United States. And yet the more I got involved, the more it became clear the war was not justified. I kept working within the framework of the NCCB to achieve a clear judgement by the bishops that from the perspective of Catholic teaching, the war in Vietnam must be condemned. Finally, in November of 1971, a resolution against the war was passed by the U.S. bishops. Since the resolution was developed from an intervention I had submitted, I felt some sense of accomplishment. It seemed to me that such a resolution from the Catholic bishops could have an important impact on U.S. policy and even more have an influence on Catholics who continued to be strong in support of the war.

While this was going on, I was also engaged in national and international meetings to stop the war.... In light of all of these efforts and this much involvement, I was stunned and hurt when I got a handwritten letter from Dan Berrigan in which he expressed anger and frustration that I had not joined in any actions of civil disobedience. Dan was very blunt, and I thought quite unfair in suggesting that I needed to be more outspoken than I had been, especially by risking arrest and jail as a way to protest very clearly U.S. Policy.

In light of all he was doing in opposing the Vietnam War, Berrigan's letter initially struck Gumbleton as "insensitive," and he set it aside from attempting to respond.

Slowly, however, I began to reflect on what he had written. It was not what I wanted to hear. Over a period of a few months, I was able to deal with his anger and I came to realize that it was genuinely out of his deep convictions and his regard for me that he would even bother to write, and to write so honestly. I came to realize that his letter was in fact a real grace to which I was being invited to respond.[22]

Well before he received that challenging letter from Berrigan, Gumbleton had been trying to challenge his colleagues. When the nation's Catholic bishops gathered in Atlanta, Georgia, in April 1972 for their semi-annual meeting, they flatly condemned abortion. The prior November they had called for an end to the war, but Tom wanted a more forceful denunciation. "I would suggest that the bombing in Southeast Asia manifests a profound disregard and a callous disrespect for human life that must be deplored and condemned as strenuously as we deplore and condemn efforts to promote abortion. It seems to me that our selectivity in dealing with important moral issues weakens very seriously our overall credibility and effectiveness as pastors and moral leaders." Some colleagues supported him, just some, not many.[23]

In the course of the war the United States pummeled Vietnam with more than four million tons of bombs, far more than the tonnage dropped by the allies during World War II.[24] At the Fall 1972 NCCB meeting, Bishop Gumbleton renewed his call for a clear condemnation of the bombing campaign. Archbishop Thomas Connolly of Seattle insisted that American peace negotiators demand that "freedom be guaranteed to the people in South Vietnam . . . otherwise we are throwing one million Catholic people to the Communist dogs." But the majority of bishops lent support to a statement close to what Gumbleton sought. The statement was better than the one in 1971, he said, "because it does refer explicitly to the bombing." While his wording calling the bombing "unprecedented" was cut, the bishops supported his amendment addressing the bombing's destruction of the land.[25] They voted 186 to 4 to call for an end to the bombing. Yet he still believed they'd not been bold enough. "The severity of the war, its duration . . . it seems to me by this time we could have made a much more forthright and very clear statement."[26]

A Trip to Vietnam

In late 1972 President Nixon ordered the "Christmas bombings" of Hanoi and Haiphong. The week after Christmas, Tom was headed to Boston to celebrate a nuptial Mass for a young woman and her fiancé, both of whom had been parishioners at St. Alphonsus in Dearborn where he first served as a new priest in the late 1950s. After he landed in Boston and was walking toward the airport exit, he ran into Robert "Bob" Manning, SJ, head of the New England province of the Jesuits. They stopped to talk, both of them deeply troubled by the ongoing war. "Both of us were saying, 'What the hell can we do?!' And so we said, 'Well, maybe we should go over there,' and so we decided we would make a trip together to Vietnam to see for ourselves what was going on and to come back and to be able to speak more definitively about it."

They flew to Vietnam in the spring of 1973. Gumbleton and Manning, together with other members of a small delegation, spent Easter week in Saigon and nearby villages. They visited families of prisoners, priests, and lay leaders, Buddhist leaders, government officials, and young men just released from prison. In a *National Catholic Reporter* story published on the heels of the trip, the bishop wrote that "there are political prisoners in Saigon's jails and in jails throughout the provinces. They are in jail not for any crime, but simply because they are in political opposition to the present government. The proof is overwhelming. And it is clear that these prisoners are subject to inhumane treatment, including deliberate and prolonged torture. I do not make that statement lightly." He described an encounter with young men who'd been released from cramped "tiger cages" designed by a firm in the United States.

> One day we met three of the members of the Young Christian
> Workers. We were gathered in a small meeting room when two of
> them came in. Both were still in a very weakened condition. One
> of them was able to walk only quite slowly. A few minutes later,
> the third young man appeared. I shall never forget that moment
> when he came in the room. None of us knew what to say. He could
> no longer walk. He edged along in painfully slow movements,
> bent over in a sort of squatting posture. It was a pitiful sight. Here
> was a young man who, before his imprisonment, was vigorously
> healthy and active.

All three former prisoners made an urgent plea, "to do whatever we could to intervene for the release of the thousands of others they knew about who were still in jail."[27] In the *NCR* piece, Gumbleton refuted South Vietnam President Nguyen Van Thieu's claim of no political prisoners. "We've been able to gather reliable testimony and documentary evidence in South Vietnam which convinced us beyond doubt there are tens of thousands of political prisoners in Mr. Thieu's many jails, that many of them have been tortured severely, and that most of them are forced to exist under the most inhuman and degrading conditions."

The same person who had perhaps blindly trusted his government earlier in his life and had never really thought about war now unhesitatingly rejected the denials made by American officials, comparing these to the

Watergate affair coming to light. "It's all of a piece. It's the same kind of deception, an utter contempt for law."[28]

The war had become a personal turning point in the life of Tom Gumbleton. For telling the truth as he came to see it and for questioning his own government, he received ample hate mail. One angry man wrote in the aftermath of the American departure from Saigon in 1975: "Gumbleton, you are a son of a bitch and a bastard. If there's anything lower than that, use the term."[29] Whatever else he was, the bishop was not a supporter of the "winners" of the war. In December 1976, he joined ninety signers, including Jim Forest of the Fellowship of Reconciliation, the Berrigan brothers, Bishop Carroll Dozier of Memphis, Dorothy Day, and leaders from other faith traditions in an open letter to Vietnam's new leaders, protesting the injustices committed by the post-war Communist regime. He signed the letter, he said, in part due to his earlier "opposition to the totalitarian regime of (South Vietnamese) President Nguyen Van Thieu and what was done to political prisoners. I'm against that injustice and oppression whoever is doing it."[30]

2

Competitive Gump

On January 26, 1930, Thomas John, the sixth child of Helen and Vincent Gumbleton, was born at home, not in a hospital. The Gumbleton family lived in a modest house on a small lot on Manor Street in Detroit's west side. During the Great Depression they could not always pay the Catholic school tuition until the end of the year. New bicycles bought for the older boys for their newspaper routes were later passed down to the younger ones like Tom. During the Second World War Helen used to send the children, ration stamps in hand, to the meat store a few blocks away. Helen had to be thrifty. She baked bread and stretched things out for her large family, adding milk to the peas, carrots, or corn, for example, and preparing a hardy dinner, usually with meat but always with potatoes.

Vincent worked at Timken-Detroit Axle Company. He had grown up in Holy Redeemer Parish in southwest Detroit, and after graduating from the parish high school he got a job as a clerk at the axle company. When Vincent and Helen were raising their family, to earn extra income he worked on the side as a notary public and did some bookkeeping for a coal company. Helen was born in Canton, Ohio, and her family (Steintrager) went north and moved into the Holy Redeemer neighborhood when her father got a job with Ford.[1] When Vincent and Helen were married, they stayed in that parish, but in 1926 they moved to the new parish of Epiphany, becoming charter members.

The kids grew up in a thoroughly Catholic milieu. Their dad used to kneel at the side of the bed saying the Rosary. "He would very often go to the early Mass before going to work, and I got into the habit of going with him, not every time he went, but quite often," Tom said, recalling the quiet and prayerful setting that always appealed to him. Like his brothers, as an altar boy Tom served the early morning daily Mass, or the one for the school kids, as well the weekend Masses. The house on Manor Street was no more than a stone's throw from the church, and Epiphany Parish provided a vibrant sense of community.[2]

The first of the Gumbleton children, Loretta, was born in 1922. Vinnie was born next, followed in short order by Jerry and then in turn, Ray, followed by Irene who was born only thirteen months before Tom. Soon after Tom was born came Jack, and then Jim. The youngest, Dan, was born in 1934. Except for Dan, who was born in a hospital, all the kids born after Loretta and Vinnie were born at home. The two oldest had suffered brain damage during their hospital births, Loretta seriously and Vinnie less so. Fortunately the other births had no complications. Six years after Dan's birth, Helen went to the hospital on Christmas Eve for what would have been her tenth child. Tom and Jack were serving the midnight Mass. Suddenly the priest announced that the community would need to offer special prayers for Mrs. Gumbleton who was gravely ill in the hospital. "He asked that people pray for her, that she was in danger of death, I don't know exactly how he put it, but it shocked me," Tom recalled. She had developed uremic poisoning and was starting to hemorrhage. Helen survived, but the baby did not make it, nor was Helen allowed to cradle her offspring even for a moment. "My mother later used to say, 'my arms would ache,' because she wanted to hold the baby."[3]

Helen, an industrious and caring mother, always rose early on Sundays to begin preparing breakfast so that everyone else could get to Mass and come home to a special meal. She did the dishes and other tasks but never had anything to drink or eat, fasting all morning before finally attending the 12:30 Mass. Back in those days, one could not eat or drink anything before receiving Holy Communion. Their father walked the kids the short distance to Epiphany. "My dad," Tom attests, "had the easier part in a way, but he had to watch all us kids in church and get us there and back safely."[4]

Vincent kept quite busy. In 1928 he signed up at the University of Detroit. He attended classes there several evenings each week and graduated four years later with a business degree. Before heading to his night classes he would try to make it home after work. On Saturday mornings he would take one or two of the kids with him to Timken. They could play on the office intercom as long as they let him get his work done. Serving as an usher and as a member of the St. Vincent de Paul Society, he was quiet, gentle, and friendly. But it was Helen's gregarious personality that stood out. She would stand on the street corner after Mass, chatting away with neighbors and parishioners. And as a member of Epiphany's Altar Society she helped take care of the sacristy, washing and pressing all the altar linens. She organized card parties to raise funds for the parish.[5]

In January 1947, during Tom's third year of high school, the family moved to a larger house a mile and a half to the south. Rising from a lowly clerk to become the purchasing agent, Vincent was doing well at Timken-Detroit Axle. The family was a little worried when Rockwell took over Timken, but Vincent stayed with the company. A strong work ethic always informed the family. Indeed, back when they were still living on Manor Street, Tom had responsibility for getting the afternoon edition of *The Detroit News* out into the neighborhood to a hundred subscribing families. Jerry and Ray rode the same bicycle route before him, as did his younger brothers Jack and Jim later.[6]

At the age of five, Tom got interested in baseball and every day started reading the sports page in *The Detroit News*. "And I used to listen to the ball games, so that when my father came home I could tell him everything that had happened, almost inning by inning."[7] When he was six years old, his dad took him and his brothers to a Detroit Tigers baseball game. Timken provided complimentary tickets, so they went to more than a few Tigers games. Tom's first decade of life was a big Tiger's decade. They won the Pennant in 1934, and a year later they won their first World Series over the Chicago Cubs. In the fifth and sixth grades Tom was in heaven, as it were, ushering at Tiger Stadium.[8]

The Gumbleton kids loved sports. Whenever weather allowed, they played one sport or another in the small backyard or out on the side street or in the nearby vacant lot. They even played right out in front of the house on Manor Street until the police put a stop to it. In those cold Michigan winters, snowball fights erupted with abandon and the kids built makeshift igloos to protect themselves. They relished ice hockey. On a side street called Orangelawn they skated to their hearts' content on ice-covered packed snow. With skates, sticks, a puck, along with a pair of stones which they placed firmly in the iced snow on either end of Orangelawn to mark the goals, they devised their own hockey rink. Tom and his sister Irene remembered how they would all listen on the radio to Hockey Night in Canada.[9]

Sports came naturally, but not music. His teachers at Epiphany Elementary were the Sisters, Servants of the Immaculate Heart of Mary (IHM). Tom's father had three siblings who joined the IHMs. Later, Irene would join the same community, as would a cousin. Among the IHMs at

Epiphany, Sister Marie Leo oversaw the music department. She was attempting to teach the fourth graders how to sing together, but Tom was a problem. "I was screwing everything up, so Sister Marie Leo very kindly said to me, 'Why don't you just move your lips and not make any sound?'" He took a seat in the back of the room, by chance next to a shelf of books. Since he did not have to sing, he thought, "Well, I might as well read." Sister did not seem to mind. "I did not keep moving my lips, and she didn't care, she was just trying to be kind to me."[10]

Tom and his brothers could be rambunctious. One time Jerry knocked Tom down. Picture the scene. All seven boys had to share the attic which had been turned into a dormitory. Jack and Tom slept in one double bed, Ray and Jerry in another, and Dan and Jim in a third. Vinnie got the single bed. On this occasion, their mother was doing spring cleaning, so all the mattresses were in the back yard airing out. The bed frames were made of metal. Tom and Jerry got to wrestling. "I don't know what we were fussing about, but he gave me a shove and I fell and cracked my head on the edge of a steel bed frame." Helen of course dropped her cleaning project and immediately called the doctor. A member of the parish, he had delivered many of the Gumbleton babies and knew the family well. He came right over, put Tom up on the kitchen table and prepared to sew up the wound, but without using any anesthetic. When he saw the needle, Tom shouted, "Get away from me!" Everybody in the family, with one exception, later testified that this is exactly what happened. According to his mother, Tom was a perfect angel as the doctor sewed up the bloody gash. "I think she was preparing to testify at my canonization or something," he laughed.[11]

Another time, when their parents were away, the boys had a pillow fight. "I got the bright idea, we were trying to duck away from getting hit by the other guy's pillow, so I'm under the bed, sticking my head out, and whoever was attempting to try to hit me, my idea was to pull back so that he would miss me. But instead of pulling back, I ducked. What happens when you're lying on your stomach and you duck?" Tom's face hit the floor. Part of a tooth broke off and flew across the room. Tom had to see the dentist several times just to deaden the pain. "I had this half tooth that turned kind of blackish, and it's the one that I grew up with."[12]

Tragedy at Birth

Loretta, born with a brain injury, never developed beyond the mental capacity of a three-year-old. Helen could not bear the thought of parting with her, but when Tom was about four his oldest sister, about eleven, began having terrible convulsions, even falling a few times on the cement outside the house. Kids in the neighborhood made fun of her. The family doctor eventually persuaded Helen to place her oldest child in an institution, a large facility named Oakdale, in Lapeer, Michigan, north of Detroit by some fifty miles. It would just be too much trying to raise the rest of the kids while dealing with Loretta. "After she got placed my parents would go over to visit her there. It was always a tough day for my mother, because Loretta, after not recognizing them at first, would remember them and was so happy to see them and at the end of the day they would have to leave, and Loretta would be crying. My mother's heart was broken."[13]

One time he saw his father grieving. "My grandfather was sick. I probably knew that, but I had no idea that it was critical. I remember dad coming home to tell my mother. He broke down and cried. I just remember very vividly how sad that was, I remember how it affected him." Vincent was thirty-seven and Tom was seven. "I had no real understanding of death, and I don't have a vivid reflection of the funeral." But Tom could remember his dad weeping. "I could see him crying, sobbing, shaking, he was with my mother, and that just hit me because it was so out of the ordinary. I'd never seen my dad cry before, and I don't think I ever did see him cry afterwards either."[14]

Vocation

When Tom was still at Epiphany Elementary, his older brother Jerry attended the Archdiocese of Detroit's Sacred Heart Seminary. Though Jerry decided to leave the seminary after his first year of high school, there were Saturdays when he had to go to the campus that year. It was not easy to catch the buses on Saturday, so their mother drove Jerry, and Tom rode along on occasion and got accustomed to seeing the grounds. "The idea of going there, I'm sure, was implanted subconsciously in my brain somewhere."

One time, he remembered, when he was an altar boy serving for Holy Thursday Mass at Epiphany he came home exuberant to tell his mother he wanted to be a priest. He had spent what felt like the whole morning in church and loved it. "I remember my mother said, 'Oh that'll be fine.' She didn't discourage me, or she didn't jump up with joy or anything. It was, sort of, 'well, we'll see,' and then I didn't mention it again to anybody until it was time to decide in the eighth grade where I was going to go to high school." One choice was University of Detroit High, a preparatory school attached to the Jesuit university. Another was Catholic Central, where his older brothers attended. For these options he would have to take an entrance exam. As decision time approached, he had made no commitment and the exam dates passed. Only one option remained, Sacred Heart Seminary, where he wanted to be.[15]

Sacred Heart and St. John's

Tom lived at home during high school and his first year of philosophy. But from the start of his seminary years he was not really at home much except on weekends because, he says, "I'd leave for school so early, had to be there by 7 a.m. and then I'd get back home late in the evening, do my chores, eat, and then go to bed." He could have boarded at Sacred Heart Seminary, and he wanted to in tenth grade, thinking it would be nice since he would then not have to ride the buses. "My mother vetoed that very quickly. It was not a money problem. I think she knew that it would not be healthy for me. When I look back, I think that was somewhat decisive because otherwise I would have been cut off entirely from normal society, so at least in the time I was at home I mingled with my brothers and sisters and their friends."

In Over His Head

In those days Tom mostly read the sports pages and wasn't giving much attention to events in the world—even World War II. His brothers Jerry and Ray, drafted into the war, came home safe. He realized they could have died but did not think about the moral questions they would face if they had to kill someone. When atomic bombs wiped out Hiroshima and Nagasaki in early August of 1945, Tom was far from the horror, working at an idyllic summer camp in northern Michigan.

A doctor and his wife managed the Catholic camp that sat by Crystal Lake one mile from Lake Michigan. The camp hosted three dozen boys, ages six to thirteen. Tom and another seminarian were camp counselors. Occasionally they would take the boys on overnight outings, and on one of those outings Tom accompanied the kids down to the banks of the Platte River. He was an excellent swimmer, to be sure, and lap swimming became a lifelong habit. But his aquatic acumen was about to be put to the test by the Platte. The river was not that deep, perhaps no more than three feet in most places, but the current could be deceptive. "I did not have enough sense to realize that this was not a very smart thing to do. We're in the river, and the kids are splashing and playing around. One kid got caught in the current and started to be swept down the river. I heard him thrashing and screaming. He was going down, and he couldn't get back on his feet." Tom, as rapidly as he could, caught up with the panicked boy. Both were now at nature's mercy, but Tom managed to get them over to the side of the river, near the bank, where he grabbed hold of a low-hanging tree branch.

> When I bumped into Al later in life, as an adult, two or three times, at whatever parish he belonged, he would always thank me. And I thought to myself, that was so irresponsible, I could have been responsible for his losing his life. That was kind of an eye opener for me about responsibility. He was always so profoundly grateful, but I realized that could have been life changing. If he had drowned, I don't know what I would have done.[16]

The nearly fatal episode tugged at Tom's conscience.

Do as Your Government Bids

While he was at camp that August, very far away in another part of the world something with profound global implications took place, twice in three days. What it meant to his own conscience and what he would do about it would have to wait many years.

> The main thing I remember is that nobody knew at the time what had happened. You know, the adults heard the radio and saw what was in the paper a day or two later, and there was this notion that some big bomb, bigger than the world had ever known, had exploded.... There was no understanding, the facts weren't out, about how many people were killed, but it was enough that the emperor agreed the war would end. Everybody was puzzled, the doubts, talking to each other, what could this be, nobody knew at the time.[17]

When Tom entered major seminary at St. John's in the early 1950s, he still had not begun grappling with the moral questions of war. "I had no understanding of the nonviolence of Jesus." The moral theology professor, Sulpician Fr. Ed Cope, a gentle, holy person, was admired by all. The Sulpicians staffed St. John's, and at the beginning of the year each student would choose a confessor. "The older students got to pick their confessor first, so after the seniors and then the juniors had selected their confessor, he was always gone by the end of the second round." Tom finally got to have Fr. Cope as his confessor in the second to his last year at St. John's. "Everybody wanted him; he was so good." Cope had been a Navy chaplain in World War II and survived when a torpedo sank his ship. Every year, as Tom recalled, Cope would take up the subject of war.

> Everybody listened carefully because we knew of his experience, and he would always start off his lectures by saying how terrible war is, that war is hell, there is no other way to describe it, it is evil, it is horrendous, and then he would go on to explain why sometimes you have to go to war. He explained the conditions and so on, but then concluded the lecture by saying, "Later on, when you're in a parish, if our country goes to war again, and I pray to God that we won't, but you will have to teach the people that their responsibility is to go to war. If the government says you must go to war, you must take their word for it. We can't know all there is that we need to know to make a decision, so you have to tell the people that it is their responsibility to let their government go to war."

No Peace on the Rink

Another friend from his seminary years, Fr. Norman Thomas, started high school at Sacred Heart a year ahead of Tom. "If anybody would be an advocate for peace," Norm says, "it would not be Tom Gumbleton." Like Tom, Norm loved the intensity of sports and both of them were intensely competitive. Norm's class frequently matched off against Tom's.

> Throughout our seminary years we had some very fierce football games. Tom may not have been the best athlete, but he was the most passionate. On the hockey rink, football field, anywhere, handball!! You know, handball isn't a contact sport, a bump sport, like in basketball or football where you bump people, but imagine the way he hit the ball! Bam! He hit it as hard as you can. That's what he did in everything, hit it as hard as you can and something

good will happen. And if you were in the way of it, you were going to get hit.

Tom was not that way off the field, according to Norm's recollection. "Once he took the football pads off, or the hockey skates, he was quiet and retiring. He was a good guy to be with, to just have fun with, he appreciated a laugh." They "hung out" together with Norm's classmate Bill Walsh and Tom's classmates Jim Maloney and Dan Walsh, among others. In that circle Tom's nickname was "Gump." Gump, Norm, and buddies did things together on the weekends, like drive around, or visit each other's homes. They played hard. One time in the basement of the Gumbleton house one of them sent a hockey puck flying into the wall.[18]

At music Tom was ever a fish out of water. In the large chapel at Sacred Heart, choir was hardly his favorite time. Mercifully, in the last year of theology at St. John's, months before his ordination in 1956 somebody tape-recorded all the parts of the Mass that were to be sung. Every night Tom could listen to the recording. If he could start on the right note, having memorized the music, he was okay, but he could never pick up a melody impromptu. But at sports he was ever in his element. Friday afternoons, during high school, there was an assembly. Monsignor Mattyn was the dean of discipline in those days, Tom remembered. "We called him Big Al, but not to his face." He would tell the students about their faults, right there and then during the assembly. Since too many demerits could get you put on a work crew, Tom assiduously avoided getting demerits so that he could spend more of his time at sports. Billy Rogell, shortstop for the Detroit Tigers, and catcher Mickey Cochrane were inspirations. Tom got to be a pretty good fielder, short stop, and catcher, though he was never great at bat. In high school and college he played half back on the football team. He played tennis. Whatever the sport was, he played it with vigor.

But ice hockey was always his true passion. Visiting Sacred Heart Seminary in 2019, he remarked as he looked over the grounds, "We played hockey out here, on the tennis court. And we built a hockey rink with snowbanks." At St. John's in Plymouth, west of Detroit, a golf course had been designed by Cardinal Mooney, the seminary's founder. But golf was one sport Tom never took up. He much preferred to swing a hockey stick. He played left wing. When he was in the seventh and eighth grades, he would go with his brothers to watch the Detroit Red Wings and was always inspired watching the greats who played left wing, like Ted Lindsey and, later, Gordy Howe. He never wanted to have to stay back from the forward line. "I wanted to shoot. I was left wing because I could send a shot from that side."[19]

In the dead of winter, the two intramural class teams, Norm's and Gump's, faced off on a frozen pond in the middle of Mooney's golf course. The golf course was blanketed in heavy snow. Norm Thomas:

> Gump was aggressive. He was cross-checking, poking with his stick, elbowing and all these sorts of things that he was good at and known for. He would take the puck and go, and if anybody got in his way, he would just go through them, straight through them. He didn't fool around with a lot of fancy stick handling. He did not have the finesse that some players had. So, there were a lot of collisions. If a player was coming down the ice on offense, and you were playing defense, you would normally expect the opponent on offense to go around you. Not Gump, hardly ever. He comes straight ahead, bangs right into you, tries to knock you over.[20]

They were both high-spirited on the ice. Next to the frozen pond there was a small hill. Norm could not recall who was at fault, but one of them, either Gump or himself, chased the other up that hill with a hockey stick! Decades hence, as old friends, they still laugh and "compete" over versions of what happened and who as at fault.

3

Doer of the Word

Ordained on June 2, 1956, Fr. Gumbleton went to work at a parish of four thousand families in Dearborn, Michigan. "I lived according to the standard they taught us at the seminary. You work inside those parish boundaries. That is where you are going to save your soul. You don't have to worry about the whole world. That is where you served God, and for me it was almost all sacramental, personal, individual piety. There was practically no concern for social justice."[1] He taught religion and through his students he got to know their parents. Soon they were forming Christian Family Movement groups. St. Alphonsus Parish was his life. "Everything would be for them, teaching, counseling, giving the sacraments, taking care of the sick. I had a day off, and it was good to play ball, go out to eat or to a movie, but the whole thing was that parish."[2]

He paid $1,600 cash for his first car, a Chevrolet. "I did not want car payments or other money worries hounding me." He had the bad habit of driving too fast, but he developed a more careful approach to pastoral ministry, taking the time to get to know the people of the parish, many of whom would become lifelong friends.[3] One day a thirteen-year-old came to the rectory's front door. She introduced herself as Christine Lynn and she said she wanted to become a Catholic. Fr. Gumbleton asked about her parents, would they be okay with this. She gave him their phone number and when he called them, they said, "If she wants to be Catholic, that's fine with us." So he gave Christine Lynn instructions in the faith over a period of nine months or so and then baptized her. He stayed connected with Christine long after his time at St. Alphonsus, doing weddings and baptisms for three generations of her family.[4]

Jan Hunt was a student at the grade school. One day she had to be taken to the hospital, suffering from acute appendicitis. Priests would often go to visit patients at the hospital, and that day Gumbleton was on assignment. He did not know where to go down the corridor to find the patient he was supposed to visit, but he heard a voice wafting through the hallway. Jan, sitting up in bed and recuperating from surgery, was singing *O Salutare* and *Tantum Ergo*. "From then on, we were pals. He would come to high school basketball games, you know, really to be part of everybody's life. In my family he was part of everything important that happened from then on."

One time Jan and her three siblings were at home with just their grandmother and their dad. Their mom was still in the hospital, having just given birth to a fifth daughter. Their dad had had a serious heart attack at home, and the doctor felt that any movement would be risky so they could not take him to the hospital. The next day Jan's sister Ann went upstairs to get a pair of shoes. When she came downstairs, she told their grandmother, "Daddy looks like he's dead." "Don't talk like that," said Grandma as she hurried up the stairs. "I thought somebody should call the rectory," recalled Jan, "so I called Tom who was on duty, and he was over in five minutes and ran up, took the stairs three at a time, to give my dad the sacraments." In the living room, a short while later, Jan asked, "He's dead, isn't he?" Fr. Gumbleton told her the hard truth. Long afterward, when reminiscing, his eyes welled up as he told Jan, "I was hoping I would be there in time for him."

At the large St. Alphonsus Parish, Tom and three or four other assistant pastors helped the pastor, Auxiliary Bishop Alexander Zaleski. "When Bishop Zaleski would have a High Mass, Fr. Gumbleton would give him the crozier," Jan recalled. He was a dutiful and loyal participant in the hierarchical structure, but he had a budding pastoral spirit. Jan played basketball, and he started coming to her games. He would stand at the gym door, she remembered. Everybody saw him and soon realized he was interested in sports as well as the parish and its people.[5]

Judy Beyersdorf (then Judy Perry) was in the seventh grade when Gumbleton first taught religion to her class. "It was the first time I had a teacher who was sharing the Gospel with us in a way that other teachers had not been able to. He lectured and asked questions, but he did not make us nervous." When she was in high school, her class had a carwash at a service station close by. When she came to the rectory, Gumbleton answered the door. She asked him if he could bring his own car over to be washed. So he handed her the keys, let her drive that Chevy, get it washed, and bring it back. Like many other students in the parish, she got to know him as a teacher and spiritual adviser. When he was later in

Rome for canon law studies, he would write postcards to her and to other former students.[6]

Carmen and Eugene Hrynewich got married at St. Alphonsus in 1959, and Fr. Gumbleton officiated at their wedding. He could be rather strict and legalistic at times, Carmen remembered. For example, "He said a singer could sing only at a certain part of the Mass." The photographer received instructions from Fr. Gumbleton, who insisted that photographs be taken only from the back and never from in front of the altar.[7] Over the years they watched him loosen up.

Slow Down

At one of his familiar haunts, the unpretentious Onassis Coney Island diner in Detroit's Corktown, Tom sat eating breakfast. It was late Sunday morning, St. Patrick's Day, 2019, and he was being interviewed for this book. After breakfast, on the road heading to Sacred Heart Seminary where he would recount many memories, he lived up to his reputation as a fast driver. The nervous passenger/interviewer asked if he had ever gotten any speeding tickets. He confessed that one day in 1958 he was on the Edward Hines Drive, on his way out to St. John's Seminary in Plymouth, sailing along at 80 mph in a 55-mph zone. A police officer stopped him. He had to follow the police car to the police station, pay the speeding ticket, and then explain it all to Bishop Zaleski.[8]

He was not so fast in coming to consciousness about systemic injustice in Dearborn. The long-time mayor, Orville Hubbard, was re-elected again and again in the late 1950s, 1960s, and into the 1970s. Hubbard let it be known that no Black person would ever reside in Dearborn as long as he was mayor. The publisher of one of the two Dearborn papers decided to challenge Hubbard in the mayoral race. The challenger, widely respected, was a parishioner at St. Alphonsus. Not only was he crushed by Hubbard in the election, but his newspaper business was ruined—in a community where Catholics were in the majority.[9] Police cars in Dearborn carried the slogan, "Keep Dearborn Clean," which meant "Keep Dearborn White."[10] The unspoken issue in the campaign was the race question. "Everybody knew it, but nobody would speak of it. I didn't even see the issue as a kind of sin infecting the parish and the whole community. Looking back, I perceive a serious failure in my ministry, but with my background and training, and the expectations I had of my priesthood, I could not have been any different."[11]

Bad Year at the Chancery

In June 1960, after Fr. Gumbleton had been at St. Alphonsus for just a few years, Archbishop Dearden asked him to come work in the Detroit head-quarters as an assistant chancellor. "I worked there for a year, and it was one of the worst years of my life as a priest. I was totally cut off from all the things I was used to doing." On weekends he said Mass and heard con-fessions, but he had little sense of being a priest. "I was the lowest guy on the totem pole in the chancery office and most of the year I was there my job was to review applications for people who wanted to get permissions to separate and divorce." This kept him busy for a few hours each morning, but he lacked the authority to grant or deny requests and had to pass the ap-plications on to another assistant chancellor. "I was sitting there every day, reading these forms, thinking 'I can't do this.'" After half a year he'd had enough. "I wanted to get out of the chancery, and so I'm working up my courage to go to talk with Archbishop Dearden and tell him that I would like to get a parish assignment, but it was a hard decision because we were trained to do whatever we were asked to do. You just obey, and as long as you obey you are fulfilling God's word."

One day he was in the lunchroom up on the eighth floor. Dearden was there having lunch that day. Gumbleton was thinking, "Maybe I'll go down and see him this afternoon," when Dearden suddenly got up, walked around the table, tapped Tom on the shoulder, and said, "I want to see you in my office." Wondering what this was about, he headed downstairs and entered Dearden's office. "You're doing really fine work and we want you to stay in the chancery," the archbishop told him. "I want to send you for further studies in canon law. I want you to go to Rome." Tom was blown over. "I'm sitting there thinking, well, here is my chance. I can say, 'No, I'd rather not go and study because I want to get out of here,' or I can say 'Yes,' and go, and who knows what it's going to be like a couple of years from now, after I come back from Rome. Maybe it will be different, and I'll be okay with it." He decided he would go to Rome.[12]

As Tom boarded a passenger ship sailing from New York to Naples in the late summer of 1961, the Catholic Church and the wider world were heading toward momentous changes. One day, as he walked the deck to enjoy the fresh air, Tom had an early taste of what was to come. A young couple, recognizing his Roman collar, began asking him questions about birth control. "Of course I had all the answers. I had gone through the seminary, and they trained us to answer every question, and I thought I knew. Well, we started discussing and soon I realized, 'What I'm saying doesn't convince this couple.' It made me begin to realize that we don't have all the answers."[13]

When he got to Rome, the air felt energized with an anticipation of the Second Vatican Council. Pope John XXIII had been elected in 1958, the same year John Dearden was appointed to Detroit. "All of a sudden here is this new pope. You'd be walking down the street and there he is in an open car, waving to the people on the street and everybody stopping to cheer, to wave. I mean, it was a small thing but very symbolic of the change that was beginning to happen."

Pope John opened the Council in 1962. Tom could not attend the Council sessions, but there were priests staying at Casa Santa Maria, where he lived, attending and translating for the bishops, so he had a ringside seat. Eminent theologians and scripture scholars including Yves Congar, Karl Rahner, Hans Küng, and Raymond Brown came to Casa Santa Maria and gave talks. "It was enough to really awaken me to the idea that there was change happening and it was going to be big."

He had grown up in a heavily hierarchical church. Authority rested in the pope and was passed down through the cardinals, bishops, priests, and then finally to the people. But as the Council unfolded, that model began to evolve, and with time his whole outlook on ministry would change.

The church is here not to convert every individual person but to insert itself into the world and to become part of the people of the world, their joys, their hopes, their griefs, their anxieties, that's where the church is supposed to be, to insert itself into the world around us, which means the people, and to bring about a transformation of the world so that it begins to look like the reign of God. So this gave a whole different thrust to my understanding of the priesthood. That was a huge shift. You're not trying to convert every person; you're trying to transform the world.[14]

But such transformation did not happen overnight. Being an introvert, Tom did not interact easily with most of the students. He got quite homesick that first year in Rome. "I didn't know what it was at first, but I was intimidated by the whole thing before I figured ways to cope." Little by little he made a few friends, especially within his own age cohort. Courses were taught either in Latin or Italian, which he did not really understand, when spoken, despite having studied Latin for six years in the seminary. He worried that he might not be able to handle it. After Christmas that first year, he began to feel less anxious. Some of the veteran students shared a survival tip: many professors gave the same lecture year after year, and one could buy lecture notes translated into English. Nevertheless, like everyone else in the program, he faced the hurdle of a single exam for each course at the end of the year. No quizzes, no conversation in class, nothing that would allow the student to impress the professor before the "do or die" oral exam. A whole year could be lost in fifteen minutes. "So, over the years people had developed a way of coping, and that got passed onto me. You got the notes, you studied those notes, and you got enough of the Latin so that you could spit back the words. All you had to do is catch what they were asking for and then give back the answer."

Three years of canon law produced a thesis on separation and divorce, comparing Michigan civil law with Catholic canon law. Defended before the canon law faculty of the Pontifical Lateran University, Gumbleton's *Separation and Divorce: A Comparative Study of the Canon Law of the Catholic Church and the Civil Law of the State of Michigan Looking Toward a Solution to the Problem of Family Break-up*, included a passage suggesting his resonance with the emerging Vatican II spirit of dialogue: "In a pluralist society, such as we have in the United States, it is right that Catholics exercise their freedom to *persuade* (Gumbleton's emphasis) others of the wisdom of their approach to the solution of problems that are common to all."[15]

To See the World of Injustice

For Easter break in 1962, Tom and a couple of other priest-students living at the Casa Santa Maria took a flight to visit the Holy Land. They added to their itinerary a brief visit to Cairo, Egypt, where, on Palm Sunday, they settled into their hotel. The next day they headed out, hoping to see where Mary and Joseph had lived with the child Jesus when they fled to Egypt. "Of course," Tom recalled, "it may not have been an historic place but there were enough traditions, so we got directions and we started off." Cairo was huge, and they were in some of its oldest parts. As they walked, the poverty of the surroundings became increasingly obvious. He had never seen anything this dire. "I'm looking around, and it just gets worse the farther you walk... animals on the loose, dirt, garbage, everything on the streets. Yet people are sleeping there. They have no place else to go." He thought, "I've got to do something, how can I look at this and walk through this area and not help some of these people?"

"I felt really helpless, and then I felt like I was disrespectful, to put it mildly, because I'm walking through this area, staring at these people like they're animals in a zoo or something. They really did seem less than human the way they had to live, and that hit me profoundly. It was one of the things that made me realize there is a whole different world that I never knew about. Deep in my interior somewhere, I made a commitment to find out about why this is, where else it is, and what can be done about it. This was the first opening I had to the idea of trying to do justice in the world." That moment unsettled him. "Sooner or later I knew I would have to act upon what I had experienced there."[16]

Before he completed his canon law studies, his parents came over to visit him. They really wanted to see Ireland. The Gumbleton heritage traced back to Germany to the fourteenth century, but Vincent Gumbleton wanted to find Irish relatives. So off they went, his parents and Tom. In Dublin they examined a book of official families, but there was no mention of the Gumbleton name. Tom's dad got a telephone book of the whole country and found the name in the listings for Derry and Cork. So they headed by car for Cork. "As we're getting close to the city, we came around the bend in the road. Right in front of us was a pub, and there was a sign that said 'J Gumbleton,' and my dad said, 'We've gotta stop!'" It was mid-afternoon and the place was nearly deserted, but a kind lady greeted them and sent them to the nearby parish where, she said, they would find Fr. William whose mother was a Gumbleton. At the parish Fr. William invited them in for supper and told them how Gumbleton ancestors from the northern part of Germany had come to Ireland in the 1500s. "That was okay with my dad, four hundred years!"[17]

When Tom returned to Detroit upon completing his canon law studies, things were changing. Dearden was eager to make Vatican II a reality in Detroit, and Gumbleton was receptive. With their backgrounds in a top-down and legalistic model of church they both had room to grow. "I got into the beginnings of new parishes and the construction and renovation of church buildings, trying to help in designing worship space most effectively for the renewed liturgy." Dearden had come to Detroit from Pittsburgh with a reputation as "Iron John," but soon Detroit would be known across the nation "as a place where a lot of priests would say, 'Boy, you guys are lucky.'"[18] Dearden appointed Gumbleton to be vice chancellor in 1965. Gumbleton oversaw the new Archdiocesan Opportunity Program (AOP), related to Detroit's Total Action Against Poverty program which was linked to the Johnson administration's War on Poverty and the Office of Economic Opportunity. The AOP fostered programs to attack the causes

and conditions of poverty. In February 1965, Tom spoke at a teacher's institute held at the University of Detroit.

> We move away from sections of the city where the poor are; we
> never walk thru their neighborhoods, down their streets, into their
> homes. But what a difference it can make in us if we begin to see
> the suffering of the poor first-hand.... Maybe this is what we need;
> to get among the poor in order to begin to understand the dimen-
> sions of the problems.
>
> This is the problem of poverty—as it exists in our society—
> today, for people—men, women, children, mothers and fathers—
> here in Detroit. But a tragic thing is that this kind of poverty, this
> kind of suffering is going on all around us, and we can be com-
> pletely oblivious of it, and more sadly, completely indifferent to it.
> The poor today have been called the "invisible" poor.... Poverty is
> a cruel fact for thousands and thousands of people in the Archdio-
> cese of Detroit.[19]

When the historic march from Selma to Montgomery took place in
March 1965, several priests and nuns from Detroit participated. A solidarity
march also happened in Detroit. Tom was not in the vanguard of the civil
rights movement, but he was beginning to open his eyes to the connections
between racism and economic injustice. As coordinator of the Urban Renewal Institute that trained priests and nuns for team ministry across traditional parish lines, he gave a sermon at Detroit's Church of the Madonna in
July 1965:

> We must be interested in one another, and we must be ready to
> help one another.... Instead so many of us can be—and have
> been—indifferent to the poor among us. There are people, and not
> just a handful, who suffer from hunger right here in Detroit. And
> so many of us have been indifferent to the cruel injustice that
> every Negro in our city and country has lived with for 300 years.
> One of the most important features of renewal within the church is
> a return to the idea that we, the people of God, must strive for holi-
> ness together, that we must pray together, that we must take part in
> the Eucharist together and that we must carry that spirit of prayer,
> love, and community into our daily lives—to all, especially to the
> poor and those afflicted most by the injustice that has been built
> into so much of our daily lives.[20]

Inter-parish sharing and cooperative team ministry brought together diverse skills and expertise, so that inner city priests, sisters, and laity could serve three or four parishes together. The Urban Renewal Institute focused on neighborhood social realities.[21] In September 1965, *Detroit Free Press* religion writer Hiley Ward described the Archdiocese of Detroit becoming "more invigorating as the days go by. This week the Archdiocese was sitting down with local Protestants to map out its proposed joint venture in race relations and related projects...." The renewal efforts were being led by young priests, among them "the new vice chancellor Very Rev. Msgr. Thomas Gumbleton in his mid-thirties and new assistant chancellor Rev. Ken Untener in his late twenties, and the Very Rev. Msgr. Joseph Imesch, Archbishop Dearden's secretary, in his mid-thirties."[22]

So much was happening, including Tom's emerging anti-war efforts, already covered in this book's opening chapter. As to the impact of Vatican II, the flux of church reform could be unsettling.

In 1965 and 1966 the cracks in the dike weren't yet showing. Great numbers of religious hadn't really left yet, but something was happening, and we wanted to get a better picture of what priests' attitudes were, so I got involved in setting up meetings of open discussions between Dearden and priests of the diocese. Dearden met with sixty or seventy priests a week for eight weeks and we followed up with a questionnaire. Among the things that came strongly back was that there was a lot of ill feeling about the pastor-assistant relationship. There was the feeling that the rectory was the pastor's home, the housekeeper was the pastor's housekeeper, and the assistants were sort of tolerated. Many had no rights and couldn't even bring their friends in to visit.

We also discovered that many priests were beginning to feel inadequate to the new pastoral demands that were being made of them. So we started a crash course on how to be a pastor for those men about to be named to the position. Also, a lot of older priests felt ill at ease with the new liturgy. Many too, were not familiar with any other kind of relationship in the rectory than the old "pastor-assistant" relationship, which often left the assistant pretty much a non-person. But the system perpetuated itself because many times the assistant who spent his priesthood in that kind of relationship was not able to act any different as a pastor than the men he had worked with previously.[23]

Guys going through a lot would come to see him. Some sought permission to leave the ministry. Young men preparing for the priesthood had no normal social development or relationships through high school, college, and theology. Some who left the priesthood looked back and realized that their ordination had come at a time when they were not prepared to make such a decision, especially the decision of celibacy. They had no understanding of what it even meant. "You know, I can say that from my own experience as well. As long as the church was that really tightly enclosed structure, the bishops could keep control of this, but after the Vatican Council more openness developed, based on the understanding of the church as the people of God."[24]

Riots and Rebellion—Summer 1967

In America and in Detroit, white racism had long been (and remains) deeply entrenched, tightly enclosed, and structural. Any number of painful realities facing the Black community could have sparked the riots and the rebellion in the summer of 1967. Gumbleton was living at Church of the Madonna Parish on Oakman Boulevard. About two miles to the south, a riot broke out after midnight when the police manhandled people they arrested at a "blind pig" bar on the corner of 12th and Clairmount. The police shoved them into a paddy wagon, and there was a scuffle. That morning, Sunday, July 24, Tom was driving south down 14th Street to where he would turn over to 12th. He could see police barricades. "They had blocked off the streets and I did not know what was going on, but I knew I had to say Mass. I pulled up to one of the police officers." Mass that morning was at St. Agnes, and he could see the church from where he had stopped. "I've got to get to that church over there for Mass," he told a police officer who at first did not budge but eventually let him through. After Mass, Tom walked over to see what was going on. Things had quieted down, so he headed back to Madonna.

That afternoon Gumbleton attended a concert at Oakland University, thirty miles to the north. Around 7 p.m. he headed home, traveling south on I-75. Detroit was in the distance. "I could see all these flames, so I turned on the radio and that's the first time I found out that what I thought had amounted to nothing in the morning turned out to be quite an incident. ...By the time I headed home there were fires going on in the lower east side of Detroit that you could see from five or six miles away." The riots, later described as a rebellion, went on from Sunday until Thursday. He managed to find his way to work each day at the chancery downtown but observed the fear on the faces of National Guard soldiers, young, white, and mostly from outside the city. "You could tell they were afraid. They were posted just outside the neighborhood where I lived, and they were checking cars coming in. They were armed but they were very tentative. They were not used to being in the city and they were not used to being in all-Black neighborhoods."

He did whatever the soldiers told him to do. "With a nervous kid, if you start acting smart or something you do not know how they are going to react." Many of his friends, including Fr. Frank Granger at St. Agnes and other priests at neighboring parishes, hunkered down. It was not safe to go out. Stores and homes were burning. A few priests made efforts to provide support for the mostly Black families in these neighborhoods. "It was a very tense time during those days. I wasn't in the thick of it, but I was in contact with those who were." Much of the Madonna neighborhood, at the north end of Detroit's core, was destroyed. Mayor Jerome Cavanagh and Governor George Romney asked President Johnson for help. Gumbleton could remember "tanks rolling down the streets in the downtown main area and soldiers coming in to take positions, to establish a curfew and keep people off the streets and bring the riots to an end."[25]

Jerry (Tom's brother) and Marian were raising their family in Precious Blood Parish, a relatively calm area. Tom often visited with them and his nephews and nieces. He happened to be at their home one of the evenings during the rebellion. For his safety, Marian encouraged him to stay overnight. But, according to his nephews Jerry Jr., Tom, Pete, and Bill, their Uncle Tom told their mom, "Don't worry, I have my collar on, they will leave me alone." He left and drove back to his parish while the violence was happening.[26]

When the tinder first burst into flame, Fr. Norm Thomas was visiting his own parents and heard on the radio that something was happening over on 12th Street. So he drove over to St. Agnes around four in the afternoon. He saw fire hoses all over. Some of the buildings were on fire. "I stayed there at St. Agnes that night and all that week. I wanted to be there to see what was happening. John Markham was an assistant there, Frank Granger was the pastor, and Arnie Duard was an assistant there as well." They had dinner together. The next day the National Guard arrived, all white, disorganized, not knowing what they were doing. On one of those days, Julian Witherspoon, a Black community leader, came to St. Agnes. "John Markham and I were outside, and Witherspoon said, 'there's a guy right in front of my house who was shot.' We said, 'Okay, Julian, we'll drive over

there.' There was a guy lying there. And a National Guardsman was standing there, and he had taken his name off his badge." A friend of the
wounded man asked the priests if they could take him to Henry Ford Hospital. Norm said, "This is your car, you drive." The wounded man's friend
beseeched Norm, "Please, Father, please drive!" Norm drove to the hospital emergency entrance, arriving too late. The victim was the last of the
forty-three people killed during those few chaotic days. The friend of the
deceased had not wanted to drive because he had taken a bullet in the
shoulder.[27]

In the years after World War II many whites started leaving for the suburbs, but after the summer of 1967 white flight only grew. Dearden would
not ignore the racism, and nor would Gumbleton. Tom had a friend who
worked at the National Bank of Detroit, so together with a sociologist from
Wayne State University they teamed up to help identify people whose
homes had been burned down. They established a program called Homes
by Christmas. "We sought out the people who needed homes and we tried
to make sure that every family that was burned out was in a home by
Christmas." They helped seventy families. Dr. Sally Cassidy, the sociologist, played a key role speaking with the families and getting the help they
needed to get set up in a new home. Then the mayor and the governor organized what they dubbed the New Detroit Committee, made up of business,
church, and government leaders. Joseph Hudson Jr., who owned the Hudson Department Store founded by his father, chaired the committee, and
Gumbleton represented the Archdiocese of Detroit.

In addition, the Archdiocese of Detroit had an annual fundraising drive,
and normally the funds were used for capital improvements to church prop-
erties. But after 1967, Dearden announced that the fund would be invested
and used to help people who had suffered from all the chaos. Gumbleton
chaired the awards committee. One grant was just $10,000, but controver-
sial. Sheila Murphy, the daughter of the founders of the Catholic Worker
house in Detroit, was involved. Years later, after she married Ken Cockrel,
an attorney and community activist, Sheila (Murphy) Cockrel became a
member of the Detroit City Council. But in 1968 she organized an effort to
train people in how to respond if police came down on them. Often when
the police came out, especially on horses, they could be brutal. "They
would charge into the crowd," Tom remembered, "and we would train people to make sure they got the badge number of any police that acted
wrongly." Community members were taught not to overreact to police misconduct. The grant upset white Catholics in the suburbs. Many of the cops
were Catholics, supported by white suburbanites who thought "their" police

officers could do no wrong.[28] Norm Thomas, involved with the Archdiocesan Development Fund, remembered that Dearden was troubled by the uproar but maintained support for the "cop watch" project even though white parishioners kept telling him, "Our money is being used to watch our Catholic cops!"[29]

Holy Ghost

Gumbleton's eyes were really opened to the entrenched nature of racism when he pastored at Holy Ghost, a mission church, shortly after the summer of 1967. Traditionally, most mission churches were established in rural areas and it was unusual for a mission church to be established in a city. Yet in this case, the main church was Sacred Heart in downtown Detroit, and Holy Ghost was more than seven miles away with many churches in between, about a half a mile from Detroit's northern border, and close to the Sojourner Truth Housing Project that had been designed in the early 1940s to house Black defense workers who were crucial to making Detroit the "arsenal of democracy." Gumbleton had lived for a while at Sacred Heart before he moved to Holy Ghost. "That's when I started to grow in my consciousness. I began to see what Norm was doing." Fr. Norm Thomas made real efforts at Sacred Heart to encourage Gospel music and to welcome a strong African American cultural basis for the parish. Black Catholics started to flock there.[30]

Holy Ghost originally had its own school but not for a good reason. Six blocks west was Corpus Christi, all white, and the people attending Holy Ghost could easily have gone to school at Corpus Christi, but that white parish was not hospitable. About half a mile to the north was St. Bartholomew's Church and they could have taken the African American community, but just like Corpus Christi they were inhospitable. About a mile to the south was the Polish neighborhood and they too were unwelcoming. Instead of resisting all this segregation, the Archdiocese of Detroit built the mission church, Holy Ghost, and the small school there for the African American community in the early 1940s. By the late 1960s, the Holy Ghost Fathers, who served both Sacred Heart and the mission parish for many years, could not staff Holy Ghost anymore, so the vicar of parishes, Tom Gumbleton, had to find a candidate to take over as pastor.

Nobody wanted to go to Holy Ghost, so I took it myself. That is when I realized the extent of segregation and discrimination in the archdiocese. Corpus Christi, six blocks away, took Black kids into their school, because at that point that neighborhood was changing so quickly, and they were losing school population and they needed students. Now, a year later, when those kids graduated from grade school and applied to Catholic high schools, the high schools would take the white kids from Corpus Christi but refused the Black kids. We called the high school principals and told them that they had to take them. They agreed when Archbishop Dearden told them that this was against church law, against moral law, "You can't do this," so they did agree to take the Black kids as well as the white kids from Corpus Christi.[31]

On many issues Tom was, according to Norm Thomas, "the one who went out and did the actual work and confronted the priests to make the changes. He was tough, I'll tell you, and some of the older guys didn't go for that." Norm ran the Urban Ministry office before he became the pastor at Sacred Heart, and he knew that Gumbleton could make things happen. "Gump was fast, I hardly ever saw him, he was working. So occasionally at night we would sit around and argue, mostly about stuff we should be doing as church, which way the church should be going. He lost all that legalistic stuff earlier. He lost it when he got in parishes like Holy Ghost and all."[32]

To Become a Bishop

Scores of men were leaving the priestly ministry by 1968, so Tom could not help but think about it himself. "Other people would say the same thing, 'Well, you know, if so and so left how can I stay, that person was such a good priest and he's gone, what am I still here for? Better people than me are leaving.'" Social life was more open. A priest could develop relationships with other people, including women. "So when I got the letter to become a bishop, that's the first time I made a decision, explicitly, to commit myself to celibacy." As was customary, the letter arrived under papal secrecy. He could not tell anyone about it except his confessor. The letter came from the Most Reverend Luigi Raimondi, Rome's apostolic delegate in DC. "The letter tells me I have to answer within twenty-four hours, by telegram." Before sending the telegram, he wanted to talk with somebody. Fr. William Lynch, who had been his spiritual director and confessor at Sacred Heart Seminary, was still his confessor, but Tom did not feel very close to him. Tom went directly to St. Aloysius Church. He prayed. Things ran through his mind. Which path to take? What would happen if he became a bishop? Could he do this? Would this fit for him? "I had some sense, you know, when you become a bishop, you become even more of a public figure than as a priest. As a priest you become somewhat of a public figure, but it's much more limited. As a bishop, even if you are an auxiliary, you are more public and you circulate among all the parishes of the diocese, not just the one parish where you are assigned." He asked himself, "Do I want to do that kind of work, pastoral work on a bigger scale than a parish and be more in the public forum?" And what about celibacy? "If you decide, you are saying yes to celibacy for the rest of your life." Alone in a pew in the silent church, he got the brainstorm to go see Dearden. "I thought, what the heck, anybody can be my confessor, and I wanted to talk with the archbishop about it."

He knocked on Dearden's door. "He was not used to having to break his routine, so he didn't jump up and smile and say, 'Oh, come on in.' I got more of the 'What are you doing here?' kind of look." Dearden was not rude, but he was surprised. "I said, 'I'm going to make you my confessor,' and I'm sure he thought, 'What the hell, what's he got to confess that he's got to come to me?' So I told him, 'I've got this letter, and I'm not sure whether I should say yes or not.' I explained to him my hesitations, and even asked him, 'Would I have to give up hockey?' He just laughed and said, 'Oh, don't worry about it, they know you, so you don't have to change, just be yourself.'"[33]

If he could be himself, he decided, he could be a bishop. He thought, "I should go to Gethsemani and see if I can get in on some conference with Merton." He wanted to make a retreat at Thomas Merton's monastic home, the Trappist Abbey of Gethsemani, near Louisville, Kentucky. "As things happened, I never set aside time to make the trip. It was just a nice thought, and then he died in December of that year, so I lost my chance. I regret that. It would have been a blessing to have met him. But I got to know him through his books and books about him."[34]

A bishop needed a crest. So Tom asked an artist friend, John Jendza, to sketch a background. The main symbol was a wheel, suggesting an active person. The spokes represented not only Detroit, the automotive capital, but also rays of light, the energy of the divine. To find a motto, Tom opened his copy of the Catholic Directory. He got no farther than Alaska when he spotted the motto of the bishop of Anchorage. *Estote Factores Verbi*, Be Doers of the Word. This was a passage from the Letter of St.

James, 1:22. It felt right. "I'm not an extrovert by any means, so I have to push myself to do public things. Turns out, I ended up responding Yes when asked, again and again."[35] He was ordained a bishop on Wednesday, May 1, 1968. Tom's sister Irene, who entered the Immaculate Heart of Mary religious community in 1949, recalled the moment of her brother's consecration. "To see my brother accepting his responsibilities, this was very impressive....He was only thirty-eight. That is extremely young. He learned as he went."[36]

4

Call to Action in Church and World

I n June 1982 at St. John's University in Collegeville, Minnesota, the nation's Catholic bishops gathered for several days of retreat and reflection. Cardinal John Dearden, who had retired in 1980, gave a reflection on collegiality. When it was Tom Gumbleton's turn to speak to his colleagues, he shared a more personal story.

> I took my four years of Scripture classes very seriously and got very high marks. But it was only after Vatican II that I began to know the Scriptures as a *living* word being heard by the Church of today in its own historical setting.... I discovered that we do not go to the Scriptures to find passages that might have a bearing on contemporary situations, but rather we hear God's word speaking to and in the present. This was a very major change in me. It influenced my prayer life, especially as I began to make directed retreats.... I began to discern much more adequately and with forcefulness what God is saying *now*, to me and to any who wish to respond to modern problems in virtue of their Christian discipleship.[1]

He went on to speak of *Justice in the World*, the 1971 statement from the world synod of bishops, which had inspired him, especially in this key passage: "Action on behalf of justice and participation in the transformation of the world fully appear to us as a constitutive dimension of the preaching of the Gospel, or, in other words, of the Church's mission for the redemption of the human race and its liberation from every oppressive situation."[2]

I can see how a convergence of a number of personal experiences relating to issues of the social order, together with new under-standings of Scripture, a profoundly different experience of what the Church is, of what its role of service to the world is, of what priestly ministry must be, and a quite new approach to prayer through a much more active entering into the experience of Jesus as recorded and made present through the *living* word of the Scriptures—the convergence of all these various experiences and understandings made it inevitable that I would come to be in-volved with issues of the public order.

In conclusion, he said, "God has been re-making me. And surely He is not through with the job yet. But I have a deep sense of being at peace with all that has happened and I am totally confident that each re-shaping of the clay is okay, even more than okay. It is a very positive and joyful experience . . . just one person's journey—nothing more."[3]

Synod '69

As he recounted in one of the interviews for this book, Tom had been centrally involved in a significant process in church reform, Detroit's Synod '69.

It was a different kind of synod, for according to canon law a synod would be the priests selected by the bishop, clerically dom-inated, and all the decisions would be made by the bishops and the priests. But Dearden wanted it to be a "Vatican II voice of the people" synod. We re-organized the whole diocesan structure. We had what we called "Speak Up" sessions in almost all the par-ishes, and people would gather in their homes. We had subject areas to discuss, including education, liturgy, social services, peace and justice, and more. It was like a huge adult education program. People shared their own ideas. It was a see-judge-act process. We had tens of thousands of people involved in this over a two-year period.

We established a parish council in every parish. The pastor would contribute to the discussions but not dominate. Most parishes did this. Then we formed the Archdiocesan Pastoral Council. We broke up the old chancery office. We now had an office of parish life, an office of clergy, a vicar of religious. Then we reconfigured the diocese into twenty-five vicariates to work as groups, with the leadership of the vicariates always elected. I was assigned the role of vicar for parishes.[4]

Synod '69 tried to make real the Council ideal, that the people are the church. "We did a lot of work so that people really felt that 'this is my parish' and that the pastor isn't the king or emperor under the bishop. It was difficult. People were so used to 'Oh Father says this, Father says that that's what we have to do,' and it was challenging for some of the older priests."[5] On one occasion in early 1970, Gumbleton spoke to a national assembly of supermarket presidents and corporate managers. While a large organization may see itself as a rock, the inner reality of that rock is a mass of swirling atoms, he suggested. A church, or a corporation for that matter, must be understood "not as a dead pile of stones but as a dynamic communion of human persons." Institutions, including the church, were dealing with racism, alienation, and the disaffection of personnel. A turbulent environment required real change in every institution.[6]

Gumbleton chaired the Synod '69 implementation committee, which including representatives from the chancery, communities of women religious, priests and parishes, and other segments of the Catholic community throughout the Archdiocese of Detroit.[7] In many ways, Synod '69 linked church reform with societal reform—the reform of the church in Detroit had to take into account efforts to reform the social order in the region. This linkage of religious and societal transformation, both at the local and global levels, was becoming crucial to Gumbleton's worldview.

Transformational Justice

Detroit's injustices in the late 1960s and early 1970s certainly helped drive Tom's growing passion for justice, and he took on a host of social justice struggles. For example, he collaborated to support the National Citizens' Committee (NCC) to Aid the Families of GM Strikers and to organize the Michigan Citizens' Committee to Aid the Families of GM Strikers during a United Auto Workers national strike.[8] And he was coming to see, more and more, the ties between economic injustice, racism, and militarism. On July 4, 1972, he was invited to speak at the Ministers' Breakfast of the 63rd annual convention of the National Association for the Advancement of Colored People:

Although I am pleased that the NAACP has assembled in Detroit, I am also saddened and angered because 62 years after the founding of the NAACP and more than a century after the Emancipation Proclamation, it is necessary for black Americans to fight for basic social justice which most white Americans take for granted. It is the shame of America that as we approach the 200th Anniversary of the founding of the nation, black Citizens and other non-white Americans are the victims of inferior education; sub-standard housing in decaying cities, employment discrimination, and unemployment rates that double the national average, inferior health services and an unconscionable degree of hunger and malnutrition.

He addressed the disproportionate number of non-white poor people who are "victims of injustices in the Administration of criminal justice," including high rates of incarceration. He spoke of the callousness toward human life reflected in the "immoral war in Vietnam," as well as the "disregard for life at its early beginnings through abortions on demand, sterilizations, intolerable infant death rates in poor and non-white segments of our society and the malnutrition or starvation among children of poor families." He concluded:

If progress is to be made then the religious institutions of our communities and nation will have to assume a leadership commitment that is aggressive and sustained. Protestants, Catholics and Jews, black and white, must join the battle collectively. National and local Church bodies have made many great, moral pronouncements but often times this has been followed by timid and inadequate follow-up.[9]

St. Raymond's and Racism, February 1971

The women religious at Detroit's St. Raymond's School were not timid. Nine members of the Immaculate Heart of Mary religious community, led by Sister Mary Margaret Slinger, the school's principal, protested a decision of the St. Raymond Parish Council disallowing disadvantaged kids from other neighborhoods to attend. The council tried to limit enrollment to people registered in the parish, shutting out the African American community. The council "generously" offered to pay the tuition for students it would not admit so that they could attend another school.[10] Having none of this, the IHMs resigned, doing so in a dramatic act of protest during the weekend Masses so that the whole parish would hear their message. Their letter to the schools' parents read, in part: "It is evident that our parish council as a group failed to base its decisions regarding the school on facts and Christian principles, but rather on the fears that stem from racist attitudes. When attempts are made to teach social justice—that is, love and concern for all our brothers—tensions and conflict between parents and teachers occur, with children caught in the middle."

St. Raymond's parish, located in an all-white neighborhood, had more than three thousand members. Most of the parents did not support the nuns. The dispute happened in the context of wider tensions around desegregation, busing, and changing demographics affecting school systems in many cities and states. White Catholic parents relied on "their" Catholic schools to avoid having to contend with busing and the goal of public school desegregation. The St. Raymond's case did not center on busing, but it certainly revealed how entrenched racism was in many Catholic communities. It was also a clear demonstration of the IHM Sisters at St. Raymond's standing their ground. And Dearden as well as Gumbleton backed them up. As vicar for parishes, Bishop Gumbleton called a news conference, denouncing racism in the Catholic Church and in U.S. society. The sisters were courageous, he said. They made their decision not "hastily, but with thought and a lot of prayer."[11]

Farley Clinton and The Wanderer

The Wanderer, an archconservative Minnesota-based, Catholic family-owned newspaper, aimed its wrath at the whole enterprise of changes happening in the church in Detroit. In October 1972, it ran a series, "Notes on a Schism in Michigan," written by Farley Clinton.

> The bishops in Detroit are certainly responsible for the task of instructing Catholics in the doctrines of the Holy Roman Church. But today the Catholic people in Detroit are, as a whole, shockingly ignorant of their religion, and many priests and nuns know less than anyone else. Just as in Holland, you have a clergy today in Michigan which hates Rome so that the teaching of the Pope is dismissed without any question.

According to Clinton, Gumbleton was leading a schism:

> Bishop Thomas Gumbleton, who was described to me by one
> bright young person at Siena Heights College (a young priest,
> from Detroit) as "obviously" the "real Archbishop of Detroit,"
> strongly approves of that newspaper for heretics [the *National
> Catholic Reporter*]. ... *The Wanderer*, however, is probably forbid-
> den, though nobody knows why.
>
> For there is a schism in Michigan, and people just don't want
> to hear any mention of the Pope's absolute jurisdiction over the
> Church that Christ founded. They don't know that this is an article
> of Catholic faith.

Gumbleton, after reading the piece, wrote CALUMNY (in all caps, in
ink) next to one particularly troubling paragraph which read:

> I [Clinton] spent eight weeks this summer with people who are
> frantic because they feel their Archbishop [Dearden] does not love
> them. He won't speak to them, and in his place he sends Bishop
> Gumbleton to speak to them; they do not see that as a sign of
> love. Gumbleton (they all said) just tells them they're wrong, and
> insults them, and goes away. Bishop Gumbleton hardly seems to
> pretend to any feeling for Detroit's Catholics, except a strong and
> self-righteous disdain. He disagrees strongly with almost every
> Catholic in Detroit about almost every question. His warmest feel-
> ings are directed almost exclusively to the Negroes and to the suf-
> fering people of North Vietnam.[12]

Social Action

Bishop Gumbleton, together with many communities of women religious,
faced ongoing attacks by reactionary forces such as *The Wanderer*. They
served to focus his energy on the enduring fight to overcome social sin in
its many manifestations. In a mid-August 1974 address to the general chapter of the Adrian Dominicans, in Adrian, Michigan, he noted:

> We can't just stand up in church and talk about the Gospel and
> come to pray together over the Gospel. That's not the whole thing.

We have to have action flowing from what we hear. We can't be
set apart; we can't be isolated and separated and feel we are
preaching the Gospel. There must be some action on our part. We
must begin to discover what the social sins are, and then begin to
take action to overcome them, become aware of them.[13]

One social sin all too manifest in the 1970s was the unjust treatment of
farmworkers. The United Farm Workers (UFW) was seeking wide national
support for its efforts to organize a union for this most oppressed class of
workers. Gumbleton was an ardent supporter of the farmworker movement
all through its *lucha* (struggle), especially the consumer boycott of iceberg
lettuce, grapes, and Gallo wine, until the union was fully recognized. A resolution by Cardinal Dearden, Gumbleton, and other bishops of Michigan
encouraged all Catholics to seriously examine the moral issues involved in
the struggle of farmworkers.[14]

Bread for the World

The crisis of world hunger was another issue that compelled his attention.
In January of 1974, Gumbleton agreed to serve as the first vice president of
Bread for the World, an ecumenical organization.

It happened because Art Simon called me up one day and asked
me if I would join an organization that he had started. His brother
Paul was a U.S. senator. They were committed Lutherans and had
a real sense of Christian mission in their lives. I found Bread for
the World to be a great organization. People, especially during
Lent, would focus on local poverty and poverty around the world
—but especially poverty close to home—and one of the things
they developed was a "letters campaign" so that every Lent people
would begin to accumulate the offering of letters. There would be
an issue that they were trying to get through Congress. That was
the idea, we are going to change public policy.[15]

Before long, Tom found that the mission of Bread for the World was
facing headwinds from the agricultural industry. In June 1974, a Des
Moines, Iowa, journalist asked Gumbleton why Bread for the World was
urging Americans to abstain from eating meat three days a week. "We're
trying to point out that some radical changes in our living and economy

are needed. Hunger is a world-wide problem, and we must look at our resources and how we use them. They must be used in a way that guarantees human life and dignity." A significant reduction in meat-eating by people in the United States would help the cause, since so much grain went to feeding cattle. "By doing a form of fasting, a traditional action going back to the Old Testament—we would help maintain a level of awareness in this country about the problem of hunger in the world. It's so easy to read about six million people starving in Africa and then forget it. But if you feel hungry once in a while yourself, it helps to keep you aware that there are many, many millions of people in the world who feel hunger all of the time."[16]

The editorial board of the Des Moines newspaper pushed back on the bishop's analysis:

> Catholic Bishop Thomas Gumbleton of Detroit said that reduced meat consumption by Americans would increase grain reserves throughout the world since less grain would be needed to fatten livestock in this country. But that is wishful thinking rather than a realistic appraisal of the effect of lower consumption of meat. A reduced demand for grain by livestock producers could result in reduced grain production. There probably would be no more for export.[17]

Resistance and criticism was to be expected as Bread for the World grew and continued to challenge the status quo. By 1981, it had thirty-seven thousand members and thirty-seven full-time staff members. Tom served as its president from 1976 to 1988. The first success had been the passage of "Right to Food" resolutions in the U.S. Congress in 1976 affirming that every person has a right to a nutritionally adequate diet. Bread for the World also helped bring about congressional enactment of grain reserves in 1977 and played a role in President Carter's formation of the Presidential Commission on World Hunger.[18]

Bicentennial Call to Action

Tom sought changes in public policy but also in church policy. He was certainly not alone in this quest. With high energy and high expectations, a new organization promoting church reform, Call to Action, was patterned after Detroit's Synod '69—but now on a national scale. By the autumn of 1976, some eight hundred thousand responses in a nation-wide grassroots consultation process had been reviewed by representative committees and shaped into a set of action recommendations.[19] Detroit was the epicenter, and Cardinal Dearden gave the opening address in Cobo Hall on October 21, 1976:

> We have come to Detroit in October of the bicentennial year, ten years after Pope Paul VI issued his "Call to Action" urging us to take up the cause of justice in the world, and two years after our own bishops summoned us to consider our responsibilities for the preservation and extension of the national promise of "liberty and justice for all." We are here to participate in an extraordinary assembly of the American Catholic community.... All of us are here to assist the American Catholic community to translate its sincere commitment to liberty and justice into concrete programs of action designed to make those ideals a living reality in Church and society.[20]

Shortly after the three-day event, Sister Kathleen Keating, SSJ, chairperson of the National Assembly of Women Religious, wrote to Bishop Gumbleton:

> Many of us left Detroit with a sense that a bright new day was dawning for the Church in the United States. People had come together from all parts of the country, representing a variety of ages, racial and ethnic backgrounds and walks of life. Some were oppressed and alienated and had come with an experience of pain. But we listened to each other, heard each other's concerns, and through the recommendations asked the Bishops to consider the needs which had been expressed. It was particularly encouraging to know that the Bishops were among us by their presence and/or their prayers. Although we realize that there were some flaws in the process, many of us know that it was the greatest experience of Church which we have felt in our lives. Our hope is that you will continue to develop the consultative process in our Church for the greater involvement of people in the life of the Church.[21]

Sister Mary Maxine Teipen, SP, chairperson of Region VII (including Michigan), of the Leadership Conference of Women Religious, also wrote to him:

The great hopes and realistic expectations which anticipated the meeting were realized in the process of the Conference. Great trust is invested in the NCCB, and we look forward to your prudent leadership so that our hopes will be sustained and so that constructive efforts will be encouraged. The members of the LCWR serving the Church in Michigan and Indiana [she wrote from Indianapolis] are giving serious consideration to the resolutions passed by the Detroit Conference.

In his reply to Teipen, Gumbleton wrote:

I was also pleased to learn that the members of the LCWR in Michigan and Indiana are studying the proposals that were made at the conference, with hopes for implementation following the bishops' meeting in the spring. There was a sense of openness and genuine hope at the conference that is hard to describe. It was one of those things that could only be fully appreciated by participation in it. I'm glad that you as an observer had the chance to see the whole thing firsthand as I did.[22]

Call to Action was intended to narrow the gulf between bishops and people. Tom wrote to one critic that this conference "was the first time in history when such a meeting has taken place—when bishops and laity (some 3,000 in all) came together to listen to each other. It is my sincere hope that this listening that took place will be followed by action on the part of the bishops on behalf of justice and peace for all people. It is to that end that we have dedicated ourselves, and to which we are responsible to our people." [23]

Decades later Gumbleton reflected back on all the hope of those heady days:

It was based on the 1971 Synod of Bishops and the call to action on behalf of justice and peace. Cardinal Krol was in charge of the International Eucharistic Conference [held in Philadelphia in August 1976], and those were the two things the bishops were sponsoring for that bicentennial year. Cardinal Dearden organized the Call to Action conference with the help of his adult education person, Jane Wolford Hughes, a very skilled adult education educator. She was the one who got Synod '69 going with all the discussion groups, and she was the one who oversaw this nationwide

Call to Action. Of course there were some dioceses that did not participate. But probably three quarters did and maybe 40 or 50 percent really did a lot because the process went on for a couple of years, the same format as Synod '69. All over the country, people participated and joined in discussions on various topics and came to the preparation of resolutions that should be adopted by Call to Action.[24]

Resolutions called for more participation for women, laity and laicized priests; elimination of sexist language; allowing local participation in the selection of bishops and pastors, and support for women's ordination; establishing a network of peace and justice commissions in dioceses across the nation; condemnation of the production, possession, proliferation and threatened use of nuclear weapons, and a ban on arms sales abroad; commitment to a policy of peace and to efforts toward disarmament; implementation of the U.S. bishops' pro-life program *and* working to pass the Equal Rights Amendment; use of investment power to help bring about social justice; the repeal of [anti-union] "right to work" laws; equal employment opportunities for people with homosexual orientation; accepting the sacramentality of Indian religious symbols; establishing secretariats for Blacks and American Indians; promoting more Black and Hispanic bishops and the appointment of an Indian bishop; support for neighborhood groups, and establishment of a commission to address rural concerns; ending discrimination toward divorced Catholics; opening the office of preacher to women, youth, and non-ordained men; support for the bishops' Pastoral Plan for Pro-life Activities and work for a constitutional amendment; respect for personal conscience on the subject of birth control; support for the work of "Dignity," the organized Catholic gay and lesbian group, and support for pastoral care and respect for people of all sexual orientations.[25]

Nearly four thousand people attended the closing Mass in Cobo Hall. It felt like a tide of hope, Gumbleton remembered.

Cardinal Dearden preached. It was a beautiful ceremony. He was the chair of all of this, so what he had to do was send a final document to the National Conference of Catholic Bishops. That was his job, get this done, give it to the conference, now it's theirs to implement. And that's where everything broke down. The final document had to be given over to the bishops, and there were resolutions in there—and this was understood, that there would be things in there that the bishops wouldn't do, and most of the people knew that, but they were giving their vision and their hopes. These were recommendations given to the bishops as a way of contributing to the well-being of our nation and its bicentennial.

Once all the bishops reviewed the resolutions, including the call for women's ordination, the tide turned. Gumbleton recalled a conversation he had with Dearden.

We were driving to Lansing for a meeting, and he expressed his profound concern and distress because he was committed to what was in his statement. If the bishops rejected it, he felt he would have to resign from the project and that would have been a huge step for him, because it would have split the conference and that had been one of his concerns as a president, from the very beginning and for those years [1966–1972], to keep the National Conference of Catholic Bishops together.[26]

In May 1977 the bishops gathered in Chicago. Dearden, having suffered a heart attack just ahead of the assembly, could not attend. Cincinnati Archbishop Joseph Bernardin was the president of the NCCB. Correspondence between Dearden and Bernardin as well as between Dearden and the NCCB staff in the months after Call to Action and prior to his heart attack show Dearden concerned, just as Gumbleton later recalled. In a March 1977 letter to the NCCB's general secretary, Rev. Thomas Kelly, Dearden called for a radical rewrite by the bishops of their own document:

The process in which we engaged in the Bicentennial consultations generated a great deal of enthusiasm. This enthusiasm has been lost in the translation. What had been a hope-filled experience for so many becomes in the response a very humdrum, ordinary activity....In reality, I am almost as much concerned about the tone of the response as I am about its content. But I think that, in every instance, there must be shown a sensitivity to the hopes of the people that were raised by our whole process. It is not a matter of glossing over things that we cannot assent to. From the beginning, people have understood this. At the same time, we must be prepared to open up to them the possibility of some reasonable dialogue that will convince them that we see lasting values in the process as an instrument by which we live as Church.[27]

The bishops made some efforts to amend their document in light of Dearden's concerns, but Vatican II's more participatory model of church, and the empowering spirit that helped engender Detroit's Synod '69 and efforts such as the Bicentennial Call to Action, would soon be eclipsed by the conservative "restorationist" ecclesiology of Pope John Paul II.

Continuing the Fight

No matter what, Tom was committed to fight for church reform and for justice in society and in the world. He continued to back the United Farm Workers and the United Auto Workers in their strikes. When the Amalgamated Clothing and Textile Workers Union launched a nationwide consumer boycott against J.P. Stevens & Co., and the UAW supported the boycott, Gumbleton was among Michigan leaders along with Detroit Mayor Coleman Young and Detroit Councilwoman Erma Henderson who lent their voices to the cause.

Many people wrote him and the archdiocese to complain about his association with labor unions. Gumbleton supported his positions by referring to Pope Leo XIII's 1891 encyclical, which clearly stated that all workers have a right to unionize. In response to a letter that accused him of aligning himself with Marxism, Gumbleton replied:

> I am not suggesting socialism or communism as an appropriate system, nor am I in favor of either of them as we understand them today. What I am saying is that our present system needs help. We must improve it, revise it, redesign it in some way, so that a small portion of the world does not have the greatest amount of the world's goods, while the larger portion is hungry, homeless, and living in poverty of such unspoken dimensions, as is the case at this moment. . . . I personally am grateful for this country, and for all who have lived and died in its name. It is precisely because I do have such high regard for the United States that I want to make it even better—more just, more willing to share the countless goods we do have, not in a paternalistic way, but because it is a matter of justice, the justice that is spoken of in the Gospel.[28]

One of the letters he received, on December 21, 1979, came from Tom Murphy, Chairman of General Motors. Writing not in his capacity as chairman of GM but "as a layman in the Archdiocese of Detroit," he hoped that the auxiliary bishop had been misquoted in allegations attributed to him "about the 'evils' of major corporations, and more specifically about 'multinational agribusiness.'" They would end up with a face-to-face meeting in Murphy's office at GM's Detroit headquarters where, though they tried to understand each other, neither would budge. Their contrasting worldviews were transparent in their correspondence. Murphy's letter stated:

> You, as a bishop, have also been quoted as condemning "multinational agribusiness" for being a major contributor to, and a basic cause of, hunger in the world. Is there any pursuit in life more contrary to the teachings of Christ than the perpetuation of world poverty and hunger? I can think of none. What are we lay people to think, then, when such charges come from a consecrated bishop of the Church and a successor to the apostles?

And in his reply Gumbleton noted:

> I appreciate the sense of concern you mentioned about the confusion that can result when a person who holds an institutional position also expresses, at times, personal views that people automatically identify as views of that particular institution. However, in this instance I do not feel that the problem you raise is really the problem at all. My concerns regarding "big business," in fact, the whole economic system of the United States, are concerns that directly flow from my responsibility as a minister of the Gospel. They are not simply personal concerns.

After citing the 1971 Synod of Bishops and their declaration that "action for justice and participation in the transformation of the world are constitutive dimensions of the preaching of the Gospel," the bishop added:

> We live in a world where big business has tremendous impact on the lives of people. I could in no way refrain from analyzing that impact and reacting to it on the basis of conscience. And among bishops I am not alone in seeing this as a responsibility of one ordained to preach the Gospel.

He appealed to GM's chairman to open his eyes to the negative impacts of the prevailing economic order:

I'm sure I do not have to expand at great length on the numbers of
poor people throughout the world who are caught up within this
system, upon whom the prevailing "socio-economic structures" im-
pose oppression and violence. Precisely as a bishop I must join in
crying out against such injustices and violence. I must try to help
people to understand that these situations are intolerable.

After citing the reports of missionaries serving in many parts of the
world, he concluded:

I am confident that no one in this country consciously chooses to
oppress people, to do violence to people in other parts of the
world. And yet, at the same time I am convinced that economic
structures do such violence. Once we recognize this, we must do
what we can to transform such systems.[29]

5

Pax Christi and Gospel Nonviolence

I n November 1972, Carroll Dozier, the bishop of Memphis, Tennessee, hosted a meeting which, nearly half a century later, Tom Gumbleton brought to mind:

> We discussed what a Catholic peace movement could be. We wanted to connect with international efforts. There was the International Fellowship of Reconciliation, and within that there were the various divisions such as the Catholic Peace Fellowship. But the Fellowship of Reconciliation was committed to no war, no violence. We thought, if we wanted this to be a popular Catholic movement, we better not go with the Fellowship because our official Catholic teaching still was just-war theology. We explored Pax Christi, a peace movement that was started by a French bishop [and a French laywoman] after World War II and then began to spread to other countries. If we want everyday Catholics to get involved, we thought, we better stay within the official Catholic framework. Supposedly there was no reason not to teach the nonviolence of Jesus, but there was hardly any place where that was ever taught.[1]

Gordon Zahn, a WWII conscientious objector, and Eileen Egan, a close friend of Catholic Worker founder Dorothy Day, were among the pioneers working to establish an American branch of Pax Christi. The meeting at Carroll Dozier's house included Egan and Zahn, as well as Joe Fahey, a

57

peace studies professor from Manhattan College in New York City, and Gerry Vanderhaar, a friend of Dozier's who taught at a local university.[2] Vanderhaar later chronicled those first connections between Bishop Gumbleton and Pax Christi. Eileen Egan wrote in November 1971 asking the Detroit bishop to consider taking on the role of episcopal moderator for Pax Christi USA. He replied to Eileen, "I would be honored to be asked to serve as moderator if your board reaches the conclusion that I am the person they want. I am hopeful that I would carry out the responsibilities of moderator in a way that would be satisfactory to all the members." Carroll Dozier had spoken out against the U.S. war in Vietnam in his first pastoral letter (that same year): "We must now squarely face the fact that war is no longer tolerable for a Christian. We must speak out loudly and clearly and repudiate war as an instrument of national policy." Detroit and Memphis had two anti-war bishops whom Pax Christi wanted on board. Egan invited Dozier to join Gumbleton as episcopal co-moderator.

A Paulist priest, Fr. Ed Guinan, along with Joe Fahey organized the first Pax Christi national assembly in early October 1973 at George Washington University in Washington, DC. Due to scheduling conflicts, neither Dozier nor Gumbleton were able to attend. The assembly seemed to go well for all who could attend, but stress between the radical and moderate wings would soon come to the fore. Guinan had close ties to the Community for Creative Nonviolence (CCNV) in Washington, whose activism could at times be "in your face." Tensions erupted between the CCNV-types and the more moderate types such as Zahn, Egan, Fahey, and the two bishops "testing the water."[3] Soon thereafter, Bishop Dozier attended a conference in Washington DC commemorating the tenth anniversary of Pope John XXIII's encyclical on peace, *Pacem in Terris*. "On the night Secretary of State Henry Kissinger was to speak," Vanderhaar writes, "several members of the Community for Creative Nonviolence, including Ed Guinan, had taken inconspicuous places in the audience. They had brought with them some laughing boxes, small hand-held devices which gave out the sound of loud, raucous laughter, intending to use them during Kissinger's talk." This was indeed a community of CREATIVE nonviolence. They disrupted Kissinger, at least until security folks sent them and their laughing boxes out the door. Dozier was not happy. "He hadn't expected Pax Christi, to which he had lent his name as a moderator, to behave in this fashion."

To find its focus, Pax Christi USA went back to the drawing board intent on engendering support among and obtaining the participation of a wider circle of Catholics, including more bishops. In November 1974, Dozier hosted another meeting that included Egan, Zahn, Fahey, and Gumbleton. From that point forward, Fahey took the lead in organizing a "mission-focusing" event set for early May 1975 at Manhattan College in Riverdale, New York.[4]

Dorothy Day, Tom Cornell from the Catholic Peace Fellowship, Zahn, Egan, Fahey, Dozier, and Gumbleton were among the participants, along with editors and writers, pastors, diocesan officials, professors, and representatives from various national organizations of religious and laity. A couple of weeks later Gumbleton wrote to Tom Cornell: "I really think the meeting we had at Manhattan College went well....As you say, we are now at least on our way."[5]

Zahn, writing in the September 1975 edition of the Jesuit magazine *America*, described with candor the rocky beginnings of Pax Christi USA. The promise of the first national assembly in October 1973 had "faded in a catastrophic breakdown of communication between the responsible officers and the operating staff, and the resulting misunderstanding spread outside of the organizational structure and escalated into hasty and unjust public recriminations." The Manhattan College gathering clarified the fact that both the just war and pacifist views had to be in the mix in some way. "The temptation to dismiss the 'just war' position as 'reactionary' or to reject pacifism as 'too radical' and of doubtful orthodoxy is always present." The split between the more radical and more measured approaches had, in Zahn's view, "reached something of a peak in the United States with respect to the Catholic opposition to the war in Vietnam." Pax Christi USA would certainly always aspire to a "Peace of Christ" vision and practice but would have to try to reach many Catholics where they were.[6]

Nonviolence Will Change Us

Though the intent was to make an appeal to the Catholic mainstream, the strongest current emerging in time for Pax Christi USA (PCUSA) was destined to be active and contemplative nonviolence. The November 21–23, 1975, annual conference, held at the Bergamo Center on the campus of the University of Dayton, Ohio, centered on "Christian Nonviolence: Challenge to American Life." Delivering the keynote, Bishop Gumbleton said: "If we want the prophecies of Isaiah to be fulfilled, the swords to be beaten into plowshares, then we have to listen to Jesus' message, his word that proclaims nonviolence and his life that lives it out. I think this is truly the challenge of nonviolence." Could God's promise of peace really be achieved? "We live in a world that is so terribly violent that it really does make us wonder if peace is a possibility. But maybe this violence is something that will move us to work for peace in the world." We must try, Gumbleton said,

> to go past what we might say is acceptable Catholic doctrine and really search out in the scripture what God is really asking of us. The theology of "just war" is based on reason. It seems to me Jesus Christ asks us to go a little bit beyond that if we can accept the challenge that he offers us. When faced with an enemy, he never struck back. Don't you think he's asking us to do the same? Isn't that really the challenge that's offered to us as Christians, his followers, really to take his words seriously? As individuals and as a people to say we will not fight violence with violence, force with force.[7]

This was six months after the fall of Saigon. "We are used to thinking of our country as a good sport, playing according to the rules, but during the Vietnam War we found out we are not so different from other violent people." Bishop Dozier then continued the theme of Gumbleton's keynote, speaking of the importance of being reconciled with our neighbor as the first step toward disarmament. By contrast, another speaker, Harvard-trained Rev. J. Bryan Hehir, a priest of the Boston archdiocese, made clear that his own outlook was still just war theology, although he could adopt a nuclear pacifism. Hehir was grounded in the school of political realism in foreign policy. But his position did not receive broad support from the more than two hundred people from thirty states who participated in the Dayton event.

Seven regions were being organized for expanding PCUSA's reach. One of these was sure to be Detroit, and another Memphis. Dozier and Gumbleton sent a letter to all the American bishops (in 1975 there were 311 total) inviting them to join PCUSA. Eight bishops signed on over the next few months. The number would grow to well north of one hundred by the time of the May 1983 U.S. Catholic bishops' pastoral letter on war and peace. (Tom's pivotal role in that letter will be explored in another chapter.)[8]

Detroit hosted Pax Christi's third annual national assembly in late September 1976 on the theme "The Peacemaker: Disciple and Citizen." How discipleship relates to citizenship was on people's minds partly because it was the nation's bicentennial year. Sr. Mary Evelyn Jegen, SND, education consultant for Catholic Relief Services, chaired the PCUSA bicentennial committee hoping to have a positive impact on the national bicentennial

Call to Action coming up in Detroit.[9] Jegen, Egan, Zahn, and others prepared "Bicentennial America: Thou Shalt Not Overkill" which read, in part:

> Our purpose in Pax Christi is to contribute to the building of peace and justice by exploring and articulating the ideal of Christian nonviolence and by striving to apply it to personal life and the structures of society. We invite concerned Catholics to respond to the Church's call "to evaluate war with an entirely new attitude" and to take an active role in making secure a peace based on justice and love.

PCUSA argued for, among other things, rejection of the possession and use of nuclear arms, promotion of and education on conscientious objection, and inclusion of complete and unconditional amnesty without penalty for those who refused on the grounds of conscience to participate in American military efforts in Vietnam.[10] These appeals helped buoy some of the resolutions (cited in the previous chapter) issued by Call to Action. Dozier wrote to Gumbleton just days after the historic Call to Action experience: "I still have a hard time believing what happened in Detroit. It was truly a movement of the Spirit."[11]

Tom felt moved by the Spirit on his own personal road into nonviolence. In the winter 1976 issue of the Catholic pacifist quarterly *Gamaliel*, he expressed his conviction:

> To someone who did not know about the life and death of Jesus, our way of life would seem rather absurd. Imagine telling a person who does not know Jesus, that we are called to a life where we must "love our enemies." Imagine telling a person about forgiving "70 times 7," or turning the other cheek, or doing good to those who hate you.... One of the most impractical parts about the Christian life is its call to non-violence. In the logic of the world, it makes no sense *not* to strike back when someone strikes me. And it makes no sense for a nation not to fight fire with fire, to rule by the strength of its military greatness. And when you stop and think about it, why should it? Human logic keeps telling us that violence works. A big man with a stick is insignificant to a small man with a gun. A country with tanks and artillery would not seem a threat to a country with an atomic bomb. But when all the countries or a good number of them each have their own supply of bombs, where does the world go from there?

Jesus answers that question. He says that guns and bombs are not the answer. He says there is another way. He says it with His life, and He says it with His death. His way, the non-violent way, is part of that unrealistic approach to life that we call the Christian way. It is an approach that says I will forgive 70 times 7; I will love those who hate me.... It is an approach to life that has been judged as too idealistic in today's or any other society. It is "The Impossible Dream" come to life.

Although impractical, the Christian must give extraordinary witness against violence. Even more, that person must be willing to forgive. Whether liberal or conservative, whether rich or poor, regardless of political preference, the Christian must choose the road not taken often enough...the road of peace, the road of justice, the road of extraordinary patience, gentleness, and love. It is a road often tangled with detours that require a loving response to a sometimes unfriendly and unreasonable world.

If this approach sounds impractical it is safe to say that without Jesus it is impossible. It was not practical for Him to go the extra mile as He so often did for those who didn't even remember to thank Him. And, of course, He was fiercely and persistently tempted to reject the will of His Father and follow a "more practical" way. But He submitted to the impractical, idealistic, non-violent way ...the way of the Cross. This approach meant pain and suffering. It also meant forgiveness and our salvation.

In terms of human logic violence is seen as the quick, practical way to get one's way (or to at least get even). It does not solve the deeper problems. In the long haul, it breeds more of the same. If you hit me with a stone, I'll hit you with a rock. Nations bomb nations and one war eventually sets the stage for another. Left to our own resources we opt for violence over and over. For the Christian, it is Jesus who breaks that cycle. He breaks it with forgiveness and love, with peace and gentleness of heart. Impractical? Very. But in the long run, it is the only answer that ultimately works for the good of all people and all nations. It is the only way to a world truly at peace.[12]

Thomas Merton had become like an "inward eye" for Tom Gumbleton. Reading one of the late Trappist monk's reflections, Tom fastened on these words:

Non-violence is not for power but for truth. It is not pragmatic but prophetic. It is not aimed at immediate political results, but at the manifestation of fundamental and crucially important truth. Non-violence is not primarily the language of efficacy, but the language of *kairos*. It does not say, "We shall overcome" so much as "This is the day of the Lord, and whatever may happen to us, *He* shall overcome."

In the margins next to Merton's prose, Tom wrote, with underlines: "It will *change us* whether or not it changes *the* situation."[13]

Making a Commitment

In 1977, Bishop Gumbleton saw to it that every Catholic bishop in the United States received a copy of a Pax Christi booklet, *The Church and the Arms Race*. And that same year, in April, he joined Carroll Dozier, Eileen Egan, and Joe Fahey for a Pax Christi International Council meeting in Dublin, Ireland. A personal memory from that trip stood out in Tom's mind more than forty years later:

> Part of the leadership for the conference was the Catholic bishop, Edward Daly. In fact, there's a famous picture of him picking ... up off the street [a person who] had been shot on Bloody Sunday [30 January 1972; the image, photographed in Derry, actually showed Daly waving a bloodied white handkerchief over the victim] and...after the opening session, he was standing in front greeting people, so I walked up to meet him and introduced myself, and as soon as I said my name, he said, "Oh, I know the Gumbletons, in Derry they were members of my parish, they lived right close by over there where a lot of the killings took place." He took me over there the next day to meet the Gumbletons.[14]

Examination of Conscience

Just what was Gumbleton thinking about the nature and the merits and possible shortcomings of Christian nonviolence? In correspondence, Rev. John Dickman of St. Gregory's Church in Samuels, Kentucky, raised concerns about the Detroit bishop's views (based on a report in the December 1978 issue of *Our Sunday Visitor*). Gumbleton clarified in his reply to Dickman that pacifism must not be confused with passivity:

> I am enclosing a copy of a Pax Christi document on the arms race and the Church. In it you'll find the statement of the Vatican to the United Nations in preparation for the UN Special Session on Disarmament. In there, the arms race is described as an act of aggression against the poor because it deprives them of the basic resources they need for a human life. This is one of the reasons why I feel so strongly that we have to stop the arms race as the Vatican urges us to do. But in addition to our wastefulness in the arms race, we tend to live a lifestyle that is far beyond what we really need, and therefore in violation of what Pope Paul VI said in his encyclical on the Development of Peoples where he indicates in paragraph #23, that no one has a right to keep for their own use, anything that is beyond their needs when others lack the very necessities of life.
>
> I mention all of this not only because I feel it is necessary for us to re-think our whole attitude toward war and develop a whole new approach toward the use of violence, but also I think we all need a profound examination of conscience with regard to our whole way of life. Unless we begin to live in a more genuinely Christian way, following the values that Jesus preached so clearly and so simply, I don't see that we are going to be able to act toward others in a very loving and compassionate way, and I see this as being profoundly immoral. I am asking that the people of the United States make some drastic changes in their use of material goods, in regard to their whole approach toward violence ... within our nation, within our homes and within our own hearts. That is a tall order, certainly, but it is also, I think, a profound challenge.
>
> I don't see non-violence as simply a passive thing. I think we really have to "hunger and thirst for justice" and I know that I can't dictate to everyone the "how" in doing that. I can only show what I believe to be the right course by the way I live and by the way I hunger and thirst for justice. The way I have chosen is the way of non-violence. I believe this is the way Jesus chose, but I realize at the same time that there are countless people who would and do see it differently.[15]

In early March 1980, Tom gathered with a crowd, including many Catholic Workers, at the Sisters of Mary Reparatrix retreat center in New York City. He recollected from his time in Rome in the early 1960s:

In discussing the morality of nuclear weapons, I often recount an experience I had when I was a student in Rome, some fifteen years ago. I discovered a place outside the city called the Ardeatine Caves, a very sobering but beautiful place. It is a monument to some people [innocent Italian civilians] who were killed in World War II. In the cave are marble tombs, with commemorative inscriptions and carvings—impressive, peaceful, prayerful. Toward the end of the war, the German government was ruling Italy and some Italian guerrillas, opposed to the occupation, had killed some German soldiers. The German general in charge of Rome ordered his troops to go into the city and round up civilians and take them to these caves. That day, 330 civilian men were randomly machine gunned and left to die. After the war, the Italian government built this monument. Whenever I recount that story people react with horror to think that people were taken indiscriminately off the streets and massacred. And the German general who ordered the deaths was convicted of war crimes at the Nuremberg trials.

But consider what happened on August 6, 1945, when we as a nation chose to drop an atomic bomb on Hiroshima. Eighty thousand men, women and children were indiscriminately destroyed in nine seconds—immediately incinerated by that bomb. Tens of thousands of others were left crippled, maimed, their lives destroyed. There are survivors who are still suffering from diseases caused by the radiation from that bomb. What is the morality of that bombing? It violates any theology of war ever taught by the Catholic Church; yet, it was not until 1976 that it was clearly condemned by the teaching authority of the Church when Pope Paul VI called the bombing of Hiroshima a "butchery of untold magnitude." What President Truman called "the most glorious day in the history of the United States" was in fact a butchery of untold magnitude.

"We must look at this attitude of Jesus," Tom continued, "to learn to develop within ourselves the mind and heart of Jesus. It is important to reflect often on His life, teaching and prayer, especially during His final days."

For Tom, pacifism was not simply a theory for debate on an academic panel. Gospel nonviolence had become deeply personal. "Such commitment to nonviolence demands a very profound conversion of mind and heart.... If we take the time to pray with Jesus, we too will be converted in mind and heart. It won't work if we try to reason it out. The only way is through a change of heart, a coming into a way of being that is the way of Jesus."[16]

Ashes

In 1978, Pax Christi USA chose Bishop Gumbleton as its first president in place of his prior role as co-moderator. Sr. Mary Evelyn Jegen became the first full-time coordinator. In March 1979, when she took up that role, the national office of PCUSA moved from New York, where Joe Fahey had been the coordinator, to Chicago. The priorities would be disarmament, primacy of conscience, a just world order, education for peace, and alternatives to violence.

At that point in time, Jimmy Carter was in the White House. Pax Christi's chronicler, Gerry Vanderhaar, documented the mid-October 1978 occasion when he joined Tom Gumbleton and Joe Fahey for a briefing on the Strategic Arms Limitation Treaty, held at the State Department:

> President Carter had recently signed the SALT II agreement with the Soviet Union. His administration was mounting a campaign to have it ratified by the Senate. After listening to speaker after speaker tell why they knew the SALT treaty would not weaken the defense of the United States, meaning our nuclear superiority, Pax Christi's three representatives all agreed that the treaty was too hawkish to deserve support.

What were the U.S. bishops thinking as a body, and the NCCB? In mid-February 1979, Tom Gumbleton voiced his opposition to ratification of SALT II. The staff of the United States Catholic Conference (the USCC was essentially the public policy arm of the NCCB), according to Vanderhaar, "believed that Gumbleton's position threatened to unravel all that they had done to have the bishops address the public policy on control of nuclear weapons."[17] Gumbleton and Dozier explained why they would not support SALT II. They made their case before the USCC Administrative Board, some forty or so bishops. Fr. Bryan Hehir, USCC's associate secretary for International Justice and Peace, made the case for SALT II. But Bishop Gumbleton argued that SALT II failed to place adequate limits on new technology, including mobile missiles and the cruise missile. When interviewed, he commented, "I wish someone would say 'You're wrong, you're missing something,' but no one has." Pax Christi's reasons for opposing the treaty differed starkly from the reasons motivating the hawkish opponents of SALT II who were claiming that the treaty would place limits on the arms build-up those hawks wanted.[18]

The administrative board of the USCC, representing the nation's bishops as a whole, decided to throw its support behind SALT II. Yet, in a statement explaining this decision, Bishop Thomas Kelly, the general secretary noted: "Discussions before the board's voice vote made it clear that the bishops feel SALT II deserves support only if it is understood and functions as a necessary, though admittedly limited, step toward true disarmament." Hehir had argued that the SALT II treaty "would amount to the first reduction of offensive weapons in the history of the nuclear arms race. The political-psychological significance of such a reduction should not be lightly discarded either as a deception or a giveaway."

But Gumbleton and Dozier could not go along with this reasoning. In reflecting on what he had been thinking since the State Department briefing the previous fall, Tom explained, "I began to ponder the fact that SALT II would legitimate the destructive power of 615,000 Hiroshima bombs, the present American arsenal. I began to wonder how I as a religious leader could offer support for an agreement that would sanction that kind of destructive power in the hands of any government." He and Dozier, and Pax Christi, were swimming against the mainstream current. Many ecumenical efforts, including the leadership of the National Council of Churches, mobilized across denominations to rally support for SALT II, viewing it as a practical step toward disarmament. Even NETWORK, the social justice lobby founded by Catholic nuns, supported it, stating that "opposition would place NETWORK in a lobbying posture that would ally us with political groups opposing the treaty for reasons different from our own."[19]

But Bishop Gumbleton kept to his principled stand. In early April 1979, in Davenport, Iowa, he asserted: "Instead of support of arms limitations, we must demand of our leaders that disarmament begin to take place." Religious opposition, he believed, was valuable even if not successful. "We're laying some sort of groundwork to confront it as a moral issue. We must not look at it on political grounds only."[20] This was a crucial aspect of Tom's outlook. One must stand on one's convictions for the power of such witness, regardless of whether such witness seemed to constitute realistic political power in a given moment. He had a longer sense of dynamic history and the role of discipleship in the unfolding history of social change.

President Carter was trying to maneuver the Salt II Treaty through the Senate, and at one point he invited a group of religious leaders to the White House. Tom was among those invited, and four decades later he could still remember—and enjoy telling the story of—an amusing moment involving Frank Cordaro, a Catholic Worker from Des Moines:

> There were a whole bunch of us in one of the rooms of the White House, maybe forty or sixty people, and Carter comes in, very pleasant and friendly and makes his pitch, and people start asking him questions and so on. So it goes on, and I wasn't in the least bit persuaded by it. Maybe I was a little too much prejudiced against it to start with, and I wasn't going to go out of there and preach that we should sign it, or endorse. But at the end, each of us walked up to shake hands with Carter. So Frank had this plan to make it kind of an act of protest. He had brought along ashes that he was holding in his hand, and when he got up to Carter, he was going to throw the ashes up in the air and say, "Here's what happens with nuclear weapons" or something like that.
>
> I don't know exactly what he was going to say, but he was going to make this point by throwing black ashes up in the air. Well, he opened his hand, and he had been sweating and the ashes were all clumped together, and it was like a black marble being tossed up in the air, and it had no effect except that the Secret Service guys were standing around the room and, I'm telling you, they were on Frank so fast, they had him down on the floor within two seconds. I couldn't help but laugh, it was so ridiculous, but Frank was doing his best to make an impression, and he sure did.[21]

In early August 1981, thirty-six years after Hiroshima, Bishop Gumbleton gave an address at the John Neumann Institute of Holy Redeemer College, in Waterford, Wisconsin. He described the bombing of Hiroshima as an "unrepented sin which is evoking an even greater evil. It started us on the path of nuclear warfare, and our participation in the nuclear arms race is a social injustice that is perhaps unparalleled in history." Americans had forgotten the "original sin" of Hiroshima. "In fact, many people do not consider it a sin at all. We were told it was acceptable because it ended the war, saving American lives. Most also felt it would never happen again. After all, we were the only nation with nuclear weapons at the time and we certainly would not use [them] again." Talk of "first-strike" capability coming from the Reagan administration was a grave concern. Even if such weapons were never used, the massive investment in the arms race amounted to a gross injustice. "Can you imagine what really could be done for the world's poor if we said that we would no longer participate in the arms race?"

In the 1970s, with the emergence of Pax Christi USA and all that he had been through in opposing America's war in Vietnam, the story which opened this book, he had prayed, observed, read, listened, talked, and traveled his way into active and contemplative nonviolence. And so he pondered, at a place aptly called Holy Redeemer, the sign of the cross in the name of the Father, the Son, and the Holy Spirit. He implored the audience to ponder something. "The first nuclear weapon test was called Trinity ... for the three elements of mass, energy and velocity. I pray you will choose the second Trinity... that of a loving father, a son who gave himself up for us, and a spirit that enkindles love in our hearts."[22]

6

With the Hostages in Iran

On November 4, 1979, several months after the Iranian Revolution, students invaded and took over the U.S. embassy in Tehran, holding several dozen Americans as hostages. It was the beginning of an ordeal that would last 444 days.

On a late Sunday night, December 16, Bishop Gumbleton's phone rang. On the line was Daniel Berrigan, asking if he would be willing to go to Tehran to conduct a Christmas Eve service for the hostages. Worried that it could make things more difficult for the hostages, Tom hesitated. But maybe such a trip could open up channels of communication, he thought.[1] Berrigan said he would get back later with more details. Some time had passed when Tom got a call from Carl Leban, a religion professor at the University of Kansas in Lawrence. Leban knew people in Tehran who were talking with the Iranian students. Would the bishop consider going to Tehran? Gumbleton told Leban about the conversation he'd had with Berrigan. Shortly thereafter Berrigan told him that if a solid opportunity were to arise through Leban, he should take it. So Leban and contacts in Tehran worked on a tentative plan including Bishop Gumbleton and the former Vietnam anti-war activist, Yale chaplain Rev. William Sloan Coffin.[2]

On Friday, Tom got a call from Fr. Bryan Hehir at the United States Catholic Conference, the public policy body for the U.S. bishops. The USCC had been working with the National Council of Churches to arrange a trip. The USCC/NCC collaboration was making very little headway. The Iranians had rejected their request to send a delegation which would have included Archbishop John Quinn, president of the National Conference of Catholic Bishops, and a representative from the National Council of

Churches. Hehir had heard that Gumbleton might be going with some other group, so he asked him for the latest word on this possibility. The content of a USCC press statement would depend in part on whether or not he was going to Tehran. Hehir did not try to persuade him against going but made clear that there could be no indication suggesting he would be going on behalf of the U.S. bishops. This troubled Tom, since he felt that if he came back from Tehran and then tried to speak about what was happening he would lack credibility. So he called Leban and asked him to talk with Hehir to explain the plans and intentions for the trip.

Conversations ensued between the State Department, the USCC, the NCC, the Iranian embassy in Washington, Leban, and others, after which Gumbleton got a phone call on Saturday, December 22, from Ali Asghar Agah of the Iranian embassy, telling him that he was being invited, along with Rev. Dr. Coffin and Rev. Dr. William Howard, president of the National Council of Churches and executive director of the Black Council of the Reform Church in America. In a chronicle he composed shortly after the Tehran trip, Tom wrote: "I was trying to find a way to kind of stall off a bit, because I really wanted to talk with Bryan Hehir first, but he said he needed to know if I was going because he had to get word back to Tehran and get the official invitation out as quickly as possible." As he got off the phone with Agah, he called Hehir who said the Vatican was okaying the plan. The papal nuncio in Tehran could see no other way to open dialogue with the students. So Hehir asked him if he would be willing to represent the NCCB and asked to accompany him as staff. The bishop was relieved to know that the NCCB wanted him to represent them. "I was sort of amused, in fact, by the way he put it, 'if I would be willing' to represent the NCCB. I guess somehow he or some of the others had felt that I really wanted to make this a personal trip only, which I did not."[3]

On Sunday, December 23, he flew to New York's Kennedy Airport where he and Hehir met Howard and Coffin. After flying to London they caught an Air Iran flight, making a brief stopover in Paris where Cardinal Léon Étienne Duval, archbishop of Algiers, joined them. At 9 p.m. on Christmas Eve they touched down in Tehran. Archbishop Bugnini, the papal nuncio, accompanied by the head of the Iranian Protocol Office for the Foreign Affairs Ministry, took them into the city by limousine with a police escort. Leaving their luggage in the hotel, they headed to the American embassy. Gumbleton recalled:

Of course, I had no sense of where we were in the city or any kind of orientation like that at all. But any way we travelled along at a good clip and got there. I was expecting that we would see the crowds of people in front of the Embassy that had been shown on TV and written about in the papers. But they took us to a back door...very quickly we met the students who were kind of running the show and they led us into a room in a small building right near the back gate of the compound.

Gumbleton, Howard, and Coffin had discussed plans for an ecumenical service, figuring that they would meet with all fifty hostages together. But the students wanted them in three separate places, each with small groups. Coffin and Gumbleton nearly got up to leave in protest but changed their minds after Dr. Howard and Cardinal Duval convinced them to stay. The Iranian students were concerned that if all the hostages were brought together some might begin to rile up the whole group, or a guard might respond violently.[4]

So, according to Gumbleton's chronicle, Coffin and Howard were escorted to other buildings. Duval and Gumbleton remained in the small building near the back gate. As they walked into the office area where they would be celebrating Mass, Tom saw four hostages, all men, seated behind a desk in a semi-circle. He moved across the room and met Marine guard Kevin Hermening, a Catholic, age nineteen, from Milwaukee. Next, he met Joseph Subic Jr., age twenty-two. Gumbleton had just stopped in to visit Subic's parents at their home in Redford Township, a suburb of Detroit, that Sunday morning.

I told him how glad I was to see him and that I had just visited with his mother and dad. And he reacted quite emotionally and just thanked me so much for that and tears came to his eyes. And I told him about how his mother and dad had asked me not to mention any names but just to say his nieces and nephews were waiting to go skiing with him as soon as they could. And that they were going to save their Christmas until he got back home and they could all celebrate together.

That brief exchange meant a lot to both of them. "Right there it made it seem to me that the trip was worthwhile. It really surprised me that I felt such a strong emotion so quickly, but it was there, and I am sure Joe did too right away." The other two hostages were Steve Lutterbach, a Foreign Service officer from Dayton, Ohio, and Jerry Plotkin, an older American businessman who had unfortunately entered the embassy for what he thought would be a quick and simple consular transaction.[5]

As they prepared for midnight Mass, one of the student leaders (she went by the name Mary, and she had engaged in the earlier tussle over how the services were to be arranged) was present. Bishop Gumbleton and Cardinal Duval were seated behind a makeshift altar, facing the hostages, ready to begin the liturgy. At that point, after Mary sat down next to the hostages, television lights came on. She read a message to the world from the Ayatollah Khomeini, attacking President Carter and mocking American Christians for failing to live up to their own sacred scripture, saying that the Iranian people had long suffered under the shah and that the U.S. president was the chief tyrant in world history. Sitting there with the four hostages and Cardinal Duval, Tom worried sick how this would all appear—with TV cameras, recorders, and Iranian students standing along the walls. What to do?

"I glanced at Mary once in a while and glanced at the students. But most of the time just kind of sat there with my head down, feeling embarrassed . . . I thought this was it, the people who warned us were right and we just got trapped into a situation where we would be exploited and used for their purposes only." Tom nearly bolted from the scene. "I thought clearly this thing could be cause for the whole trip to be totally misunderstood and rejected." But what about the hostages? For their sake he was there. He thought, "I came to see these guys and no matter what happens I will just stay here and see them."[6]

When Mary finished Khomeini's diatribe, the bishop began the liturgy. He asked Kevin Hermening to do the first two readings and then shared the Gospel reading and tried to give a homily worthy of the situation. "I just really tried to draw out of the Scripture lessons from Isaiah, Titus, and Luke, something that could give them a renewed sense of confidence and trust and real hope. Jerry Plotkin, who was Jewish, joined in the liturgy and they all held hands together as they prayed the Our Father. It was meaningful prayer memorably embodied. You could almost feel the pressure coming through the grip of their hands."

At the sign of peace, Tom was allowed to greet and speak briefly with each hostage. "In each case they just said again they couldn't thank me enough for coming and how much this meant to them." Joe Subic and Steve Lutterbach were on the verge of tears. When Mass ended, TV cameras and microphones turned on as Kevin read a statement, followed by Joe, Steve, and Jerry. They included a call for the return of the shah to face justice. They gave some explanation of how the people of Iran had been oppressed by the U.S.-supported regime. Afterward Joe, looking down, told Tom in a very quiet voice that the whole thing had been staged. "We had to do it. It would have been a lot worse for us if we did not." Steve whispered something similar, adding that the bishop need not keep this to himself when he got back to the States. In a very low voice, Steve said, "Just tell the truth."

After the four hostages were taken away, Bishop Gumbleton and Cardinal Duval waited for a second group. (Duval, who did not speak English, had been invited by the Iranian students as a hero of anti-colonialism. During the Algerian revolution when France attempted to crack down on its colony, Duval had renounced his French citizenship, throwing his support to the revolution.) The second group was half the size of the first group, this time just two persons, both women. One was Kathryn Koob, director of the Iran-American Society in Tehran. A cousin of hers had given the bishop a card for her. "It just seemed so providential that Joe Subic, whose parents I met, and now Kathryn, whose cousin I had met, were in my groups." The other woman hostage was Elizabeth Ann Swift, the embassy's ranking political officer. Koob, a Lutheran, and Swift, an Episcopalian, were happy to participate in a Roman Catholic Mass. This was ecumenism by necessity. Bishop Gumbleton tried to give the homily. "I was really feeling very emotional myself and found the feeling kind of welling up in me and so I found it hard to speak, but I did. And each of them wept a bit. The difficulty of the situation was sort of contradictory and contrasting, a kind of sadness and suffering, but at the same time of joy and hope."

At some point Tom asked the two women if they would like to pray out loud. "Kathryn did for a minute or two, and it was a very beautiful prayer, very expressive of deep faith and a lot of strength. Ann kind of wept quietly. And I couldn't help but have tears in my eyes too." They started singing Christmas carols, and Tom, never good at carrying a tune, was a good sport trying to join in. Cardinal Duval assisted in the service. "But with his inability to speak English, there wasn't very much that he could share. And I wasn't smart enough to think that they might understand French." As a matter of fact the two women did understand French. Koob spoke with Duval for a short while. Both Koob and Swift also spoke Farsi and likely had some idea what the guards or students were saying, but Gumbleton could tell that neither of them knew what was happening back in the States. They had been isolated even from one another.

Given the signal from their captors that it was time to end the gathering, Kathryn began singing "Hark the Herald Angels Sing." Tom noted in his chronicle:

So we stood there and sang again. And then they moved down over to the door, standing by the door and singing. I walked over with them. We just stood there at the doorway. The guards were waiting for something. I don't know if they had to wait for a car to put them in or what. But they were standing by the door singing loud and clear and even with a sense of joy, a strong sense of conviction about what they were singing. And that's the way they walked out. They walked out singing with their heads up.

Tom had never seen "people in such difficult straits, women who had been kept in isolation and still had such a strong conviction about who they were and what they stood for." Both encounters, with both sets of hostages, gave Tom the conviction that the precious moments together helped them renew their determination. Cardinal Duval told a group of people at the papal nuncio's quarters the following evening that these had been the most memorable liturgies he had celebrated in over fifty years as a priest. "And I felt the same way," Tom wrote. "There's been no experience in my life that's been quite the same as this one."

Rev. Coffin and Rev. Dr. Howard had completed the services which they had conducted with other hostages. It was 5 a.m. on Christmas morning when they all got into the car for a police escort back to the hotel. They held a press conference on Christmas day and met at the office of the Iranian Foreign Ministry with three U.S. personnel, including the *charge d'affaires* Bruce Laingen, who had been seized as hostages at that office. The day after Christmas they went again to the Foreign Ministry, this time to meet with Iran's foreign minister, Dr. Sadegh Ghotbzadeh, who gave them a history of the current crisis and explained that the ayatollah had made clear to the students that the hostages were not to be harmed. Ghotbzadeh had to be delicate, however. He could not challenge the students too much since he knew that the army would back them up, as would the masses. Only Ayatollah Khomeini could control the students, it seemed. As for the revolutionary council, some might have viewed matters the way Ghotbzadeh did, but others were more strident.[7]

Meeting with Clergy

Ghotbzadeh, urging the American delegation to visit the main theological school in Tehran, made arrangements for a "dialogue" with twenty leading clergy of Tehran. It was not a dialogue free of duress, of course. One of the

Iranian clerics spent an hour railing against all the wrongs the United States had done to Iran. William Sloan Coffin then threw fuel on the fire, launching into a rant about all the times the United States had intervened after the Second World War in various countries, overthrowing governments. Gumbleton observed:

> Now a lot of it was true, but it seemed like the wrong thing to be saying in that sort of circumstance, especially if it was filmed and it was going to be shown back home. It would have actually inflamed the American people. We had been trying to tell the Iranians that we can't risk arousing the anger or the sense of outrage of the American people any more than it was, and yet what Bill was doing would absolutely guarantee to do that.[8]

Gumbleton and Howard tried to shift the tone, but another Iranian cleric pointed again to U.S. wrongdoing. Some people gave personal testimony of what they had undergone during the U.S.-backed shah's brutal reign—years spent in prison, family members killed, others tortured. "It would seem that almost everyone in the country would know of others who had suffered or some relative who had suffered. It just has to have been a national experience that few other countries have undergone." Tom tried to persuade the Iranians that both sides would need to appreciate the intensity of feelings. He hoped more Americans would come to understand what Iran had been through under the shah and that in turn more Iranians would come to understand what was going on in the United States. He pleaded with them not to use any of the footage for Iranian television or any other propaganda purpose, and then asked that they all join together based on their shared faith in God, "to be united in prayer for each other, for our peoples and for the resolution of the crisis."

Gumbleton's post-trip chronicle included his observations about the flurry of TV and print interviews, details about the flight back to the States on December 27, and some notes about a de-briefing in Washington DC with the State Department, including Secretary of State Cyrus Vance. The religious delegation met with families of the hostages, mostly those who lived close to the DC area. "It was kind of a mixed feeling in the crowd. Some were sort of tentative about it, others were waiting with great anticipation of our visit." Tom visited with the sisters of Kathryn Koob and the mother of Ann Swift. Howard, Coffin, and Gumbleton met in separate rooms with the families of the various hostages each of them had been with. "I had the fewest. So we went off into a side room. And I began to tell them about my experiences. Again, it was obvious that they were hungry for any kind of information, any detail, anything that would tell them a little bit about their loved one."

Something from the whole saga especially affected Tom thereafter:

> Every time I say Mass now, at some point in the Mass I have a very good recollection of that Mass in the Embassy on Christmas Eve. And it just makes me feel very close to those hostages with whom I had celebrated that Mass. Ann Swift and Kathryn Koob with whom I celebrated communion service later. Something or another will come back into my consciousness and it keeps me feeling very close to them. I feel a very strong bond with them and certainly a responsibility to keep on praying for them and trying to do everything I can to make their situation understandable to the American people and, at the same time, try to make the concerns of the Iranian people understandable also.[9]

After Being with the Hostages

On Monday, December 31, the Associated Press reported on a story also covered by ABC, NBC, and CBS. "Four Americans held hostage in the U.S. Embassy in Tehran read statements during filmed Christmas services last week, some of which were critical of the U.S. government for refusing to return the deposed Shah to Iran for trial." Bishop Gumbleton told the AP that he was convinced that the hostages knew they were participating in a "propaganda ploy" and that they hoped the American people would realize that it was staged.[10]

Before the first month of 1980 ended, Gumbleton, along with Howard and Coffin, had been interviewed by dozens of media outlets, appearing on television programs such as the MacNeil/Lehrer Report and the Phil Donahue Show. And over the next several months Tom visited with or talked on the phone with various family members of hostages. He received a copy of a letter from Kathryn Koob to her family which was sent to him by Kathryn's sister, Mary Jane Enguist. Mary Jane thought he "might like to see Kate's letter written after your Christmas visit." Koob wrote:

> I was awakened about 2:30 and taken to a place where a Christmas tree had been set up and two priests were there—a candle and small table set up as an altar. Ann Swift was there too. She and I,

and as it turned out the Bishop from Detroit, whose name I still don't know, and the Cardinal from Algiers! I was in such a state of shock, not much registered. It passed so quickly! I had asked if a minister could come, but I never dreamed that one would come from the States!... When I introduced myself to the Bishop I said, "My name is Kathryn Koob," and he said, "I met your cousin at the airport in Detroit." I finally managed to blurt out "Lorna May" and he said, "Yes." He didn't know why she was there, but she was. We had a service and he offered communion to us and we took it gladly. Somehow, under the circumstances, Catholic or Protestant, Lutheran or Episcopalian, just didn't seem to matter. The Bishop then gave Ann and me his lectionary—lessons for every day from Advent to Pentecost. And it is used!

She could not sleep until much later afterward, but when she did finally wake up again, "the lectionary really was by my chair and I knew that the whole Christmas Service had really happened."[11]

Advocacy

In early spring 1980, at Carlow College in Pittsburgh, Pennsylvania, as part of a lecture series called "Toward a More Compassionate Society" that included Coretta Scott King, Tom Gumbleton said that the people of the United States should try to look with compassion into Iranian bitterness over the quarter century of the U.S. backing of the shah.[12] And then when Carter broke all diplomatic relations with Iran and cut off trade, Bishop Gumbleton voiced his views that these moves could put the hostages in "greater danger than ever" and that the U.S. should negotiate rather than escalate.[13] After a late April rescue attempt cost the lives of eight servicemen when a helicopter crashed, Tom made a statement:

There is no evidence in the president's remarks that he was saying we'd made a horrible mistake, that there was an unconscionable risk to the lives of the hostages and the deaths of the eight servicemen is a horrible waste of human life.... I think this disastrous, bungled attempt to solve this thing through force will make the militants and religious fundamentalists in Iran all the more suspect of our motives and ambitions. Now the students at the embassy will not let anybody in to see their captives. Why should they? They will think that anyone who's seen them lately might have been carrying secret messages about the attempted rescue.[14]

In early May, he played a lead role in getting strong language opposing the use of military force to solve the hostage crisis into a nearly unanimous resolution by the NCCB.[15]

The former Shah Mohammad Reza Pahlavi died of cancer in late July. A Detroit newspaper reporter asked Bishop Gumbleton whether he thought America was headed on the wrong path.

> Our government ought to be more forthright in our complicity over there during the 26 years of the shah's rule. Since we were so strongly supportive of him and it is now quite clear there were many human rights violations, and there were strong feelings among the masses that the shah's leadership was destroying their cultural and religious heritage, I would see no reason to refuse on our part to say yes, perhaps it was a mistake on our part, we did that kind of thing.

The United States should pledge not to interfere with their government, he added. "It is something we could and should do."[16]

Aftermath

The hostage crisis that began on November 4, 1979, ended early in the morning of the inauguration of President Reagan in January 1981. The yellow ribbons people had tied around trees throughout the ordeal could finally be untied. The hostages were free! When a *Detroit Free Press* reporter called Gumbleton, he expressed relief. "As you know, I am very close to some of the hostages and their families.... We will all now have to concentrate on welcoming them back with much patience and love."[17]

In early February 1981, Tom reflected on the whole affair.

> Yellow ribbons will be looked upon in the future as a significant reminder of our American hostages and their flight to freedom on January 20, 1981. But when the parades are over and the flags have been folded up again, there are a few thoughts that I hope will remain with us.

First of all, the joyous spirit that has accompanied our fellow Americans home: they are free at last! We thank God for their safe return. Surely the Lord's hand guided them and kept them from despair.

We thank many people, who, because of their persistent efforts, made freedom possible. President Carter said many times throughout the 444 days of the hostages' captivity that a day didn't pass that wasn't filled with efforts for their release. Sleepless nights followed by long days of struggling must have overlapped one another, as hundreds of people searched for a peaceful end to this terrible ordeal. We would be remiss if we didn't express genuine thanks to President Carter and all our leaders, as well as to the Algerians and so many others, who labored so long for the Americans' freedom.

The second thought that comes to mind is the tremendous anger which I feel in a deep and personal way, over the mistreatment of our hostages during their captivity. Though I was aware of the long and difficult days of solitary confinement and the anxiety of mock executions, I was angered even more when I read about worms in their food, days and weeks without seeing the sun, and beatings. Who could read about these things and not be angry? And yet, if we stop there, what can we possibly hope to accomplish? If our anger overtakes our will and our judgment, who can be helped by that? Somehow, with time, we have to go beyond our anger and frustration. Somehow we've got to find a way not to let anger fester within us until we are destroyed.

I think often of the father of Gary Lee, one of the hostages, who is pastor of a church in California. His insights help me to believe that we can reach beyond our anger. And who better to show us the way than someone who spent over 14 months waiting to see if his son was even alive or would ever be free? Reverend Lee prayed to God that his son and all the hostages would be cleansed from bitterness as they left their captors. He prayed that these 52 would leave their hatred and their revenge behind them as they boarded that plane for Algiers. Is this possible? Somehow, we've got to believe that it is. Can it happen overnight? Hardly. But it must happen eventually if these 52 people are ever to resume their lives again as whole human beings.

But this applies not just to these 52 or even to their families and friends. It must happen to us—to you and to me—and to every

American. We've got to rid ourselves of the desire to "get even." If we do not, we are doomed to a path of destruction.

Beyond that, we have to reach a point where we can even begin to see the other side, where we can search out the reasons for the anger of so many Iranian people, an anger that has been building up for over 25 years. Our relationship with Iran cannot be dismissed simply as history. Though we can never condone their taking of hostages, we've got to try to understand the whole pattern of this relationship. And that is probably the hardest task of all.[18]

7

Taking Up *The Challenge of Peace*

altimore Auxiliary Bishop Frank Murphy, a member of Pax Christi
USA, requested an addition to the agenda for the November 1980
meeting of the NCCB. A few other bishops signed on to Murphy's
request for a plenary examination of church teaching on war and peace in
the nuclear age. The *varium* was accepted, so at the meeting Murphy asked,
"Do we need to speak more specifically about the nature and numbers of
nuclear armaments, about the morality of their development and use, and
especially about the morality of diverting massive human and material resources to their creation?" Some bishops expressed concerns about the government's nuclear posture while others were more supportive. Gumbleton
then stood up and weighed in:

> If we need any convincing of it, a very quick review of what has
> happened in our country in the past thirty-five years since we en-
> tered the atomic era will help us realize that there is an urgency
> today that means, in fact, that time is very short before the nuclear
> holocaust could happen. We went for a long time after August 6,
> 1945, with the unspoken presumption that even though that terri-
> ble thing did happen—and many of us would have said it had to
> happen—it would never happen again.
>
> As we move on out of the seventies and into the eighties, we
> find ourselves now with a further evolution of our public policy
> that says we are moving toward a counterforce strategy with first-
> strike capability. We are also finding out that our leaders are telling
> us that a nuclear war, a limited nuclear war, is possible, something

which none of us would ever have believed before—and rightly would not have believed before.

We've just elected a President who has stated his conviction that we can have superiority in nuclear weapons, an utter impossibility. We have a Vice-President who has clearly stated that one side could win a nuclear war and that we must be prepared to fight one and to win it. When we have that kind of thinking going on, it seems to me we are getting ever closer to the day when we will wage that nuclear war and it will be the war that will end the world as we know it. We are at a point of urgent crisis. We have to face this question and face it very clearly.[1]

Soft spoken but intense at the same time, he seemed to strike a chord. The bishops voted to form an ad hoc committee on war and peace. Archbishop Joseph Bernardin (then of Cincinnati), known as a consensus-builder, took the lead, asking John O'Connor from the Military Ordinariate, Gumbleton from Pax Christi, and "middle-grounders" Dan Reilly of Norwich, Connecticut, and George Fulcher of Columbus, Ohio, to join him. The other members of the committee were scripture scholar Sr. Juliana (Julie) Casey, a provincial leader of the Sisters, Servants of the Immaculate Heart of Mary in the Detroit area, representing the Leadership Conference of Women Religious; and Fr. Richard Warner, head of the Indiana Province of the Holy Cross Fathers, representing the Conference of Major Superiors of Religious Men. Staff included Fr. Bryan Hehir and Mr. Edward Doherty. Bernardin wrote to the team at the outset, "It will not be easy!"[2]

Pax Christi USA members had high expectations. Frank Murphy and sixteen other PCUSA bishops wrote to Archbishop Bernardin in mid-March 1981, asking that the committee probe these questions: Can the nuclear arms race between the superpowers be continued without greatly increasing the risks of war? If the indiscriminate use of weapons of mass destruction is morally wrong (as Catholic teaching clearly holds), how can the threat to use them (a threat considered to be essential to deterrence), be morally justifiable? Is it right, then, for our country to possess nuclear weapons?[3] Questions and suggestions from every corner of the country came in, and the committee also sought out the insights of various scripture scholars, theologians, theorists and activists in the peace movement, defense establishment-types, and former or current members of the federal government.

At the committee's first session in July 1981, Gumbleton urged them to lift up "the specific contribution of Jesus' message, nonviolence."[4] One month earlier, Archbishop Raymond Hunthausen delivered a "Faith and Disarmament" speech in Tacoma, Washington, decrying the nuclear first strike-capable Trident submarine soon to be stationed at the Bangor naval base on the Hood Canal. "We must take special responsibility for what is in our own back yard. And when crimes are being prepared in our name, we must speak plainly. I say with deep consciousness of these words that Trident is the Auschwitz of Puget Sound."[5] Gumbleton praised him. "It's the task of a religious leader to challenge the presumptions of society. I'd say he's done exactly the right thing."[6]

Among the strongest voices challenging the bishops to be prophetic were communities of women religious. In October 1981, Sr. Mary Lou Kownacki, coordinator of Benedictines for Peace, wrote to the bishops. Nine hundred and fifty Benedictines for Peace (including members of men's religious communities as well as women's) were fasting and praying together one day a week to help inspire the bishops ahead of their annual meeting in the nation's capital the next month. Kownacki wanted them to know they would not be alone. "On Sunday evening, November 15, at 8:00 p.m., we will gather outside the Hilton Hotel to begin an all-night prayer vigil for peace and for the Spirit's clear guidance of our Church leaders in their crucial task of interpreting the good news of peace."[7]

About a year after the Bernardin committee began its work, at a retreat in Santa Barbara, California, Gumbleton told a large audience about the progress thus far. "We attempted in the beginning to write a biblical, theological vision of peace, and how to build peace in the world—what is the call of the Christian to peace." The first draft of the emerging pastoral letter on war and peace included a section on "just war" theology.

In fact, one of the criticisms we've received is that we developed that too much and underdeveloped the pacifism side of it. At the same time, I think it is very important to have a thorough and well-founded explanation of the Catholic theology of the so-called Just War. In fact, and this is sort of a tragic thing, during the Vietnam War when I began to be a bit more aware of the truth of these matters, I did quite a bit of speaking about that war, and its evil. I was at a parish in Detroit one evening, speaking about the Vietnam War, and in a real sense, speaking against it. I wasn't trying to force my opinion on anybody, but I was trying to lay out for people what their options were. I was making a point that because it wasn't certain that this was a just war, a young person really had a serious obligation to consider whether or not he had to go into the army. After the talk, a couple came up to see me. They were the parents of a young man. They said they only wished I had come to the parish two weeks ago. Their son had just gone into the service. He hadn't wanted to go; but they had told him he had to go *as a Catholic*. [Gumbleton's emphasis] They were very sincere, and of course, very upset.

Though personally committed to Gospel nonviolence, Tom had to consider just war theology and grapple with the morality of nuclear deterrence. Some people who testified to the committee, he told his Santa Barbara retreat audience, "say that in fact, the only thing that's preventing the horror of a holocaust is the possession of strategic nuclear weapons, as a deterrent. They claim if it were not for this deterrent over the last 37 years, we most likely would have had a holocaust already, and if you give up that deterrent, you bring on a nuclear holocaust." Somebody might argue that "if you dismantle that deterrent precipitously and without care you might bring on a nuclear holocaust." He admitted that he had to pause and think it over. "And in trying to make a moral decision in this regard, you really have to consider that as carefully as you can, because the existence of the world is at stake." Bernardin's committee was trying to determine what to do, what to argue. One thing they knew for sure was that deterrence and the possession of nuclear weapons amounted to a terrible and sinful situation.[8]

Fr. Bryan Hehir could recall in 2020 how Tom never tried to ignore moral complexities: "Tom fulfilled his role on the committee, but it would be an injustice to him to say that all he did was to represent his own position and the people he represented. He took very careful engagement with every issue that we dealt with. He was well prepared. He was smart and he was civil in the way he would conduct himself in the debates within the committee."[9] And Tom himself described what it had been like working with the committee.

I got stacks of suggestions. O'Connor did the same with the military. O'Connor would wait until the last minute after a couple of days of committee work and discussion and the committee was ready for a vote. Overnight O'Connor would talk with his military friends and return with suggestions for change. At least once, we already had taken a vote and he requested a revote and offered a suggestion from the military perspective. All of us had to deal with it and sometimes it got put in, but often I would object to O'Connor's language and managed to get some modifications. Though we disagreed during our committee work, it was not stressful or personal. We just had our different convictions. Bernardin made sure everybody's point of view was presented. He was an excellent chair. Hehir was a very good staff person. He listened back and forth and could summarize and find the right words to accommodate two or more points of view.[10]

Ensnared in Factories of Death

The committee invited experts to testify, from defense officials to biblical scholars. One expert had designed nuclear weapons. Robert Aldridge spent over fifteen years with the Lockheed Missiles and Space Company, leading an advanced engineering group on the Polaris, Poseidon, and Trident missile designs. His testimony was professional, personal, and powerful:

I am a veteran of World War II and saw combat in the Pacific. I was in the Philippines when the atomic bombs were dropped on Hiroshima and Nagasaki. Later I became an aerospace engineer and helped to design every generation of submarine-launched strategic weapons that the U.S. Navy has. I left that work in 1973 when I saw that the new Trident missiles were going to be aggressive weapons. I consider the arms race, and in particular the nuclear arms race, the greatest deception ever perpetrated on the American people. This is being done mainly by promoting a massive hysteria regarding the Russian threat. I do not deny that the Soviet military is a real threat which could annihilate us, but it has been grossly misrepresented in an effort to stimulate and perpetuate public fear. Meanwhile, U.S. programs are escalating the arms race and moving toward a world-threatening instability.

I am a convert to Catholicism. After Janet and I were married I started taking instructions to become a Catholic. I was attracted to the Church because it seemed to provide more spiritual guidance than I had previously experienced along with a demand on the faithful to put that faith into practice. The Spirit seemed to be very present in the Church's teaching. Twenty-five years later things had changed. I was struggling with the morality of helping to build nuclear weapons. I was convinced it was not the kind of work Jesus would do but the Church was silent on the matter. If anything, the priests and bishops seemed to condone nuclear weapons and even invested in the companies manufacturing them. I did resign from that job, but my family and I had to make that decision alone. At the time I was facing the most severe moral crisis I had yet encountered, the Church—the source of guidance in matters of faith and morals—was rapidly losing credibility in my eyes.

It is a sad fact that the Church just isn't relevant in the shops and offices of the arms industry. People in that occupation almost invariably succumb to the profit incentive and look out for "number one." If a person does show a spark of conscience, he or she is dismissed as either weak or radical. I don't believe I am overstating when I say it is virtually impossible to cultivate a conscience and continue that work. Some do sublimate into superficial good activity but fail to come to grips with the morality of their everyday work. One reason for this is the lack of firm and sincere spiritual direction.

Church leaders must not be silent. Aldridge urged a pastoral letter that would provide "meaningful spiritual guidance to the faithful who are ensnared in the factories of death."[11]

A very different message came from President Reagan's defense secretary, Casper Weinberger, who hosted the peace pastoral committee for an afternoon at the Pentagon in May 1982. Tom asked Weinberger about nuclear deterrence. "Is this simply a threat, or do we really intend to use them?" Weinberger's solemn reply, "Well, of course, we don't want to use them, but when we have to, we will." This knocked Tom off his feet. After Weinberger finished the rest of his remarks, Tom scribbled notes: "He operated off the conviction that we are weaker—'we must increase arms in order to disarm'—He wants to increase our capabilities. He claims that we are not trying to get superiority, but we must build up so that they have incentive to reduce." Weinberger had been candid in his forecast, "You have to assume a certain degree of irrationality even to consider using these weapons" and "nuclear war is obviously the last resort—but it could be 'just.'"[12]

The First Draft

In the same month as the committee's meeting with the secretary of defense, they released the first draft of their pastoral letter. Keeping his Pax

Christi network apprised, Tom shared the draft pastoral letter with fifty
or sixty theorist-activists. One of them, his good friend, the sociologist
and pacifist Gordon Zahn who had helped shape Pax Christi USA,
wrote back to Tom. Gordon wanted his good friend to fight for a more
prophetic pastoral:

> You will recall that at one of our EC [Pax Christi USA Executive
> Committee] meetings over a year ago, you expressed concern that
> the bishops' committee might be presented with a pre-packaged
> statement by Bryan Hehir, simply to approve. I'm happy that has
> not been the case, but I'm not too sure that much the same thing is
> not happening *after* all the consultations and discussions have
> concluded.... Instead of keeping the focus on the bishops' pri-
> mary area of expertise and responsibility—moral judgment and
> guidance—it too easily slips over into considerations of national
> security, deterrence theory, and the like. These things are not to be
> ignored, of course, but they should be fit into the framework of
> Christian morality—morality should not be "adjusted" or trimmed
> to fit the needs and objectives defined by political or military
> leaders and experts.
>
> I know you are alert to these dangers in the proposed draft
> and will do everything possible to counter them. I would go be-
> yond this, however, and suggest that you be prepared to insist
> upon some kind of minority dissent if these things are in the later
> and final versions. That will be necessary to give opponents the
> required leverage to work for a broadening and deepening of the
> pastoral's teaching in the future. It would really be tragic if all
> the fine work you have done over the past several years would be
> undone or seriously weakened by your apparent participation in,
> and acceptance of, positions against which you have struggled
> for so long.

Gordon and Tom had just been to a huge peace rally at the United Nations in New York City, where Detroit's "peace bishop" had spoken
prophetically. Tom replied to Gordon from Collegeville, Minnesota, where
he was on retreat with his fellow bishops.

> I understand your concerns about the Peace Pastoral.... I think it
> has a direction and a scriptural base that is something different
> from anything else which the Bishops' Conference has done. Also,

there's a section in the pastoral on pacifism which I want to call to your attention. This is the first time the Conference of bishops has taught so clearly that pacifism is a very important part of the total teaching of the Church, and held it up as not only an ideal, but a very real way of life that Catholics are called to. I hope that after a careful reading of it, you'll agree with me that this really is a major advance.... It's not a totally pacifist document, but I doubt that any of us expected it would be. I think it clearly sets us at odds with American national policy and allows for conscientious decisions on the part of many people to object and work against that policy in every way that they are called to do.[13]

Zahn wrote back again a month later, worried that the draft was giving cover to deterrence.

It may still be possible to modify, if not eliminate, the implied approval of deterrence . . . I'm sure you are aware that a goodly number of our friends are very concerned about this aspect of the draft pastoral.... One of the worst things that could happen at this juncture, I think, would be a split among our "peace bishops." I'm sure there will be opposition from both sides of the issue in November [when the bishops would next meet], but I would hate to see you in the uncomfortable position of having to defend a 'tolerance' of nuclear deterrence—unless it is placed within rigid limits.

When Tom got back to Gordon, he acknowledged the challenges facing the committee (not to mention the larger challenge of finding common ground among three hundred bishops from across the nation and political spectrum) that had to involve compromise and attempts at consensus, and thanked Zahn for his sensitivity to the complexity of all the issues. "It is more than I would have expected from some others—but exactly what I have come to expect from you. Just thought I would let you know that I really do appreciate it. Work continues on the draft. Pray, and keep your fingers crossed!"[14]

Don't Fudge

As the work continued that summer, John Quinn, archbishop of San Francisco, wrote to the war and peace committee:

I believe that it is necessary to make a clear distinction in regard to the use of the word "deterrence" as it appears in this document. Deterrence can mean two things. It can mean the mere possession of nuclear weapons and it does seem to be understood in this sense in various parts of this document. Deterrence, however, is also used to mean the threat and the intention to use nuclear weapons, not the mere possession of nuclear weapons. It is this second meaning which deterrence has in the actual policy operative at the present time. This does not seem to be clear in the document.

We seem to envision possession as some sort of static state. In actual reality, possession means the continual design, improvement and production of more and more sophisticated kinds of nuclear weapons. This needs to be taken into account in framing any statement of this nature which we would make.

In the margins of Quinn's letter, Tom wrote "most important" and underlined it twice. He was thinking about what Caspar Weinberger had said about deterrence.[15]

Quinn sought clarity, but another archbishop from the Pacific side of the country wanted nothing to do with deterrence. In a personal note to Tom, Archbishop Raymond Hunthausen reprised a conversation he'd just had with Jim and Shelley Douglass, theorist-activists at the Ground Zero Center for Nonviolent Action located aside the Bangor nuclear submarine base. Archbishop Hunthausen's call to conscience was poignant.

It seems to me that a crucial question for the writers of this document is the question of purpose: to whom is this written, and to what end? I would urge that the document be seen as expounding the Gospel. I think that the present document states strongly the thrust of the Gospel toward peace, justice, and nonviolence on a theological level but does not follow through with an uncompromising call for conversion and the following of God's way in the "practical" realm. The fact that for so long we have failed to live up to the Gospel call to nonviolence does not invalidate that call— it raises questions instead about our visions and assumptions....

I do not believe that anyone can predict the results of acts done in faith and hope, and for the bishops of all people to make statements that show so little respect for human beings on the other side of an issue, and so little hope in the security provided by God, is very sad. Why does this statement assume that success— continued American preeminence in world affairs, as now—is necessarily the end to be achieved? Is it not possible that success might take some entirely other form in God's eyes? If we are to consider Christ a success, what does that say about the security of arms? Is it not a form of idolatry to sacrifice the world's very life on the altar of national security?

I would like to see this document become an uncompromising preaching of the Gospel. I would like to see it recognize that use or possession of nuclear weapons is foreign to the mind of Christ. I would like to see it call for a conversion on all of our parts, a conversion to reliance on God for security, and for mutual support in acting out that conversion. I would like to see it recognize that people are not uniformly capable of such faith/action, and that there is forgiveness and compassion for those whose consciences do not yet reach that point—but it should be clear that that point is the point which must be reached. A document like this one must be clear and uncompromising in the way it states its message. We are all quite good enough at fudging on the Gospel demands. We don't need an official document to do it for us.

I would like to see it define security as other than national arms, success as other than world domination, and justice as a global ideal which must be achieved if peace is to come. I would like to see it stripped of its hopelessness—and its attempts to predict the future—and proclaiming instead the hope that if we begin to live the Gospel, God will be with us. If God is with us, good will come from whatever happens. That, it seems to me, in the ultimate hope, denied by arms. There is no end that God cannot transform. There is no reason for people of faith to devastate God's earth out of a desire for security. God is the only security that matters.[16]

Debate over Deterrence

Hunthausen had good reason to be concerned. His colleagues, it seemed apparent, were not unequivocally rejecting nuclear deterrence. Nor was Pope John Paul II, who weighed in with an evaluation of deterrence in a June 1982 statement submitted to the United Nations:

In current conditions "deterrence" based on balance, certainly not as an end in itself but as a step on the way toward a progressive disarmament, may still be judged morally acceptable. Nonetheless

in order to ensure peace, it is indispensable not to be satisfied with
this minimum which is always susceptible to the real danger of
explosion.[17]

Thinking about what Hunthausen had written and what Weinberger had
said, pondering the stark contrast in their outlooks, Tom wrote to Bryan
Hehir later that summer:

> I feel even more strongly that when we speak about the Pope's
> judgment that deterrence is "morally acceptable," we must use the
> whole quotation, because he is, in fact, speaking about a certain
> kind of a deterrent (and only this kind is morally acceptable), i.e.,
> a deterrent that is intimately joined with genuine steps towards
> disarmament. This is clear because the Pope says explicitly that
> the deterrent "as a step on the way toward progressive disarma-
> ment" is the only morally acceptable deterrent. I think what the
> Pope is saying becomes clear when you compare his description
> of deterrence with our actual deterrent. Ours is not within a
> framework where disarmament is going on. In fact, the Wein-
> berger 5-year plan for escalation, the plans to develop a strategy
> of protracted nuclear war in which we are determined to prevail,
> make our deterrent clearly something other than what John Paul
> was describing.[18]

But this was hardly how John Paul II's statement for the UN was inter-
preted by Weinberger, who wrote to Bernardin in September: "I am particularly pleased that your committee's draft pastoral letter directly recognizes
and supports the right to legitimate self-defense and the 'responsibility to
preserve and pursue justice.' I was also heartened by the statement of Pope
John Paul II to the Second Session on Disarmament of the United Nations
General Assembly." Yet Weinberger found troubling the letter's "implica-
tion that the policy of deterrence itself should be forsaken if complete nuclear disarmament is not imminent. The truth is that the continued safety
and security of all nations requires that we maintain a stable military balance even as we negotiate reductions." The path from deterrence to disarmament would be difficult. The draft pastoral letter had failed, in Weinberger's judgment, "to discuss the real opportunities before us in the area of
negotiations.... The President has made clear that no nuclear weapons system is excluded from possible arms limitations, but clearly we must mod-
ernize our forces as we negotiate."[19]

Dare to Preach the Gospel

How could the bishops or the pope preach the Gospel *and* provide moral cover for nuclear deterrence? The Leadership Conference of Women Religious called for the kind of prophetic language of a Hunthausen and bishops such as Leroy Matthiessen of Amarillo, Walter Sullivan of Richmond, and Michael Kenny of Juneau. The steering committee of Benedictines for Peace wrote to Bernardin and the committee in late July:

> First, we are concerned that the text in its present form may unwittingly accomplish precisely the opposite of what we think is needed, namely your voices raised authoritatively as bishops of the church against the nuclear arms race and the nuclear threat to future generations. Your reasoning, leading to your "qualified endorsement" of a whole range of behaviors from the manufacture to the stockpiling to even the use of nuclear weapons under certain conditions, will put you on record as being the first ecclesiastical voice to justify what is occurring. It was our hope that you intended to speak against the nuclear horror and all that contributes to it.

They questioned the draft's superficial treatment of Christian pacifism in the first centuries. "The first generation of disciples clearly felt impelled to follow the nonviolence of Jesus unconditionally.... Dare to preach the gospel of nonviolence even when it is unseasonable. That is your episcopal responsibility." The Leadership Conference of Women Religious, representing tens of thousands of sisters, urged the bishops to find their voice:

> We do not believe it is your purpose to teach military doctrine and so to lend the Pentagon and the United States government an authoritative role in the interpretation of the gospel.... The United States government has adequate access to the American people. It does not need to teach its doctrine through your pastoral letter, nor does it need you as its spokesmen. The church and all humanity, however, do need your clear voice at this time.[20]

In a letter to their good friend, Srs. Joan Chittister and Mary Lou Kownacki were adamant: "Dear Tom, Please fight to your nonviolent death for these points of consensus. It would be impossible for us to accept

any pastoral that does not, at a minimum, contain these consensus statements: 1. No use of nuclear weapons, ever, under any circumstances. 2.
No threat to use nuclear weapons.[21]

Tom shared their sentiments. The ineradicable challenge was how to
help achieve a prophetic pastoral letter by the whole NCCB, or at least a
solid majority vote, when not all the bishops were of the same mind. Meanwhile, Cardinal Terrence Cooke, archbishop of New York, wrote to Bernardin and the committee, referencing the statement of John Paul II to the
Second Special Session of the UN on Disarmament. Cooke argued:

> There is certainly a moral imperative to work with all the power
> that is within us toward mutual and verifiable disarmament. As we
> do so, the interim situation can be agonizingly long and fraught
> with danger. It is not, however, necessarily to be judged as im-
> moral. In fact, the Holy Father says, "it may still be judged
> morally acceptable." There can therefore be, in light of this teach-
> ing, sound application of the principle of double effect [one effect
> intended; the other unintended], provided we are in fact doing
> everything possible to eliminate weapons of massive destruction
> from the nations of the world and to make impossible the waging
> of war in our time.

After reading Cooke's letter, Tom scribbled frustration in the margins
of his copy: "I suppose he would say the Weinberger 5-year plan [which involved the modernization of nuclear weapons] is an effort to eliminate nuclear weapons!"[22]

We're on Thin Ice

A second draft of the pastoral went public at the end of October 1982. Tom
conceded that the question of nuclear deterrence remained "the hardest part
of our whole letter on war and peace. We're on thin ice with it."[23] The draft
included three criteria for evaluating deterrence: (1) If nuclear deterrence
exists only to prevent the use of nuclear weapons by others, then anything
that would encourage nuclear war-fighting capabilities must be resisted. (2)
Sufficiency to deter is an adequate standard; the quest for nuclear weapons
superiority must be resisted. (3) Since deterrence can be acceptable only if
used as "a step on the way toward progressive disarmament," each proposed addition to the nation's strategic system or any change in strategic

doctrine must be evaluated as to whether it will render steps toward arms control and disarmament more or less likely.[24]

Such nuance looked like thin ice to the peace movement. More palatable were the draft's calls for a bilateral nuclear freeze, recommending "immediate, bilateral, verifiable agreements to halt the testing, production and deployment of new strategic systems" and rejecting first-strike weapons.[25] The bishops voted in November 1982 to endorse the second draft. The Reagan administration raised concerns about the implications of passages such as: "As a people we must refuse to legitimate the idea of nuclear war.... No Christian can rightfully carry out orders or policies deliberately aimed at killing non-combatants."[26] National Security advisor William Clark leaked a letter to the *New York Times* telling the nation's bishops they were making it difficult for the administration to pursue disarmament *and* maintain national security. In an interview with a Detroit journalist, Bishop Gumbleton pushed back: "Clark's letter, while he had every right to send it, was not a very honest way to deal with us. For him suddenly to put something in the public press makes you wonder about (the administration's) motives."[27]

Battle of the Bishops

On the PBS *McNeil-Lehrer* news program Gumbleton was asked what could happen if the U.S. were to disarm but the USSR did not do likewise? Christians who had undergone martyrdom in the past might have to face it again. Syndicated columnist Kevin Phillips reacted to Gumbleton's stand as "mind-boggling."[28] Conservative Catholic intellectuals such as Michael Novak and William Buckley tore into the second draft. Mainstream media spotlighted contrasts between the bishops themselves. *U.S. News & World Report* featured "Battle of the Bishops: Should Church Oppose Nuclear Arms?" with two interviews—Hannan vs. Gumbleton. Philip Hannan, the archbishop of New Orleans, asserted that the pastoral letter should be scrapped. He had been a chaplain in World War II and parachuted into Europe with the 82nd airborne division. The draft pastoral, he said,

> does not acknowledge adequately the greatest problem that we face right now, which is the deprivation of the human rights of hundreds of millions of people behind the iron curtain. That should be our primary concern. It certainly is to the Holy Father, John Paul II. Our nuclear deterrent helps contain the terror. The Holy Father has said, and I agree, that the violation of conscience by the

Communists is the most painful blow that can be inflicted on human dignity. In a sense, it is worse than inflicting physical death. This letter belittles the enormous problem of resisting Communist enslavement.

Even the threat of first use of nuclear arms could be just. "We need this option to achieve deterrence." The refinement of nuclear weapons could deal with the problem of indiscrimination in their destructive capacity. The United States must have the military capacity to defend against Soviet aggression.[29]

Bishop Gumbleton was asked about Archbishop Hannan's suggestion that they drop the letter. Why not scrap it? "Because this is the most dangerous issue before the public today. It is the most dangerous in the obvious sense—physical danger. But it is also the most dangerous moral threat that we confront." Should the United States dismantle its nuclear arsenal even if the Soviet Union is not willing to do likewise? "Yes," but Tom explained, "when you make judgments about what is morally right or morally wrong, you can never base your judgment on what someone else does." Moral judgments made regarding the United States apply also to the Soviet Union. "It isn't a one-way morality."

He stood on principle, but the interviewer pressed. Wouldn't there be considerable risk in asserting the immorality of a strategy which the government claims is essential to national security? "I'd agree that it puts us in a difficult spot. No one wants to be in a situation where you are in opposition to the public policy of your own country. And so, yes, it's very difficult. But that's precisely what the role of the church should be—to make value judgments a government can't make." How would he try to persuade Moscow to accept the argument that weapons and war should become things of the past?

Obviously, this won't happen immediately, but we can begin to take some steps in that direction. What has to happen, of course, is that there has to be a different kind of relationship between the Soviet Union and the West. We can begin to build a relationship where we're not simply enemies always. If you project someone as your enemy, there is no basis for trust, and you're always going to feel threatened and be threatening to them, and you're going to intensify hostilities. If we act differently, we might begin to draw Russia into friendship with us.[30]

Sinful Situation

The pastoral letter's ambiguity on deterrence never sat well with Gumbleton. In early January 1983 he wrote to Hehir: "What we must make clear is that we are not declaring the evil of deterrence morally acceptable, but that we are saying it is morally acceptable to be part of this sinful situation under certain strictly applied conditions: (a) we do not accept this policy as an end, but rather we are determined to change it, and (b) we demand that the deterrent posture be a first step toward progressive disarmament."[31]

Everyone on the drafting committee knew that Rome would expect to have the final say on certain aspects of the pastoral letter. On January 18–19, 1983, Vatican officials hosted an "Informal Consultation on Peace and Disarmament" attended by Archbishop John Roach of St. Paul and Minneapolis, president of the NCCB, Cardinal-elect Joseph Bernardin (Bernardin had been "elevated" to the College of Cardinals and was now serving as the archbishop of Chicago), Msgr. Daniel Hoye, secretary of the NCCB, and Fr. Bryan Hehir. The Vatican also invited delegations from France, the Federal Republic of Germany, the United Kingdom, Belgium, Italy, and The Netherlands, all on the frontlines during the Cold War era.

Cardinal Ratzinger, prefect for the Sacred Congregation for the Doctrine of the Faith, chaired the meeting, accompanied by Cardinal Agostino Casaroli, Vatican secretary of state, along with other Vatican staff including Rev. Jan Schotte, secretary of the Pontifical Commission on Justice and Peace, who documented the proceedings. In his opening remarks to the audience of one hundred and fifty (all men), Archbishop Roach cited three factors which convinced the bishops to write the pastoral letter. One was the teaching of the popes and the Second Vatican Council on modern warfare. The second was questions and challenges put to the bishops by individuals and groups across the country. Third was "the conviction many of us have that the direction and dynamic of the nuclear arms race is profoundly wrong, that it is growing more dangerous and that the Holy Father's call at Hiroshima for a moral conversion must be addressed in concrete specific ways in each country."[32]

Cardinal Bernardin reported on the work of the drafting committee. On nuclear deterrence, he said, five characteristics in the second draft differed from the first draft: (1) Pope John Paul's statement on deterrence at the U.N. Second Special Session on Disarmament figured prominently; (2) the new draft restricted the morally acceptable function of deterrence to the one purpose it is said to have had: preventing the use of nuclear weapons in any form; 3) it developed criteria for assessing specific elements of deterrence strategy; 4) these criteria were used for making specific judgments on actual deterrence strategy and policy; and 5) "the pastoral recognizes those negative elements of nuclear deterrence policy which make any moral support of it so difficult." He explained how they had tried to thread the needle:

> Specifically, it is clear that as Catholic bishops we cannot approve any policy of deterrence which involves an intention to do what is morally evil. The moral complexity of deterrence, however, centers upon three elements: the possession of nuclear weapons with massive destructive capability; the threat to use these weapons; and the intention which undergirds the policy.... The Second Draft does two things. First, it makes a moral assessment of deterrence: one of strictly conditioned moral acceptance. Second, it does not try to solve all the questions of moral theory concerning deterrence which are presently debated by theologians, philosophers and policy analysts.[33]

In a detailed report delivered via Archbishop Pio Laghi, the papal nuncio in Washington, DC, to Bernardin and the drafting committee in early March, the Vatican's Schotte summarized Cardinal Ratzinger's messages at the meetings in Rome, presenting them as if all the participants affirmed them:

> Everyone agreed that both the interdependence of nations and the communion of the Churches among themselves would demand that basic agreement in these grave matters should be established between the Episcopal Conferences and with the Holy See, in order to provide guidance along the path to peace for the People of God, and all people of good will. [A national conference of bishops] does not have a 'mandatum docendi.' This belongs only to the individual Bishops, or to the College of Bishops with the Pope. When a Bishop exercises his teaching authority for his diocese, his statements are binding in conscience. Taking into account that the stated purpose of the U.S. Pastoral Letter is to form individual consciences and to offer moral guidance in a public policy debate, how can it be made clear when, in a statement of a Bishops' Conference, the Bishops are speaking as Bishops who intend thereby to exercise their teaching authority?

Another passage read: "The Draft Pastoral Letter seems to presume that a certain dualism has existed in the whole tradition of the Church with regard to the problem of war and peace: a tradition of nonviolence on the same level as a tradition of acceptance of the just-war principles. Does this correspond to the historical reality?" And still another question: "Taking into account the geo-political context and fundamental moral principles, how is the morality of deterrence to be judged? Can it be said that the use of nuclear weapons is illicit? If one grants that use is illicit, can it then be said that the possession is illicit? Or can possession aimed at promoting disarmament be judged morally acceptable?" Beyond making it clear that the bishops must not reject deterrence entirely (and sending this message with the subtlety of its questions), the Vatican's report on the meeting questioned the teaching authority of a national conference of bishops. The draft pastoral, so Rome had decided, mixes different levels of authority:

> Hence grave questions of conscience will arise for Catholics. A clear line must be drawn between the statement of principles and practical choices based on prudential judgment. When Bishops offer elements for reflection or when they wish to stimulate debate —something that for pastoral reasons they might be called upon to do in present day situations—they must do it in such a way that they clearly differentiate this from what they are bound to propose as *'doctores fidei.'* It was the consensus of the meeting—also seconded by the U.S. Bishops—that the Pastoral Letter in its present draft makes it nearly impossible for the reader to make the necessary distinctions between the different levels of authority that are intertwined. The desire of the meeting—offered as a contribution in a spirit of collegiality—was: that the Pastoral Letter at least be rewritten to state clearly the different levels of authority, and this for several reasons. First, in respect for the freedom of the Christian so that he or she be clearly informed about what is binding in conscience. Second, in respect for the integrity of the Catholic faith so that nothing be proposed as doctrine of the Church that pertains to prudential judgment or alternative choices. Third, for reason of ecclesiology, that the teaching authority which belongs to each Bishop not be wrongly applied and therefore obscure its credibility.

In his copy of the Schotte report, Tom underlined "also seconded by the U.S. Bishops," writing in firm ink next to this, "Not So!"[34]

If Rome could influence the pastoral letter, Washington could try also, especially given the close relationship between Ronald Reagan and the Pope.[35] Prior to the January 18–19 meeting in Rome, Reagan's national security advisor William Clark wrote to Bernardin:

> Clearly, the goal of the United States Government, and the purpose of its military strategy, is the prevention of war by demonstrating the attacker could not possibly emerge from a conflict in a position of net gain. This would clearly convey to any potential aggressor that he could not hope to achieve significant political and or military objectives through either a resort to nuclear aggression or by a threat to do so. For moral, political and military reasons, the United States does not target the Soviet civilian population as such. There is no deliberately opaque meaning conveyed in the last two words. We do not threaten the existence of Soviet civilization by threatening Soviet cities. Rather, we hold at risk the war-making capability of the Soviet Union—its armed forces, and the industrial capacity to sustain war. It would be irresponsible for us to issue policy statements which might suggest to the Soviets that it would be to their advantage to establish privileged sanctuaries within heavily populated areas, thus inducing them to locate much of their war-fighting capability within those urban sanctuaries.
>
> It is precisely because we do not want to make war upon innocent Soviet civilians—or at all—that we do not want to drive the Soviets into loading up their cities with offensive forces. Paradoxically, this is best avoided by using the kind of scholastic distinctions in our public expressions which then give rise to some of your concerns. However, recent public statements by the Chairman, Joints Chiefs of Staff, Secretary of Defense and myself should make clear to reasonable men and women that Soviet cities and their populations are *not* the aim of a deterrent strategy developed to avoid war. Additionally, the United States does not announce its targeting strategy publicly and unequivocally, nor should we, for to do so would give the Soviets a decided advantage. Ambiguity in this sense is as much a moral as a practical imperative for responsible U.S. officials. Ambiguity in deterrence is constructive because it fosters doubt which hinders the opponent's choice of one or another course of aggressive action.[36]

In a "Confidential Memorandum" of February 9, sent to Archbishop Roach, Bishop Gumbleton, Bishop Fulcher, Bishop O'Connor, Bishop Reilly, Msgr. Hoye, and Fr. Hehir, Cardinal Bernardin summarized personal talks he had with the Pope, and with Cardinals Casaroli and Ratzinger, earlier that month. On February 3, Bernardin had met with John Paul II for lunch. The Pope made it clear to him that the various hierarchies should be on the same page. The bishops' conferences of Western European countries must be heard because they were on the frontlines with the Soviet Union and its satellites. The Vatican worried about the potential consequences if a final draft of the pastoral letter included an outright rejection of deterrence. In his discussions with both the Holy Father and the Cardinals, Bernardin reported in the confidential memo, he had indicated that efforts would be made in the final draft to give more credit for what the United States was trying to do.

> Moreover, we would try to represent correctly what the Government's actual stance is. But I explained that we could not approve of every dimension of their strategy; I could not envision the Government's being totally pleased with our document, no matter how the final nuancing turns out. I added, however, that what we say—as is the case now in the 2nd draft—will be in the form of an objective moral analysis of specific realities rather than an attack on the motives, etc., of governmental leaders.[37]

The Voices of Women—the Strongest Voices

Rome, Washington, the pastoral letter drafting committee, and the National Conference of Catholic Bishops who would ultimately "author" the letter, were all male-dominated. Keenly aware of this, the Leadership Conference of Women Religious (LCWR) continued to push. The LCWR Region VII—Michigan section, wrote to Tom and the rest of the drafting committee in March 1983 encouraging him to make a "clearer explication of the relationship between economic interests and military spending, and the effects of this relationship on the poor both in this country and abroad."

Michigan's LCWR community, while commending the inclusion of an LCWR representative, Sr. Julie Casey, on the ad hoc committee, stated: "Nevertheless, we cannot help but feel that the pastoral letter might have had even greater richness had you included the thoughts of more women, the traditional seekers and keepers of peace."[38]

When a third draft of the pastoral was released, the Reagan administration did its best to spin it in their favor, but on April 10, 1983, Bernardin and Roach pushed back: "We could not accept any suggestion that there are relatively few and insignificant differences between U.S. policies and the policies advocated in the pastoral." The third draft, like the two prior drafts, arose from consultation and dialogue with the wider Catholic community and civil society and not from the Reagan administration, they insisted.[39] In an interview with the Associated Press, Bishop Gumbleton also refuted the administration's claims: "It's actually a stronger letter than before. It's absolutely false to imply the bishops have backed down in any way. They seem to be trying to co-opt us as having been backed into their corner. But we're not trying to...please them. Nor are we trying to get into a fight. But we haven't turned away from anything."[40]

Nonetheless the *National Catholic Reporter* editorialized that the third draft "pleases the U.S. administration beyond its greatest expectations . . . This has been the bishops' most significant political bout with the U.S. policy-makers in recent history....Under pressure, the bishops backed down."[41]

Among all the correspondence Tom received throughout the whole pastoral letter process, and especially in reaction to the third draft, one letter Sister Janice Link sent to him in April that year shined with austere clarity:

Dear Bishop Gumbleton,
Having heard you speak several times and being very moved by your sincerity and honest search for truth, I turn to you. After having become somewhat acquainted with the 3rd draft, I became very concerned about the changes. Particularly of my concern was the weakening of your position on "halting" testing and development of nuclear weapons to "curbing" the above. You are very important, not only to us as Catholics, but to all people for your stand on justice and caring for humanity. We need you to continue to *stop* our insane efforts toward nuclear disaster. Please amend the draft to again take a *firm* stand against using our resources for nuclear warfare.[42]

The Final Draft of The Challenge of Peace

To no one's surprise, it was John O'Connor who had pushed for the language of "curbing" to replace "halting." In early May 1983, the bishops were going to vote on the final draft of *The Challenge of Peace*. Detroit Archbishop Edmund Szoka, Dearden's successor, authorized plans for a major outreach effort to get ready for the letter's public release. Gumbleton and Sister Julie Casey coordinated with Cathy Wagner of Detroit's Justice and Peace office and others in the chancery, preparing a peace education program. Harry Cook, religion writer for the *Detroit Free Press*, interviewed Gumbleton and Casey. "We want to use every means possible to bring the contents of the letter into people's consciences," said Tom. "The pastoral letter seeks to fulfill the teaching ministry of which bishops are responsible. As moral leaders, we obviously must challenge concepts and patterns of thought and behavior which are lacking or flawed from a moral point of view." Sr. Casey felt that Michigan Catholics were ready to make the most of the letter. "People are excited that their bishops have addressed this issue forthrightly. And people— especially the younger people—are worried that we may not survive if something isn't done to stop the arms race. And they are looking to their leaders for help."[43]

Early May 1983

More than three hundred reporters from many nations, newspapers, and television stations packed the Palmer House Hotel in Chicago. Harry Cook, the intrepid religion reporter for the *Detroit Free Press*, wrote just after the bishops voted to restore the word "halt": "The bishops were faced with four hefty booklets of amendments to the letter's third draft when they convened Monday morning.... By their 6 p.m. adjournment, they had plowed through eighty-five substantive amendments, many of which would have weakened the letter's impact. But the prelates beat back every effort to tone down the language of the letter."[44] The next day, May 3, Cook filed an update: "The bishops of the U.S. Catholic church voted 238-9 Tuesday to adopt a controversial pastoral letter that condemns the nuclear arms race and directly challenges the Reagan administration's policy of nuclear deterrence. ... After two grueling days of debate and more than 450 amendments to the 151-page document, the bishops approved the letter."

Harry Cook knew Tom's life story well, so he added: "Passage is a personal triumph for the Most Rev. Thomas Gumbleton of Detroit, who for years was a solitary voice among U.S. Catholic prelates for non-violence and pacifism.... After the vote late Tuesday afternoon, Bishop Gumbleton smiled broadly as he was greeted with hearty handshakes and embraces by some of the bishops who not so many years ago shunned him as a radical."[45] Cook placed the Chicago meeting in the larger context of changes since the Second Vatican Council:

The Bishops were talking about nuclear weapons, defense strategies and deterrence. Making no effort to hide it, they were politicking hard and fast. It was democracy writ large—some might say run amok—in an organization that used to be run directly from the top, in an era in which these shepherds of flocks were considered by the hierarchy's higher-ups to be merely upper-class sheep expected to follow the dictates of the chief shepherd in the Vatican. ...There was Joseph Cardinal Bernardin—chairman of the drafting committee—sounding less like a prince of the church than a patient legislator trying to protect the language of a pet bill as he defended the highly nuanced, often deliberately vague but politically sophisticated language of the letter....

There was Bishop Thomas Gumbleton of Detroit again and again politely but firmly battling his fellow committeeman, Cardinal Bernardin, trying—often in vain—to clear away the complex verbosity of the text to make it crystal clear that the bishops meant business.

There was the forlorn and lonely figure of the Most. Rev. Philip Hannan of New Orleans, a chaplain in the 82d Airborne Division which fought in Europe during World War II, going to the microphone fully two dozen times in two days to chide Cardinal Bernardin and his committee for "selective memory...for ignoring the threat of atheistic communism on the very borders from which you naively want to remove the weapons of defense." At one tense point in the prelates' deliberations, an angry Archbishop Hannan shook his finger at Cardinal Bernardin and said, "You don't know what you're talking about. You haven't seen combat. You couldn't be saying these things if you had." So it went for 17 grueling hours over two days....

One sixty-ish reporter for a Midwest newspaper, who was born and reared a Catholic, sat in the press gallery and shook his head over the prelates' proceedings. "If my dear, devout Irish Catholic mother were alive to see these guys, these holy men fooling around with amendments, points of order, parliamentary maneuvering and caucuses, she'd damn near die," he said. "Boy, have things changed!"[46]

The Challenge of Peace: God's Promise and Our Response was a significant achievement, calling on the Catholic Church to be a community of conscience, denouncing the arms race, affirming personal conscience, lauding those who adopt nonviolent alternatives to violence, and clarifying that Catholic teaching begins with a presumption against war and a commitment to seek peaceful alternatives. Quite significantly, it employed and inspired a widely participatory process.

Forty years after it all, Tom talked about what pleased him most:

> The enthusiasm which it received when we took the final vote at the spring meeting in Chicago. It was voted on in the final session of the meeting which was opened to the press, a very unusual practice. It was packed with press from all over the world. The committee gave a presentation to the bishops prior to the vote on the final draft... committee members sat on stage with Bernardin in the middle. I sat at one end and O'Connor at the other end. Bernardin made a joke about it—he was keeping the two of us as far apart as possible because we categorically had different points of view.

And what disappointed him?

> At the time I was very happy with the outcome because I trusted the bishops would do some periodic review and evaluate and determine deterrence was the wrong approach. After ten years there was an evaluation. It left open the deterrence statement of 1983. ... Yet after the ten-year review, the bishops never dealt with it again. Ray Hunthausen never agreed with the Bishops' Conference decision to accept and include John Paul II's statement [expressing conditional moral acceptance of deterrence], even though he voted for the 1983 document. He was adamant against deterrence as a policy. Hunthausen was right.[47]

8

Moving Beyond *The Challenge of Peace*

Not long after *The Challenge of Peace* came out, columnist Michael Novak criticized the bishops as too partisan on various social concerns. He wrote that one bishop (apparently sympathetic with Novak) contrasted former paratrooper "just warrior" Archbishop Philip Hannan of New Orleans with "pacifist" Bishop Gumbleton. "In the 1950s we were all Hannans, now we're all Gumbletons."[1] The Catholic War Veterans convening in Philadelphia that summer warned that the peace pastoral could have an adverse effect on U.S. foreign policy. William Gill, a leader of CWV:

> I am convinced that the only way that our bishops wrote this was the influence of the Pax Christi group—Gumbleton, Hunthausen in Seattle, Sullivan down in Norfolk—these are the guys. [Pax Christi] is supposed to be a peace group.... It sounds real good. But then, oh man, in this country they've just gone crazy.... Gumbleton is the national president of this group.... I just can't believe some of the stuff that seems to come out of this guy....[2]

Undaunted, Gumbleton promoted *The Challenge of Peace* and advocated on behalf of peace activists who were, in his view, trying to put into practice the pastoral letter's best vision. On August 9, 1983, at cruise missile engines–producer Williams International Corporation in Commerce Township, Oakland County, Michigan, four activists scaled a fence and poured blood-colored dye into a pond, evoking Nagasaki (August 9, 1945) and the horror of what happened when victims not instantly incinerated by the atomic blast sought a moment of refuge from their terrible and fatal pain in the city's waterways. The activists were charged for trespassing and contempt of court because they had violated a prior injunction against protests, and sentenced to thirty days in jail. Later the circuit judge of Oakland County, James Thorburn, issued a second order of contempt because the activists would not promise never again to violate his injunction. The *Detroit Free Press* editorialized, "These shenanigans [by Thorburn] sparked two Michigan bishops to write a stinging letter to the judge, declaring that he has 'no right to determine a matter of conscience.'"[3] The two bishops, Rev. Edsel Ammons of the Michigan Area United Methodist Church, and Gumbleton, wrote:

We understand the judgment of the court related to the breaking of civil law, for which those involved were responsible, was necessitated by the laws of the state. Persons who engage in civil disobedience do not expect to be excused or protected against whatever punishment attaches to their activities. It is a standing principle that civil disobedience as an act of conscience does not shield one against the consequences of the violation of the law. The judgment of the court in regard to the breaking of civil law is not in question. On the other hand, we must strongly protest any action that is taken to compel a change of position relative to matters of conscience. Again, the court has every right to decide matters of law; it has no right to determine a matter of conscience. To endeavor to do so is a clear violation of the First Amendment freedoms granting separation of church and state. We are responding, of course, to the report that the court has insisted that Reverend Hall, Father Judd, Ms. Jaeger and Ms. Choly betray their consciences by agreeing never to engage in a similar protest of conscience. This letter is offered in strong reaction to any request by a civil or legal entity to impinge on matters of religious faith and conscience which are beyond civil litigation and judgment. Such an act of conscience is and always has been construed to be a decision of the most personal kind and one that is reached out of such personal struggle between oneself and one's God.[4]

More protests ensued at Williams International. The next summer, Rev. Bill Kellerman nearly missed his wedding to Jean Wylie at his own church, Cass United Methodist in Detroit. He had violated Thorburn's injunction and was detained along with four women, Sr. Margaret Dewey

(Adrian Dominican), Sr. Sheila Gainey (IHM), Patricia Mentzer, and Mary Girard, all of whom fasted to protest what they felt to be an unjust judgment. Tom visited them in the Oakland County Jail. They were, he said, "acting out of a very profound question of conscience."[5] On the seventh day of the fast, Gumbleton, Ammons, and other religious leaders went to the jail to support the fasters. Their press release read, in part:

> We recognize the protesters as people of conscience and people of great value to the community they serve; we have felt their absence. ... They are being held in jail in exchange for a promise that they will never protest at Williams International again. Requiring such a promise is wrong—and it is a threat to the religious and political freedom of all Americans. We pray for the protesters' health—we stand in solidarity with them—we urge their immediate release.[6]

Put Your *Body* on the Line

A handwritten note to Tom arrived in August 1984 from a federal prison in Sandstone, Minnesota. Maryknoll Fr. Roy Bourgeois, an activist protesting the training of Latin American military personnel at the School of the Americas in Fort Benning, was doing time for civil disobedience. (His story will be developed in chapter 10.) Several of the bishop's prophetic speeches had filtered into his prison cell. He quoted from one: "We have got to be disposed to share the Cross. We must be ready to take a resolute stand and embrace the 'foolishness' of the Cross. As disciples of Jesus, we must come to regard as normal the path of persecution and the possibility of martyrdom.... We must be ready to choose to do what is right, regardless of the consequences...." Bourgeois then made his point:

> Strong words indeed. I've been hearing these words from you and many others for over 5 years now. It's reaching a point where I'm asking if these are only words. In all honesty, Bishop Gumbleton, your words have become meaningless to me. You certainly *say* good things. Yet, I ask what is the difference between your actions and say the person who is for building more nuclear weapons? I really would like to know how many more nuclear weapons we must build before you "cross the line." I really would like to know how many will have to die in Central America before you stop talking and put your body on the line.

When Gumbleton wrote back, he said:

> I wanted to have a chance to think about it and pray about it before
> I tried to respond to it. I don't have any extraordinary statements to
> make. I did take your comments seriously and in a good spirit, be-
> cause I know that's how they were intended. I'd be less than hon-
> est, however, if I didn't say that the letter disturbed me. It did. I
> recognize the witness you and others give regularly by going to
> jail. The idea has crossed my mind many, many times. But at this
> point in my life I am not convinced that it is the right path for me.
> I'm just not sure that civil disobedience is the answer for me. I
> can't know what's best for other people, and certainly you've
> made your decision to witness in this fashion only after much re-
> flection, prayer, dialogue, etc. My conscience tells me that at this
> time I can do more good, both in a public and private way, by the
> kind of ministry that I'm doing.

But he would not rule out civil disobedience:

> On the contrary, it might well be in my future. It's something that I
> continue to consider, and if I decide that that's how I can best
> serve, you can be sure I'll do it—even though, admittedly, with
> great difficulty.
>
> It's what I believe for me at this time, and it's as honest as I
> can give it. I hope you know that my decision in no way reflects
> on what other people do, or on what I think they should do. You
> have my greatest admiration and support, mostly because I believe
> you're doing what you feel the Lord is calling you to do at this
> time. All I'm saying is, so am I.[7]

In November of 1985, Frank Cordaro, founder of the Des Moines,
Iowa, Catholic Worker House, organized a retreat in Bellevue, Nebraska,
the headquarters of the Strategic Air Command. Bishop Maurice Dingman
of Des Moines and Gumbleton invited their colleagues from every diocese
in the nation to meet there for prayer and discussion. At the retreat's end a
group of bishops would cross the line into the SAC headquarters. However,
as the *Des Moines Register* reported, they "failed to gather enough support
from other bishops and it was indefinitely postponed."[8]

Meanwhile Gumbleton, Dingman, and other Pax Christi bishops pushed
the NCCB to review the peace pastoral's ambivalence on deterrence. "Two

and a half years after the promulgation of the pastoral letter, in fact, the evidence strongly supports the conclusion that our nation's policies are not taking us far beyond a 'minimum' deterrence and do not give evidence of moving toward 'progressive disarmament.'" A review committee led by Bernardin was formed in January 1986. Tom served on this review committee.[9] At one point he made a statement covered by Religious News Service: "There has been little progress in arms control; in fact, many would judge that this period has been one of the most serious regressions in the history of arms control. The judgment of many that the conditions necessary for the 'conditioned moral acceptance' of deterrence are not being met seems well-founded." In response, the *Arizona Republic* claimed that the "radical prelate" was ignoring the Reagan-Gorbachev summit, the ongoing Geneva arms-control negotiations, and the complexity of arms control efforts. Gumbleton and others like him exemplified "the modern affliction of moral earnestness. All that is needed to be morally serious is passion and *pronunciamento*. Imprecise thinking is a necessary prerequisite for this kind of moralizing in which zealotry counts above all else."[10]

Fr. Bryan Hehir, who played a central role staffing the peace pastoral letter process, also staffed the review committee. Lucid in his recollections decades later, Hehir recently described Tom's approach during the pastoral drafting process and in the ensuing years:

Tom would not have written the document on conditional acceptance had he been in charge of it, totally. But the fact is that once the pope weighed in that settled the question. It had to be the center of our document because it came directly from the pope and everyone understood that the Vatican understood what we were doing. The peace pastoral letter process attracted a great deal of attention, so there is no doubt that the pope had us in mind, though not just us because there was a debate in Europe similar to this.

After the letter was published Tom was a great person to keep pushing and asking, well how do you assess the conditions? And those were complicated questions. If you got reductions in arms and those became quite deep in the post-Cold War period, do you count that as a partial fulfillment of the conditional, or do you look at the fact that the arms race still goes on, that proliferation globally has expanded, does that indicate that conditionality ought to be withdrawn? We did not have, in my mind, a single formula for deciding what counted as a plus or minus in terms of the conditional, because in the end you were trying to say, should you forsake the idea of deterrence entirely because of this fact or that fact, or should you see in deterrence the basis by which you can conduct arms control discussions? Tom just kept raising publicly and using the voice of Pax Christi as well as his own to keep measuring those questions.[11]

In June 1986, seeing no noteworthy progress toward arms control, Tom said that the "bishops are going to have to face up to these facts." First-strike weapons including the MX and the Pershing 2 missiles deployed in Europe must be rejected. "While I have to be careful not to pre-empt the work of the committee, in my opinion, both of these conditions are not being met." Deterrence could be morally justified only if part of a framework moving toward a different (not deterrence) security relationship between the superpowers, and given that the moral justification of deterrence could rest only on the prevention of the use of nuclear weapons, any new addition to the arsenal could be justified only if it led away from rather than toward the probability of use.[12]

He kept challenging the bishops to reject deterrence and stayed close to activists. On August 6, 1986, Hiroshima Day, a hundred activists trespassed onto the Wurtsmith Air Force Base in Oscoda, Michigan. They were among some three hundred people who participated in a peaceful demonstration across the street from the home of B52 bombers and nuclear cruise missiles. The public affairs officer for Wurtsmith, Captain Roger Davis, said the right to demonstrate would be respected, "but we cannot allow them to interfere with our mission. That mission is deterrence, and by that we hope to continue to guarantee the rights these people used today, one of them being freedom of speech."

This demonstration was part of the first Faith and Resistance Retreat organized by Tom's close friend Bishop Ken Untener of Saginaw, along with Bishop Judith Craig of the Detroit Conference of the United Methodist Church and Bishop Coleman McGehee of the Episcopal Diocese of Michigan. Standing next to them, Gumbleton said, "We are convinced that God is working here. We are answering a call. Jesus told the people the kingdom of God was with them." Rev. Bill Wylie-Kellermann, holding his infant daughter in his arms when he crossed the line, said in a soft voice picked up by a reporter: "You tell them we brought babies, not bazookas."[13]

That same year, the Catholic bishops produced another pastoral letter, *Economic Justice for All*. Gumbleton felt it could have included a stronger critique of capitalism. "There are many fundamental deficiencies with the capitalistic system that need to be addressed. For one, greed. It is the basic premise of capitalism. You cannot escape from consumerism in capitalism. It causes enormous waste and is therefore sinful. The free market, or capitalism, is not working justly in the international order. With the present system it is inevitable that the rich will get richer and the poor will get poorer." He was pleased that the pastoral made a clear link between unemployment and the arms race, since arms production is often capital intensive rather than labor intensive. "The arms race in the Third World is the reason for poverty and turmoil, and stress in the world is due to an unjust economic system. It is increasingly clear that if we want peace we must work for a just economic order."[14]

Capital investments in nuclear weapons research and development, manufacturing, and testing were massive. In mid-January 1987, demonstrators gathered at Cape Canaveral to protest the first-strike-capable nuclear missile, the Trident 2. Four thousand activists arrived from across the country, one hundred and fifty of whom had marched from Kings Bay, Georgia, 217 miles away, to the main gates of the Cape Canaveral Air Force Station. They protested the planned placement of nuclear Trident submarines at Kings Bay. Tom spoke at a vigil in a nearby church, "Can't we hear God say to us, 'Your conversion lies in tranquility and peace—in complete trust. The very future of our planet depends on this conversion. We can follow a way of violence, a way of death and a way of sin, or we can pray to be converted." The next day he encouraged the thousands of protesters to "keep working to save our bodies, our lives and our souls" and to reject Trident 2 as a "choice to die" being made by the United States.[15] Well over a hundred activists crossed onto government property after a three-mile march. He described them as "demonstrating, in a very dramatic way, that they refuse to participate in something they judge to be morally evil. It's a matter of trying to resist evil in one of its most terrible forms." They raised a ladder next to the ten-foot-high perimeter gate and draped pieces of carpet over the strands of barbed wire so that they could get over.[16]

Tom did not climb the ladder that day. By late February 1987 he still had not engaged in civil disobedience, but he was about to do so. "I think I have to, if you get to the point where you're convinced the political process isn't working and will not work and understand that this is something that's greatly evil...you have to take the next step. I still have some sense that maybe we'll turn it around."[17] Although he had no arrest record, the FBI had a file on both him and Seattle's Archbishop Hunthausen. The *National Catholic Reporter* had submitted a Freedom of Information Act request. *NCR* revealed its findings in mid-February 1987. The FBI and

CIA had been keeping a file on Gumbleton dating back to the late 1960s. The Michigan State Police also had records on him. He told the *Detroit Free Press* that some portions of the file reports "were blacked out, and I guess you can appeal that and try to find out what it was, but I never bothered. I'd be curious to find out if I'm being watched that much, but I really don't care. Anything I do, as far as I'm concerned, anybody can know."[18] Accounts of the government watching two Catholic peace bishops made international news. The *Miami News* editorial board wryly suggested that all the FBI needed to do if it wanted information on Hunthausen and Gumbleton was to ask them. "They are motivated by a foreign ideology, the same one that influenced another FBI target, Dr. Martin Luther King Jr. It's the Bible."[19]

Crossing the Line

In the spring 1987 issue of Pax Christi USA's quarterly magazine, Gumbleton extended an invitation to Pax Christi members from across the country:

> It is time to resist our participation in government policies that conflict with the gospel. We must change public policy in accord with the clear teaching of the peace pastoral....I invite all of you to come to the Nevada desert to pray at the place where all U.S. nuclear weapons are tested. And if you are called, I invite you to join in a nonviolent act of civil disobedience to protest our national policy of testing and stockpiling nuclear weapons.[20]

Many anti-nuclear protesters traversed the boundary line on May 5, right after they celebrated a Mass just outside the gate. Bishop Charles Buswell of Pueblo, Colorado accompanied Bishop Gumbleton in crossing the line. UPI reported:

> Gumbleton, Buswell and 96 other protesters, including nine clothed in black religious robes, were loaded into three buses and taken to nearby Beatty, Nev., where trespassing citations were issued by Nye County sheriff's deputies. The protesters were released on their own recognizance and will not be prosecuted, in accordance with a policy announced April 30 by Nye County Dist. Atty. Phil Dunleavy when he dropped more than 400 misdemeanor prosecutions against test site demonstrators.[21]

This was the first time Catholic bishops had been arrested at the Nevada Test Site or at any other protest of United States nuclear policy, although in 1984 New York Auxiliary Bishop Emerson Moore had been arrested for protesting South Africa's apartheid system.[22] "What I have been saying and what we are doing is consistent with the church's teachings," remarked Gumbleton, just before walking over a cattle guard onto the test site. "We have a moral imperative to protest the making of new nuclear weapons."[23]

Bishop Maurice Dingman had intended to join Gumbleton and Buswell but could not make it due to a stroke. Sr. Mary Lou Kownacki, Pax Christi USA's executive director, crossed the line alongside Gumbleton and Buswell and read aloud Dingman's statement: "In my powerlessness to move, I experience the powerlessness of all who feel unable to act against the spiraling nuclear arms race. So I ask you, in the name of Christ the peacemaker, to carry me across the line with you, in spirit, as a gospel witness to a fragile and broken world that desperately seeks peace."[24]

Pax Christi USA's summer newsletter noted that "although the action of the two bishops was symbolic of a more active commitment of the Church to peace, it was the presence of the 300 other participants in the action which gave substance to the witness of the whole Church." Young and old, priests, sisters, and laity, all "came by car, by plane, by bus—from 30 states in the nation and from as far away as Italy, Australia and Canada. They came from middle America and from the margins of America. For two days they formed a church community of peace."[25]

In November, speaking at Seattle's University Baptist Church, a faith community well known both for providing sanctuary to Central Americans fleeing violence and for protesting the Trident nuclear submarines at the nearby Bangor base which Archbishop Hunthausen protested by embracing war-tax resistance, Tom took a moment to reflect on his first arrest. "I was given a June 2 court date, 31 years to the day from when I was ordained a priest. I had come to the point where I had to resist through civil disobedience the public policy of my nation. Maybe I finally started listening to what I had been preaching."[26]

Buoyant Mood

In mid-June 1988, one hundred thousand people came together for a New York rally and march coinciding with the United Nation's Third Special Session on Disarmament. Speakers included Coretta Scott King and Thomas Gumbleton, with musicians including Pete Seeger. More than five hundred peace, religious, social justice and labor organizations sponsored the event.[27] Mary Lou Kownacki fondly recounted her memories of the day:

> In NYC, we had a huge gathering, people coming in from all over the nation. There was a march and then there was a special Pax Christi Mass. I was supposed to give the homily because I was the national coordinator at the time, and there were leaflets all over NYC, "Come to the Pax Christi Mass, homilist Mary Lou Kownacki." Archbishop O'Connor was the Ordinary at the time and his office called Tom and said, "You know, a woman cannot give a homily, that's a canon, so she is not permitted to give the homily." So Tom called me and said, "You will not be able to do it, but this is what we'll do, I'll stand up and I'll say, weren't these beautiful scriptures, hello everybody, and then I'll call on you to give testimony." So I said, "Alright Tom." We're all on the altar and the place is jammed, it's festive, people dancing, and it's time, so I'm sitting there waiting for him to get up, and he looks at me and he says, "Forget them, you go up there and you give it." So at those critical points he let's go of the consequences. He didn't get up, he didn't say one word, I got up and gave the homily.[28]

The mood was buoyant. But what of the nation's Catholic bishops and their peace pastoral letter? The review committee on which Tom served had been tasked to evaluate whether the government was meeting the conditions on deterrence. Gumbleton estimated that fifty to sixty (the NCCB had roughly three hundred or so bishops) shared his conviction that the Conference ought to finally denounce U.S. deterrence policy once and for all. The June 1988 report approved by most bishops did not take this stand.[29] Jerry Powers, working on international justice and peace issues for the USCC, helped Bryan Hehir staff the review committee. Tom was not pleased with the review committee's restricted mandate. "He wanted the anniversary document to say unequivocally that the conditions regarding nuclear deterrence were not being met. Cardinal Bernardin was clear that the committee did not have a mandate to reconsider the key judgments of the peace pastoral, including its strictly conditioned moral acceptance of deterrence."[30]

Deliberations among bishops and staff never matched the enthusiasm of peace rallies and demonstrations. On Saturday, May 6, 1989, dozens of antinuclear activists were arrested protesting the Trident-missile submarines being stationed at the Kings Bay Naval Submarine Base. The Trident 2 had a preemptive first-strike capacity. Bishop Gumbleton, standing with three hundred protesters, asked, "How can we be one with the people of the Soviet Union when we target their cities with weapons like these?"[31] Three days later, in Nebraska, he told reporters: "I've decided to make a public statement by crossing the line because this country is involved in an evil policy, and that policy has to be changed."[32] He joined thirty-six people in civil disobedience at the Strategic Air Command headquarters, Offutt Air Force Base, near Omaha. "By crossing the line you are publicly declaring your conviction," he said. "Whether it changes public policy or not, you maintain your own integrity. Later, it could help change public policy. There comes a point where, if you are a faithful follower of Christ, you have to resist. Whatever the cost, if the evil needs to be resisted and there is no other way, and nothing else will change it, I must resist. That is where my faith journey has brought me. I hope I can always do it in gentleness, faithfulness, and love."[33]

On January 15, 1990, at St. Anthony's in Detroit he delivered the homily, saying that Rev. Dr. King had taken on racism, classism, and militarism with a force more powerful than violence, nonviolent direct action. "The most magnificent part of his vision is to return good for evil, love for hatred, peace for violence, forgiveness for assault—to bring freedom, equality and justice not only to our nation but to all the nations of the Earth."[34] From May 24 through May 28 that same year, Bishop Gumbleton participated in the International Citizens Congress for a Nuclear Test Ban, held in Kazakhstan (part of the Soviet Union then) and co-sponsored by the Nevada-Semipalatinsk Anti-nuclear Movement and the International Physicians for the Prevention of Nuclear War. He wrote about it afterward: "About 600 participants from the Soviet Union, the United States and 15-20 other countries came together to demand an end to nuclear testing. A huge demonstration and outdoor rally with thousands of protestors made very concrete for me the depth and scope of people's convictions." The group from Kazakhstan would begin a peaceful migration from the Semipalatinsk nuclear test site to Hiroshima and Nagasaki, eventually arriving at the Nevada nuclear test site in September 1991. "Nuclear testing is still one of the greatest moral and physical dangers we face today. As the Nevada-Semipalatinsk Anti-nuclear Movement crosses the globe and draws us into it, we build hope for the future of our earth."[35]

Continued Reliance on the Just War Theory

In 1993, ten years after *The Challenge of Peace*, the bishops released a new statement, *The Harvest of Justice Is Sown in Peace*. It continued to rely on just war reasoning, even though it suggested that an ethic of nonviolence could have a place not in personal conscience but also in public policy. With the support of other Pax Christi bishops, Tom tried to convince the Conference to see that the just war tradition "continues to destroy us spiritually." By always relying on this just war tradition, they could not clearly condemn wars.[36] In the summer 1993 edition of *Pax Christi USA*, he wrote about "structures of violence" killing people:

> Almost one billion people on the planet contend with absolute poverty, are in fact dying in numbers that are overwhelming— 250,000 children every week, for example. It is as though Hiroshima happened every two or three days. How do we peacemakers remain oblivious to this? Especially when we know the world's resources are sufficient to provide every person on earth with enough for a fully human life. . . . On this anniversary we must commit ourselves to live up to the demands of being such a community by giving up our addiction to violence—both the violence of war and the violence of structures.[37]

Sr. Dorothy Vidulich, Washington correspondent for the *National Catholic Reporter*, was at the Omni Shoreham Hotel in DC when the nation's bishops approved *The Harvest of Justice*. She had been in Chicago ten years earlier, and she wrote about that historic moment when *The Challenge of Peace* was completed. "That evening we threw a party to celebrate . . . free beer, songs, even dancing; a veritable pacifist chorus line, Pax Christi activists (like Gordon Zahn, Jesuit Fr. Richard McSorley, Benedictine Sr. Mary Lou Kownacki, Eileen Egan, Joe Fahey) and peace bishops Thomas Gumbleton, Francis Murphy, Walter Sullivan and Maurice Dingman gathered around Carroll Dozier who celebrated from his wheelchair."

A decade later? "For their 1993 reflection, the bishops again consulted outside their circle. This time around, the bishops stated that nonviolence has a new importance and can even be effective as a public option for a nation." The savagery of modern warfare even left them skeptical about the just war theory, but they held onto it. That was not enough for many people who had been at that celebration in 1983. "And it wasn't enough for Bishop Gumbleton. Knowing he would change nothing, but determined that the point be made, three times Gumbleton—with the determined vigor of a peace protester on the steps of the Pentagon—was on his feet and at the mike." Gumbleton "in his unyielding nonviolent way," urged them "to abandon the just war theory, to renounce nuclear deterrence and to place

restrictions on rich nations, on multinational corporations and on banks regarding their attempts to receive payments on Third World countries'
debts." The bishops reacted, many nodding in agreement and "probably just
as many hid a bored yawn.... But Gumbleton held the floor, unflinchingly
making his points. He obviously knew he wouldn't get the two-thirds vote
required to pass his amendments, but he was hopeful 'the bishops will
begin a real analysis of what modern war has become and how we can follow the model of Gandhi—the poor peace man—and Jesus.'"[38]

Personalizing Advocacy

In early May 1995 Tom had been fasting for eleven days and planned to do
so for at least another week. He explained the purpose of the fast. "We're
drawing attention to the fact that the Nuclear Nonproliferation Treaty is up
for renewal at the United Nations, and this is an important opportunity for
nations to discuss how we're doing with eliminating nuclear weapons."
That treaty went into effect in 1970 and was scheduled to expire soon. With
nearly 170 nations debating the terms of its renewal, he said, "Right now,
the argument is over how much accountability will be built into the treaty
when it is renewed." Joining in the fast with him were Daniel Ellsberg,
William Sloane Coffin, Robert Lifton, and Helen Caldicott, among others.
Relying only on juice and mineral supplements, Tom called his action a fast
of repentance. "We're calling our nation to repent for our use of nuclear
weapons on Hiroshima and Nagasaki. We are the only nation that has ever
used such weapons against people."[39] On Monday, May 8, at a midday rally
the fasters stood in vigil at the 'Isaiah Wall' across from the UN. Etched on
the wall were the words from Isaiah: "They shall beat their swords into
plowshares, and their spears into pruninghooks. Nations shall not lift up
sword against nation. Neither shall they learn war anymore."[40]

Tom personalized his advocacy very often. In June 1997 he went to
Tallahassee's Federal Correction Institution to visit with an inmate. He
walked into the prison on Monday, June 16 for several hours of prayer and
conversation with Michele Naar-Obed. At the shipyard in Newport News,
Virginia, she had made her way with three others onto the USS Greenville
and then, evoking those lines from Isaiah, they wielded simple hammers to
pound on the submarine's tubes where Tomahawk cruise missiles could be
positioned. They poured their own blood on the launch tubes. Michele, a
member of the Catholic Worker Jonah House in Baltimore that was also the
home of Plowshares activists Philip Berrigan and Elizabeth McAlister, re-

ceived an eigheen-month prison sentence. Tom spoke to the press about Michele. "I came away being very enriched. She is a very profound person. She is very aware of God being in her life." She had been isolated from her family, including her husband Greg, her young daughter Rachel, and her friends. "I was very impressed with the strength of her convictions—which I share—that nuclear weapons are evil."[41] After she was released from the federal prison, he wrote to her probation officer asking that a judicial order be lifted. "The order prohibiting return to her residence leaves Michele, her husband and their three-year-old daughter virtually homeless. Jonah House is important to her and the family because it is highly respected by the wider Baltimore community for its constancy, faithfulness, non-violence, service to the poor and concern for the future of our world. In truth, it is their home."[42]

Working for the Elimination of All Nuclear Weapons

That autumn, as part of a Pax Christi delegation together with his successor PCUSA Bishop-President Walter Sullivan, Tom conducted a five-hour meeting with officials at the Lawrence Livermore National Laboratory near Oakland, California. "There is simply no commitment on the part of the U.S. to eliminate these weapons. I am convinced that the U.S. is in violation of our treaty commitments," he commented after meeting with Lab officials. Livermore continued developing and testing nuclear weapons despite treaty commitments, including the Comprehensive Test Ban Treaty and the Nonproliferation Treaty.[43] Gumbleton returned again in July 1998 as part of a "Citizens Weapons Inspection Team" of the Lab. Standing at the south gate, intent on inspecting the Nuclear Ignition Facility, he spoke: "This inspection comes on the heels of recent inspections by UN teams in Iraq and recent nuclear testing in India and Pakistan. Sanctions are in place in all three nations, when it is our country that possesses more nuclear weapons than any other nation in the world. We are also the largest arms merchant, often supplying weapons to both sides of the conflict."[44]

That same year he also tried to enter the top-secret nuclear weapons facilities at the Los Alamos National Laboratory in New Mexico. United Nations weapons inspections teams were in Iraq at the time. The "citizen verification team" he was part of wore UN style blue jackets. He announced to the press that the United States was "violating international law and violating the law of God. The only moral course we can take is to eliminate these weapons." He highlighted the hypocrisy of imposing

sanctions on Iraq for *allegedly* doing the very same thing that the United
States was *actually* doing—building and testing (and threatening to use)
nuclear weapons.[45]

This was one peripatetic and persistent prelate. In late April he flew to
Geneva as part of a delegation of Pax Christi USA and Pax Christi International, to testify before representatives of 187 nations who met together for
a preliminary review of the Nuclear Nonproliferation Treaty to be formally
reviewed in 2000. He spoke to the representatives of all these nations. "You
meet at a propitious time. With a new millennium rapidly approaching, the
people of this planet yearn to enter the new century free from the threat of
nuclear holocaust." Gumbleton pleaded with them "to take decisive action
to set the course for the abolition of all nuclear weapons on Earth."[46]

Denouncing Deterrence

In October 1998 Pax Christi USA published *The Morality of Nuclear Deterrence: An Evaluation*, undersigned by more than 90 PCUSA bishops and
produced by a team led by Walter Sullivan and Tom Gumbleton. Leading
up to the fifteenth anniversary of *The Challenge of Peace*, they reviewed
the pastoral letter's conclusions in the new global context:

> Throughout the Cold War the nuclear arsenal was developed and
> maintained as the ultimate defense in an ideological conflict that
> pitted what were considered two historical forces against each
> other—capitalism in the West and communism in the East. The
> magnitude of that conflict was defined by the mutual exclusivity
> of each other's ideology. Nuclear weapons and the policy of Mutu-
> ally Assured Destruction were accepted as the inescapable context
> of that particular struggle. Today the Soviet Union no longer ex-
> ists. The United States is now aiding its democratic successor, the
> Russian Federation, in dismantling the very nuclear weapons that a
> short time ago were poised to destroy us. Yet, the Cold War
> weapons amassed throughout that struggle have survived the
> struggle itself and are today in search of new justifications and
> new missions to fulfill.... It is absolutely clear to us that the pre-
> sent U.S. policy does not include a decisive commitment to pro-
> gressive nuclear disarmament. Rather, nuclear weapons policy has
> been expanded in the post-Cold War period to include new mis-
> sions well beyond their previous role as a deterrent to nuclear at-

tack. The United States today maintains a commitment to use nuclear weapons first, including pre-emptive nuclear attacks on nations that do not possess nuclear weapons.

The policy of nuclear deterrence was being institutionalized, and nuclear deterrence had been expanded well beyond the role of deterring the use of nuclear weapons by others. The U.S. was intent on retaining its nuclear deterrent into the indefinite future. "Nuclear deterrence as a national policy must be condemned as morally abhorrent because it is the excuse and justification for the continued possession and further development of these horrendous weapons. We urge all to join in taking up the challenge to begin the effort to eliminate nuclear weapons now, rather than relying on them indefinitely."[47]

The New Millennium

In the years that followed, Thomas Gumbleton maintained his witness against the threat of nuclear war in countless demonstrations and countless acts of witness. He was arrested again in 2000 at the Nevada Test Site.

On Hiroshima Day, 2001, Tom and fourteen others were arrested at the Y-12 nuclear weapons production plant in Oak Ridge, Tennessee. The fissile radioactive material for the Hiroshima bomb came from the Y-12 Plant. The same place produced components for a new generation of nuclear weapons.

He was back at the Oak Ridge site again on August 10, 2003. After entering the grounds he was arrested with many others, shackled, and placed in jail for a few hours. Years later he commented that many peace activists over the decades had endured a great deal more than whatever he went through, spending much longer periods incarcerated—sometimes months or years—for their nonviolent acts of conscience.[48] Yet the example of a Catholic bishop committing civil disobedience for the cause of peace might have a special impact on others. The threat of nuclear weapons, he believed, raised fundamental moral questions that every Christian should evaluate in the light of the Gospel. In a 2021 conversation for this book, he put it this way:

If *The Challenge of Peace* were really used as a teaching tool, the Catholic Church would have a much different stance toward what's going on in the world right now with nuclear weapons, their continued development, the threats to use them. . . . The failure of that letter is that it has never been used that much. It was and still is one of the clearest statements concerning the morality of nuclear weapons and nuclear war.

You don't have to be committed to nonviolence to be opposed to every use or even any threat to use nuclear weapons. Just war theology absolutely rules out such weapons because they violate two of the main criteria: the requirement to declare war, because they would be used before any declaration, but also the indiscriminate killing because here is no way to control them; you would kill tens of thousands, and you might end the world as we know it. You don't have to be a follower of Jesus on the path of nonviolence to be opposed to nuclear weapons. You don't have to be a pacifist to be opposed to nuclear weapons.

Although he was fully committed to nonviolence as a personal practice well before the time of the peace pastoral letter, he'd worked to get a consensus among the bishops with regard to their appeal for U.S. public policy. "I worked with the committee to put forth Catholic doctrine. We weren't trying to go beyond what the Church accepted and taught, just war theology. That was our basic teaching on war. My concern has always been that we don't even live up to the just war theology let alone try to hit the ideal of nonviolence."[49]

Did he think it had been a mistake to try to build consensus?

I'm not so sure it was. It would have been the easier thing to say, "Well, I'm an absolutist on this issue," but the pope wanted us to put in a condition on deterrence and I went along with it. On the face of it, it was reasonable. The Conference was not committed to that peace pastoral the way I was, and the way Ray Hunthausen was. So five and ten years later they still would not make the moral judgment that we were not moving toward disarmament. I can't say what was in the minds of the bishops at the time. I took it that we would periodically check whether the condition was being fulfilled or not, and if it was not being fulfilled then we would have to say no and come out against deterrence completely. The only way we justified deterrence was on the condition of moving in the direction of disarmament, and we never moved in that direction.[50]

PART TWO

9

My Brother Came Out

In the summer of 1974, Brian McNaught, a reporter and columnist for *The Michigan Catholic*, came out of the closet in an interview with *The Detroit News*. Nancy Manser, the *DN's* religion editor, had decided to do a story on homosexuality and religion, and reached out to McNaught, having learned that he was the founder of a newly forming Detroit chapter of Dignity. Across the country chapters of this organization were emerging with a mission to foster respect for the rights, pride, and *dignity* of Catholics of same-sex orientation. In his mid-twenties, McNaught was well liked and respected at Detroit's progressive diocesan newspaper, so he had some reason to hope he might get official support from the Archdiocese of Detroit.

When he came to work on the Monday morning following the Saturday publication of his interview, Margaret Cronyn, *The Michigan Catholic*'s new editor, called him into her office. "We're dropping your column," she told him. Angry readers were canceling their subscriptions and upset advertisers and parishes were pressuring the paper. When Manser soon thereafter called McNaught asking if there had been any reaction to her story, he told her, "Yeah, they just dropped my column." The next day *The Detroit News* headline, "Catholic Newspaper Drops Column by Homosexual," brought on a deluge of protest. Gay students at the University of Michigan picketed outside the office of *The Michigan Catholic*. Dignity USA heralded McNaught's cause. Despite all the support he received, the intensely negative reaction from conservative sides of the Catholic world left Brian feeling lonely. "The day before the article appeared in *The Detroit News,* I was the privileged son of a prominent Irish Catholic General

Motors family of seven. The next day I was 'a homosexual.'" His own newspaper was cutting off his widely read weekly column and he had not yet found a new home in the gay community. "It was scary. I prayed a lot."[1]

On Labor Day, priests, women religious, and laity attended a Mass at Holy Trinity Church in Detroit's Corktown, where Monsignor Clement Kern told the gathering: "All of us, gay and straight alike, have come here today to affirm ourselves before God in faith; to accept ourselves without regrets or self-pity; and to seek a good and full life in keeping with our potential for growth and God's call." Dozens of people joined in a silent march to the Archdiocese of Detroit's chancery office to witness to their belief that God loves all people regardless of sexual orientation. Cardinal Dearden had called Kern and asked him to cancel the service. Kern, gentle but firm, told Dearden, "Cardinal, I just can't do that."[2]

Aside from Monsignor Kern, McNaught was getting support from other sectors, but not from the bishops. In early September he launched a hunger strike, declaring that he was "seeking a response from the church to commit themselves to a program of education, and a commitment to end discrimination where they saw it."[3] In mid-August, Gumbleton had met with Brian to try to explain how official Catholic condemnation of homosexual acts could somehow cohere with support for the dignity of all persons. Brian had hoped for more support from the bishop widely recognized as progressive.[4] He went ahead with his hunger strike. Then, three weeks into his fast he received a letter from Bishop Gumbleton and Bishop Joe Imesch (also an auxiliary) in response to a letter he had written to Dearden and all the bishops of the Archdiocese of Detroit explaining why he was fasting. He was losing weight and energy, and the two bishops expressed their concern. "From the outset let us say that we respect the motives behind your fast, and the sincerity of your efforts." The Church would not endorse or condone overt homosexual acts, they wrote, but "we have a serious obligation to root out structures and attitudes that discriminate against the homosexual as a person. We will exert our leadership in behalf of this effort."[5]

In light of these encouraging words, Brian ended his fast of twenty-four days. Paul Diederich and co-leaders of Dignity/USA wrote to the pair of bishops thanking them for their "sensitive understanding and concern for Brian in his fast, and for the seriousness of his message. Moreover, we appreciate your firm commitment of the Church in Detroit, to root out the structures and attitudes of oppression towards Homosexuals, both within and outside the Church." But Dignity/USA's praise was premature.[6] McNaught was soon fired from his job as a writer for the diocesan paper. The paper gave a different rationale for the firing, but the real reason was obvious.[7] Though they had noble intentions, Gumbleton and Imesch, like Dearden and so many other bishops across the country, were part of a discriminatory church structure and culture. Could any bishop find his way out?

Dignity chapters challenged the Catholic bishops to change their outlook. In 1976, at the Bicentennial Call to Action gathering in Detroit, McNaught was Dignity's voting delegate. He called for church efforts to promote respect for gay and lesbian people and their fight against discrimination. As noted in Chapter 4, Call to Action affirmed these calls in its resolutions. In 1977, the Catholic Theological Society of America published *Human Sexuality: New Directions in American Catholic Thought.* One of its authors, Fr. Anthony Kosnik, was an influential moral theologian in the Detroit area whom Tom Gumbleton knew and respected. Kosnik and his co-authors called for a fresh perspective on homosexuality, breaking through old stereotypes and grounding church teaching in new evidence coming from the biological and social sciences. There were some strides being made in the church in those years and into the 1980s, but they were slow.[8]

Michael Hovey Coming Out

From August 15 to 17, 1986, Pax Christi USA held its thirteenth annual national assembly at Emmanuel College in Boston. The national council's meeting took place in conjunction with the larger assembly. At the council meeting, the issue came up as to whether Pax Christi would make a statement denouncing violence against gay people. Michael Hovey, a native of Detroit and a conscientious objector after five years serving in the Navy in the 1970s, had been working closely with Gordon Zahn on CO-issues and so he accompanied Zahn to the council meeting. Afterward there was a social. A group gathered around the RV of Bill and Mary Carry, Pax Christi stalwarts from Michigan who always traveled to events around the nation in their RV. About ten people were relaxing, enjoying cocktails. Hovey had been thinking about the council meeting and the fact that Eileen Egan was opposed to Pax Christi saying anything about gay people. Egan, not anti-gay at all, felt that the issue was outside the scope of Pax Christi's mission. So that evening Hovey decided to speak up. "As a gay man, I'm not sure that Pax Christi itself should say something because, you know, we are a peace group, we're not a general human rights group, but I just want to tell you that as a gay person this is important." Bill Carry asked him how his parents reacted when they found out that he was gay. Others asked him how it had felt to sit through the council debate earlier in the day.

So Hovey told them his story. He had not "come out" until he was thirty-two years old. He had been living in Boston when he got a call from his sister, Patti. Their parents had moved back to the family home in Romeo, Michigan, from Florida, and Patti worried that people in small town Romeo would gossip about their brother Steve. She decided to tell their parents that Steve was gay.

> Mom broke down in tears and said she was worried about how this could negatively affect Steve, losing his job or getting sick. I asked my sister, "Then what did you do?" She answered that she told Mom, "Look at Mike, he's gay, and he's had a wonderful life." I was stunned that my sister had come out about my brother and me without asking us. I asked Patti how Mom then reacted. Mom started crying harder and asked our dad, "What are we going to do?" Dad answered, "They're our sons and we love them, what's there to do?" About three weeks after that phone call from my sister, my parents came to Boston to visit. I sat down with them. We had a heart to heart. We were all relieved, my brother included, to bring this out in the open. The wonderful thing about coming out to anyone, especially parents, is that a burden is lifted of hiding behind the truth.[9]

Like everyone else at the evening social, Bishop Gumbleton, president of PCUSA, listened intently to Hovey's story. It was cathartic for Hovey, opening up and sharing something with people he cared about.

The next day the National Council of Pax Christi made a strong statement: "[I]t is absolutely imperative at this time to utter a word against what we sense and fear to be an increasing marginalization and oppression of men and women of homosexual orientation.... Wherever we exploit or reject or condemn our brothers and sisters for what they are (or, more cruelly, for what we think they are), we fail in our mission as peacemakers. Therefore, Pax Christi USA is challenged to address specifically the attitudes and acts of violence directed toward women and men of homosexual orientation in our society."[10]

Gumbleton would soon feel the transformative impact of another story, this time from a member of his own family.

My Brother

Tom was one of three Catholic bishops, including Ken Untener of Saginaw, Michigan, and Bill Hughes of Covington, Kentucky, speaking to about five hundred people at a New Ways Ministry symposium in Chicago on March 28, 1992. Their task was to offer a sense of what a bishop's pastoral response ought to be to gay and lesbian people. The papal nuncio had warned them not to attend, but they decided to go anyway. Gumbleton had two presentations ready in his head, one about the pastoral role of a bishop, the other more personal. As he neared the podium, he said to himself, "I am going to do it, I am going to tell my own story."[11]

He had not spoken to anybody about this before, but he hoped that what he was about to share could help people understand the barriers still to be overcome, such as a priest chaplain in a general hospital being so rigid as to not even enter the room of an AIDS patient to anoint or bless and pray with that person. "From the doorway he tells the patients that they must repent of their evil ways." But, Bishop Gumbleton admitted to the Chicago assembly, if it was difficult for many bishops to really be examples of openness to the gay and lesbian community and to instill this openness in others, he wanted to speak honestly about his own life difficulty. "The seminary formation I received was reinforced by the culture in which I grew up. It did not prepare me in any way to minister effectively to gay and lesbian people."[12] The hushed crowd listened as Tom described a letter he had received from his brother Dan out in California in the late 1980s, declaring to his family that he was gay. "Dan and his partner have a very good relationship. It is humbling for me to acknowledge that I would not even deal with that letter for several months. I simply refused to respond. For a while, I was unwilling to visit him."

Before saying more about how he and his family reacted to Dan, he talked about a Cuban immigrant named Olga, a seventy-year-old mother and widow he met when on a ministry visit to St. Francis House, a group home for AIDS patients in Tampa, Florida. (For many years Tom would fly to Florida to spend the long Thanksgiving weekend working with Sr. Anne Dougherty and St. Francis House.) Olga told him that she was fortunate to have the two best sons in the world, "one on earth and the other in heaven. It is for the one in heaven that I have become an activist for gay rights and AIDS education. I promised my son, Raul, who died from complications of AIDS in June 1990, that as long as I lived, I will fight AIDS with all my heart and work for the dignity of gay society." Raul was a proud man, and she was a proud mother. When her son came out, she said, she was shocked at first. "I wanted to die, but I looked at my son and I knew God loved him every bit as much as I did. So, I took him in an embrace and that embrace lasted as long as he lived. I was able to have peace, serenity, and acceptance. It was God who showed me the way, which is why I know God approves of what I'm doing these days." Olga was a blessing, Tom said, because "she helped me to be much more accepting of my brother and his partner."[13]

Not long after that emotional meeting with Olga he had an encounter with his own mother back home in Michigan. The family letter from her youngest son Dan had really unsettled her. In 1989, about a year before she died, she asked Tom, "What's going to happen to Dan? Will he go to hell?" She was well versed in Catholic teaching, but she looked to her son The Bishop in this moment of bewilderment. They were together on the front porch of her house late that evening. "She was almost afraid to die with that terrible fear that somehow her youngest son would end up in hell just because he was homosexual. Because I had come to know Olga and to imbibe from her something of the compassion, the love, and the pride that she felt, I was able to speak with my mother in a very understanding way, which I might not have been able to do otherwise."[14] Dan was not going to hell, Tom told her.

When he told this same story for Catholic Parents of Gay and Lesbian Children at a retreat center in Stamford, Connecticut, a couple of years after the Chicago address, Gumbleton was self-critical, saying he had been poorly prepared to be a pastoral minister to gay and lesbian people when first ordained in 1956. He would hear confessions and at times people who were gay would confess to committing acts with other men. He would admonish them, "You know, you probably won't fall into that sin if you separate yourself from the places where that happens. Get away from the occasions of sin." He thought this was good counsel. "Well, I wasn't even beginning to understand the whole situation."

In Chicago for the New Ways symposium he had decided he had to "come out" in a way himself, and say, "I'm a bishop and I have a gay brother and it's okay and he's part of our family, his partner is accepted as part of our family, they visit, and it's okay, and I have discovered since then that this was a very important thing for me to do, because speaking at New Ways Ministry had a very important impact on the people there."[15] His Chicago story made major news in the *National Catholic Reporter.* There were soon stories, including a feature story in the *Detroit Free Press* and broad coverage through the AP.[16] "There weren't very many bishops saying anything like that," he recalled in a 2020 interview, "so I began to get very involved in responding to letters from gay priests, women religious, and lay people, and I met with dozens of them for sure, and did an awful lot of work. That became a whole new kind of area of ministry for me because there just were not many Catholic bishops they could go to."[17]

Brian McNaught's Call

In the autumn of 1992, after he had learned about Bishop Gumbleton's growing involvement in ministry to the gay and lesbian community, McNaught wrote congratulating him. In reply, Gumbleton wrote:

> Dear Brian,
>   When I reflect on your experience in Detroit at *The Michigan Catholic,* I now have a better sense of how very, very difficult it must have been for you. Truly you were ahead of your time in calling for understanding for the gay community. I'm sure those days were filled with frustration and loneliness. I'm personally grateful that you persevered. My affiliation with New Ways Ministry and my experience in working with HIV positive and PWA's [people with AIDS] have opened my eyes. Know that I will continue to do all I can to work for justice and understanding for the homosexual community.[18]

McNaught had become a nationally known diversity trainer and author. He called the bishop, yearning to understand what had happened to draw him into the cause. Over the phone Tom confessed, "I was totally unhelpful and insensitive to you. I didn't know anything about homosexuality. I grew up with a fear of asking questions about sex." He wished he'd been more supportive. "I have sad feelings of failure about what happened to you. We failed you. It was a real loss to the newspaper and to the diocese." The case had bothered him for years, enough to get him thinking and reflecting. As he was wont to do on any social issue that commanded his attention, Gumbleton began reading to try to understand things better. Fr. John McNeill's influential *The Church and the Homosexual* was helpful. A series of educational programs for clergy regarding sexuality and diversity were conducted in the Detroit area during the years after the McNaught case, and these were helpful. And then there was Tom's experience working with people suffering from AIDS. He served on the board of St. Francis House where he met Olga. His brother Dan's coming out had had a profound personal impact, he told Brian.[19] McNaught wrote about all this in *Now That I'm Out, What Do I Do?*

> Twenty-some years ago, I wanted something very different from the bishop than I got during our recent telephone conversation. In 1974, I wanted his approval and I wanted him to defend me. Fortunately for me, he could do neither. As a result, I learned to give myself approval and I learned to defend myself. Twenty-some years ago, I wanted the bishop to embrace me. The embrace I experienced recently was not the one I wanted in 1974. It was better. It was an embrace *with* Tom and not *from* the bishop. The conversation we had on the telephone was deeply healing for both of us. To the casual eye, a former Catholic gay man and a heterosexual bishop crossed paths briefly and reminisced on their past. For me, two spiritual pilgrims met in the desert again, celebrated their common goal, hugged each other in affirmation, and continued on their journeys grateful to know the other was out there somewhere.[20]

Listening and Learning

In May 1993, Andrew Sullivan, a gay Catholic born in England and brilliant editor of *The New Republic*, was interviewed in the Jesuit magazine *America*. Gumbleton, who was moved by what Sullivan had to say, later wrote about it. "It made me realize how inadequate and even hurtful my efforts were. I was so clearly a part of the Church that 'refuses to come to our aid, refuses to listen to this call [quoting Sullivan]'." Sullivan had described what it was like growing up with no support.

> No one taught me anything except that this couldn't be mentioned. And as a result of the total lack of teaching, gay Catholics and gay people in general are in crisis. No wonder people's lives—many gay lives—are unhappy or distraught or in dysfunction, because there is no guidance at *all*. Here is a population within the church, and outside the church, desperately seeking spiritual health and values. And the church refuses to come to our aid, refuses to listen to this call.[21]

Tom thought more deeply about what it must have been like for his brother Dan.

As I look back I can see a pattern in his life that I didn't pay any attention to at the time....He was gay, but not wanting to admit it even to himself; he got married and seemed to have a good relationship. He and his wife had four daughters, and they lived together for about fifteen years. But then they moved away....Not being able to tell anyone, gay men and lesbians often move away from where they are known. He and his wife moved to the West Coast. He was hiding who he really was, and his marriage really wasn't working out. It came to the point where he knew he had to be honest about who he really is.[22]

As he was coming to better understand his brother, Tom was undergoing a profound personal transformation. In late October 1994 he went to Minnesota's Twin Cities for a three-day series held in various parishes, "A Shepherd Listens and Speaks with God's People." Dawn Gibeau of the *National Catholic Reporter* captured an emblematic moment:

Bishop Thomas Gumbleton rarely wears a miter, but he wore one October 28 at the Basilica of St. Mary in Minneapolis. Adorning the miter was a cross, and on the cross a pink triangle. A wide border rimmed the miter, the multicolored stripes of the gay/lesbian rainbow. The miter was a gift from Bill Kummer and Leo Bowe, two of the planners of Gumbleton's Oct. 27-29 visit to the Twin cities, and it was stitched by Poor Clare Sr. Caroline of Bloomington, Minnesota. The Detroit auxiliary bishop wore it appreciatively as he walked to and from the "eucharistic liturgy of liberation," a Mass followed by a question-and-answer session.

Each Twin Cities parish event included a listening session. "Gumbleton listened to gays and lesbians, to bisexuals and transgender persons, to gay priests and to heterosexual parents of homosexual children." A man asked him how he felt about gay marriage. The questioner had grown up Catholic, had been away from Catholicism for more than a decade, and had a committed relationship with another man, but told the Detroit bishop that he "really would like to be part of the Catholic church, but I refuse to be part of a church" or to tithe "to something that's working against me." The bishop responded, "It's something we're struggling to understand." Would he bless a same-sex commitment ceremony? Although "we need to support gay and lesbian people in their relationships," he replied, he could not do so because the Catholic Church had not yet arrived at "a clear, public stance on that." He tried to be transparent. "I tend to keep pushing forward, but I feel it is important for me to stay within the church. If I were to be suspended, I could not work within the church. So I do have to not do certain things that would bring about the end of my ministry in the church." The Catholic Church had failed homosexual persons, their parents and siblings, he acknowledged, saying how important what "we are doing here" was in the listening and dialogue. He believed that the public sharing of stories could help to bring about change.[23]

Advocacy Opportunity

On November 14, 1995, in Washington, DC, on the evening of the second day of the U.S. bishops' annual meeting, Bishop Gumbleton received the "Bridge Building Award" from New Ways Ministry (NWM). Turnout was in the hundreds for the event held strategically at the same time as the meeting of the NCCB and at the same hotel. At a news conference ahead of the award ceremony, Gumbleton remarked, "We must become an open church that truly respects each person and accepts them in the way God made them." Dan attended the ceremony and spoke. "I just want to thank my brother Tom," he proclaimed from the podium. "There are millions of people who need your ministry."[24]

The next day National Public Radio's "All Things Considered" interviewed the two brothers. Years afterward, Dan reflected back:

> I have had an enormous impact for thousands of people I have not met, only because I came out to my family. I could not live with that life, that double-life sort of thing, and for my own mental health I had to do this, and it was a risk and I did this and Tom realized what was really a natural phenomenon, and with his changing his own understanding...he had to think through a lot of things...so I think Tom did accept that challenge from me....I feel like I have had a major influence on Tom and then the two of us have done a lot of unknown good for a lot of people.

He could not forget what happened during the NPR interview:

> The interviewer said, and this kind of threw me, "Bishop Gumbleton, how do you feel about the fact that you're sitting here with your brother and you're at the bishops' conference and you know your brother doesn't go to church anymore?" Tom said, "Well, I'm

very disappointed," and I thought, oops! And then he said, "but not in Dan. I'm disappointed in the church that they cannot understand the love that Dan shares and the beauty of gay love." I got all choked up and felt pretty darn proud.[25]

Only a month before the award and the NPR interview, Tom had been at the aforementioned retreat center in Connecticut meeting with parents of gay and lesbian children, sharing how his brother's coming out had put in play so much:

> I have been going to different places and talking about this whole matter, and I must say that I have had correspondence with people all over the country, and to me it's been a very enriching experience. I've heard from people who have gone through a very hard time, gay people, lesbian people, priests who are afraid to let their bishop know they are gay, and they don't know who to turn to, and they've written to me and shared their stories with me, and parents, many parents throughout the country have written to me and I've been able to write back and been able to communicate with people and help, I think, in a lot of ways. And I've been very blessed because I've met many people who have helped me to understand even better what I was struggling with a few years ago and how we all have to work our way through it...and you discover that there are many people who are suffering a lot, and it's so important to reach out, so important to support one another. Within the church we need to develop much more pastoral ministry so that the alienation and hurt and the pain will be eliminated and that our gay brothers and sisters, or your gay sons and daughters, will know that they are fully welcome within our church community.[26]

An Objective Disorder

In October 1997, the NCCB released a pastoral booklet, *Always Our Children*, directed to the parents of homosexual children and with suggestions for pastoral ministers. What led to this pastoral message began a few years earlier when, in July 1993, Gumbleton wrote to Cardinal Bernardin, then serving as the chairperson of the NCCB's Marriage and Family Life Committee. Tom had sought the support of several other bishops who signed onto his letter to Bernardin, which read, in part:

An enormous task of reconciliation and understanding between gay and lesbian people and the Catholic community awaits us. Lesbian and gay people and their families and friends experienced much pain following the publication of the 1986 *Letter to the Bishops of the Catholic Church on the Pastoral Care of Homosexual Person* from the Congregation for the Doctrine of the Faith. *Some Considerations Concerning the Response to Legislative Proposals on the Non-Discrimination of Homosexual Persons* from the same Congregation in 1992 only increased the alienation.[27]

The 1986 document from Cardinal Joseph Ratzinger, prefect of the Vatican office on doctrine, not only upheld the longstanding view judging homosexual acts as gravely wrong but included this language:

Although the particular inclination of the homosexual person is not a sin, it is a more or less strong tendency ordered toward an intrinsic moral evil; and thus the inclination itself must be seen as an objective disorder. Therefore special concern and pastoral attention should be directed toward those who have this condition, lest they be led to believe that the living out of this orientation in homosexual activity is a morally acceptable option. It is not.

National Catholic Reporter's Tom Fox, in his 1995 book *Sexuality and Catholicism*, noted that whatever else "the Vatican had said, what was heard loudest were the words 'objective disorder.'"[28] As to the June 1992 Vatican directive to the U.S. bishops, also cited in Gumbleton's letter to Bernardin, Fox zeroed in on its two claims: first, that discrimination against homosexuals in certain situations is not unjust and may even be a good idea, including in the employment of teachers or athletic coaches, in housing or in adoption and foster care of children; second, that efforts on behalf of gay rights amounted to an attack on the traditional family and its "family values" and could easily be used to support a "homosexual lifestyle." The 1992 document from Ratzinger stated:

Recently, legislation has been proposed in some American states which would make discrimination on the basis of sexual orientation illegal.... Such initiatives, even where they seem more directed toward support of basic civil rights than condonement of homosexual activity or a homosexual life-style, may in fact have a negative impact on the family and society... the proper reaction to crimes committed against homosexual persons should not be to claim that the homosexual condition is not disordered.[29]

In Gumbleton's view, this statement was "clearly based on an ignorance of the nature of homosexuality. It is also totally in conflict with Gospel values that condemn discrimination and insist that we recognize the dignity inherent in all persons.... It is impossible to imagine Jesus supporting this call to discrimination."[30]

New Ways Ministry repudiated the Vatican's support for legal discrimination against gays and lesbians. That NWM statement, "A Time to Speak," with more than fifteen hundred signers including Gumbleton and Walter Sullivan of Richmond, Virginia, and Charles Buswell of Pueblo, Colorado, ran as an ad in the November 13, 1992 issue of the *National Catholic Reporter*. In his report, Peter Steinfels, *New York Times* religion writer, placed Gumbleton "among a small number of unusually outspoken bishops, and their direct public disagreement with a Vatican document is unusual."[31]

For Gumbleton and the other bishops who joined him in that July 1993 letter to Bernardin, their reaction to Vatican's dogmatism had energized their effort to encourage a genuinely *pastoral* message. NWM had approached Tom initially with the idea of asking the NCCB to address a message to parents and ministers of homosexual people. Tom obliged with the appeal to Bernardin, who wrote back in mid-August, letting Tom know that although he was about to hand the role of chair to another bishop, he would "make sure that it gets on the Committee's agenda for the next three-year period."[32]

In 1997 the Bishops' Committee on Marriage and Family Life issued *Always Our Children*. The purpose of the message, stated the bishops,

> is to reach out to parents trying to cope with the discovery of homosexuality in their adolescent or adult child... we intend to speak words of faith, hope, and love to parents who need the Church's loving presence at a time that may be one of the most challenging in their lives. We also hope this message will be helpful to priests and pastoral ministers who often are the first ones parents or their children approach with their struggles and anxieties.

Always Our Children supported fundamental rights. "It is not sufficient only to avoid unjust discrimination. Homosexual persons 'must be accepted with respect, compassion and sensitivity' (Catechism of the Catholic Church, no. 2358). They, as is true of every human being, need to be nourished at many different levels simultaneously." The language was affirming. "All in all, it is essential to recall one basic truth. God loves every person as a unique individual. Sexual identity helps to define the unique persons we are, and one component of our sexual identity is sexual orientation. Human beings see the appearance, but the Lord looks into the heart (cf. 1 Sm 16:7). God does not love someone any less because he or she is homosexual."[33]

Always Our Children had, of course, gone through a drafting process. Significant sentences were deleted from the final version. One cut passage had read: "Judging the sinfulness of any particular act is a matter ultimately between God and the individual person. This is the function of one's conscience, which the Second Vatican Council described as the divine voice echoing in our depths, as a law written by God in human hearts. A person must always obey the certain judgment of his or her conscience." Chuck Colbert, a member of the board of the National Lesbian and Gay Journalists Association, listened to Bishop Gumbleton read the deleted passage to a large audience at the annual conference of Call to Action held that autumn in Detroit.

Some bishops, Gumbleton said, were concerned such language would imply that the church was changing its doctrine prohibiting homosexual activity. But that teaching "puts a homosexual person in a terrible bind because…it seems absolutely clear that genuine homosexual people have been homosexual from their earliest years. It isn't something they chose in their teenage years or as an adult." And the bishops underscored this point, that sexual orientation is not something freely chosen and yet genital homosexuality is contrary to church teaching. "How, then," Gumbleton asked, "does a person deal with the teachings of the church and stay faithful to the teaching? Every person has to come to a point of personal growth where we fully integrate sexuality into our whole lives—not repress it. Each person, struggling to be a whole person, must deal with this serious question of conscience." Colbert took Gumbleton at his word. "For an increasing number of us," Colbert observed, "it's the church's very own teaching—a carefully formed conscience as the ultimate guide in every moral decision—that empowers us to remain good, faithful gay Catholics and be sexually active, in spite of hurtful pronouncements from the Vatican." He found especially encouraging these words Gumbleton had shared: "Primacy of conscience is a very important piece of Catholic teaching. It's not up to any one of us to judge anyone else."[34]

Dignity USA National Convention in Denver, 1999

Denver, Colorado was host for the August 5–8 national convention of Dignity USA. Archbishop Charles Chaput discouraged Colorado's Catholics from participating, but Tom came to the Adam's Mark Hotel in the mile-high city to speak words of encouragement to members of Dignity USA. He asked the more than three hundred members in the hall that day to please forgive the bishops. "We ask for your forgiveness for the ways we have hurt you in the past. We need bishops to speak out in defense of gay people. We must make gay people welcome in every parish." He encouraged them to follow their conscience. When he finished his address, the assembly gave him a standing ovation. An observer noted, "Some members of the audience cried as Gumbleton told how his brother Dan announced to the family in a letter that he was gay." Asked if the Catholic Church would quit opposing gay marriage, he said this was his hope.[35]

His address and the Q & A were widely covered and well received by many influential leaders, including Michigan State Senator Jackie Vaughn III, associate president pro tem of Gumbleton's home state senate.

> Bishop Gumbleton, you are a shining example of the progressive side of the Catholic Church. Your remarks were both compassionate and heartfelt, and the hope and understanding you showed to the audience is worthy of high praise. You obey the teachings of the church, but you feel the church has not done enough to meet the spiritual needs of people with alternative lifestyles. The love in your heart is so great, I trust the community will never forget the contributions you have made and continue to make.[36]

Gumbleton replied:

> Years ago, if you asked me if I would be ministering to the gay and lesbian community, my answer would have been—probably not. Now, however, I can honestly say that it has been a blessing in my life. I am a private person, and I never intended to share the story about my brother, Dan, who is gay. But I felt it was the right thing to do, and my life and ministry took a turn I never would have predicted. And I couldn't be more pleased. I feel blessed.[37]

He received dozens of letters after the Denver talk, especially from people who had felt alienation and ill-treatment from the church.

Nevertheless, after the Dignity convention he also received a letter from an unhappy Archbishop Chaput. While the archbishop respected Gumbleton's desire to reconcile Dignity USA with the Catholic Church, he reprimanded the Detroit auxiliary bishop: "I have to say I was very disappointed with your presentation here in Denver. I do not think your remarks, at least as reported in the press, served the mission of the Church here locally, and I believe your presence at meetings like Dignity's recent convention may mislead a great many people."[38] Chaput also wrote to Cardinal Maida, Tom's superior in Detroit. "To be frank, I do not understand why Tom does not see the collateral problems created by his involvement in such meetings."[39] Gumbleton had communicated with Chaput before the convention, informing him that what he would say would be consistent with official teaching.

Responding to the reprimand, Gumbleton made it clear to Chaput that what he had said in Denver was "totally in line with *Always Our Children* —just as I said it would be in my first letter to you." He told Chaput that he continued "to be overwhelmed with the number of people within and outside the Church who feel alienated and condemned simply because of who they are. I am committed to continue teaching and ministering to them, in the hope that they will know they are loved by God just as they are. I wish the bishops would discuss this issue at our national meeting in an open and direct way as well."[40] Over the years, Gumbleton would face not only reprimands from some prelates. There were those who would not even permit him to come to their dioceses even though communities within those dioceses had invited him.

The Vatican Takes Action

Rome made life onerous for the gay community and for allies such as the co-founders of New Ways Ministry. In July 1999, the Vatican decreed that Sister Jeannine Gramick and Father Robert Nugent had to end their ministry to gay and lesbian people and their families. New Ways Ministry had begun twenty-nine years earlier. A statement decrying the decree appeared in the edition of the *NCR* released while the Catholic bishops were meeting in the nation's capital in mid-November. More than forty-five hundred individuals and groups from all fifty states, DC, and thirteen other countries, signed "Jubilee Justice Begins at Home," an appeal to Rome to reinstate Gramick and

Nugent and to work for reconciliation with lesbian/gay Catholics. The sign-ers, Gumbleton among them, called on the U.S. bishops to "lead by example and establish serious and open dialogue with lesbian and gay Catholics about the full reality of their lives and the kind of ministry they desire."[41]

Stepping out of the NCCB meeting, Tom spoke on behalf of Gramick and Nugent at a November 15 press conference in Washington DC. Ironi-cally, Detroit's Cardinal Adam Maida had been assigned by the Vatican back in 1988 to lead a commission examining the activities of Nugent and Gramick. As early as 1984 Rome had asked them not to conduct their work "without faithfully presenting the Church's teaching regarding the intrinsic evil of homosexual acts." In July 1999, NCCB President Bishop Joseph Fiorenza of Galveston-Houston, Texas, announced that "the commission chaired by Cardinal Maida did not find this ministry to be 'without positive aspects' for homosexual persons and their families." Nevertheless the Vati-can's Congregation for the Doctrine of the Faith declared that it "was obliged to act" on account of deficiencies in their ministry and "not because it was a ministry to homosexuals as such." Cardinal Maida for his part in-sisted that the commission he headed "never lost sight of the realization that ministry to the homosexual community is both sensitive and neces-sary." However, "such ministry can cause more harm than good if it is con-ducted in the midst of controversy and ambiguity."[42]

The double-talk only further spurred Tom to write to all the country's bishops:

> I believe that the work of Sister Gramick and Father Nugent has been a gift to the Catholic community for decades; it has been af-firmed by hundreds of letters and statements to the NCCB from re-ligious congregations and laity who know them and their pastoral approach. These two individuals reflect the best spirit of the 1997 statement, *Always Our Children*. Each of them played some part in its development. Many gay and lesbian Catholics and their fami-lies are understandably angered, hurt, and bewildered by this deci-sion [the Congregation of the Doctrine of the Faith's decision to permanently prohibit them from pastoral ministry to lesbian and gay Catholics and their families]. Many Catholics who yearn for a more just Church find it difficult to reconcile the Church's call for compassion with severe censure to those who model compassion.

He reminded his colleagues that many of them personally knew Gram-ick and Nugent and had sponsored NWM programs. "We need to find some mechanism of reconciliation for these two individuals, for lesbian and gay Catholics and their families, and for the Church's ministry itself."[43] A small number agreed with him, including his old Detroit chancery colleagues and good friends Joe Imesch, bishop of Joliet, Illinois, and Ken Untener, bishop of Saginaw, as well as Bishops Charles Buswell of Pueblo, Colorado; Walter Sullivan of Richmond, Virginia; Joseph Sullivan of Brooklyn; Leroy Matthiesen of Amarillo, Texas; Raymond Lucker of New Ulm, Minnesota; Juan Arzube of Los Angeles; Frank Murphy of Baltimore; William Hughes of Covington, Kentucky; Jack Snyder of Jacksonville, Florida; and Seattle's retired Archbishop Raymond Hunthausen.[44]

At the November 15 news conference, Tom's anguish could be felt: "Over the past almost ten years now, I have been involved in an extraordinary and very enriching ministry to gay, lesbian, bisexual and transgendered persons. So I feel that today, in some way, I can speak for them in identifying the pain and hurt that they have experienced so often from the church in the past. That pain is being reinforced now by the action taken against Father Nugent and Sister Gramick."

Meanwhile, Cardinal Maida, interviewed by the *Detroit Free Press*, dismissed the efforts of his auxiliary and the thousands of people who had appealed to the bishops. "Once the Holy See has spoken to an issue like this, I can't imagine that changing. And I think it would be wrong for our conference of bishops to get involved in this." He made one thing clear: "I am the only one who can speak for the archdiocese in the name of the church. Bishop Gumbleton is on a solo mission here."[45]

Solo

As the new millennium began, Tom was indeed being relegated to a "solo mission" more and more—and not just on the issue at the center of this chapter. On the issue of LGBTQ rights and where the Catholic Church stood, the Vatican compounded the trials of Gramick and Nugent, perhaps to send a chill to other like-minded ministers. Now not only were they prohibited from participating in pastoral initiatives for lesbian/gay people and their families, but they were no longer to write or speak on homosexuality. They could not even openly discuss how they had been treated.

Gramick belonged to the School Sisters of Notre Dame and Nugent to the Society of the Divine Savior, the heads of which asked them to comply with Rome. Nugent reluctantly decided that he would obey but Gramick decided otherwise. On May 25, 2000, she spoke (excerpted here):

A command to not speak or write about the Notification [of the Congregation for the Doctrine of the Faith, 14 July 1999, that presented details of the Vatican investigation] and its ecclesiastical processes is similar to ordering a woman who feels she has been unjustly treated to remain silent. Is this not a violation of the basic human right to self-defense? A woman religious does not surrender her human rights by virtue of her state of life....I have gravely considered the requests of my community leaders....I feel pained that the Vatican and my community leaders now ask me to silence myself. After finding my voice to tell my story, I choose not to collaborate in my own oppression by restricting a basic human right. To me this is a matter of conscience.[46]

Gramick had appealed to Sister Rosemary Howarth, Superior General of the School Sisters of Notre Dame, and Gumbleton had written to Sr. Howarth on her behalf:

I am writing out of my very strong conviction about what I perceive as "grave injustice" against Sister Jeannine Gramick. I know Jeannine and have heard her speak on several occasions. Her ministry to gay and lesbian Catholics is of the utmost importance. Never has she spoken against Church teaching. What her internal convictions are, based on her conscience, cannot be the subject of any human inquiry. Conscience is a matter between an individual and God.[47]

Although Gramick's religious community had long supported her work, they said that if she now continued in this ministry, they would have to dismiss her. She did a lot of praying and mercifully found that another religious congregation, the Sisters of Loretto, would accept her. They have backed her work with New Ways ever since.[48]

Louisville 2002

Tom Gumbleton and retired Bishop Leroy Matthiesen, of Amarillo, Texas, were among the speakers for the NWM symposium in Louisville, Kentucky, in early March 2002. "We don't put people out of the church for following their conscience," said Gumbleton, thinking about Gramick and Nugent among others. Matthiesen emphasized conscience, "our most sacred core and sanctuary, where we are alone with God, whose voice echoes in our depths."[49] Gramick was there, now as a member of the Sisters of Loretto. Archbishop Thomas Kelly of Louisville had received a letter from Archbishop Bertone of the Congregation for the Doctrine of the Faith: "Because of the confusion and scandal which will inevitably arise from this event, this congregation asks your excellency to inform organizers of the symposium that they do not have permission to celebrate the Eucharist as part of their conference." New Ways Ministry never received a direct order from Kelly. He simply shared the Bertone letter with them. They went forward with the Eucharist and Matthiesen presided, commenting later, "I was not given any instructions from the Vatican or Archbishop Kelly not to do the Mass. The example of Jesus was not to exclude but to include."[50]

The head of the Vatican Congregation of Bishops, Cardinal Re, wrote to Gumbleton in May. The Congregation for the Doctrine of the Faith could not allow Gumbleton's continued participation with New Ways. There should have been no celebration of the Holy Eucharist. "In spite of this clear and authoritative intervention, your active participation in the *New Ways Ministry* March Symposium has been the cause of grave concern of this Dicastery and a source of scandal to the faithful." Gumbleton was required to cut his ties "and no longer support, attend, or make any presentation at any meeting or activity of the organization or of other organizations which hold positions contrary to Church doctrine or discipline."[51] In October, Gumbleton wrote to the NWM board: "With this letter, I am submitting my resignation as a member of the Board. . . . I am not happy with this, but I agreed to go along with the request rather than get involved in an extended controversy. I have and I will continue to support the Board if you are willing. I hope you are."[52] His name might be removed from the NWM letterhead, but he would not stop going to the meetings and supporting the work.[53]

"A Hero's Journey"

In mid-November 2002, three gay Catholics were refused communion at the Basilica of the National Shrine of the Immaculate Conception. The priest who turned them away had been the secretary of Cardinal Maida. Fr. Michael Bugarin later realized he been mistaken in turning them away. "A priest can't judge the state of a person's conscience when he stands up for communion," Gumbleton remarked at the time. Mike Perez, Ken Einhaus, and Kara Speltz were there in silent vigils with Soulforce, a gay rights group protesting the discriminatory stands of the bishops.[54] Months later the three were in court to face a charge for entering the lobby of the Hyatt Regency Hotel on Capitol Hill where the U.S. bishops were. In the lobby they had gotten down on their knees in hopes that one of the hundreds of bishops at the NCCB meeting would serve them communion. Instead, they were sentenced to six months and fined $350. When Judge Mildred Edwards, a Catholic, heard the case she suspended the sentence. One factor in her decision was testimony given by Bishop Gumbleton who flew into DC to advocate on behalf of the defendants. Edwards later wrote to Gumbleton: "Thank you for taking the time to come to Washington to testify this week. It was an honor for me to see you in my courtroom. I am so grateful for your prophetic witness to the gospel values of peace and justice, and for your pastoral concern for the marginalized."[55]

In late October 2004, Tom joined eighty Detroit area Roman Catholics, including at least twenty clergy, in signing a public letter opposing Proposal 2. This proposal was aimed at adding language to the Michigan constitution requiring public institutions to deny domestic partnership benefits to any couple whose union was outside the traditional definition of marriage. The Michigan Catholic Conference had been campaigning to promote the ballot proposal. The signers of the public letter argued that there was more than one valid moral stance that a Catholic voter could hold, and they made it very clear they would vote NO on the proposal.[56]

Not long after this, Archbishop Gabriel Montalvo, the papal nuncio, called Tom to Washington. Apparently Cardinal Maida had read the *Detroit Free Press* and saw the group letter opposing Proposal 2 with his auxiliary bishop's name on it. Instead of bringing the matter directly to Gumbleton, he took his concerns to the Vatican. Rome then asked Montalvo to speak with Gumbleton. He was with Montalvo when, to his surprise, down the steps came Maida. Tom stood his ground and calmly explained his rationale for signing the public letter. In the prudent judgment of some eighty signers, he told them, Proposal 2 would "create serious and undue hardships for a whole class of citizens." He never heard any more on the matter from either Maida or Montalvo.[57]

In July 2009, Dignity USA planned to present their Lifetime Achievement Award to Bishop Gumbleton at their fortieth anniversary convention in San Francisco. Tom wanted to accept this, seeing it as a pastoral opportunity. He wrote to San Francisco's Archbishop George Niederauer to explain his rationale in wishing to come in person to accept the award.

I believe the example of Jesus as the Good Shepherd, which was our reading this past Sunday, supports this approach to these members of our Church. I have tried in my ministry to follow this example of Jesus. I have tried always to focus first on a lesbian/gay person's self-image, on the totality of the person and tried to guide them to an awareness of God's unconditional love for them. However, for many of them their experience of the Church is all too often one of being made to feel different, inferior, and marginalized. I have found that many lesbian/gay people want to stay in communion with their Catholic roots, but they feel shunned and rejected. Perhaps my presence at Dignity USA's 40th Anniversary can help heal some of the hurt and rejection they've experienced over the years.[58]

Niederauer urged him not to accept the award. The atmosphere was too charged, he claimed, and various groups would use the apparent contrast between the two of them "in unfortunate and public ways."[59]

Tom was finding himself more and more at odds with bishops around the country and in Detroit as well. Dearden, his mentor, had been replaced by the more conservative Szoka, then by Maida, and then by Vigneron. By the time Archbishop Allen Vigneron was in charge, the cause of marriage equality had become a paramount issue in U.S. society. In 2013, he proclaimed that "pro-marriage equality Catholics" should refrain from Holy Communion. Tom Nelson and Linda Karle-Nelson, parents of adult gay children, lifelong Catholics, and leaders in the support group named Fortunate Families, held a prayer vigil in front of the chancery protesting Vigneron's statement. "He's not going to keep me from the Eucharist," said Tom Nelson. "Somebody's got to stand up and say, Enough!"[60]

The question of how marriage was to be defined would soon reach the highest court. On Friday, June 26, 2015, the U.S. Supreme Court, in a 5-4 ruling, determined that the right to marry is constitutionally guaranteed to same-sex couples, overturning various state bans on same sex-marriage, including Michigan's. Vigneron had led the seven Catholic dioceses in Michigan in fighting to maintain the state's constitutional ban. The Michigan Catholic Conference responded to the Supreme Court decision by asserting that Catholic teaching defends marriage solely between a man and a woman. Linda Karle-Nelson, Tom Nelson's spouse, told a reporter for the *Detroit Free Press* what she thought about the SCOTUS decision: "We're just ecstatic. We were hoping, hoping, hoping for so long. And this has been a very emotional time. The experience of people over time really motivated the court to decide the way it did. We're hoping the church will take some consideration of the experience of the people and come to some new decisions." The *Detroit Free Press* asked the opinion of Gumbleton, who suggested that the bishops ought to "follow the lead of Pope Francis, who said about gay people, 'Who am I to judge?'"[61]

In 2019, an Italian journalist asked Tom about official Catholic language that still framed homosexuality as objectively disordered. "No parent [should ever] tell a child that he or she is intrinsically disordered. For the church to teach such a thing is insulting to the parent and child. I've had parents become very angry if that is even suggested, and I don't blame them."[62] He again told the journalist the story of how his brother came out, how Dan's courage challenged him, and how much it troubled him that his own church could lead their mother to worry that Dan would go to hell.

Brian McNaught has aptly described Tom's transformation over the years. "I think Tom has, in the words of Joseph Campbell, made "the hero's journey" and I'm thrilled. He was not an ally on gay issues in 1974. He just did not have any information. But he has made the journey. We need more bishops in the church who have done what he's done."[63]

10

Accompaniment and Solidarity in Central America

T HE ASSASSINATION of Salvadoran Archbishop Oscar Romero, on March 24, 1980, awakened people throughout the world to the violence engulfing El Salvador. Immediately, the United States inserted itself into that civil war. Congress grew alarmed that the Sandinista guerrillas' triumphant overthrow of U.S.-supported dictator Anastasio Somoza in Nicaragua the previous July would be replicated in neighboring El Salvador.[1] The day after Romero's assassination, members of the House of Representatives initiated efforts to send military advisors to El Salvador along with $5.5 million in aid. These advisors were called "trainers," to avoid memories of the quagmire in Vietnam.

Though unfamiliar with the state of affairs in El Salvador at the time, Gumbleton had known of Archbishop Oscar Romero. After speaking with San Francisco Archbishop John Quinn, who had attended Romero's funeral, he quickly grasped the reality. He recalled Quinn's description of the funeral violence: "They opened fire upon the crowds, right there at the cathedral, which again shows you they had no sense of compassion or care about killing people even during religious services. This is when I really began to become aware of the situation in El Salvador."[2]

He connected personally with El Salvador a few months later at Maryknoll, New York. He had traveled there to speak on the Gospel's call to nonviolence in Maryknoll's summer program for missionaries who had returned to the States to reconnect with their community and to be updated on current U.S. policy. Ursuline Sr. Dorothy Kazel introduced herself to him following his presentation. She and laywoman Jean Donovan were part of the mission from the Cleveland Diocese to El Salvador. They worked with Maryknoll Sisters Ita Ford and Maura Clarke.

Dorothy explained to Tom how terrible it would be if the Church were to abandon the Salvadorans, such poor and endangered people. "We don't want the violence, but we are caught up in it." The guerrillas were from the families in the village where she was ministering and the government soldiers would capture, torture, and kill villagers. Dorothy said she did not see how she could support the guerrillas but felt it would be wrong to tell them to drop their weapons. Tom recalled, "I told her this is the challenge of the Gospel, to somehow bring about nonviolent revolutionary change."[3]

The missionaries' dilemma echoed Archbishop Romero's statement in an interview with a Venezuelan journalist ten days before his murder.

My relation with the [popular] organizations is one of a shepherd, a pastor with his people, knowing that a people has the right to organize itself and defend its right of organization. And I also feel perfectly free to denounce those organizations when they abuse their power and turn in the direction of unnecessary violence. This is my role as pastor: to animate the just and the good, and to denounce that which is not good.[4]

Dorothy and Tom corresponded after her return to El Salvador. Yet he could not have anticipated what happened next. On December 2, 1980, Dorothy and the other churchwomen had been raped, murdered, and then thrown in a ditch. The three nuns were buried in El Salvador, and Tom made a point of attending the memorial Mass for Jean in Cleveland. As he said, "I felt great empathy for these missionaries, working in a revolutionary situation, facing extreme repression."[5] These deaths, along with Romero's, compelled him to pay close attention to Latin America, especially El Salvador and Nicaragua. He learned that during the 1980s his nation had increased its engagement in the civil wars in both countries through military aid. As this involvement became more public, citizens in the United States increasingly protested these policies.[6]

Gumbleton identified more and more with the spirit of Oscar Romero, grappling with how he might most meaningfully respond to the suffering of the Salvadoran and Nicaraguan people. Paul Letcha, a Detroiter and seminarian studying with the Passionist community in Chicago, urged him to act. Letcha wrote:

I just want to ask if there is anything you can do that would influence the new [Reagan] administration towards curtailing their military assistance to El Salvador? Are your brother bishops aware of
the concerns of our brothers and sisters in El Salvador? In Latin
America? Why is the Church so weak and slow to speak out
against injustice?...Archbishop Romero fought against the economic policies of the families of the country who hold the power.
Please speak on this.

Gumbleton responded: "The people who are suffering there...make
this whole situation an intolerable one. And yet there is a deep sense of
frustration at not really being able to help those people in a direct and concrete way. I for one feel this in a personal way, especially since one of the
sisters who was murdered in El Salvador just a couple of weeks ago was a
close personal friend of mine."[7] In the years that followed he would continue to search for ways to help and provide effective solidarity to the suffering poor of Central America.

The Call of Salvadoran Refugees

The growing tide of violence in El Salvador drove thousands of refugees to
escape into the United States. By 1983, there were more than five hundred
thousand undocumented Salvadorans in the country.[8] In response to this
crisis, people like Eileen Purcell of San Francisco focused on providing
these refugees sanctuary. Joining with other interfaith leaders, she helped
establish the East Bay Sanctuary Coalition, which began operations on the
second anniversary of the assassination of Oscar Romero, March 24, 1982.
The Coalition sought endorsements from religious leaders across the country and Bishop Gumbleton responded immediately. As Eileen has said, "He
identified with war refugees coming to this country; he was one of the first
bishops to do so early on."[9]

Meanwhile, many thousands of Salvadoran refugees had fled to neighboring Honduras to escape the bombing of their villages. By 1986, the
largest of the UN-sponsored refugee camps in Honduras, Mesa Grande,
held about twelve thousand Salvadoran refugees.[10] Eileen Purcell made numerous trips to the camps, observing how these refugees organized themselves into committees and held popular assemblies to foster community.
Eventually, the refugees told her that they wanted to return home and called
for international support to accompany them.

The UN opposed such a return, calling it suicidal. Yet the vicar general of the Archdiocese of San Salvador, Monseñor Ricardo Urioste, asked, "What would Jesus do?" Eileen, then leading the SHARE (Salvadoran Humanitarian Aid, Research and Education) Foundation, together with Jose Artiga, the executive director of the Interfaith Office on Accompaniment, conceived of the Going Home Campaign to motivate internationals to take up the refugees' request for accompaniment.[11] In the summer of 1987 Tom accepted Eileen's invitation to serve on the steering committee of the Going Home Campaign.

The campaign responded to the refugees' appeal that internationals accompany them both on their journey home and in their resettled communities. The refugees believed the presence of others would provide them protection under the assumption that the Salvadoran government would not attack while internationals were present. "From the Salvadorans themselves has come a plea that we 'accompany' them on their return to their homelands from which they have been ruthlessly and murderously evicted by U.S.-backed troops.... They were trying to make a human statement. It goes: These are our lands, our homes, our farms, our villages. We are entitled to dwell in them. We intend to do so."[12]

In December Gumbleton traveled to El Salvador to visit recently repatriated refugees from Mesa Grande, the first of four repatriations. These fearless, tenacious refugees, in the face of opposition by the UN, Honduras, El Salvador, and the United States, determined they would return to rebuild their villages. The war continued and they did not want their children to learn to beg and their elders to die in a foreign land. Tom invited three friends from the Detroit area to join him, Mary and Bill Carry and Sue Sattler, IHM, co-author of this book. They merged with eight others from across the United States. Oscar and Guillermo Chacón, Salvadoran brothers who had escaped death threats by fleeing to the U.S. in the early 1980s, led the delegation.[13]

Each of the three rural communities they visited, Copapayo, Guarjila, and Santa Marta, was located in a conflict zone. The Salvadoran government opposed internationals accessing such communities and set up a complex procedure requiring visitors to obtain *salvo conductos* (safe conduct passes) in order to travel to these militarized areas. Yet even if they secured the permit, the travelers met with repeated delays and sometimes denial of access en route to the villages. Visitors experienced, in a very limited way, the power of the Salvadoran military over Salvadorans' daily lives.[14]

Once in the communities, the visitors were amazed at the peasants' achievements: the tall growth scythed, tents for shelter, worship, education, and health set up and an elected *directiva* (coordinating committee) established. What they had achieved in the six weeks without, of course, electricity, equipment, or government assistance, astonished and inspired the delegates.[15] One delegate asked a refugee if there was a message for the people and the government of the United States. The refugee replied:

> This war could not happen if it were not for the help the U.S. is providing to our government. We are sad when we know that so much money is being given to our government in El Salvador and used to perpetrate abuses of all kinds, sometimes massacres of entire villages. This is nothing we have been told but what we have experienced and seen and can tell you about our own relatives having been victims of these abuses.... Every time you come to see us; we are filled with hope. There is one more eye looking at us.[16]

When asked what motivated his ongoing support for the Going Home Campaign, Tom shared this:

> You can't know the situation of the poor and their suffering from the violence...unless you see some of it firsthand, experience it, and come to understand their life from their perspective. Otherwise, if there aren't people doing this, getting the firsthand experience and trying to share it with others, we will never be successful in changing those structures of violence that need to be changed, and ultimately that's the main goal, to try to transform our world into as close an image of the reign of God as possible, which means that everyone has the opportunity to share in the gifts that God's given for all.[17]

Travel to El Salvador required a travel visa for entry, entailing the submission of several documents. The Campaign urged delegates to obtain congressional support letters addressed to the president of El Salvador and the chief of staff of the armed forces of El Salvador.[18] During his orientation for the Fall 1989 delegation, Oscar Chacón advised the delegates that the Salvadoran government was increasing surveillance on those arriving at the airport and was denying entrance to visitors whom they considered suspect.[19] Specifically, Chacón expressed concern that Bishop Gumbleton might be barred from entering. So the delegates strategized to address this prospect. They resolved to stand in front of and behind him as he moved through the immigration line and chose three delegates who would remain with him if he were detained. They also brought phone numbers of key people in the United States to notify them if he were detained.[20]

Their advance planning proved wise. Immigration authorities took Tom's passport and removed him from the line. The designated delegates remained with him; their passports also taken. Officials directed all four to return to the U.S. on a flight leaving shortly for Los Angeles. Feigning an inability to comprehend Spanish, they remained in the terminal as the other delegates left for their hotel in San Salvador. The detained delegates found a wall phone with a direct line to the States and called Eileen Purcell to alert the SHARE advocacy network. They also reached Tony Rothschild, staff to Detroit Congressman George Crockett Jr., chair of the Foreign Affairs Subcommittee on Western Hemispheric Affairs, and several Detroit media. By 11 p.m., only four hours after his landing in San Salvador, the Detroit TV stations reported on the bishop's detention.[21] A few security guards stayed with the four delegates in the airport overnight. The following morning Salvadoran government representatives arrived to meet with Bishop Gumbleton, compelled by the controversy the phone calls had evoked. The officials told him he could be released into the country if he signed a statement which they presented to him. This statement, he noticed, prohibited his participation in any political activities. He feared that the Salvadoran government's interpretation of the term "political" could encompass religious services as well as any other activity the government decided to oppose. He recalled that Archbishop Romero had frequently been accused of political activity when he celebrated Mass.[22] So he indicated that the word "political" would have to be defined in writing in the document before he could sign it. The government representatives left and returned with a definition of "political" that he concluded would allow him to safely carry out the activities he had planned during his visit.[23]

In time, he learned he had been detained because he was considered a subversive by both governments, the Salvadoran and U.S. In addition to the Salvadoran pressure, the U.S. embassy in El Salvador had already singled out Tom shortly after his initial trip to El Salvador two years earlier. A program officer of The Lutheran World Federation, Phil Anderson, had been called to meet with David B. Dlouhy, U.S. Embassy chargé d'affairs in San Salvador. During the meeting Tom was characterized as "the most radical member of the U.S. Catholic Bishops Conference...who is into very questionable stuff."[24]

As soon as the delegates were reunited at the hotel in San Salvador, they learned of violent attacks the day before. A bomb had exploded at the headquarters of a labor federation, FENASTRAS, killing ten people and injuring twenty-nine others. That same day another bomb had exploded in the office of COMADRES, a human rights organization.[25] The delegates visited the sights of these attacks and joined in the community's mourning. Surely, this solidarity would have been deemed "political" if Tom had not had the foresight to require the word be narrowly defined prior to signing the statement.

Within a week of returning home, another violent attack occurred that helped alter the direction of the Salvadoran civil war. During the night of November 16, 1989, six Jesuits, residing at the Jesuit-run University of Central America (UCA), were dragged out of their rooms and forced to lie face down in a garden. Members of the Salvadoran army then machine-gunned them in the back of their heads. The priests' cook and her daughter were also murdered to eliminate witnesses. All of this occurred in a state of martial law imposed by the government to restrict movement during a guerilla offensive that had brought the civil war to urban areas, including San Salvador. Overwhelming evidence indicated these murders were committed by government troops. Yet when a witness said she had seen men in military uniforms near the Jesuit residence that night, U.S. Ambassador William Walker suggested that they could have been rebels dressed in military uniforms.

Undeterred by the escalating violence, the United States government continued to support the military and their affiliated death squads. Four days after the massacre, Congress approved continuation of funding for El Salvador at the rate of over a million dollars a day. The only hope for the truth to emerge came when Speaker of the House Thomas Foley appointed Representative Joseph Moakley to lead a task force to investigate the UCA murders.[26] The task force faced difficulty in getting cooperation from either the U.S. or Salvadoran governments, yet it published regular reports that made headlines in both countries. "Their searing honesty made it impossible for the George H. W. Bush administration and the Salvadoran government to cover up the crimes and move on."[27] The first report issued five months after the UCA tragedy noted that five of the nine Salvadorans arrested for the massacre were trained at the SOA. The next report, released four months later, "accused high-ranking Salvadoran commanders of withholding, destroying, and falsifying evidence." Congressman Moakley also blamed the American government for withholding information. "What we need now is a Truth Commission report on our own government." After meeting Salvadorans afraid to be seen meeting with him in public, Rep. Moakley appealed to Americans to speak for those who have been silenced, saying they could do so without fear of being tortured or disappeared.[28]

The search for truth and justice for the UCA assassinations meandered on for decades, long after Moakley's death in 2001. Finally, thirty-one years after the assassinations, Spain successfully prosecuted a notorious graduate of the SOA for the murder of those priests who were from Spain. On September 11, 2020, in Madrid, Spain, Colonel Inocente Orlando Montano was convicted of the killings of the five Spanish Jesuit priests. Montano was vice-minister of public security on the night of the slayings.[29]

In 1990, soon after the UCA killings, José Artiga summoned religious leaders like Gumbleton to the site of a bombing to interview survivors and sustain them in their terror and grief. The victims were repatriated refugees who had returned to Corral de Piedra in October 1989 and had recently renamed their village to honor Ignacio Ellacuría, one of the assassinated UCA Jesuits.[30] José described the horror of their experience. "The people had returned to their homes. The military attacked them from a helicopter and one of the rockets hit a family that we had accompanied a few months earlier."[31]

José recalls that the delegation had permits from the Salvadoran High Command to make the visit, but the local military checkpoints would not let them pass. Hundreds of people from the community had come to the checkpoint to welcome the delegates, but the military had lined up across the road to make sure nobody passed. Notably, U.S. military "advisors" were with the Salvadoran troops. The delegation was demanding the right to go the village and celebrate Mass with the people. After some hours, many of the delegates felt they should just proceed, leaving it up to individuals to decide whether they would go or stay behind.

What was Tom Gumbleton going to do? "At that point I thought about it. I didn't think they were going to shoot anybody in the delegation from the U.S., but then again you didn't know exactly what would happen. I was aware that it was a dangerous moment." About ten of the delegates joined the people and started walking toward the wall of the military, arms-linked and fearful, but the military slowly parted as the delegates walked through to reach the community.

Tom was going to walk with them, but because the local bishop had arrived he stayed behind to participate in the negotiation process that ultimately ended successfully. "So, as a result," Artiga recalled, "everyone was able to go. We were there facing the very same military that had killed so many for so many years, military trained in the United States. For Tom to be there was a powerful symbol of accompaniment."[32]

When they reached the village to view what had happened earlier that month, Tom remembered, "it was immediately clear why they did not want us to see for ourselves what had happened or hear firsthand accounts from eyewitnesses." The villagers, especially the children, had fled from the low-flying helicopters to the one structure that was a brick building. It was a communal structure where people came to grind their wheat and they thought it was the safest.

I felt anger and the deepest sadness when I stood inside the tiny house where the rocket had torn through the roof. Fourteen people were huddled there, terrified by the exploding bombs and rockets. ...Four children and one adult were killed immediately. Even ten days later, when we were there, very tiny pieces of the bodies were still embedded in the walls. At one point, someone who was picking up pieces of shrapnel to show us found a piece of the skull of a baby. I couldn't bring myself to hold it, although others took it and held it very respectfully and prayerfully.

He brought home with him two pieces of rocket shrapnel the U.S. government had financed. He would look at these pieces daily and find a renewed determination to advocate for a cutoff of military aid to El Salvador.[33]

Negotiations in El Salvador began in 1990, resulting in a peace treaty signed in January 1992. It is generally accepted that the political victory achieved by the guerrillas' insurrection, the international outcry after the UCA murders, and pressure from Moakley's investigation were key factors leading to the treaty. The Salvadoran ruling elite and American officials were forced to accept a negotiated settlement after years of unsuccessful aggression by the U.S.-trained Salvadoran military.[34] The Peace Accords created the United Nations' Truth Commission which released its report in March 1993. The findings substantiated the wisdom of trying to close the School of the Americas, or SOA, a military school at Fort Benning, Georgia, for training military and security forces from Latin America: "Two of the three officers cited in the assassination of Archbishop Romero are SOA graduates, including death squad founder and leader Roberto D'Aubisson. Three of five officers cited in the rape and murder of the four U.S. churchwomen are SOA graduates. Nineteen of twenty-six officers cited in the November 1989 murder of six Jesuit priests, their housekeeper, and her daughter are SOA graduates."[35]

As an introvert, Tom Gumbleton's natural inclination would not have led him into the crisis in El Salvador. Yet his conscience compelled him to respond to the cries of the victims of injustice there—first made known to him by Dorothy Kazel. Eileen Purcell has lauded his accompaniment. "Every time Tom was in El Salvador he was on a list. They were killing priests. And he didn't hesitate. He took risks that were real. He accompanied the people and lived his faith as a servant leader. In El Salvador the people say that Oscar Romero has an address in Detroit, and that is Tom Gumbleton."[36]

He traveled to El Salvador for nearly thirty years to accompany the people, advocate for justice, and celebrate the anniversaries of the martyrs. His last trip was in December 2015, to honor the four churchwomen thirty-five years after their torture and murder.[37]

Advocacy to Change U.S. Policy in Nicaragua

Tom Gumbleton embarked on the first of many visits to Nicaragua in December 1986. After returning from his initial trip, he told the press: "We've been lied to in order to promote the current war between the Sandinista government and the U.S.-backed Contra rebels."[38] He had been following the consequences of the July 1979 Nicaraguan revolution, having learned about the country's reality from friends who traveled there after the revolution. Many went as participants in the solidarity program, Witness for Peace. Detroiter Bill O'Brien wrote to him from Nicaragua in November 1979, "It means a lot to the folks here that people in Detroit are interested and excited about Nicaragua...." Tom responded, "I continue to be encouraged by all that you are doing for the Nicaraguans. Also, from your letters I have an even clearer sense of the sufferings of the people, and certainly you must be suffering right along with them. I continue to keep you and all of them in my prayers and thoughts every day."[39]

By 1981 the United States had begun sending aid to the Contras, a counter-revolutionary group struggling to overthrow the new Nicaraguan government. As U.S. involvement grew, Gumbleton voiced his opposition to this policy. His stance was consistent with legislation passed in Congress, the Boland Amendments, 1982–1984, which outlawed assistance intended to foster the overthrow of the Nicaraguan government.[40]

After Congress appropriated $27 million in non-military aid to the Contras in 1985, he joined an ecumenical effort, Quest for Peace, to raise an equivalent amount of humanitarian relief. He joined with two hundred Protestant, Catholic, and Jewish clergy on the Capitol steps in early March to promote this campaign. They strongly opposed Reagan's latest proposal for $100 million in military aid to the Contras which he had submitted to

Congress on February 25, 1986.[41] Bishop Gumbleton read the statement on behalf of the group, accusing the administration of exaggeration, misinformation, and outright falsehood. Signers claimed the administration had been deceiving the public in seeking military and so-called humanitarian aid. Most notably, they alleged the administration had been covering up numerous credible reports that the Contras had been committing human rights atrocities against innocent civilians. The Contras were not freedom-fighters as described by President Reagan. The United States should not conduct its foreign policy by funding paramilitary groups to subvert sovereign nations.[42]

Later that day, on the PBS MacNeil/Lehrer NewsHour, he and Elliott Abrams, assistant secretary of state for inter-American affairs, discussed Reagan's $100 million request in new aid to the Contras. After an examination of the foreign policy in support of the Contras, the show continued with Abrams opposing Tom's public statement presented on behalf of the religious leaders. Abrams defended the administration's goal of financing the Contras. He claimed the administration did not cover up alleged abuses by the Contras and pointed to atrocities committed by the Nicaraguan government. The United States wasn't concealing anything. "It would be funny if it weren't a little bit sad. We don't cover anything up.... But the notion that we're covering anything up is—it's incredible."[43]

They also debated the Catholic Church's attitude toward the Contras, with Abrams contending that the Catholic Church in Nicaragua, in the person of Cardinal Miguel Cardinal Obando y Bravo, the archbishop of Managua, did not share the view expressed in the religious leaders' statement. To this assertion, Gumbleton replied:

But, Mr. Abrams, you don't have to tell me who is the church in Nicaragua. It's not Cardinal Obando. The church is the people. That's who the church is.... No, if you could only understand that the church is represented by those three million people, 80 percent of whom are Roman Catholic. That's the church. And the people who minister in the parishes and in the villages and in the hospitals and in the dispensaries, they are the ones telling us that they're free to practice their religion. They are not being persecuted.

Abrams: "Maybe you're right and maybe I'm right, but I don't call you a liar, and the charge of outright lying does not help the American people cope with this issue very much."

Gumbleton: "It is a very sad thing that we have to say that our government is lying. And yet, in the documentation which we published today we listed at least fifteen separate areas where the facts show clearly our government says one thing; the facts are the opposite."[44]

As the debate intensified, the bishop asserted:

"I don't claim to be the Church in Detroit. No bishop is a church. ...I am standing up for the Church in Nicaragua, and they are the people who are suffering because of the Contras. They are the people who are being killed with the weapons we are supplying."

Moderator Lehrer: "Is there anything...the Reagan administration could say to change your position on this?"

Gumbleton: "Well, the one thing that they could do to change my position would be to withdraw the request for aid. Then I would be supportive of them. I am not going to support any kind of further aid to the Contras to do further atrocities in Nicaragua."[45]

Uncovering the Truth about United States Policy in Nicaragua

In his message to Congress in support of this massive military aid package for the Contra commandos, President Reagan had called them "Freedom Fighters" and "the moral equivalent of the Founding Fathers." The converse was true. The immorality of the "Contras" "had been well-documented by human rights organizations which cited them repeatedly for the deliberate use of terror: raping, torturing, and murdering civilians. Their commanders came from the ranks of the overthrown dictator Anastasio Somoza's hated National Guard. Their 'cold-blooded executions' had even been denounced by one of their own leaders, Edgar Chamorro, once a prized asset of the CIA."[46]

Predictably, Bishop Gumbleton's advocacy in Nicaragua drew opposition from some Catholics. About forty people from a group called Catholic Laity United picketed outside the Archdiocese of Detroit offices on March 17, 1986, demanding the bishop's expulsion and denouncing what they termed his pro-Communist views. The following day, Gumbleton issued a statement quoting the American Catholic bishops' position that "direct military aid to any force attempting to overthrow a government with which we are not at war, and with which we maintain diplomatic relations, is illegal and in our judgment, immoral, and therefore cannot merit our support."[47]

He also received a large volume of mail from supporters and detractors after the PBS appearance. He responded to each letter, including that of Joe Cortina from Tampa, Florida who told him "You can go to hell, or go to the communists, but don't spread your lying filth any more in my country. You don't belong with decent people."

> Dear Mr. Cortina:
>
> [Y]our letter has probably expressed more contempt that almost any other (hate mail). . . . My position is based upon conversations with priests, religious and lay missionaries who are personal friends, and who have the firsthand experience of living and working in Nicaragua, some for many years. It is they who are putting their lives on the line in the name of justice; it is they who are responding to hatred and violence with love and compassion. I believe in their work and in the testimony they give. I apologize for upsetting you so much and I regret that you have the impression that I think so little of the United States. Nothing could be further from the truth. I love my country and because of that love, will continue to challenge her to act—even at great risk—in a Christian way.[48]

Congress approved Reagan's request for the $100 million in aid, $70 million in military aid and $30 million in non-lethal "humanitarian" aid on August 13, 1986. Only a couple of months later, in October 1986, a cargo plane providing support to the Contras crashed in Nicaragua. This accident led to the exposure of an illegal U.S. operation diverting to the Contras the proceeds from prohibited sales of arms to Iran. The weapons sales were intended to encourage the release of American hostages held in Lebanon. This venture, led by Lt. Col. Oliver North, a National Security staff member, directly contradicted congressional policy.[49] The illegal practice, famously called the Iran-Contra scandal, led to televised congressional hearings by the Tower Commission. The commission's report in February 1987 "condemned the Reagan administration for swapping arms for hostages at the same time it pressured other countries not to deal with Iran."[50] Eventually fourteen administration officials were indicted and eleven of them convicted. Nevertheless all sentences were vacated on appeal or the guilty were pardoned by President Gorge H. W. Bush one month before the end of his presidency.[51]

Accompanying the Victims

Tom Gumbleton's solidarity with the people of Nicaragua continued throughout the decades that followed, up to the present, even in protest when a later Sandinista government, under Daniel Ortega, took an increasingly authoritarian turn. His travels to Central America and acts of witness and solidarity extended as well to Honduras and Guatemala, on occasions too numerous to describe. In summary, it is worth describing his support for two particular American women, Dianna Ortiz, OSU, and Jennifer Harbury, whose lives were tragically shaped by U.S. policies in Guatemala. They each invited him to join them in their search for truth, though their Guatemalan experiences differed significantly.

Dianna's ordeal began in 1989 soon after she moved to Guatemala to minister among indigenous people. As a Catholic sister working with poor Mayans, she was immediately and unintentionally caught up in the struggle between the army and the guerrillas. The previous year the Guatemalan bishops had issued a pastoral letter condemning the unjust distribution of land in which two percent of the population owned two-thirds of the land. Because their ministry was intended to improve the Mayans' lives, the military viewed religious workers as aligned with the Mayans and the army saw the Mayans as natural allies with the guerrillas.[52] After about a year of Dianna's ministry in Guatemala, the local bishop received letters accusing her and the other nuns with whom she served of meeting with subversives. Dianna herself began to receive death threats and her mail was intercepted. Yet she remained determined to live in solidarity with the Mayan community in San Miguel.

On November 2, 1989, while she was in Antigua praying in a convent retreat center garden, Guatemalan Security Forces kidnapped her. They then transported her to the Antigua Escuela Politécnica, a large military installation located near the American Embassy. They immediately took her to a downstairs cell for interrogation and identification of people in photographs they showed her. Every time she answered a question she was burned with a cigarette.[53] She later described many terrible abuses, including being lowered into a pit filled with the human bodies of men, women, and children, alive and dead. She saw rats feasting on these bodies. She was forced to participate in the torture of another woman and was gang raped. They accused her of being a whore and told her no one would believe her even if she managed to survive.[54]

Eventually, "Alejandro," apparently the Guatemalans' "boss," arrived. News media reports about the missing nun were circulating in Guatemala City. Speaking in American-accented Spanish, this tall, fair-haired man cursed the Guatemalans for "disappearing" a North American nun. He took her away, telling her he was transporting her to a safe haven at the American embassy. While stuck in traffic, Dianna jumped from the vehicle, afraid he was actually driving her to her death. A Mayan woman recognized her on the street, having seen her on the news, and came to her aid. The woman contacted Dianna's religious community and eventually got her to safety in the papal nuncio's residence.[55]

Within forty-eight hours of her escape, she returned to the United States and described feeling that "everything that made my life worth living dried up." A doctor examining her reported that he saw 111 second-degree burns on her back. She did not recognize her family in New Mexico or her Ursuline sisters in Kentucky. Stripped of any memory of her life prior to the abduction, frightened by anything that reminded her of the torture—men with cigarettes, squirrels she mistook for rats—Dianna was disoriented for many months.[56]

She turned to Chicago's Marjorie Kovler Center for the Treatment of Survivors of Torture to recover. There the clinical supervisor, Mario Gonzalez, described what was occurring: "Ortiz's symptoms—extreme anxiety, depression, insomnia and severe memory loss—are typical of torture survivors. ... The obvious result of the experience of torture is that of disorientation and confusion.... In order to protect itself and suppress those painful experiences that continue torturing even in the form of memories, the mind creates a kind of blockade.[57] The therapy helped her gain perspective on her torture.

At Kovler the therapists had tried to teach us that torture was political, not personal, that we were attacked as part of a strategy involving the broader society. I never understood. It seemed personal when it was my own skin that was burned, my own memories that were obliterated. Seeing the list [Religious Killed or Disappeared in Guatemala since 1976], I understood, finally, that the Guatemalan army may not have had any personal issue with me. It was the 'Sister' in front of my name that had made me a target—like the Sister and Father and Brother in front of all these other names. The attack on me was actually an attack on the Church.[58]

She also began to recover through meeting others who had either been tortured themselves or had loved ones tortured. Perhaps the person in this group with whom she most identified was Jennifer Harbury, an attorney, whose husband had been "disappeared" in Guatemala. Harbury invited Dianna to join a coalition of U.S. citizens who had suffered directly or indirectly from Guatemala's political violence. Soon Dianna was co-chair of the coalition and before long she and Jennifer became close friends and colleagues in their determined search for truth and justice.[59]

Harbury was the widow of Efraín Bámaca Velásquez, a Mayan leader of the resistance forces in the thirty-five-year-long Guatemalan civil war. He vanished in the mountains on March 12, 1992. She tirelessly sought the truth about her husband. Was he alive according to reports of those had seen him being tortured, or was he dead as had been reported to her by Guatemalan and U.S. officials?[60] Being with Jennifer gave Dianna strength. "Her words were what made me stronger. I clung to them and pictured myself a tall, strong sunflower, standing straight up and opening." Dianna continued to spend time with her even though she knew Jennifer was not trusted nor leveled with by U.S. government representatives.

Jennifer's rebuttal to this scorn was to seek the truth. She had been lied to by various U.S. agencies and given conflicting information about her husband's status. After over two years of frustratingly unsuccessful efforts to discover the truth, she launched a hunger strike in Guatemala City in October 1994 in front of the National Palace. Throughout this strike she was accompanied by human rights advocates from the United States who traveled in a variety of delegations to support her. Nearly three weeks after the strike began, some members of the Washington, DC, community in which both Jennifer and Dianna lived, Assisi Community, were planning to travel to Guatemala. Given the prominent position of the Church in Guatemala, the organizers had hoped to include several North American bishops in this delegation. Yet only Bishop Gumbleton, solicited to join the delegation by another member of the Assisi Community, Marie Dennis, agreed to go. "Another bishop who was also invited would have nothing to do with Jennifer's hunger strike. He said it was tantamount to suicide, which, as a representative of the Church, he couldn't condone." This attitude seemed to ignore Jennifer's needs and appalled Dianna.[61]

Once in Guatemala City, the delegates learned from Jennifer that the TV program *60 Minutes* was coming to film a segment. This would significantly expand Harbury's campaign to publicize her search for the truth. "Interviewer Mike Wallace was going to cover not only Jennifer's story, but

Guatemala and the atrocities that were occurring day after day.... Exposure on *60 Minutes* could be an invaluable tool in the effort to curb the army's campaign of terror."[62]

The timing of this trip coincided with the fifth anniversary of Dianna's abduction—a date that had annually caused her harrowing flashbacks.[63] Yet she joined the delegation, and they visited the Politécnica, the building where she had been detained and tortured. Tom recalled how she walked around it, leaning against it, touching it. "It was as if she was making sure nothing could happen to her again. She was fragile yet courageous in trying to confront firsthand the trauma of the whole experience and to move beyond it."[64] Both Jennifer and Dianna experienced continual frustration in their efforts to uncover the facts.

Eventually, three years after her husband's disappearance, Jennifer learned the truth during the second week of another fast in Lafayette Park across from the White House.[65] The information came indirectly. A State Department official, Richard Nuccio, the department's point man in Guatemala, had learned about a CIA cover-up. He told Rep. Robert Torricelli, a member of the House Intelligence Committee with a security clearance, about this cover-up and CIA complicity in the torture and murder of Jennifer's husband. Torricelli informed Jennifer that her husband had been murdered by a former CIA "asset."[66] Torricelli's assertion resulted in an Intelligence Oversight Board (IOB) probe into the behavior of the CIA in Guatemala. The scope of the investigation included both the disappearance of Efraín Bámaca and the kidnapping of Sister Dianna Ortiz.

Ortiz continued in her own efforts to expose the truth. On Palm Sunday in 1996 she began a six-week vigil in front of the White House. She viewed her actions as a means of revealing the appalling suffering of Guatemalans.

> Many of you know my story. What is overlooked is that my experience is a daily reoccurrence in Guatemala. Six people a week, on average, are killed for political reasons. Two a week are tortured. The total death toll may never be known. The army's counterinsurgency campaign has left an estimated 200,000 dead and another 45,000 disappeared, victims of the dreaded death squads. This staggering death toll is far higher than that of the dirty wars of Argentina, Chile, and El Salvador.

As her vigil persisted, people joined her. Some committed civil disobedience by standing or kneeling in front of the White House, as standing still there for any amount of time is against the law. In the first ten days of civil disobedience 125 people had been detained. Tom was among those handcuffed and arrested.[67] Shortly after his return to Detroit, he wrote thanking Dianna for her witness. "You are very courageous, and what you are doing is important for you and also for all victims of tyranny throughout the world. I will be praying in solidarity with you every day.... Your sufferings dramatize how Jesus continues to endure violence and hatred in the 'little ones' of this world even now, but also your courage and commitment to life gives all of us renewed hope in the power of the Resurrection."[68]

Tom Gumbleton rejoined Dianna Ortiz the following month and, along with about thirty people, was arrested for demonstrating without a permit. Dianna's lengthy protest hoped to pressure the Clinton administration to release information about her case.[69] She ended her vigil at a May 6th press conference during which she revealed the fruit of her painful work with sketch artist drawings of Alejandro along with other scenes depicting her torture.[70] Despite the vigil, her advocacy led to very limited results, causing her intense frustration. In June 1996 the presidential IOB report, resulting from Torricelli's intervention, was released. Yet, it also proved lacking. U.S. victims of human rights abuses, including Dianna, complained the report "failed to provide information on their cases and on the CIA's role."[71]

Finally, in September a *Washington Post* article disclosed the extensive U.S. role in training Latin American military officers to torture. "U.S. Army intelligence manuals used to train Latin American military officers at an Army school (the SOA) from 1982 to 1991 advocated executions, torture, blackmail and other forms of coercion against insurgents, Pentagon documents released yesterday show." The manual had been distributed to thousands of military officers from eleven South and Central American countries, including Guatemala, El Salvador, Honduras, and Panama.[72]

The types of torments named in the report matched Dianna's experience and the treatment of many Guatemalans. Her kidnapping and torture occurred while former Defense Minister General Hector Gramajo, trained at the School of the Americas, served as the Guatemalan commander.[73] Though unsuccessful in identifying Alejandro, her prolonged search for truth and justice helped expose the suffering of thousands of innocent Guatemalans.These human rights violations were the subject of investigations by the Guatemalan Historical Memory Project, founded and coordinated by Guatemalan Bishop Juan Gerardi. His work reported on and verified the abuses even though the Guatemalan government denied them. "The four-volume report documented more than 14,000 acts of violence, producing more than 55,000 victims, most of them Mayans."[74] The report attributed 89.7 percent of the violations to the army and security forces.

In April 1998, two days after Gerardi presented the report, he was bludgeoned to death in his garage with a concrete block. Two high-ranking members of the Guatemalan security services were eventually convicted. Tom wrote to the people of Guatemala through the Guatemalan Office of Human Rights of the Catholic Church expressing his sorrow over Bishop Gerardi's assassination. "Monseñor Gerardi stands in the company of Monseñor Oscar Romero and all those who have given their lives for the poor and oppressed. May his martyrdom give those of us who remain the courage to continue our efforts towards building a peaceful and just society."[75]

President Clinton later made front-page headlines in 1999, saying, "What we did in Guatemala was wrong." Dianna's reaction captured her perspective on her nation's actions in Guatemala: "Are a few words all we owe when we created and maintained an army that slaughtered hundreds of thousands? With that sort of impunity, what will keep us from doing it over and over again?"[76]

Advocacy and the SOA Watch Movement

For many years, one of the chief targets of protest for those concerned about U.S. involvement in violence and human rights abuses in Central and Latin America was the U.S. Army's School of the Americas, which provided training to military and security forces in the Americas, many of whom were documented as responsible for torture, assassinations, and massacres. Among those who led the way in focusing attention and protest on the School was Maryknoll Father Roy Bourgeois. As Tom noted, "While Bourgeois had not met Archbishop Romero, it is impossible to overstate the effect the archbishop had on him. The story of Romero's transformation and raw courage would become a cornerstone of Bourgeois' life, inspiring him time and time again, focusing his mission and fueling his actions."[77]

The U.S. role in training troops from Central and Latin American countries had begun in 1946 in the Panama Canal Zone. In 1985, under the terms of the Panama Canal Treaty, it had to relocate. Now known as the School of the Americas (SOA), it moved to Fort Benning, Georgia as part of the U.S. Army Training and Doctrine Command (TRADOC). Over the years the SOA trained nearly 59,000 Latin American military, policemen and civilians.[78]

Known among the persecuted people in Latin America as the "School of the Assassins" for "having trained so many of the dictators, torturers and death squad leaders in their countries," the SOA has also been described as "the biggest base for destabilization in Latin America." Roy Bourgeois founded SOA Watch and nurtured the organization into a movement to close the SOA.[79]

Tom Gumbleton's experiences in Latin America led him to support Roy Bourgeois's public critique of the SOA. Bourgeois's efforts to close the SOA, his fasting, protesting, civil disobedience, and imprisonment eventually seemed to bear fruit. In 1998, prominent people like actor Martin Sheen joined 7,000 people to gather for the annual November demonstration at Fort Benning. Of these, 2,319 engaged in civil disobedience.[80] Congress began efforts to significantly defund the SOA. Rep. Moakley, a legislator very familiar with military atrocities in El Salvador, proposed legislation to reduce the SOA budget by $2 million, money designated to recruit and transport Latin American soldiers to Fort Benning.[81] Catholic Church leaders of the peace movement also joined in these efforts.

Bishop Walter Sullivan, bishop-president of Pax Christi USA, requested that the NCCB International Policy Committee endorse a resolution to close the SOA. Tom wrote to individual bishops urging them to sign the SOA resolution. Yet, other bishops opposed the measure. Bishop Francis Roque, with the Archdiocese for the Military Services, USA, wrote bishops asking them to affirm their support of the SOA. He included an article by Louis Caldera, secretary of the army, articulating the "bad apples" argument, claiming that only a few of the SOA graduates had violated human rights. "The facts are that less than 1 percent of the school's 600,000 graduates have ever been linked to human rights violations and fewer still have had allegations substantiated against them."[82] Tom critiqued this "bad apple" contention.

> While it is true that the large majority of SOA grads have not been *convicted* of human rights violations, the low conviction rate reflects the incomplete records and nonexistent monitoring system of SOA graduates. Few perpetrators of human rights abuse are identified, much less indicted, much less convicted, much less incarcerated, or otherwise punished or rehabilitated....Of the few perpetrators of atrocities in Latin America who have been publicly identified, a disproportionate number are SOA graduates.[83]

Meanwhile Army Secretary Louis Caldera, concerned about the growing awareness of the SOA's record of abuses, wanted to halt the increasing support the SOA movement was generating. "We're not going to allow the army's reputation to be dragged through the mud every year....[We] don't want to go through another fiscal year with this torture." He proposed changing the name of the school, moving it, and modifying its curriculum. Moakley called the proposal "perfume on a toxic dump." The Clinton administration, undeterred by Moakley's criticism, supported Caldera's proposed changes. A task force evaluated the military training programs. This work led to a Congressional vote to close the SOA in December 2000 and to reopen it on January 17, 2001, under a new name, Western Hemisphere Institute for Security Cooperation (WHINSC).[84]

Two months later Tom joined nine other bishops, and on their behalf again circulated a letter with a petition calling for the closure of the renamed SOA. "We appeal to you to sign this petition in support of the four churchwomen, Archbishop Romero, Bishop Gerardi, the six Jesuits and the two women killed with them, and in support of all who plead for justice and call for the closure of the SOA."[85] Bourgeois described his ultimate goal for the SOA: "We want this School closed because it is a School of Thugs. It is a School of Terrorists. It is a School that brings shame upon our country and upon us and our laws and what we should be standing for."[86] Yet the resolution before the NCCB failed, and the school remained open.

*Tom and his sister Irene, First
Communion, May 2, 1937,
Epiphany Church, Detroit*
(Courtesy Thomas Gumbleton)

*Graduation, Sacred Heart Seminary
High School, 1948*
(Courtesy Thomas Gumbleton)

A newly ordained priest, 1956
(Courtesy Thomas Gumbleton)

*In 1968, the youngest bishop in the
United States*
(Courtesy Thomas Gumbleton)

Gumbleton with Vietnamese priests in Hanoi, 1973
(Courtesy Thomas Gumbleton)

Bishop Gumbleton with retired Bishop Carrol Dozier of Memphis in 1984
(Credit: National Catholic Reporter/Steve Askin.)

Stations of the Cross with the Benedictine Sisters of Erie, PA in the 1980s
(Credit: Pax Christi).

Bishop Gumbleton with Franziska Jägerstätter, whose husband Franz was beheaded by the Nazis for refusing to take a military oath in 1943
(Courtesy Thomas Gumbleton)

Bishop Gumbleton supports Sister Diana Ortiz during her fast outside the White House in 1996
(Credit: Rick Reinhard)

Bishop Gumbleton with Cardinal Christoph Schönborn of Vienna at the beatification ceremony for Franz Jägerstätter in 2007
(Courtesy Thomas Gumbleton)

Bishop Gumbleton is arrested in Washington DC during an anti-war protest
(Credit: Linda Panetta/Optical Realities)

*Bishop Gumbleton
visits a gravesite
in Colombia*
(Credit: Linda Panetta/
Optical Realities)

*In El Salvador, at the
cemetery in Chalatenango
where three U.S. nuns,
murdered on December 2,
1980, are buried*
(Courtesy Thomas Gumbleton)

*Protesting the School of the
Americas*
(Credit: Pax Christi)

With children in Afghanistan
(Credit: Linda Panetta/Optical Realities)

Protesting the war in Iraq
(Credit: Linda Panetta/Optical Realities)

With children in Iraq
(Credit: Linda Panetta/Optical Realities)

*Bishop Gumbleton serving
meals to children in Haiti*
(Credit: Linda Panetta/
Optical Realities)

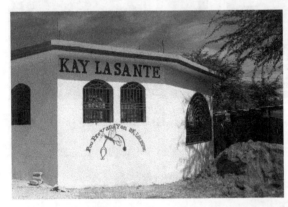

The Kay Lasante Clinic in Haiti
(Courtesy Johanna Berrigan)

*With a malnourished
child after the
earthquake in Haiti
in 2010*
(Courtesy Johanna Berrigan)

Thomas Gumbleton receiving Bridge Building Award from New Ways Ministry,
poses with his brother Dan Gumbleton, Bishop John Snyder of St. Augustine, FL,
and Francis DeBernardo
(Credit: Courtesy New Ways Ministry)

In 1994 Bishop Gumbleton wears a
miter adorned with rainbow colors for
a "Eucharistic liturgy of liberation" at
the Basilica of St. Mary in Minneapolis,
followed by a listening session for LGBTQ
Catholics
(Courtesy Thomas Gumbleton)

(Credit: National Catholic Reporter/Arthur Jones)

*In vestments for Christmas liturgy
at St. Leo's, late 1980s*
(Courtesy Thomas Gumbleton)

At a board meeting for New Ways Ministry, 2012
(Courtesy New Ways Ministry)

Bishop Gumbleton in his office at St. Leo's, 1998
(Courtesy Thomas Gumbleton)

11

Crises of Iraq, 9/11, and Afghanistan

When Saddam Hussein invaded neighboring Kuwait in early August 1990, George Bush Sr. responded by greatly increasing troops and equipment in the Gulf region. Pax Christi USA condemned the Iraqi dictator's aggression *and* called for the immediate withdrawal of all foreign combat forces from the region. Bush's buildup changed from a deterrent force to an offensive force that could attack Iraq.[1] Were security interests really at stake? Or, Pax Christi asked, had Bush deployed a military force "to guarantee the free flow of oil to the U.S., a nation that consumes a disproportionate share of the world's resources?" PCUSA urged the National Conference of Catholic Bishops—and appealed to all American citizens—to scrutinize the actions of their government.[2]

When the bishops assembled in Washington, DC, in mid-November 1990, Bishop Gumbleton petitioned his colleagues to sign a new Pax Christi USA statement asking Catholic soldiers to become selective conscientious objectors. "We want to make it clear that what the president is doing is developing an offensive capability," he explained. "This is not just about influencing public policy, but we have to offer moral guidance to people who face concrete questions about participating and whether it is acceptable to engage in an offensive war."[3] David Crumm, with the *Detroit Free Press*, reported: "Outside the formal conference, several bishops admitted they still regret the slowness with which their conference came to oppose the Vietnam War—and want to oppose war in the Gulf even before it breaks out." Bishop Michael Kenny of Juneau, Alaska, one of Tom's Pax Christi colleagues, admonished the NCCB assembly: "We don't hesitate in telling Catholic people what they should do in terms of abortion...or in terms of condoms. Aren't we willing to be as clear and direct in telling them what they might do in terms of weapons that might bring incalculable destruction?" With Kenny and other PCUSA bishops, Gumbleton sought bold language from the NCCB, especially on the matter of conscientious objection. "The troops in the Middle East need our moral guidance. They can't wait for continued discussion that we can carry on interminably while they risk their lives and their spiritual lives as well." Other prelates cautioned against being too critical of the government.[4]

The debate was then closed to the public, but two days later the NCCB issued a statement saying that "the use of weapons of war cannot be a substitute for the difficult, often time-consuming and frustrating work of searching for political solutions." Bishop Gumbleton's appeal for language supporting soldiers seeking selective conscientious objection failed to get majority support. Nevertheless, the bishops warned against an attack on Iraq, and Cincinnati Archbishop Daniel Pilarczyk, the Conference's president, wrote to President Bush spelling out the criteria of a just war: "I fear that, in this situation, moving beyond the deployment of military forces in an effort to deter Iraqi aggression to the undertaking of offensive military action could well violate these criteria." Not ruling out war as a last resort, Pilarczyk implored Bush to exert every alternative means.[5]

Just three weeks after this, Tom flew to Iraq to visit hostages and seek their release. Hussein was holding several hundred foreign nationals, and relatives of some of the hostages accompanied the bishop. "We're definitely going to ask for the release of those with family members there and for all the hostages," he told a reporter. "I don't think you can overlook the need and the comfort we can bring to those over there. If someone wants to put a political twist on it, let them." Might Hussein use the visit for propaganda purposes? "The families understand that, too. They've wrestled with it, but when you get down to it, there's lives at stake, so it's worth being used."[6]

Tom was in Baghdad when the news broke that Saddam would free all foreign hostages. "It's certainly something beautiful to share," Tom said. "I'm surprised how grateful they all are I'm part of it." There were about nine hundred American hostages, and among them was Kevin Bazner of Farmington Hills, a Detroit suburb. Kevin's wife Dawn, who with their two children had also been held hostage but had been released earlier, traveled with the Detroit bishop as part of the delegation. Kevin was one of seventeen Americans released that same day. The release of the hostages was good news, to be sure, but as Tom was standing in the lobby of the Melia al-Mansour Hotel, he felt less than sanguine. "Part of this seems totally unreal. I was walking through the hotel garden today and thinking I shouldn't be here, in the sense of the unreality of it all."[7] He celebrated a liturgy for some of the released hostages and their families and told a journalist, "I leave feeling that what we had hoped for was accomplished. I also feel a certain sadness for the people of Iraq and Kuwait. I don't sense the majority of people in the U.S. want to probe into what causes one country to invade another, the sense of injustice that many Arabs feel."[8]

The Air War

At St. Frances Cabrini Catholic Church in Allen Park, southwest of Detroit, Bishop Gumbleton was conducting a prayer service with children preparing for confirmation. The children and their parents exchanged the sign of peace. Someone came over from the rectory to let the bishop know that war had begun. On that day, January 16, 1991, bombs began to rain down on Iraq. The bishop announced the news to the congregation, and after the service he told a reporter how he felt upon hearing that America had launched an attack on Iraq. "I thought of our soldiers and then of the churches I visited in Baghdad and the people I visited, and I began to wonder how they cope with this. I can only say that I felt very, very sad."[9]

On the next Tuesday evening, January 22, two hundred religious demonstrators conducted a candlelight vigil and protest near the White House. Bishop Gumbleton was there. At a pre-rally press conference, Pax Christi's national council chairperson Marie Dennis called for an immediate ceasefire and appealed to the Catholic bishops of the United States to raise their voice against the war. In his remarks, Gumbleton called the air sorties over Iraq, happening at that very moment, worse than President Nixon's 1972 Christmas bombings of North Vietnam. And Benedictine Sister Joan Chittister asked some piercing rhetorical questions, drawing applause even from the press corps:

Aren't we on the verge of becoming what we hate? We have dropped more tonnage on Iraq in the last five days than we did on Hiroshima. Is this what democracy's all about? To blast the questions and the questioners into oblivion? We have participated in the massive arms race in the Middle East. We gave Iraq tacit support for their invasion of Iran. Aren't we really showing the world that the wealthy warmakers don't need to negotiate? They can simply demolish the opposition.[10]

A Bunch of Sheep

On a crisp autumn day in 2019 we were heading by car from Detroit to Erie, Pennsylvania, to visit Joan Chittister, Mary Lou Kownacki, and all the Erie Benedictines with whom Tom had grown close over many years. Something still troubled him, he said, about what happened when the bishops met in November 1990.

> Some of us made sure the threat of war was on the agenda. The Conference readily said we must try to oppose the likely war. Since it was too late to write a pastoral document to circulate all around the country, we authorized the president of the NCCB to write a letter to President Bush explaining why, according to Catholic teaching, this war would not be justified. Bush totally ignored it and went ahead in January with the war. What upset me, and still does, is that even though almost every bishop was behind that letter and supported its arguments, when the war started, they were silent. Almost nobody said anything! The bishops didn't say, "Look, people in the military, you've got to examine your conscience, if you're following Catholic teaching about just war here are things you've got to consider." Not a word! It was as if our letter had gone right down into the sewer, and nobody cared. To me that is just a terrible failure of leadership. We seemed so bold in November but then, once the war started, we just became a bunch of sheep.[11]

From January 17 to February 28, 1991, the United States conducted 110,000 aerial sorties over Iraq, unleashing 88,500 tons of explosives equivalent to seven and a half Hiroshima bombs. Nearly every facility vital to civilian life became a target. Over 150,000 thousand defenseless people died.[12] Gumbleton was in the region during part of that very air assault. On Friday, February 15, in Amman, Jordan, he accompanied Palestinian Liberation Organization activists and others in a peace proposal to try to end the Gulf War. Then, in a Baghdad press conference he said he hoped there would be "public pressure against the terrible suffering and slaughter going on in Iraq. I can't believe most people in the United States are at all comfortable with that." The issues could not be solved without paying attention to other occupations in the region, he argued in concert with other activists. Iraq should pull out of Kuwait, to be sure, but Israel should pull out of its occupied territories, Syria should withdraw from Lebanon, and Turkey should leave Cyprus. The economic sanctions against Iraq should cease.

Saddam proposed a similar peace plan, but Bush summarily rejected it. Why cast aside the offer? Tom asked. "It seems like a very real opportunity. We've had so much bloodshed and suffering."[13]

Days later, just before celebrating the Sunday liturgy back home at his parish, St. Leo's, he told a reporter, "I'm very saddened by the whole thing. I feel very strongly that the war in the Middle East is an adventure with no gains. There will be a lot more suffering." The reporter noted that the Rev. Robert Schuller, pastor of Crystal Cathedral in Garden Grove, California, had great confidence in President Bush. Bush told Schuller before the war began, "I don't believe my critics have done as much praying as I have."[14] At St. Leo's that Sunday people prayed for twenty-two relatives of parish members who were in the military in the Gulf region. And Tom told the reporter, "This is such an evil thing. To have that much killing—that much suffering going on when there's no clear reason to believe we're going to end with a more just or more peaceful situation in the Middle East."[15]

Six weeks after it began, America seemed to have won, the war seemed to have ended. The "Vietnam Syndrome" seemed to have been overcome. But Tom did not see it that way. At the Newman Center in Port Huron, Michigan, on Tuesday evening, February 26, he remarked, presciently:

> The whole problem of terrorism will become far worse if we don't get at the causes of injustices. Yes, there are grave injustices in the Middle East. But there is no way to resolve them with war. Violence only begets violence. War usually doesn't resolve issues. War lends itself to resentment and further hostility. Is the flow of U.S. and Iraqi youths' blood worth more than the flow of cheap oil? Maybe we will answer that question with more realism in the future. Or perhaps we will decide that oil is worth the price of blood. If that is our choice then I say, "God help us."

Very few American soldiers had died, and for this he expressed relief. But, he said, "Think about the 100,000 Iraqi troops that have been killed and the tens of thousands of innocent Iraqi citizens. This war is bringing intense suffering to the 4 million people in Baghdad."[16]

Voices in the Wilderness

The Iraqi people suffered intensely not only during the 1991 war but in its wake —a long wake. In early September 1997, six members of Chicago-based

Voices in the Wilderness set out to document the impacts that UN sanctions were having on food and medicine shortages. Bishop Gumbleton was part of this delegation, led by Voices in the Wilderness founder Kathy Kelly. Kelly had followed his story ever since she had used *The Challenge of Peace* as a teaching tool in her religious education courses. His peace work had emboldened her to participate in anti-nuclear civil disobedience. They would become good friends. Tom recalled that first trip:

> We took drugs and medical equipment to give to Iraqi hospitals and clinics. We flew from New York to Amman, Jordan, stayed there overnight, and went by automobile on a long drive across the desert to get to Baghdad. It was a difficult journey. There were checkpoints along the way, and you never knew exactly what was going to confront you. It was dangerous in some ways, not so much physically, but there was the possibility of getting arrested, and you always had your Iraqi minder with you.[17]

Iraq had been given UN approval (since December 1996) for an oil-for-food/medicine exchange, but the amount allowed, $2 billion worth of oil every six months, was hardly sufficient. Sanctions had been imposed in 1990 by the UN under heavy pressure from the U.S. If carefully targeted, sanctions could be effective but otherwise they only hurt the people. War by another name, in Gumbleton's view. "The hidden nature of the war being waged against Iraq is tragic. Editorials seldom appear and we see no front-page stories even though these sanctions have caused the deaths of more than one million people, constituting one of the greatest human rights abuses of our time," he said at the time. Archbishop Gabriel Kassab of Basra in southern Iraq appealed to President Clinton and the people of the United States:

> The blockade imposed on us has impoverished our people, depriving the poor of even plain bread and the simplest medicines. Basra, Iraq's second largest city, has no potable water supply and little electricity. Epidemics rage, taking away infants and the sick by the thousands. Those children who survive disease succumb to malnutrition which stunts their physical and mental development. Our situation is unbearable.[18]

Kassab had Gumbleton's ear, so when the American bishops convened in November 1997, Tom urged them to condemn the embargo. He had written in early October to the chair of the NCCB's international policy committee, Archbishop McCarrick:

I recently visited Iraq and saw first-hand the devastation the US/UN embargo is inflicting on innocent people, especially women and children. I visited hospitals and homes, spoke with doctors, nurses, and parents.... When our Secretary of State Madeline Albright was asked about the sanctions and whether it was worth the devastation caused to the children she said, "It is a hard decision, but we think it is worth it." I just cannot justify this line of thinking. Clearly this is a violation of our moral teaching that counter-population warfare is not justifiable.... To me, this is a matter of grave urgency. I request that the NCCB forward a resolution to President Clinton demanding an immediate end to the sanctions. We must demand that the people of Iraq be given an opportunity to recover from the devastating effects of the war and begin to rebuild their country and their very lives. It is true that the sanctions are based on a United Nations resolution. But there is no doubt that they would be lifted if the U.S. government requested an end to them.[19]

Despite Gumbleton's appeal, the bishops refused to condemn the sanctions. Many seemed caught on the horns of a dilemma. Patricia Lefevere, writing for the *National Catholic Reporter*, explained:

Only minutes into their Nov. 10–13 semiannual meeting here [at the Hyatt Regency in DC] the issue surfaced when a soft-spoken but impassioned Bishop Thomas Gumbleton... recently returned from Iraq, tried to sway his 270 fellow bishops with the specter of one million Iraqis dead since 1990. He said the figure included 600,000 children. Quoting his guide, Chaldean Bishop Gabriel Kassab of Basra, of Iraq's second largest city, he described "innocent civilians" dead or suffering for want of food and medicines, which have dwindled during the seven-year, U.S.-led blockade of Iraq by the international community. "Those children who have survived have stunted growth," Gumbleton said. But when it came to a vote—one that pitted Gumbleton's pleas for action against Newark Archbishop Theodore McCarrick's submission of a five-paragraph "informational" statement on the crisis—Gumbleton's pleas fell five votes short of the two-thirds majority needed. Even before the start of the session, the two bishops stood at the top of the escalator leading to the Hyatt Regency conference area wrestling with the issue.[20]

Many years later the shocking truth would get out that McCarrick had been a career perpetrator of sexual abuse. But at that November 1997 meeting he carried the day. A statement crafted by him and others, "Called to Global Solidarity: International Challenges for U.S. Parishes," suggested ways parishes could reach beyond their own boundaries to serve those in need and to work for global justice and peace. Gumbleton told *NCR's* Lefevere that this so-called call to global solidarity was hardly "designed to disturb the consciences of U.S. Catholics in any way. Global solidarity ignores the counter-population warfare," exactly what America had been waging against Iraq since 1990 when the sanctions were put in place. If the American bishops really wanted to be in solidarity, they would challenge militarism and what drives it, he insisted.[21]

Tom could count on many of his colleagues, but rarely a majority. In January 1998 he appeared at the National Press Club with an open letter to President Clinton signed by fifty-four bishops. Fifteen of them joined him in a hunger strike. Their letter declared: "Sanctions have taken the lives of well over one million persons, 60 percent of whom are children under 5 years of age. The 1991 bombing campaign destroyed electric, water and sewage plants, as well as agricultural, food and medical production facilities. All these facilities continue to be inoperative, or function at subminimal levels." They encouraged others to fast, to hold prayer vigils, and to consider civil disobedience.[22] Gumbleton spoke to the press on their behalf:

> I am appalled that the United States takes the lead in imposing these devastating sanctions on the people of Iraq. I implore, end the sanctions, find another way to address the problem, look for the root causes that led to war in the first place and try to negotiate a solution to those problems. We must not kill defenseless innocent people.
>
> If you saw what we saw, you would be outraged. People just don't know that. Put yourself in their shoes. Imagine watching your child dying of hunger, or if there are not medical supplies to take care of your child, imagine if you were suffering that way, your outrage, your pain. If only we could put ourselves in their shoes.[23]

In early February, speaking on the Cornell University campus, he described what it had been like to look into the eyes of a hospitalized Iraqi child who lay at death's door. "This youngster had come to terms with dying. A 10-year-old should be filled with life and energy and looking forward to life."[24] He continued with his characteristic soft-spoken but passionate conviction: "For eight years we have waged a counter-population war against Iraq (in the form of economic sanctions). I hope I can convince all of you tonight to stop this embargo against Iraq and to prevent another war with it. What I saw there is some of the worst suffering I have ever seen."[25]

In the third week of the liquids-only fast, on the evening of February 11, Gumbleton and Pax Christi members from Michigan prepared to fly from Detroit to DC. He previewed the purpose of their trip:

> On Thursday, February 12th, the [seventh] anniversary of the bombing of the Amariyah Shelter in Baghdad, Pax Christi USA, Pax Christi Metro Washington, and the Dorothy Day Catholic Worker House together with other groups are sponsoring a Prayer Vigil at the White House at noon. I intend to be there to speak and probably will be arrested along with others praying at the White House. It's one more attempt to raise the issue of the immorality of the embargo and the even greater evil of another planned military attack against the people of Iraq.[26]

He had been to see the ruined Amariyah shelter in late summer of 1997. American bombs had killed between a thousand and fifteen hundred civilians in the strike in 1991. The woman who showed him the ruins had lost her husband during the Iran-Iraq War in the 1980s. On February 12, 1991, she had lost her seven children. The only reason she survived is because at the moment the bomb hit, she was outside doing the family's laundry. Tom tried to convey her unimaginable grief, telling her story. "It has been one of the most terrible atrocities of any war that I know of." He read aloud a letter signed by seven Iraqi Christian clerics: "The sanctions are killing our people, our children, the ones Christ has given us to protect. They are killing our beloved Muslim brothers and sisters. They strike at our poor and our sick most of all. In the name of God's people we ask you: Tell your government to end the sanctions against the Iraqi people. End the seven years of war against Iraq." Along with other activists he was arrested for protesting without a permit.[27]

According to a mid-1990s report by United Nations Food and Agricul-
ture Organization scientists, over five hundred thousand Iraqi children
younger than age five had died because of malnutrition or disease made
worse by the UN Security Council-imposed sanctions. Former Attorney
General Ramsey Clark referenced this report during a March 1998 interview: "You can't just kill 500,000 children. We have sanctions on every day
that are killing more people than the bombing would. The sanctions are
killing several hundred a day, relentlessly and remorselessly. Someday
we're going to wake up and see that we killed all these people because of
our hatred of Saddam."

In May, Gumbleton, Clark, and Kelly headed to Iraq again, this time
with eighty leaders and activists from labor, community, religious, student,
and anti-war organizations. The delegation led a week of internationally coordinated efforts, "The Iraq Sanctions Challenge," defying sanctions and
travel restrictions. David Sole, a chemist from Detroit, spoke to the press in
Amman, Jordan, as they set out overland by truck. "We are united in our
opposition to the genocidal sanctions that have killed over 1.5 million people." The delegation had medical aid valued at $4 million.[28] "We have
come in defiance of our own government. We do not feel any people can be
forced to ask permission of a genocidal power," Ramsey Clark announced
in Baghdad on May 9. Standing next to him, Gumbleton vowed to do all he
could to help motivate more and more Americans to "force our government
to end the sanctions policies."[29] The Iraq Sanctions Challenge violated the
Trading with the Enemy Act—delivering medical supplies to "the enemy."
This could lead to a $1 million fine and up to 12 years in jail—*if* charges
were pressed. "Before we left for Iraq," Tom noted, "each of us received a
letter from the U.S. Department of Justice which stated we would be subject to the fine and possible imprisonment if we went. But I never heard
back from them after I came back. Because it's very clear this country
doesn't want a public discussion of what's going on over there."[30] They
transported medicines to Baghdad, Fallujah, Karbala, Mosul, and Basra.
Afterward, he wrote with dark ink in tiny cursive on the manila cover of an
office file folder:

*I went back to Iraq with a feeling of "what's the use?" Even $4
million of medicines is nothing in relation to the overwhelming
needs. Then I met Dr. Abdul-Abbas in the hospital in Basra. He
was tired. His face was sad. But as he walked up to us and recognized us, his eyes lit up, his whole demeanor changed. "You make
me happy. I smile from my heart. You make me strong." For him*

*and all the people of Iraq, we must keep going back until we end
the sanctions.*[31]

In the years that followed, Tom continued to press his fellow bishops to
condemn the ongoing sanctions against Iraq, and to speak out against the
incalculable toll they were exacting on innocent civilians.

A few, especially members of Pax Christi, responded. But by and large
his words and actions had little effect.

9/11 Horror

And then came the terrorist attacks of 9/11. Five days later, in the Sunday
homily at his parish, St. Leo's, Tom tried to fathom the horror that had
struck.

> Think about the ones on the airplane or some of those in the upper
> floors who got on the phone and began to talk to the people they
> loved the most, and had to say, "Goodbye." They knew they were
> going to die in a matter of minutes.... And I'm sure that in those
> few minutes they had, they wanted to say all the things they had
> never said—how much they loved their wife or their son, their
> daughter... how much they wished they had cherished them even
> more... at least they had those few last moments to say, "I love
> you, I love you."... We must keep on reaching out and deepening
> our love, cherishing our children, cherishing one another.

Across the nation, prayer services were taking place. He told his St.
Leo's community: "All our leaders have gone to those prayer services,
our political leaders and church leaders throughout the country.... We
need to come together in prayer to listen, to listen to God." He asked,
"Are we listening to discover the ways to peace?" Eighty percent of
Americans thought that we must "do the very thing that was done to us,
kill people to get even, to teach them a lesson." Was this the way of
Jesus? "Over the last few weeks our Sunday Gospels have time and again
reminded us that we who are disciples of Jesus must listen to a different
way, follow a different path. We must stand out against the ways of the
world around us that are so often leading to disaster. And if there is any
time that we really need to try to understand how to follow Jesus, it's this
time in which we live right now." An Iraqi doctor had spoken to him in

anguish, he remembered. "You could see the pain in his whole being because he said that "when the parents bring their little children to me, and they want to say that I am going to heal that child, I can never say it. I know that child will die because I don't have the medicines. I can't get the food that child needs to grow and be healthy. That child will die.'" At a school in Iraq, Gumbleton said as he continued the homily, once they became aware that Americans were coming to visit, the kids were terrified and wanted to run home. "Why? Well, because they had been bombed just a week or so before. And some of their classmates had been injured with shrapnel flying around. The windows of their school had been knocked out. And they thought we were coming to finish them off, to kill them. Those children in Iraq are living in that kind of terror all the time. We bomb Iraq two or three times a week. And it's being done in my name and your name. And then we wonder, why do people hate us?"[32]

For an *NCR* piece that week he recapped some contextual history. George Kennan, the famous State Department analyst, in the late 1940s saw clearly how America's control of the world's wealth, with 50 percent of it and yet just 6 percent of the world's population, would breed resentment. "But instead of committing the United States to working throughout the world to bring everyone up to our economic and democratic levels, Kennan said the United States must develop the pattern of relationships that would enable us to maintain the disparity. And we're still doing it." Gumbleton added, "You have these kids in Palestine cheering [over the September 11 attacks]. They're products of 50 years of refugee camps. They've been kept down for a half-century. Every time they've lifted their heads to demand a hearing, demand change, an *intifada*, they're crushed back down. Humiliated. They see the United States behind it, operating through Israel. So, they see the United States humiliated. They cheer." How are we to overcome terrorism? Tom asked. "America has gotten to the point that we really are dominating the world." Pacifists "are caught in the bind of having empathy and utter compassion for those suffering from what happened in New York and Washington and trying to get people to begin to think about the terrorism that has gone on in the world before, and who is responsible. That we, the United States, have built up this anger."[33]

He would once again be the minority voice crying in the wilderness when the American bishops made a statement heavily influenced by Boston's Cardinal Bernard Law. In early October, American bombs began to drop over Afghanistan, the haven of those who launched the 9/11 attacks. In November a majority of prelates affirmed the right to respond militarily in Afghanistan to the terrorist attacks. Gumbleton denounced the bombing.

"It is causing death and suffering to huge numbers of people. If we're religious, moral leaders, we ought to be looking for a different set of guidelines and that should be the Gospel."[34] The bishops voted on November 15 for their official statement on military force against international terrorism. "Without in any way excusing indefensible terrorist acts, we still need to address those conditions of poverty and injustice which are exploited by terrorists." So they were not ignoring root causes, yet they did not reject the use of military force. Gumbleton was one of only four bishops who did not vote with the majority. "What kind of wisdom is it to carry out a war," he asked, "when we know the only outcome is going to be further war?"[35] Once again, as time would tell, he may have been hauntingly prescient.

The bishops, with Law in the lead, had shown their hand in a letter to President Bush shortly after the 9/11 attacks. Along with diplomatic and legal efforts, measured military action—consistent with the just war moral tradition—should not be ruled out. Gumbleton objected to their depiction of the terrorist attacks as an act of war. The attacks were a crime against humanity. Those responsible should be apprehended and tried. "So it ought to be dealt with by the whole community of nations," he told Gustav Niebuhr of the *New York Times* just before the United States launched what would become its "forever war" in Afghanistan, the graveyard of empires.[36]

My Brother Was Killed On September 11

Colleen Kelly had never met Bishop Gumbleton, but thinking he was the right member of the Catholic hierarchy to try to reach, given his reputation as a strong advocate for peace, she faxed the following letter to him from her parents' home in Long Beach Island, New Jersey, on the afternoon of November 10.

Dear Bishop Gumbleton,

I am writing to you today to offer support and encouragement for what I hope will be an ongoing discussion among the bishops. My brother, William Hill Kelly Jr., was killed on September 11th at the World Trade Centers. There is no scale on which my family can begin to measure our loss. Nor are there any words to adequately express our sorrow. My family is quite clear however that we would never want another family, whether Afghan or American, to feel the way we do now. My family runs the spectrum from pacifist to Marine, but we have tried to listen very carefully and respectfully to one another these past two months. We all agreed on the need for justice....

It is hereafter that our opinions begin to diverge. My youngest sister feels that in the face of this horrible evil, the only way to change people is to show them love, not more evil! Christ-like? Yes. Foolish and naïve in human terms? No, not when you really think. I have other family members that feel the bombing of Afghanistan is now appropriate. They feel this is the only way to remove the oppressive Taliban in order to send humanitarian aid, some innocents may die in order for many others to live.

Personally, I adamantly oppose the bombings. I have no other argument other than it is not "Christ-like." I do not know what Christ would do in these current times, but I am certain he would not advocate the bombing of anyone. The deepest, truest part of our collective heart knows this truth. You and I and my family live in a very human world however. So how can we reach this true place?

One stumbling block seems to be the lack of choices given the American public concerning our response to September 11th. Our country sees no other way because we have been presented with no other way. This is my urgent request of the bishops. Can you begin the discussion of the other way, Christ's way? Could you help provide moral guidance to a majority that is voicing support for a bombing campaign, but with reserve and ambivalence. Could you open a dialogue of alternatives, concrete ideas leading to Christ's truth in our hearts? Could you pray that we may all be open to God's difficult and sometimes divisive message?

On a final note, I want to thank you for your bravery and out-spokenness on many issues. It gives me great comfort to know there is Catholic leadership speaking out strong and clear against violence. I read with great interest parts of your August 19th homily on transforming fire. I could not help but think of my brother trapped on the 106th floor of Tower 1. Although I know my brother's death will never be in vain, it helps me to think of Jesus' transforming fire and all that he wants for our world: jus-tice, peace, love. In the end there is nothing but love.

With love,
Colleen Kelly[37]

Gumbleton remembered how he felt when first reading this letter from Kelly. "It was a very moving plea that just knocked me over."[38]

All the nation's Catholic bishops were assembled just a few days after that letter had been received by Tom. He rose to read from it. Jean Stokan, a veteran activist in Central America concerns, had decided immediately after 9/11 that she wanted to volunteer with Pax Christi, so she was working with Gumbleton. She remembered what happened: "He read it, made his plea, and the bishop chairing the meeting sort of dismissed Tom and his pacifism, saying that pacifism is fine as an individual response but not what the bishops were about as an institution."[39]

Not long afterward Colleen Kelly met Kathy Kelly of Voices in the Wilderness (the two Kellys are unrelated) who had organized a walk for peace from Washington to New York City. The walkers, including other family members who had lost loved ones in 9/11, began in late November and arrived in Manhattan in early December. Colleen met them at a forum held at Xavier Parish, a Jesuit parish on 16th Street. Kathy had invited Colleen to be one of the forum's speakers. Afterward Collen and her husband invited the other 9/11 family members to the White Horse Tavern, which happens to be the pub where Dylan Thomas and other famous writers used to hang out. "We sat there talking amongst ourselves and someone started taking notes." Those notes soon morphed into the vision and goals of an organization to be known as September Eleventh Families for Peaceful Tomorrows.

Colleen met Tom in person some months later at St. Peter's College in Jersey City, New Jersey, where the bishop was giving an address.

> I just remember, it seems weird to talk about the Catholic Church this way, but to hear a bishop speaking about nonviolence in a way that did not do back spins and adjustments to try to talk about the just war. He was speaking real truth about the Gospel message, and I had never seen a crowd that big come to see a bishop speak. I was by myself that night and I remember waiting. So many people wanted to talk with him, and when I got my chance, I said, "Hi, I'm Colleen Kelly, and I wrote that letter," and immediately he gave me a hug. It was very emotional. We spoke only briefly that night, but it was a very powerful moment. Here was a Catholic bishop doing something I had not imagined a Catholic bishop doing.[40]

More War

When Pax Christi USA convened, in late July 2002, for its thirtieth anniversary national assembly on the campus of the University of Detroit Mercy,

Gumbleton gave the keynote address to the eight hundred PCUSA members in attendance. Among his remarks, he said:

We come out of a century which was the most violent in all of human history. A new century, a new millennium is upon us.... To put your faith in Jesus means choosing to believe what Jesus says, no matter how strange it may seem—and choosing to reject the claims of evil, no matter how sensible and attractive they may seem.

On October 7 [2001], when President Bush announced the war strikes on the Taliban and al-Qaeda targets in Afghanistan, he said, "We are a peaceful nation!" Then a few days later while speaking at the FBI headquarters, he declared, "This is the calling of the United States—the most free nation in the world, a nation built on fundamental values that reject hate, reject violence, reject murderers, and reject evil." He says we are a peaceful nation, and that's what we stand for. He would call it, I'm sure, "peace America, or *pax Americana*."

But what is this *pax*, the bishop asked. "Pax Americana: bombing, killing, wherever we decide. As Madeline Albright put it, 'We are America. We are the indispensable nation. If we have to use force, it's because we see further than anybody else.'" He cited one of his most cherished quotes, from John McKenzie's *The New Testament without Illusion*. "If Jesus did not reject violence for any reason whatsoever, we know nothing of Jesus. Jesus taught us how to die, not how to kill." Tom told the story about what had happened the prior November when the bishops were deciding how they would respond to the September 11 terrorist attacks and to the October 7 retaliatory attacks on Afghanistan's Taliban.[41] He had shared from Colleen Kelly's letter, he told the PCUSA audience, but most bishops had not seemed to hear its message.

The Catholic bishops of the United States supported the bombing, the war. And I'm sorry to say it continues that way. I was utterly appalled on January 29th when President Bush was giving his State of the Union message outlining our plans to attack the "axis of evil" and continue to glorify our response, violent response to September 11th, two Catholic cardinals sitting in the audience jumping up to clap with everyone else. Another cardinal after September 11th and after October 7th wrote a letter to President Bush

...congratulating him on how well he has responded in this just use of violence.

I tell you all of this only because it becomes very clear to me that Colleen Kelly's request is not going to happen soon...the U.S. bishops are not going to show us the alternative way. It's going to be up to you, and anyone in this country who really understands *pax Christi*, who really is ready to reject *pax Americana*. So we must be the ones that will begin to show the new way.

He called out to the Pax Christi assembly, "Will you reject the claims of evil pax Americana, no matter how sensible and attractive they may seem?" Hundreds responded, "Yes!" "And will you believe what Jesus says, and follow him, no matter how strange it may seem?" Again, "Yes!" If any new war against Iraq were to be declared, "We must say, No! When you sign that pledge you really are saying, 'I am ready to get out in the streets and do civil disobedience if they attack.'" The pledge read:

If the United States sends combat troops, invades by proxy, or otherwise significantly escalates its intervention, I pledge to join with others to engage in acts of nonviolent civil disobedience at U.S. Federal facilities, Congressional offices, military installations, or other appropriate places. I pledge to engage in nonviolent civil disobedience in order to prevent or halt the death and destruction such U.S. military action causes the people of Iraq.[42]

Afghanistan

"Afghanistan has been nearly totally destroyed by twenty-three years of almost incessant war. From the Soviet war in the 1980s, through intense factional fighting and the Taliban war of the 1990's, to the United States 'war on terrorism' in 2001–2002, the poor majority of Afghanistan have been pummeled time and time again."[43] Marie Dennis wrote these words in late June 2002. Dennis, currently senior adviser to Pax Christi International, was working with the Maryknoll Office for Global Concerns when she joined Gumbleton and eighteen others in a week-long fact-finding mission to Afghanistan in June 2002. Tom was "a deeply pastoral presence and an astute observer of the tragedy we witnessed." They had seen profound tragedy. "Meeting the children, Ameena and Ehsanullah, was particularly poignant. U.S. bombs had inadvertently hit Ameena's house near Kunduz, killing her mother, all her brothers and sisters, her aunts and uncles and her cousins, including a two-day-old baby—sixteen people in all." A bomb "gone astray" killed Ameena's entire family—only her father survived, distraught beyond words. Ehsanullah, just seven years old and from the Quargha neighborhood in Kabul, told what happened when he and his cousin thought they were opening a package of biscuits until what was in fact a cluster bomb exploded, causing severe injuries.[44]

That trip was seared into Tom's memory as well: "We visited places where lots of kids had been damaged by the bomblets. If someone came along, especially a child, the child would pick it up, hold it in his hand, and the heat would blow it up. They were in the midst of all these bomblets and landmines."[45] He created a heartfelt Christmas card to send to friends that year. On the front was a photograph of an Afghan girl, missing part of a leg and with the fitted prosthetic placed right in front of her. Somehow, she was smiling and next to her photograph were words from Psalm 72: "The mountains shall yield peace for the people and the hills justice. God shall defend the afflicted among the people and save the children of the poor...." On the back of the card, he wrote:

Dear Sisters and Brothers: The deepest meaning of Christmas, the feat of God's becoming one of us, is the special identification of Jesus with the poor. As he later proclaimed, God anointed him "to proclaim good news to the poor, to heal the broken-hearted, to give the blind new sight and to set the down-trodden free." The photo of the little girl was taken in my recent visit to Afghanistan. During this visit to this shattered country, we met with hundreds of women, children and men who are victims of the U.S. bombings, and even after the bombings, victims of the landmines and cluster bomblets left behind.

The United States had not signed the international treaty banning the use of landmines. "In fact, in advance of the possible war with Iraq, Pentagon records show the U.S. military has stored land mines in Bahrain, Qatar, Oman, Kuwait, and Saudi Arabia." In this remarkable Christmas card he described how he and others in the delegation walked through a rehabilitation hospital in Kabul where victims of land mines and cluster bombs were being cared for.

The vast majority of the staff are also amputees, some double amputees. As we walked through the facility, they would almost methodically lift up their pant leg to show us their prosthetic, or they would remove their prosthetic to show us their limb. And although this was generally followed by a handshake, or an arm-shake for those without hands, it was always followed by what seemed to be a look of gratitude. Ironically, many of them knew that we (being from the U.S.) were in part responsible for their terrible plight, but there was no visible hatred nor condemnation. We felt welcomed.

As a way to celebrate the authentic significance of the birth of Jesus, I invite you to join in the effort to rid Afghanistan of these deadly devices and to outlaw the use of these weapons forever.[46]

NCCB Stance

Afghanistan had become one object of retribution for the attacks of 9/11, but George W. Bush, encouraged by Vice President Cheney, wanted to finish the job his father had started in Iraq. When the bishops came to DC for their autumn 2002 assembly, Boston's Cardinal Bernard Law again took the leading role even though his credibility was beginning to be questioned after the *Boston Globe* broke the news that he had been less than transparent regarding the clergy sexual abuse crisis. He was still chairman of the bishops' International Policy Committee, at the helm of the bishops' views on Afghanistan, and now he was charting their course.

With nearly three hundred bishops together in one large room, Gumbleton stood up at the microphone and called on Law to drop all the just war talk. "I would hope we would speak right out of the Gospel and just forget about 'just war.'" Law acknowledged Tom and other pacifist bishops such as Walter Sullivan of Richmond, Virginia. "There are those prophetic voices who, out of conscience, articulate and powerfully so, an absolute pacifist position. This statement will not do that."

When Bush's father had launched Operation Desert Storm in 1991, Law was the one who led the effort that justified it. After 9/11, he provided the leadership that gave qualified endorsement to the war on Afghanistan.[47] This time round, however, Law helped craft a statement which expressed "serious questions about the moral legitimacy of any preemptive, unilateral use of military force to overthrow the government of Iraq." Tom Gumbleton had given his all to try to influence the statement. It was hardly an absolute pacifist statement, but a few days afterward Tom told *The Michigan Catholic*, "I was very pleased with the fact that we were able to amend it in a way that made it even stronger, and we now have a clear statement of opposition to the war on the part of the Catholic bishops." He was happy that the bishops had at last affirmed selective conscientious objection. "The last

time, in the first Persian Gulf War, there were hundreds of military personnel who said, 'I can't support this war—it's against my conscience,' but
they got no support from military chaplains."[48]

Pope John Paul II had sent his DC diplomat, papal nuncio Pio Laghi, to
plead with George W. Bush not to attack Iraq. And the U.S. bishops were
on record opposing an imminent war. One might ask, had Gumbleton un-
derappreciated what the bishops had been trying to do over the years? Jerry
Powers worked with the bishops on international policy. The bishops did a
lot on Iraq and matters including the sanctions:

> We argued that some form of sanctions was morally justifiable.
> NCCB statements acknowledged that there were serious problems
> with the sanctions and that what was needed was a move to "smart
> sanctions," but Bishop Gumbleton always wanted moral rejection
> of sanctions *en toto*, and he always wanted the NCCB—and those
> of us working on these matters—to remove draft sentences which
> expressed criticism of the Iraqi government because he felt that
> would divert attention from the sanctions issue. He wanted a clear
> refutation of sanctions, period.

Not long after 9/11, according to Powers, ethicist Mary Ann Glendon,
who would serve as President George W. Bush's ambassador to the Vatican
later on, headed a subcommittee of the NCCB's International Policy Committee (the committee chaired by Law), and its purpose was to address the
post-September 11 reality. Glendon and team produced a draft position in
short order, relying on just war arguments, against the use of force in Iraq.
NCCB statements on Iraq in 2002 and again in 2003 used just war criteria in
arguing that the use of force would not meet just war norms. "These statements," according to Powers, "acknowledged the contingent nature of pru-
dential moral judgments based on applying just war criteria and were, in
part, geared to catalyze a moral dialogue while raising serious moral concerns about intervention," hoping to persuade the Bush administration that
going to war with Iraq could not be justified. Gumbleton's proposed amendments time and again were to delete the just war arguments and to simply
make a clear Gospel-based nonviolence case against military intervention.[49]

September Eleventh Families for Peaceful Tomorrows, in Iraq

In early January 2003, Kathy Kelly organized another delegation to Iraq,
this time with Tom, Rudy Simons of the Detroit Area Peace and Justice

Network, and citizens including Colleen Kelly and three other Americans
who had lost family on 9/11. September Eleventh Families for Peaceful Tomorrows sought nonviolent diplomatic alternatives to war. Colleen Kelly
recalled this trip:

> It felt very safe to me that somehow if I was traveling with a
> bishop nothing bad was going to happen. Of course that is not true,
> but the fact that Tom was going was a huge relief to me. I hate to
> fly, and it also allayed the fears of my family of origin. My family
> was against the idea. It's a very loving family but the trip was a
> real issue. You can imagine, my mother and father had lost a son
> and in their minds the possibility of losing a daughter in Iraq just
> overwhelmed them, so having Bishop Gumbleton on the trip was
> like a talisman or a special shield against anything bad happening.

The group was picked up at the hotel in Baghdad and driven by regime
underlings through dark tunnels so there was no way they could figure out
where they were, she said. Once they got to their destination:

> Iraq's Foreign Minister Tariq Aziz came into the room, there were
> formal introductions, and then the first thing Tom said was, "We
> would like to address the human rights abuses of the Iraqi regime."
> I remember sitting there thinking, this is how it's done, you meet
> with the perceived enemy, you don't layer over things, you bring
> up what's important. There would be more we focused on, includ-
> ing our worries about what could happen in Iraq with civilian ca-
> sualties, but we made it clear to Aziz that this was not going to
> simply be these 9/11 families coming to Iraq worried about Iraq
> civilians. We made it clear we were worried about all people and
> all loved ones everywhere being killed because of violence, no
> matter the source.[50]

Anti-war rallies spread. Saturday morning, February 15, 2003, the *Detroit Free Press* headlined, "Here and Around the Globe, a Plea for Peace"
and began the story: "While the U.S. military digs in for war with Iraq,
Thomas Gumbleton will be among the millions standing up today in an
expanding worldwide cry for peace." A large rally was happening in Detroit as were antiwar rallies all across the globe. Millions of protesters
demonstrated against the rush to war in those weeks before "Shock and
Awe" commenced. Journalist Frank Provenzano focused on one protester:
"Gumbleton, a Catholic bishop from St. Leo's Church in Detroit, is one of

Michigan's most high-profile peace activists. The outspoken critic of U.S.
foreign policy will address a noontime crowd that is expected to number in
the thousands at an antiwar rally in Grand Circus Park in downtown Detroit." Bishop Gumbleton, wrote Provenzano, is rooted "in the doctrine of
nonviolence and firsthand experience seeing the impact of the 12-year
economic sanctions on Iraq. He makes his point by holding a fragment
from a cluster bomb dropped from a U.S. fighter jet during the 1991 Persian Gulf War."[51]

Abayomi Asikiwe, with the *Pan-African News Wire* based at the Pan-
African Research and Documentation Center at Detroit's Wayne State University, reported on the February 15 demonstration in Detroit. Thousands
marched. There were passionate speeches. When it was Gumbleton's turn
to speak, he said:

> I just returned from my seventh trip to Iraq. It is impossible to ex-
> aggerate the sense of terror the people of Iraq feel as they await the
> bombs to drop again. There were four people from the "September
> 11 Families for Peaceful Tomorrows" in this delegation who gave
> special meaning to the journey.
>
> As we left Iraq, Pope John Paul II met in Rome with diplo-
> mats from every country which has representation at the Vatican.
> No to war! And he mentioned Iraq twice in his speech. He insisted
> that war is not inevitable and that if it happens "it is a defeat for
> humanity.'" This war cannot be morally justified. This is my
> strong conviction. We must do everything possible to stop the war
> and end the sanctions.[52]

Shock and Awe

Late on Wednesday, March 19 (early Thursday morning March 20 in Iraq,
where it mattered) the United States hit Iraq with its Colin Powell doctrine
of overwhelming force. Tom caught a plane for Philadelphia, gave a speech
denouncing the war and then went on to New Jersey to tell a Camden audience: "We are on a path of death and destruction that will make it all the
more difficult to solve the problems that exist in our world." Intervention in
Iraq was part of a pattern including meddling and violence in places such as
Chile, Guatemala, Iran, Afghanistan, and Panama, and elsewhere, he argued.[53] On March 26, he joined a protest action in DC. They'd been singing
and praying until taken into custody for climbing over barricades the police

had placed to close off Lafayette Park (across Pennsylvania Avenue from the White House). Mairead Corrigan Maguire, Nobel Peace Prize recipient for her efforts to bring peace to Northern Ireland, Nobel Peace Prize recipient Jody Williams for her leadership of the International Campaign to Ban Landmines, and Daniel Ellsberg, known for his revelation of the Pentagon Papers, were among the sixty or so people arrested with Gumbleton.[54]

On September 3, 2003, ANSWER (Act Now to Stop War and End Racism) Coalition, building momentum toward a mass anti-war mobilization day planned for late October, hosted a speakers' panel at the DC National Press Club.

Gumbleton challenged the nation's religious leaders:

I am here today to join with millions of people in the United States and, I am sure, throughout the world in calling upon President Bush and the U.S. government to end the occupation of Iraq and to bring our troops home and, as quickly as possible, to transfer to the United Nations the responsibility of overseeing the rebuilding of Iraq through bringing together international resources to help heal this country which has suffered so much in the last twenty-three years of almost continuous warfare.

I am calling upon religious leaders throughout this country to take up this charge to lead the way for the people of the United States to become aware of the evil that we have perpetrated in Iraq for so many years and to reject the policies of the U.S. government. And I make a special appeal to the Catholic Bishops in the United States to come forward in a very loud and clear way to express, as a body, our rejection of the current policies of the U.S. government, which are so clearly immoral and ill-advised. If these policies continue, they will bring further suffering, death, violence, and chaos into the country of Iraq. My hope is that we can very quickly end this occupation and that the world community will see its responsibility and that, under the leadership of the United Nations, it can carry out that responsibility to rebuild Iraq. And then, as quickly as possible, we must allow the people of Iraq to determine their own destiny.... Give them a chance to live once more in real human dignity and with all the resources they need to have full human lives. It's the only way we can begin to build genuine peace, not only for Iraq, but throughout that whole area. My hope is that the religious leadership of this country will truly lead in making this happen.[55]

A reporter asked the Detroit bishop how much support he was getting from other religious leaders.

> Before the war the U.S. Catholic bishops made a rather clear statement against the war, but it was not clearly presented in parishes around the country. At the present time, I am not aware of very many bishops being willing to speak out against the continuing occupation, and that is one of the reasons why I said publicly today, and I will repeat it everywhere I can, that it is a responsibility of religious leaders to identify immoral actions of their government and to denounce them and to call people to resist them. And so I am hoping that there will be, not only among Catholic bishops but religious leaders of every faith, enough who will speak out and call their people to resist what is going on, to try to bring genuine peace to the people of Iraq, to heal their sufferings, to end the killing of those people. That's a responsibility that I hope religious leaders will live up to. The Catholic bishops of Iraq themselves have pleaded for an end of the war, an end of the occupation and have denounced what is going on, so perhaps bishops in another part of the world will listen to them and know that they are speaking for their people and for all the people of Iraq. So I'm hopeful.[56]

The Last Visit

On Sunday, January 11, 2004, St. Leo's parishioners raised their arms with outstretched hands to give their pastor an affectionate send-off for his eighth trip to Iraq. "I'll be trying to sharpen my own understanding so I can critique better," he told a reporter. "We all have a heavy responsibility to urge our government to do something that will result in peace, not civil war." He was hoping to celebrate liturgy in Basra with his colleague and good friend, Archbishop Gabriel Kassab. "I go to places where there is suffering and oppression and violence, but also where U.S. influence is an important factor. We, as citizens who are committed to our values, must try to influence government policies, to make them consistent with our values."[57]

Turns out he could not visit Archbishop Kassab and the people of Basra. The flight into Baghdad had been perilous enough. The pilot had to fly the plane into the airport in a spiral pattern to avoid being an easy target.

On January 17, Tom and other delegation members stood outside the Provisional Authority's Green Zone compound to observe squatters demonstrating against efforts to eject them from a bombed-out building. The next morning a car bomb went off, killing thirty-one people and wounding many more, right where the delegation had been the day before.

His objective upon his return from Iraq, he told *The Michigan Catholic,* would be to urge Americans to "pressure our government to bring the troops home and allow the people of Iraq to move forward, and to bring other nations into it. We should rebuild that country and give its people a chance." The $1 billion per day for military purposes in Iraq ought to be redirected toward rebuilding the country. "The (American troops) we talked to don't understand what they're doing there, and they're always sitting ducks in danger of being killed. They don't speak the language, they don't understand what people are saying all around them and wouldn't know it if someone were warning them a car bomb was coming at them."[58]

After that final trip to Iraq, at St. Leo's he put all of his heart out on his sleeve. Ever since shortly after 9/11, his Sunday homilies have been recorded for "the Peace Pulpit" in *NCR.* One can hear the pain in his voice:

I was overwhelmed, really, by what I experienced in Iraq this time. As you know, I have been there seven times prior to this trip. The first time was before the first war. At that time Baghdad was a marvelous, beautiful, active city. Now it is in shambles. Five million people living in a terrible situation. It is always ready to erupt into violence. That's what has happened! The lives of innocent people in Iraq, now in the millions literally, have been destroyed. What is left is hatred and resentment that make it all the more difficult to resolve the problems that provoked the war. We could reconnect with the people in a loving, peaceful and just way. We could bring peace. We could end the violence. We could give true freedom to the people of Iraq and enable ourselves to live in a greater spirit of freedom, freedom from fear at any moment of an attack. It is possible! The agenda of Jesus is what can make it happen. We've heard that agenda this morning: "Proclaim Good News to the poor. Heal the broken-hearted. Give the blind new sight. Set the captives free. Lift up the downtrodden. Proclaim God's year of favor." That's the agenda of Jesus. Each of us must ask ourselves: Am I ready to say "amen" to that agenda? Am I ready to follow it?

Am I ready to urge the leaders of my country to give up violence and to use our resources in a loving way for the people of Iraq and people in other places who are desperately in need of being lifted up, of being given their freedom and of being healed?[59]

Many years later, Tom thought back to that final trip and remembered some young folks, in their late teens and early twenties, with whom he met.

They were distressed, deploring the fact that their whole life has been in a war. They've never experienced peace in their country. And that is really tragic. They told stories about how they have known nothing but violence, bombing, running for shelter. It is a terrible way to have to grow up. I'd hate to grow up like that. But that's something we don't think about either. Look at the kids in our own country growing up and afraid to go to school. Every time they hear about a school shooting it scares them, and they go to school, they practice what to do if some shooter comes into our school. Well, can you imagine a seven- or eight-year-old kid running for cover or thinking they are going to be shot? That is the tragedy, the trail of fear and distress and anxiety that a child grows up with and yet we let it go on and on and on.[60]

Asked how he felt about what he'd tried to do since first getting involved in Iraq concerns in 1990, Tom said, "I felt then, and I feel now, a deep sense of compassion for the people of Iraq but also a sense of shame. It was our country that was causing their suffering. We had been totally dishonest with our relationship with Saddam Hussein. We had misled the people of the United States. Our government misled us into war because they just decided they wanted to get rid of him."

Dominican Fr. Thomas Merkets, a member of the Dominican monastery in Baghdad whom Tom met on one of his early trips, came to mind. Fr. Merkets was livid over what the United States was doing. "Merkets was so right. We made a mess over there that people are still suffering from. We had no business doing what we were doing, and it was just bringing more suffering to the people of Iraq." The Dominican priest had told Tom, "Saddam Hussein is a brutal dictator, but we'll get rid of him our way. We don't need you, the United States, to destroy our country to do it. You are a country that is two hundred years old. We've been around for five thousand years, and we've known all kinds of dictatorships and we've found ways to survive."

No person in Iraq had made more of an impression on Tom than Gabriel Kassab. In mid-September 2000, Basra's Archbishop Kassab had visited Detroit. His own brother, a medical doctor, lived in Michigan. In a public address at Southfield Manor just north of Detroit, Kassab described Iraq's plight and pleaded for a change in American policy. Over the years Gabriel and Tom became soul mates. "When he came to Detroit, I visited with him. In fact the cross I wear when I do church services is a gift that he gave me when he came here." Tom keeps that cross in the left pocket of his shirt, near to his heart.

I wanted to be close to the people of Iraq and always have them in mind. I always wore the cross whenever I celebrated Mass. It's the only accoutrement that I ever wore. To me, it's a very important symbol. I have the cross even today. It reminds me of those years, from 1990 until today, and the terrible evil things that we did to Iraq and the reparations that we should be making.[61]

12

With the People of Haiti

aitians established the world's first Black independent republic in 1804. Not so many years after its own 1776 declaration of independence, the United States of America refused to recognize Haitian independence, fearing that the precedent could inspire a revolt against slavery in the young USA. President Wilson, a century hence, sent Marines to invade Haiti. The United States occupied the country for two decades and then backed one oppressive regime after another. Haitians suffered horribly, especially under the brutal dictatorship of the Duvalier family (1957–1986). A rapid series of military coups followed. Nevertheless, throughout the country's history there had been movements to overcome oppression, whatever its source, and in the 1980s a grassroots movement was flourishing. Fr. Jean Bertrand Aristide became its most prominent leader.[1]

In December of 1990 Haiti held the first free and fair elections in its history. Aristide won over 70 percent of the votes. Pax Christi USA, which had begun to focus attention on Haiti a few years earlier, sent a team that observed the December 16 election, including Mary Lou Kownacki, OSB, Pax Christi USA's national coordinator. "It was a real resurrection moment," Kownacki said. "The people showed such determination in making sure the election went on as planned, despite all odds. This was a moment of victory for a country whose history is marked by so much tragedy. We at Pax Christi have made a commitment to Haiti, and we feel that this election was a very positive step in the country's future."[2]

The inauguration did not take place until February 7, 1991, and the new president did not appear publicly throughout most of the interval due to threats on his life. There was an attempted coup in early January by sup-

porters of the former Duvalier regime. When the Aristide inauguration finally took place, Mary Lou Kownacki described the moment as "a taste of
the reign of God on earth as it is in heaven. It was probably the most hopeful place on the planet to be."[3] And yet it may have been one of the most
precarious hopes as well. Pax Christi USA sent a delegation to meet with
Haitian church, grassroots, human rights, and government leaders, to see
how Pax Christi could help. President Aristide needed all the support he
could get even though he was very popular with the impoverished majority
of the people, because from the outset his new administration faced, among
other counterforces, a very negative U.S. press.[4]

Only nine months after he had been elected, he was ousted by a military coup. The overthrow led to a mass exodus of forty thousand Haitian
refugees to the shores of the United States. The Vatican, under Pope John
Paul II, had never wanted Fr. Aristide to be engaged in political life, and the
Haitian bishops did not support him either. Jean Bertrand Aristide had
grown up in a poor peasant family and was ordained a priest as a member
of the Salesian religious order in 1982, but in the late 1980s his political activism led the Salesians to oust him from their order.[5]

After the coup, Aristide was in exile in the United States. In November
1992, Bishop Gumbleton invited him to come to Michigan. He spoke on
Monday, November 30, 1992, in Dearborn. Gumbleton introduced President Aristide and told the story of how during the inauguration ceremonies
a person cried out in hunger and the new president fed him with his own
hands. In Dearborn, despite the coup and everything he and his country
were going through, Aristide exuded hope. Haitians had danced in the
streets when he was elected. Many Haitians at the Dearborn lecture joined
him in a Creole chant, translated as: "Alone we are weak; together we are
strong. All together we are the flood. We do also want you Americans to
help restore our democracy. We are the victims of history."[6]

By March of 1993, with Pax Christi USA Tom Gumbleton had been to
Haiti three times since the coup in 1991. He tried to encourage bishops in
Haiti to speak out against the repression. Many actions were happening in
Michigan and around the U.S. to respond to Haitians asking for solidarity,
especially for the refugees who under the new Clinton administration were
still being forcibly returned to Haiti. Representative John Conyers of Detroit and Bishop Gumbleton were among the many voices demanding that
the Clinton administration give Haiti a clear message that the military
government was unacceptable, and that Aristide should be allowed to return to his rightful role.[7] But on what terms? The Clinton White House and
State Department worked to pressure Aristide into forming a government

that would include military leaders. "Democracy" would be restored, and Aristide would be back in office, but on stipulated conditions. Like Conyers and many other advocates, Gumbleton wanted a true and full restoration of Aristide's powers: "President Aristide is the champion of the poor, it's that simple, and that's the majority of the people. The poor are totally behind him because he's going to give them a chance for a decent human life."[8]

People Are Living in Fear

In October 1993, the Detroit bishop wrote in the *National Catholic Reporter*: "Do you know a country where they pull people out of church and kill them, and no bishop speaks out?" Most Haitians would readily recognize how the question applied to their country. "The Catholic Church," wrote Bishop Gumbleton, "is really two churches: the church of the elite and—the vast majority of the people—the church of the poor. And the bishops are almost without exception tied to the church of the rich." He had just been in Haiti, and he had seen poverty and affliction many times, but this time the poverty was overlaid with severe tension. "People are living in fear. Unarmed and poor, they are defenseless in the face of the violence from the military and the police (who are in fact part of the military)." In September, Antoine Izmery, a prominent businessman and supporter of Aristide, was dragged out of his pew in Sacred Heart Church in Port-au-Prince. Gumbleton wrote about this:

> As he stood in silence [in the church sanctuary] with his arms extended, they [armed soldiers in civilian clothing] shouted accusations at him and struck him, then pushed him toward the door. He was knocked down twice and then pushed into the street, where he was knocked down again. As he lay on the street, a soldier pressed a gun against his head and fired it. Izmery died within minutes. It all happened in the presence of U.N. observers, his family and friends and people in the church and out on the street. Those who were there are still traumatized by its blatancy and extreme cruelty.[9]

Several Benedictine Sisters from Erie, Pennsylvania, including Mary Miller and Mary Lou Kownacki, were in Haiti for the Izmery funeral. Mary Lou recalled: "We really felt we had to be there for the funeral as an act of solidarity, though it was kind of risky at the time. We really weren't sure

how the military would react to it. But any time you go into Haiti you cannot be sure."[10] Mary Miller remembered how Tom handled it:

> We were in the same church where Izmery had been dragged out
> and murdered, and we were sitting in this one section of the
> church, and Tom was over in another part sitting by himself, a very
> solitary figure, because he knew what he was going to do, and he
> knew the danger of it. He sat there for perhaps twenty minutes in
> this great solitude, I am sure, ready to offer himself up, he knew
> the danger, it is still a strong visual in my mind. Then we went out
> to the place where Izmery had been killed. You could look up from
> that intersection, where there was still dried blood on the pave-
> ment. You could see a jeep with army people sitting in it, 500 feet
> away from us. We walked out of the church together, we walked
> over to the spot, Tom knelt down, kissed the spot of the blood stain
> and prayed. The army people didn't approach, but it was a scary
> moment. Tom was willing to sacrifice his life and be another mar-
> tyr in Haiti. Those two images, him sitting in the church, solitary,
> and him there kneeling at the spot where the man had been mur-
> dered. Two images seared into my mind.[11]

The funeral liturgy took place on the second anniversary of the overthrow of Aristide's government. In the prior two months more than one
hundred people had been killed.[12]

A State of Terror

On the last Sunday of August 1994, unknown assailants gunned down the
Reverend Jean-Marie Vincent in Port-au-Prince as he stood at the gates of
his home during a rainstorm. Vincent was forty-nine years old, had long
worked among Haiti's poor, and was a strong supporter of Aristide, once
shielding him from an assassination attempt. Gumbleton had just returned
from another trip to Haiti, and reacted to the news:

> It's a tremendous loss for the church in Haiti, especially the poor
> to whom he was committed. I'm so angry at the total failure of the
> U.S. government to do anything but give mixed signals about this
> situation. They make statements claiming the junta must be de-
> posed, then they announce that Haiti is on the back burner. Are

they insensitive? Callous? Inept? Or are they trying to make sure Aristide never returns to Haiti?

The Vatican had only mentioned the death of Rev. Vincent on its radio broadcast but had made no comment. "The Vatican, the bishops of Haiti and all of the bishops of the world ought to be standing together and insisting that the killings stop." Bishop Gumbleton joined Pax Christi members and other activists who stood in vigil outside the White House on the first Wednesday in September to demand the restoration of Aristide.[13]

Aristide was finally able to return in mid-October 1994. He called on the people of Haiti to refrain from violence against those who had overthrown him. He wanted accountability and justice, but not vengeance. "Help us file charges against those who committed crimes," he said during a Mass at the cathedral in Port-au-Prince for Marcellus Denis, a school principal who had been beaten and tortured in Aristide's hometown of Port-Salut. Denis died in early December, and the funeral Mass at the cathedral included some 250 people, one of whom was Gumbleton. Denis had once told Aristide that he would "die a thousand times" for him. At the Mass, Aristide wept openly: "What I say here has no sense, no value if we can't prevent other people from dying in the same conditions. We must take away the weapons from the people who did these things." Among those in attendance were several top military officers who may have had reason to look down rather than face Aristide as he spoke.[14] Tom had accompanied Aristide on his return flight from exile:

> I was very happy to be part of that group that took him back to his rightful place and I saw the enthusiasm with which he was met upon his arrival in Port-au-Prince. He had less than a year of his term left, and many people advised him that he should not count the times that he was in exile, but he refused to do that. He did not want to go beyond the five years of his original term, and he could not according to the law run immediately to succeed himself, so he was out of office for five years and then again five years later he won overwhelmingly again.[15]

Jean-Juste and the Emergence of the Kay Lasante Health Clinic

Indeed, the very popular Aristide won the presidency for a second time. But he faced yet another coup, and once again he was exiled. In 2004, around the time of this second coup, Tom Gumbleton met Fr. Gerard Jean-Juste. Jean-Juste was Haitian but had emigrated to the states and served as a priest in Brooklyn, founded the Miami-based Haitian refugee center, and then went back to Haiti in 1991 and became pastor of St. Claire, a poor parish in Port-au-Prince. This absolutely poor parish (through donations to the Berkeley-based What If Foundation founded by Margaret Trost) would feed a couple of hundred kids in the afternoon after school. Otherwise the kids would have no real meal all day. Gumbleton recalled how the seeds were planted for what eventually became Kay Lasante:

> We helped with serving the meal. Afterward we were sitting around talking and Jean-Juste said, "Well you know, there's a lot of support for this meal program, but what we really need is some health care. There is no place for people to get health care, you know, the rich people go to Florida to get what they need, and there are some clinics and so on, but they charge and they're not very nice to the people." Johanna Berrigan ran a clinic in north Philadelphia, one of the poorest areas in the city, and she said, "Well, we run a clinic and we could help start one here."

Johanna Berrigan and Mary Beth Appel, of the Catholic Worker House of Grace health clinic in Philadelphia, soon joined Tom in conversations with Dr. Paul Farmer about how to best implement the idea. Farmer's Partners in Health program had already been working in Haiti and advised them to make sure that the whole staff of any new clinic be Haitian.[16]

Empowerment mattered at both the local (health clinic) and national (governmental) levels. On a Thursday evening in late June 2004, Bishop Gumbleton called out "The Truth about the Coup in Haiti" in a talk he gave at Sacred Heart Catholic Church in Detroit:

> We have been inundated over the last few years about the war on terror both here and abroad. Our energies and focus have been channeled to Afghanistan, Iraq, Israel and Palestine. But for most of us, the war on terror was never a focus in the poorest nation in the Western Hemisphere, Haiti. Why? Because the terror being perpetrated on the people of Haiti was often backed and always ignored by the U.S. Government. Anti-Aristide forces used terrorist tactics to oust the most popularly elected President in the Americas. Now, Haiti is being run by a government that the majority of the people do not want and have not hoped for. The situation for

these men, women and children continues to worsen and gains made by President Aristide, like minimum wage, are losing ground. Terror is ruling Haiti and its people while President Aristide sits in exile in South Africa.

We must ask for clarity and transparency for the role the U.S. played in the coup. We must request the U.N. to monitor the process through to its end. As members of the wealthiest nation in the world, we must take responsibility for our Haitian brothers and sisters. We must trust their capability to elect the leader that they choose democratically. We are called to work together, in solidarity and peace, for a unified Haitian people by leaders who are just and seek to uplift their people through the virtues of Democracy. We need not look any further than our own shores for the roots of terror. Let us plant new seeds of justice today![17]

A few months later Tom Gumbleton was back in Haiti for a delegation trip which included visits to jails and prisons, meeting with human rights activists, and efforts to document the abuses and killings happening since the coup. Not long after the delegation returned to the United States, the Haitian police arrested Fr. Jean-Juste. The February 2004 coup that ousted President Jean-Bertrand Aristide's government had led to a climate of human rights abuses and arbitrary detentions like that of Jean-Juste.[18] Political supporters of Aristide were being subjected to arbitrary arrests, indefinite incarceration without trial, and violence by the regime in power, and Tom knew this firsthand through visits he had made to St. Jerome in Petite Riviere, Haiti, St. Leo's sister parish. Tom was in Haiti again in November 2004 and he visited with Fr. Jean-Juste in prison. When Tom visited him at the nation's penitentiary, at least half of the twelve hundred prisoners were being detained without trial.[19]

Just as he had come to admire Aristide, so too he had come to admire Jean-Juste. On the very last Sunday of August 2005, in a homily at St. Leo's in Detroit, he spoke about Fr. Jean-Juste. The first reading of Scripture was from the prophet Jeremiah, chapter 20:7–9. The mocked prophet complains to God about all the derision he is facing, but still he knows that he must speak God's word, because "it becomes like a fire burning in my heart, imprisoned in my bones." Tom drew a parallel between Jeremiah and Gerry Jean-Juste,

who has been overwhelmed by God's word and in spite of the fact that he's rejected. The poor, who of course are the majority, accept him, but the other priests and the bishops of the country, the wealthy people, they reject him, they laugh at him, and they make sure he's thrown into prison where the conditions are horrendous. He was in isolation in a tiny cell in darkness all the time. But when we visited with him both times this past week, it was amazing. They bring him from his cell, and he sits down to talk with you. You sense how tired he is and how, well, in some ways, discouraged. But then as you begin to talk, he gets energy. He gets strength, and by the time we finish the visit, we say a prayer together. He leads the prayer, and he challenges us to be faithful, to be strong, to be courageous, to work for justice, to bring peace into the world. He's the one who's leading. It's amazing.

Tom asked his St. Leo's parishioners to "listen deeply to what God says to us and during the week pray each day God's word. Listen deeply. Let it become a fire inside of you, like it did in Jeremiah, like it does in Jean-Juste. He has his prayer book with him, and he prays the scriptures every day in that jail cell."[20]

In those years when Fr. Jean-Juste was subjected to arrests and other forms of repression, Gumbleton tried to the get high church officials in Haiti to help, and at one point while on a trip to Rome in early 2006 he met with the archbishop in charge of the curia office for priests. He continually faced this message: Jean-Juste must convince his own bishop and others in Haiti that he would disengage from politics. But, Gumbleton persisted: "How could Gerry do this? It depends on how 'politics' is defined. In Haiti, being with the poor is seen as political by the upper class, by the bishops. It is not a choice for a man of the Gospel."[21]

Despite international support for his release, it was not until nearly the end of January of 2006 after he was diagnosed with leukemia, that Haiti's interim government granted him provisional release for medical treatment in the United States.[22] Fr. Jean-Juste died at age sixty-two on May 27, 2009.

Earthquake and Aftershocks

A magnitude 7.0 earthquake struck Haiti on Tuesday evening, January 12, 2010. As soon as it was feasible to fly in with medical supplies, Tom arrived in Port-au-Prince with Johanna Berrigan and others. He celebrated his eightieth birthday (January 26) in a pup tent. Matthew 25, the guest house they usually stayed at, could easily collapse, so they camped out in a soccer field with hundreds of displaced Haitians. The earthquake killed more than two hundred thousand people and left much of the nation a rubble. Almost every Haitian lost someone close. Later in homilies back in Michigan Tom described what he had seen and felt:

> I had an extraordinary experience of how the poor are blessed in this regard....I saw this myself on more than one occasion, when I celebrated the Eucharist in an open field with hundreds of people. Their singing and their joyfulness, even in the midst of their suffering, was incredible. It's because they deeply trust in God and no matter what happens, they know that God is present to them, God loves them, and somehow God will bring them through their suffering to a new and better life. Think of what it might be if we had a world where every one of us had that deep awareness that everything we have is gift. Would we be selfish?[23]

A field hospital was set up in the soccer field.

> There were about 1,500 people there, not all needing medical care, but just sleeping on the ground, and every morning, as I woke up, I woke up to the singing of hymns. In spite of their suffering, in spite of all that happened, these people showed a tremendous faith in God and God's presence among them. Every morning, someone would begin to lead prayers and to lead hymns, and it was so peaceful and so beautiful.[24]

In June he was back in Haiti, and he then reflected on that experience in a homily the following Sunday:

> As I was there this week, it became clear to me that this is an almost unbelievable catastrophe. I've been there before, as you know, but this time it seems worse than it's been and it's over five months now since that earthquake happened. All kinds of aid have gone down there and lots of people have gone down, but so much is not happening that should be happening. As you probably know, people are living in tents in Port-au-Prince, almost a million of them.

He had visited a tent community right on the edge of a slum in Port-au-Prince, Cité Soleil, city of the sun, "but it's an extreme, unbelievable slum

area." He was in a tent-village of over five hundred people, all with disabil-
ities. No one had come with food or medicine. They were struggling to get
by, with no water and no electricity. Then, a couple of hours later, when he
got ready to leave, a little child followed him back over to where his car
was parked.

> As I opened the door, he saw on the floor of the car, a container—
> one of those plastic containers that you might take home food
> from a restaurant—and he jumped right away and took it, but then
> when he opened it, it was empty. You could just see the total dis-
> appointment. He thought that he was going to get some food;
> there wasn't any. There was half a bottle of water there and he
> said, "Water, water," so of course I said, "Yes, take it." So he took
> it and drank some but then shared it with another little child that
> was with him, so they had some purified water at least then. One
> of the things that really hit me hard was the fact that as I was
> walking through this village, and then I stepped aside because it
> was kind of overwhelming. I picked up my rosary that I had been
> saying and I happened to be at the third mystery of light—you
> know, the new mysteries that John Paul II instituted. That third
> mystery of light is the public preaching of Jesus where Jesus pro-
> claims the good news, "The reign of God is at hand," and I
> thought, how can we say that "the reign of God is at hand" when
> I'm standing here looking at what's going on? The reign of God is
> when everyone has what you need for a full human life and these
> people have nothing. They've been struggling for five months
> barely to survive. So for me, it became very clear that if I'm
> going to respond to who Jesus really is, and if I'm going to try to
> follow him, I must deny myself more and share more of what I
> have with people like this in the world.[25]

Driver, Translator, Community Organizer, Teacher

Daniel Tillas first met Tom Gumbleton about fifteen years before he was
interviewed for this book in 2021. Daniel described his roots in Cité Soleil,
known as the most terrible slum in Port-au-Prince:

> It is a dirty place, a place where nothing happens, and that's where
> I have my work, my service, and the fact that Bishop Gumbleton

would actually go there was a sign of real sincerity. It was not easy. I remember days when we were in Citi Soleil, visiting hospitals, visiting activists, and there were gunshots, and we couldn't even leave. I recall these days. Even after incidents like this, Bishop Gumbleton would go back again and again, over and over, to this place that is marginalized and really poor. I remember after the earthquake, for example, we went to Citi Soleil to see how desperate things were. Even the NGOs with money would not go there. I took Bishop Gumbleton to pay a visit to one of the tent cities that was an awful situation, he shared with the people, he prayed with them, and we sat down with the people. Even before the earthquake it was the most marginalized community in the country. Even when we could not leave due to gunshots, he still would go back to inspire children who were part of the program that I started. I initiated with some friends a Pax Christi Haiti chapter in Port-au-Prince, and we focused on nonviolence, and we started an athletics program to teach young kids the value of nonviolence to overcome the gang mindset and guns culture that was proliferating in 2005 and beyond.[26]

In 2004, Daniel was a translator educating himself in English by meeting people in the various delegations that came to Haiti and offering his services as a driver and guide. "From Gumbleton and others with him, I got this strong sense of not being alone in the struggle. Often groups would come and visit but would return to the States and you would never see them again. But with Bishop Gumbleton and others I had the sense that they would follow up. I always felt myself as part of their team."[27]

Indeed they did follow up. They created the health clinic inspired by Jean-Juste, Kay Lasante, which came into being before the 2010 earthquake. Tillas thought Gumbleton could be stubborn. "I see Bishop Gumbleton coming back, he just keeps coming back to Haiti. 'Okay, he is back!' I have experienced this. 'All you need to do for the country, Tom, you have done it. Don't even try to do more.' But he keeps coming at a level of solidarity one would not expect."

Gumbleton and Johanna Berrigan kept coming back. They had learned in October 2016 from Donahue Jabouin, Kay Lasante's administrator, about the case of a woman, Ms. Florida, suffering from very serious breast cancer. Florida and her family turned to Kay Lasante. The staff at the clinic did all they could for her, providing dressings to protect the wound, medications, supplies for use at home, and efforts to get her to the Partners in

Health hospital in Mirebalais, the best place in Haiti for cancer patients, but two hours away by car, and because the PIH (founded by Paul Farmer) was already overwhelmed with so many patients, two months away on the calendar. Eventually she did get treatment at Mirebalais, but it was too late for surgery.

Kay Lasante continued to provide palliative care. During Lent of 2017 Johanna and Tom were back in Haiti when Ms. Florida's son called Kay Lasante to say his mother was just too weak to get to the clinic anymore. Johanna and Tom decided to make a "home visit" but to get there they would have to climb a steep hill. Tom was eighty-seven, and even to Johanna, twenty-five years younger, the climb looked daunting. They could grab nothing but a twig or the edge of torn tents along the slope where people were trying to live. Johanna wrote about the home visit:

> At the very top of the hill was a two-room concrete structure. We had reached Ms. Florida's house. The visit was transformative. We were shown gracious hospitality. There were two chairs brought in for us, wobbly on the uneven dirt floor. The only other furniture was the bed in the corner, covered with brightly colored sheets, on which Ms. Florida sat. There were a couple of colored basins hanging on the wall, used for laundry and dishes. The opening in the concrete, where a window might be, was covered by a beautiful white lace curtain. There was no electricity, and no water. Ms. Florida was being lovingly tended to by her daughter, who smiled shyly to acknowledge us, but then proceeded to braid her mother's hair—just as her mother most assuredly once braided hers.
>
> It was a beautiful time of sharing and prayer. After months of praying for her from a distance, it was an honor to pray with her in person. She understood—even accepted—that there was little else we could do. She spoke with us about how Donahue, our [Kay Lasante clinic] administrator cared for her like a son would, and inquired about "her daughter" Ms. Menard, our nurse, who had taken such good care of her. As we took our leave, she was smiling. Shrugging, and speaking softly, with a touch of resignation in her eyes, she said she was sorry she didn't have anything to give us, but she knew we would receive blessings for coming to visit her.[28]

Daniel Tillas, who along with Donahue Jabouin accompanied Tom and Johanna on that climb to the home of Ms. Florida, took a photograph of

Tom being supported by Ms. Florida's son as they walked the narrow and steep trail. Daniel sent the photograph to Tom and Johanna afterward. "I find hope in humanity through this picture over and over. I am so glad I got to know people amazing like you guys who inspire my nights for getting the strength to wake up the next day."[29] Daniel, exuberant and tenacious, shared a hopeful message, an apt coda for this chapter:

> Bishop Gumbleton would say, "Don't call me bishop, call me Tom." I wanted to start peace advocacy in Haiti, and he gave me advice. The Catholic Church has played a role of distancing between the hierarchy and the people. Gumbleton's humility was such a shock to me, we don't expect a bishop to be humble. We do not expect a bishop to be driven in a junk car. I remember how he would get out of the car and wait for me when the car gave us trouble. When I am old, if there is one person I would like to be it is Bishop Gumbleton because of his humility and his care and knowledge.[30]

> Haiti needs the kind of solidarity that Bishop Gumbleton would come here for. A presence that would remind the people of Haiti that they are not alone in the struggle, but also a way for U.S. citizens to be aware and to be educated about what is going on right now in Haiti. A lot of what is going on in Haiti is connected to the U.S., after years of relationship. Right now the people of Haiti are suffering, and I wish that more and more people from the U.S. could keep coming, to really understand what is really going on, not just what is in the news and does not reflect the reality, so that something new could happen in Haiti.[31]

13

Two Graces in a Small Village

On August 9, 1943, a thirty-six year old farmer, husband, father, and sacristan, Franz Jägerstätter, was beheaded because he would not take the Wehrmacht Oath of Loyalty, which stated: "I swear before God this sacred oath that I will render unconditional obedience to the Führer of the German nation and Volk, Adolf Hitler, the Supreme Commander of the armed forces, and that, as a brave soldier I shall be ready at all times to stake my life in fulfillment of this oath."[1]

On August 9, 1985, his widow, Franziska Jägerstätter, welcomed Bishop Gumbleton to the tiny village of St. Radegund in Upper Austria. The farming community of St. Radegund had maybe one hundred people at most.[2] Tom Gumbleton, serving then (from 1985–1990) as the vice-president of Pax Christi International, came to St. Radegund on that day for the annual memorial honoring Franz for his courage of conscience. Franziska was a gracious host, gentle, resilient, a vigorous spirit in her seventies.[3] At the memorial Mass that evening, Gumbleton began his homily:

> I want to thank Frau Jägerstätter and her family for inviting me
> here to celebrate the liturgy this evening, and to participate in the
> prayer and procession this afternoon. It is for me a very profound
> honor and privilege. For me, and for people in many parts of the
> world, it is very clear that Franz Jägerstätter is an extraordinary
> witness of faith, prayer and love, a witness who is willing to be
> even a martyr because of the strength of the conviction of his
> faith.[4]

Franz Jägerstätter had paid the ultimate cost of discipleship. After his conscription papers arrived in late February 1943, he went to the army barracks in the town of Enns, and on the second day of March he announced that he would not participate in the war. He was sent to a military prison in Linz. Months later after being moved from Linz to a prison in Berlin, he was guillotined. A Catholic chaplain, visiting him on the night before he was executed, pointed to a document that had been placed on a table. The document was the Wehrmacht Oath of Loyalty. If Franz would sign the oath, his life would be saved. He would not sign it.[5]

This courageous and conscientious soul would one day be beatified. On October 26, 2007, the beatification rite took place in Linz as thousands packed the Linz cathedral. Among the two dozen or so bishops who concelebrated was one bishop from the United States, Thomas Gumbleton. Among the procession of priests were three prominent American peace activists, Frs. John Dear, Robert Cushing, and Roy Bourgeois. Tom Roberts, covering the ceremony for the *National Catholic Reporter*, described a "certain sense of disturbing history" pervading the place:

> The cathedral where the ceremony occurred was just steps from the bishop's residence where Jägerstätter once made his case—and received little support—for refusing to join the army. The cathedral also is just blocks from what was once an Ursuline convent, taken over by the Nazis, who used it as a prison and torture center. It was there that Jägerstätter was held for about two months before being transferred to Berlin, where he was eventually sentenced and executed.

Roberts also conveyed a sense of resilient hope embodied in Franziska with her daughters, that day of the beatification. When they were introduced, the "congregation erupted in spontaneous applause that lasted for half a minute."[6]

Tom Gumbleton had first learned about Franz Jägerstätter in the mid-1960s when he read *In Solitary Witness: The Life and Death of Franz Jägerstätter*, by Gordon Zahn. "This helped me through a time of discernment, a time of trying to make what, in some ways, were hard choices, going against the popular opinion. But Franz's story, his witness, influenced me profoundly." Jägerstätter, through Zahn's 1964 book, impacted a great many people including Daniel Ellsberg, who in 1971 revealed secret government documents ("the Pentagon Papers" as they would come to be known) that told troubling truths about the U.S. war in Vietnam. Revelations in these documents helped widen public opposition to the war. On occasion Tom would tell the story of how Jägerstätter inspired Ellsberg's own costly decision of conscience:

> He not only destroyed his career, which had been very promising within the government, but he risked jail and because it could even be called an act of treason, risked death. But at one point, he told me, among the many influences in his life was becoming aware of Franz Jägerstätter and his witness against his government during World War II. That had a tremendous effect in the United States, the revelation of these documents. It helped change the public attitude very quickly.[7]

Jägerstätter's witness had helped to inspire Tom's stand against the American war in Vietnam as well as his advocacy on behalf of so many conscientious objectors, including selective conscientious objectors (opposed to a particular war as unjust), for decades to come. In his homily for the Mass on the Feast of Blessed Franz Jägerstätter in May 2010, in St. Radegund, Tom shared:

> We see the example of Franz, refusing to subject himself to civil authority, his government, when that government wanted him to do something that was against the will of God. God is first and supreme in our lives. How we need to carry this out is something that each of us must determine. It will not always be a case of having to go against a government law, a government rule, a government decree. Sometimes it will simply be trying to face up to criticism from those within our own community, within our own church community, and trying to do what is right, be responsive to God's sovereignty and not to any other human authority or human power that might be exercised over us. God is supreme, God alone we must obey. This is what Franz teaches us....
>
> No matter what they did, no matter what the consequences, Franz knew that Jesus was always there to be with him and would not only be with him in this life, but forever. Nothing can separate us from the love of God made present to us in Christ Jesus. I urge us, all of us, we must try to deepen our understanding of this truth, our awareness of this truth, and let it be the source of our

confidence, even our joyfulness in making God supreme in our life
and always, no matter what the cost, following the way of Jesus.[8]

Jägerstätter paid the ultimate price of discipleship. Gordon Zahn's *In
Solitary Witness* gave the impression that Jägerstätter was, as the title indi-
cates, a lone witness against the Nazi war. But through the research and
writings of the Austrian scholar Erna Putz, Tom learned that there were
other Catholics in Austria who opposed the Nazis at great personal cost.
Forty priests of the Linz diocese, sharing the views of outspoken Bishop
Johannes Gfollner (bishop of Linz from 1915 to 1941) who denounced National Socialism, were arrested and put in concentration camps where
eleven of them died. Franz himself was moved by the courageous sermons
of Bishop Gfollner. Zahn was not mistaken, however, in giving the reader
of his influential book a sense that Jägerstätter must surely have felt very
alone at times as he faced down the certain consequences of his life and
death decision. The overwhelming majority of Austrian Catholics, from the
laity to the hierarchy, did not condemn the war. Few took so clear a stand as
did Franz.[9]

At a Pax Christi Florida gathering, just a few days before the beatification ceremony in Linz, Tom reflected on the courage of this Austrian
peasant:

He was in his early 30s when he was finally called up to be conscripted in Hitler's armies. As a peasant farmer, he was not called
at first because they needed farmers to produce the food for the nation and for the army, but then as the war turned against the Nazis
and they began to be defeated in Russia, North Africa and so on
...the command came for Franz to be conscripted into the army.
Now he had already spoken out very strongly against Hitler and
Hitler's ideology because he was the one person in his tiny village
of St. Radegund who voted against the joining together of Austria
and Germany that Hitler was insisting upon. That was back in
1938. Franz was known as someone who was speaking out against
Hitler and Hitler's ideology, so it was not a surprise to the people
that he was going to say no, but they tried to talk him out of it.
They resented the fact that he was showing what, in fact, all of
them should have been doing. Many, in fact the parish priest and
the bishop of the diocese, tried to convince Franz. "Wait, you must
go. You must serve your country like all the others are doing. Be-
sides, you have three children and a wife. If you don't go, they

will kill you." They tried to convince him that he had to go, but
Franz continued to say no.

Tom also heralded the courage and steadfast sacrifice of Franziska:

Imagine the emotional experience that will be [the beatification
ceremony], I think, especially for Franziska, because at first, she
was among those who were trying to tell Franz, "No, for the sake
of your family, don't do it. Don't resist Hitler like that." But then
she was persuaded, and she fully committed herself to what he was
going to do. Then she lived on, taking care of the farm, providing
for the children as they grew up. She was heroic and is still a very
heroic person. One time when I was visiting there, she got out a
scrapbook with photographs in it. I think it will give us a sense of
how hard it had to be for her and for Franz. She had taken a picture of the three children, who at that point in 1943 were around 6,
4 and 2 years old. The three children are standing there with a sign
on which is written three words: "Father, come quickly." They
were begging their father to come home. She showed that picture
to Franz when she visited him in the prison in Berlin. How it must
have torn his heart to have to say no to his children on that occasion, but he was saying yes to his children in a much more important way, by living and witnessing to the truth of Jesus in spite of
the cost.[10]

Many years earlier and joined by good friends Bill and Mary Carry,
Molly Fumia, Julius Gasner, and Gordon Zahn, all with Pax Christi, Tom
was in Linz to celebrate what would have been Franz Jägerstätter's 80th
birthday (May 20, 1987). In the *Pax Christi USA* issue that followed this
celebration, Gordon Zahn described this event: "The sacristans of that entire
region of Upper Austria had gathered to honor the life and death of Franz
Jägerstätter, a sacristan, who had been beheaded by the Nazis in 1943. It
was moving to watch the man's widow, Franziska, nearly 80, as she per-
formed the sacristan's duties which she had taken over from her husband."[11] At that event, Gumbleton tried to convey what he imagined it
would be like to walk in the shoes of either Franz or Franziska:

I try to imagine the anguish he must have felt in what must have
been the dark night of his own soul. I imagine for myself how
deeply lonely and exhausting his wrestling match with God must

have been. It wasn't only that he had to stand up to the military establishment, or to the power of the state, or even to the advice of people of good will who told him that he was going too far, that he could serve with Hitler's army in good conscience. His own martyrdom surely occurred when he knew that the wisdom of God demanded even this, his absolute separation from his wife and daughters in death.

To live through the execution of the heart and still have the executioner to face—what an almost unspeakable thing it can be to know God and try to act in God's name.

It is not enough, Franz Jägerstätter came to know, to be privately, individually moral, in the face of evil embedded in the very structure of the social system. It is not enough to be a good husband, a good father, a good citizen. When the public authority leads us away from truth into nightmares of human destruction and then persuades us that they are doing good, the believing person who has known something, some little bit, of God and of human love, must stand in the public arena and say no. The believing person says, I will not blind myself. The believing person says, in the company of other men and women I will try to find out the truth about this evil, however uneducated I am, however inarticulate I am, however much I will not be paid attention to, however much I don't count for much. The believing person says, I will try to speak God's name into this madness and stop it.

That is what Franz Jägerstätter came to know. That is what his life and death spoke to. His story is new, his life takes root in our own imaginations, because he confronted social sin so clearly. Perhaps that is where holy men and women are made—where the ancient truths of revelation and the demands of the time or the age intersect within a person's heart. Franz Jägerstätter knew that collision, knew the cost of adhering to the word of God in the face of evil.

There is one more thread in Franz Jägerstätter's story that I think is significant for us, and for a Church in search of models of the Gospel life truly lived. The witness for which we honor Franz Jägerstätter was a joint witness. His decision to resist to the death was made with Franziska. It was not made without pain or terrible soul-searching for both of them, but it was made, with humble clarity of conscience. His was the dramatic action; hers was to live out that act of resistance.... Theirs is a marriage that never broke the communion of life—the active resister with God; the woman of faith and endurance, struggling to live daily in the presence of God. It is a marriage consecrated to the work of peace.[12]

For her ninetieth birthday, Tom sent a personal note to Franziska, expressing gratitude for two extraordinary lives:

[Franz's] example, however great a blessing it was, wasn't the only gift God gave me. After I got to know you, I felt even more rewarded when I realized what an unshakable witness you have been over the years. Despite your grief and family commitments, your courage and faith have been an overwhelming testimony of what it means to follow Jesus. I have learned from you and my life is richer from learning this. Two graces in a small village. God is good.[13]

14

Ministry in Detroit and Michigan

The degree to which Tom Gumbleton is widely known as pastor of St. Leo Church in Detroit relates more to his being removed as pastor in January 2007 than to his long tenure there. Yet to truly understand the man, one needs to observe his ministry at St. Leo's, from 1983 to his forced departure twenty-four years later. This ministry nurtured his full-hearted pastoral commitment to the people of Detroit. The journey to becoming St. Leo's pastor began unusually.

I had been working with the members of St. Leo Parish to balance their budget in my role as their regional bishop. I told them to close the church building because it was too expensive to maintain in the winter and to celebrate the Sunday liturgy in the school. A few months later, I came to celebrate the Sacrament of Confirmation on a Sunday morning. I walked into the church where the parishioners were holding the liturgy. I was surprised it was open.

Then I saw its beauty, especially the extraordinary stained-glass windows with the light shining through them. I could understand why people would not close the building for fear it would not open again. They were right. Closing the church would have been a terrible mistake. I admired the parishioners' determination. At this same time, I had been looking for a pastor to serve there with no success. I knew I was ready to take on a parish as pastor because it had been six years since I served as a pastor and I missed it. When I met with the parish council, I promised the people I would be present every weekend and a good part of the time in between.[1]

A few years before he arrived at St. Leo's, the 1980 census documented that the Black population of Detroit had become the majority.[2] Yet the Catholic Church lacked the ability to meaningfully minister to Black Catholics. Friends, other priests who were pastors of several of Detroit's African American parishes, inspired him. He had interacted frequently with them as their regional bishop and now would have the opportunity to follow their pastoral practice. Life-long friend, Rev. Norm Thomas, pastor of Sacred Heart parish, became his primary guide. Norm had enculturated "Black cultural traditions of spirituality in the music, style of prayer and so on. It was the only place in the archdiocese where Black people could celebrate in their own traditions without an imposed white style. The music was different; the style of liturgy was different."[3]

Years later Tom recalled how St. Leo's deepened his understanding of racism and white privilege. "I've come to understand far better than I ever did before how terrible the racism has been within the Catholic Church. As I work within an African American community and people trust me enough to tell me what their experience in the church really has been, I've learned how much hurt and injustice was perpetrated against African Americans."[4]

Sr. Cathey DeSantis, CSJ, a long-time friend who ministered and worshiped at Sacred Heart for decades, explained Tom's transformation.

He didn't go to St. Leo's saying he was going to do something specific. He was open to the reality and he really evolved in terms of race consciousness at St. Leo's. None of the other issues he was involved with—Central America, his peace work—none of that involved a real heart change like understanding and confronting racism did. He shifted to no longer see Black people as the objects of one's charity. One of the most important things about Tom is that he was open to a kind of transformation. The St. Leo folks made him what he is today. He would talk about it. He was open to hearing experiences that weren't very comfortable for him.[5]

His St. Leo's ministry also showed the intrinsic interconnection between his advocacy at home and his advocacy abroad. At a national demonstration opposing U.S. policies in Central America and South Africa, he declared, "As a pastor in inner-city Detroit, I have seen the bitterness of poverty and injustice. We must weed out racism, not export it with foreign policy."[6]

Parish staff, parishioners, and colleagues saw him as a humble pastor whose priorities were service to those in need, outreach to the community, and a worshiping community reflective of African American spirituality.

Keir Ward, music director at St. Leo's beginning in 1987, learned firsthand Tom's commitment to fostering Black Gospel spirituality. Keir recalled the bishop saying "we serve the Black community, and this worship service should reflect that and in all the other ways, and he wanted the community to feel comfortable to come in and worship as well. He was trying to make it fully inclusive... an experience that was authentically African American, while also being Catholic."[7] Keir described Bishop Gumbleton's lifestyle and approach as pastor:

> He lived in the church office, which was a little building on the side of the church, a very small place. He lived in a room where he had an air mattress. He had his desk there, like a night stand, and a clock radio—just very, very simple. His mind was just not on material things. He always had a good car, but it wasn't flashy. He needed something reliable, a new car, because he was on the go, but it was always something modest. He knew everybody by name. He met with everybody, whether it was a tither who gave $2000 or the person who didn't have anything to give. It was always amazing to me how he was able to pastor our church, as busy as he was, go out of town a lot, and was still able to address those issues that were right there.[8]

Angela Thomas-Weldon, pastoral associate since 2001, offered a caring critique of the bishop's pastoral approach.

> He gave me his office when I came. The rectory at St. Leo's was the old boiler space. He would sit in a chair. He would read; he would pray. His table was a TV tray table. He had a little desk; it was just simple. He gave and gave, and I thought he was spoiling the people. I remember one time saying to him, "You got to stop giving out money to people, you just gotta stop." He says, 'Oh, it's fine.' I said, 'No, it's not. They're taking advantage of you; they know you're here.' Here is a white man; they are using him as a money tree. He never put himself above or saw himself as being above anyone. It wasn't paternalistic. He paid for it a lot.

He has been robbed, but he didn't run away. People broke in; they've broken into the church, into the rectory. We are in the inner city; this happens. One time they broke in, and he was there, they knocked him down, roughed him up a bit. We always told him to be careful. I'm from the ghetto; I was raised in the ghetto. Everybody is not out to say "thank you" and be on their way. He never showed fear. I think he believed the Lord was taking care of him.[9]

The parish offered worship, sacramental preparation, religious instruction, spiritual guidance, and even a grade school. In addition, because it was located in one of the poorest Detroit zip codes, St. Leo's ministered to those in the neighborhood, Catholic or not, including those lacking shelter. Gumbleton especially valued the St. Leo Soup Kitchen ministry. It had begun with a few older parish women preparing bag lunches in their own kitchens.[10] Sr. Mary Ellen Brennan, RSM, the pastoral associate when Gumbleton went to the parish, hired Joe Micallef to do maintenance. Joe was a crusty Maltese man, proud of his heritage and of the beauty of St. Leo's Church. Gradually he took on responsibility for the soup kitchen and moved it to the church basement where it grew to serve approximately three hundred guests each weekday.[11] The bishop wanted the soup kitchen to be an integral part of parish life, so he suggested opening it on holidays so the guests could celebrate and the parishioners could prepare and serve the meals.[12]

Consistent with this priority, he asked the congregation during a Sunday homily to ponder where Jesus would stop first if he were to visit St. Leo's; Jesus would go to the soup kitchen. Joe did most of the fundraising for the soup kitchen. Gumbleton wrote letters to other pastors to introduce Joe and encourage them to invite him to meet with their parish council or Christian Service commission. This successful outreach enabled the soup kitchen to expand to Saturdays. Parishioners from these parishes would serve the lunch on Saturdays and, in some cases, bring the food as well. He also wrote an annual fundraising appeal letter and Joe contacted the Knights of Malta, which provided support to set up a medical clinic. Eventually, with the help of the parish and several community partners, including Metro Detroit Call to Action, the guests could enjoy showers, dental and medical services, a washer and dryer, and a library and clothes closet, in addition to a warm meal and carry-out food for a second meal.[13]

He found inspiration in his parishioners' lives, especially older Black Catholics who had suffered from the impact of racism in the Church much of their lives. One of these memorable people was ninety-year-old Almena Jones. At her funeral he described the many ways she served the parish: in the soup kitchen, as a lector, and as a nurturer of the children. Reflecting on the words of Isaiah that we are called to be a light to the nations, Tom described her:

> On the day she died I had been at a meeting and as I pulled into the parking lot, I saw one of the soup kitchen guests, and she came running up to me, and she was weeping. She said, "Mrs. Jones passed." These are people that are not formally members of our parish, but they come here every day, and Mrs. Jones was very often downstairs while we were serving the meal, and she would get to know these people. She was a light to them, and brought God's light, God's goodness, God's love to people.[14]

The parish grade school had opened in 1890 with four grades, one year after the establishment of St. Leo Parish.[15] The Sisters of Charity provided dedicated instruction for one hundred years until 1991 when the few remaining sisters retired to Cincinnati. Yet Tom was committed to keeping the school open and hired a new principal, Mary Lou Van Antwerp, an experienced, committed Catholic school principal.

> Even though people could not afford the tuition, he wanted the school to continue in what is a very poor area. He always looked for all those things that support the dignity of the person. He said, What do the people need?" and that is what we would get. So that's really his complete acceptance of people as persons; did not make any difference, rich or poor, whether they were clean or dirty, whatever they needed, his goal was to provide that for them.[16]

A major school improvement he facilitated came through a chance encounter on an airplane. An airline attendant recognized him as a priest and asked if she could meet about a personal pastoral concern. They met and she later introduced him to Tom Wheeler, a successful businessman who had created a family foundation, who asked how he could help the parish. Tom directed him to Mary Lou. She described the school's need for computers.[17] Wheeler transformed a storage room into a computer lab for the students. He paid to have electricity brought into the room, repaired the roof leakage, carpeted the room, and bought furniture and computers. Wheeler hired a person who spent months developing the curriculum and then paid his salary for several years. He gave all the teachers bonuses; one year each got $1,000. "Anything that room needed to become a computer lab, he did it."[18]

St. Leo School welcomed the neighborhood children, Catholic or not. The pastor raised money to subsidize their tuition and he ensured the school got money the archdiocese set aside for inner-city schools. Mary Lou explained he did this until it was too much to continue. Teachers' salaries were still too low despite his fundraising. "So, in conversation with a friend and educational consultant, Sheila Turney, he investigated how the school could become a charter public school. He consulted with the archdiocese, met with parents and with the proposed management company, and got state-required university authorization. He presented the concept to parents. They agreed to proceed. Tom did all of the work with the consultants and the parish council to complete the process."[19] St. Leo School closed on June 30, 1998, and George Crockett Academy, the charter school, opened on July 1. The principal and nine teachers out of about twenty remained. The name change resulted from several options being considered. Tom suggested George Crockett Academy because of recently deceased Congressman Crockett's outstanding career in civil rights, locally and nationally, and the parents agreed.[20]

Ministry in the city often included bringing comfort and support to prisoners and their families given the extremely high incarceration rate of Black males.[21] Soon after Gumbleton arrived at St. Leo's, a parishioner, Eloise Treadwell, requested that he write her son, Robert, who had been sentenced to life in prison in 1974 after being found guilty of first-degree murder. Tom began correspondence with and then advocacy on behalf of Robert that continues to the present. In the nearly fifty years since his sentence Robert has earned three college degrees, volunteered with the NAACP, created a child's coloring book, raised funds for Hurricane Katrina victims, and been a model prisoner. Despite the bishop's letters to the multiple parole boards, three successive governors and other advocacy, Robert remains in prison. Through their correspondence they have created a bond that Tom described in a letter to Robert: "I have experienced God's presence in the friendship we share. I thank you for this and I pray that we will continue to know and spread God's love throughout the coming year."[22]

The parish tried to respond to the many other needs of the local community. Daretta Williams, a single mother of four, whose common sense and compassion enabled her to serve the public well, succeeded Mary Ellen on the parish staff. Daretta coordinated parish outreach to the neighborhood. Every weekday morning the parish office was open to respond to requests for help with diverse needs, such as money for paying utilities, rent, or transportation; help accessing medical care, or other assistance from the St. Vincent de Paul Fund.

St. Leo's informally sponsored a new organization, Core City Neighborhoods (CCN). Sr. Theresa Blacquiere, RSM, approached Tom describing her desire to set up a community development organization to improve the quality of life in the neighborhood. He welcomed the idea and donated rental space for the organization's start-up office. Soon after, a nearby Catholic church closed. That rectory became available and was donated to CCN. Tom served on the CCN board of directors for its first decade.[23]

After the Sisters of Charity retired from the school, Tom offered the building rent-free to New Steps, a case management program for pregnant, crack-addicted women. He saw this as an opportunity to offer another vital service at a time when crack addition was rampant in Detroit. He also supported New Steps by raising significant funds for it through his outreach to parishes and through his membership on the New Steps Development Council.

The parish celebrated many milestones in their pastor's life, such as birthdays and anniversaries of his ordination as a priest and also as a bishop. He expressed his gratitude for these celebrations in Sunday bulletins. On the occasion of his fiftieth anniversary as a priest, in 2006, he wrote in part: "What can I say? You are great! You made my celebration a parish family event, which is exactly what I wanted. As I mentioned last Sunday, almost half of my 50 years as a priest has been here at St. Leo's. You have taught me about the love of God and love of others more powerfully than I could have learned anywhere else. You are truly a community of disciples of Jesus, and I am blessed to be called to serve in your midst."[24]

Funerals of two of his family members, his mother, in March 1990, and his brother Jack, in April 2002, were celebrated at the parish. He wrote on the Sunday after his mother's funeral, "Words will never be able to adequately express the gratitude and love I feel for each of you as I reflect on the passing of my mother to eternal life.... Death is never easy. But your kindness and strength carried us through those difficult days. On behalf of my family and myself, we are truly grateful."[25]

Advocating for Detroit Parishes

In September 1988 Cardinal Edmund Szoka announced that fifty-six parishes, more than a third of the city's parishes, could close by the following July. Many in the archdiocese rose up in opposition over this initiative. "I don't think you could find a single historical parallel to this," said Msgr. John Tracy Ellis, the eminent Catholic historian.[26] Detroit was dealing with economic disinvestment evidenced in the closing of factories and stores and the departure of hundreds of thousands of people to the suburbs. Many of the city churches, like St. Leo's, were often the only stable presence in neighborhoods. In a televised announcement the cardinal stated: "Our bottom line is we want alive, vibrant parishes that really make a difference in the community."[27] Many urban Catholics saw the closings as a contradiction and rallied to strongly oppose them. They complained that the project was handled "too much from the top down," and "there was too little effort to get the people most affected by the results involved in the process."[28]

The final closure decisions were to be based on the results of a 408-question survey inquiring about such factors as parish income from collections, sacramental activity, and number of families.[29] The people protested, challenging the appropriateness of the criteria to judge the viability of a parish. "What happened in Detroit hit the country very, very hard," said Msgr. John Egan of Chicago, a widely recognized spokesman for the Catholic urban ministry. It "came with such a dramatic impact to the church across the United States that it has affected the morale of priests in the inner city everywhere."[30]

Bishop Gumbleton discussed the recommendations being drafted with Cardinal Szoka and Bishop Patrick Cooney, who supervised the committees drafting the closing plan. He described his difference with them over whether their plan would strengthen the church. "My judgment is that we will not end up with these large parishes." Yet he added, "I'm not infallible either. I could be totally wrong. I'll be ready to rejoice if I am wrong. I'll be right there at the head of the line to congratulate him (Cardinal Szoka)."[31] As the process continued, the protests grew. On March 9, 1989, the Detroit City Council held a hearing on the pending church closures. Cardinal Szoka and Americans United for the Separation of Church and State warned that the hearing would violate the "constitutional precept against intermingling government and religious affairs." But Tom disagreed. "I see this as a compliment to the Catholic Church. It says our parish churches are very important to the city. They're not going to try to tell the archdiocese what to do; they're going to try to figure out what they should do when the churches close."[32] About 150 people attended the hearing during which Gumbleton spoke as board chair of CCN. The archdiocese said that all social services now being offered by the closing churches would be maintained by the remaining city parishes with assistance from the archdiocesan staff. Tom's pastoral experience led him to doubt that would be possible.[33]

Ultimately, effective July 1, 1989, thirty-one Detroit parishes were closed and twenty-five more were determined to be "questionably viable" and given one more year to improve their status or be closed.[34] Tom grew increasingly concerned about the controversy these closures were stirring, so he went to see Archbishop Pio Laghi, the papal nuncio in Washington, DC, to make sure he was aware of the divisiveness in the Detroit church resulting from closures. Shortly thereafter, Cardinal Szoka was appointed to oversee the church's economic affairs in Rome. Tom did not assume his visit resulted in the move as it may have been in the planning stage prior to his meeting, but he believed it necessary for the sake of the archdiocese for him to communicate in person the severity of the problem.[35]

Supporting the Catholic Urban Ministry

Born out of intense anger and frustration arising from the parish closures, the Detroit Catholic Pastoral Alliance (DCPA) became a source of hope and formation for the church's urban ministry. What matured into the DCPA resulted from the months of organized protests over the church closings. As more and more people participated in the rallies to keep churches open, it became obvious that the DCPA board would have to hire someone to keep the momentum going. Sr. Cathey DeSantis was hired and the work of the DCPA, in its present form, began. Fr. Norm Thomas also continued to play a major role in developing the organization. Soon there were programs of anti-racism training, housing development, and services for youth and seniors to serve the needs of parishioners and neighbors.

One of the key DCPA programs, the Ministers of Service Training Program, had begun in the late 1970s when Norm created the program for his parish. He recognized that lay women and men could do almost anything a deacon could do. Other pastors recognized the same thing, and the program grew. In 2005 the DPCA took over the initiative and parishes sent their candidates to the DCPA for training. Centralizing the program made it more efficient and enabled a stronger faculty. Tom taught the canon law course and participated in annual installation of the Ministers of Service. The need for the Ministers of Service program evolved from Vatican II's encouragement for laity to serve as deacons but the qualifications for the diaconate were set very high. Tom explained that "you had to be a college graduate in to order to apply and take a theology course. So, we had genuine leaders in the city who just did not qualify."[36] This was especially true for Black Catholics from the World War II era. They were not among the nearly eight million World War II veterans who actually benefited from the GI bill. Congress provided all veterans the same benefits but the segregationist practices of most institutions of higher learning effectively excluded a huge proportion of Black veterans from earning a college degree.[37]

Tom Gumbleton's commitment to the DCPA has always been rooted in his longstanding belief that the church had been failing to appropriately serve Catholics in Detroit. "In spite of our rhetoric of wanting to be a church of the poor, the poor are easily forgotten if they aren't part of your congregation. We've seen the archdiocese close churches, saying, well, 'Our people have left'—as though there are not people here. Part of the task of the church is to proclaim the good news wherever there are people. Now whether we've moved away more easily because the people left are Black, or not, I don't know. That could be part of it."[38]

Promoting Social Justice in Public Policy

Drastic cuts in human services in the 1991 State of Michigan budget prompted parish leaders in the Archdiocese of Detroit to come together to advocate for just social policies in Michigan.[39] They formed the Catholic Caucus, a non-partisan advocacy group, to promote economic justice in the light of the Gospel and Catholic social teaching. Tom and Faith Offman, Christian Service representative from St. Robert Bellarmine Parish, served as founding co-chairs for the first thirteen years. The membership grew to nearly three hundred parishes. Jacques Pasquier, of St. John Fisher Parish, and Beverley McDonald of Detroit Sacred Heart Parish, followed them as co-chairs while Tom and Faith remained on the steering committee. He helped sustain the caucus by sending annual letters to pastors requesting financial support "to promote public policies consistent with Catholic Social Teaching."[40]

In October 1998, after eight years of holding Catholic Caucus meetings at Sacred Heart Seminary in Detroit, he received a phone call from Bishop Allen Vigneron, the seminary rector, informing him the group would no longer be welcome to hold the meetings there and that Cardinal Maida concurred with this decision. Hoping this had resulted from a misunderstanding, Gumbleton arranged for himself and Faith to meet with Maida.[41] He wrote Cardinal Maida in advance, outlining the history and mission of the Caucus. He emphasized its role in helping "Catholics to live their Faith" and urged the cardinal to work with the co-chairs to resolve the problem.[42] The controversy arose from an article in *The Wanderer* objecting to the presence of a speaker, H. Lynn Jondahl, at a recent Catholic Caucus meeting. The archconservative newspaper described his association with groups that espoused abortion, gay rights, and euthanasia. Yet Raj Chablani, caucus staff person, noted that Jondahl limited his remarks "to political responsibility and poverty issues, welfare legislation, and how it would impact recipients and service providers, how to restructure welfare programs so they are more efficient and how term limits for state legislators will impact the service industry.[43]

Many lay and clergy members of the Catholic Caucus wrote to Cardinal Maida objecting to this arbitrary prohibition. One such letter described the value of the Catholic Caucus: "The Catholic Caucus is the one group in this diocese that has managed to gather people from all types of parishes to work for social justice particularly as it affects the poor who are dependent on government programs. It is a remarkable group that is doing what no other group in this diocese has been able to do. It is truly sad when their work is discouraged by the church that should be supporting them in every way possible."[44] The cardinal responded by agreeing with the letter writer but adding that regardless of what a speaker presents, "one must also take into account the public 'persona' of the speaker." Despite this concern, the cardinal's meeting with the co-chairs successfully resolved the problem.[45]

Afterward Cardinal Maida wrote to Tom and Faith. "Based on our conversation and the mission statement that you gave me, I feel confident that the Catholic Caucus of SE Michigan intends to remain faithful to Catholic social justice teachings and in full conformity with Catholic doctrine and discipline." He asked that the speakers' resumes and backgrounds be reviewed by archdiocesan staff, specifically the Christian Service Department and Monsignor John Zenz, and permitted the group to resume meeting at the seminary.[46] The crisis passed and the group's public policy advocacy continued.

Fostering Adult Catholic Learning: The Elephants

A continuing Catholic education series arose out of a convocation of the archdiocesan priests. Fr. Tom Lumpkin described its origin. "The priests gather annually at a resort area, stay in a motel, have meetings and discussions. There is always a time for questions for the cardinal. At this particular one with Cardinal Maida they were asking questions and he would not really answer the questions, especially about the priest shortage. He would say there wasn't really a priest shortage and there is a priest for every situation. But everybody knew there was a huge shortage, and the situation would get worse."[47] Following this gathering, a group of priests decided that since the cardinal wouldn't raise important issues or let the priests discuss them with him, they would do it on their own. They described this endeavor as embodying the saying, "the elephant in the living room." Nobody wants to admit that it's right there and they then referred to themselves in shorthand as "The Elephants."[48]

Eleven priests met in a planning group to consider their options. In May 2004 Lumpkin and Gumbleton prepared a draft letter of invitation on behalf of this group. After circulating it, they along with a handful of other priests, signed the letter to all of the archdiocesan priests inviting them to a meeting the following month. Michael Himes, a Boston College theologian, would speak on Vatican II ecclesiology. They chose this topic in light of the group's concern "that the ecclesial vision of Vatican II has become dimmed. Current policies and practices seem to reflect more of a pre-Vatican II than post-Vatican II perspective. Topics of great importance to the life of the Church are barred from an open discussion. Theologians whose work has enlivened Catholic thought are no longer welcome to speak."[49]

Soon the attendees of the presentations included lay participants as well. The planning group would identify topics that otherwise did not get discussed publicly, and then bring in a speaker. Once they identified potential presenters, Bishop Gumbleton would invite them since he usually knew them. More than fifteen years later, Lumpkin noted, "Elephant sessions have become the place where many people in the archdiocese get their adult education and where they can live out and experience their understanding of the Catholic faith. It fits with how they understand their faith."[50]

He emphasized that the high quality of the speakers was primarily due to Bishop Gumbleton. "Our presenters have come because he is the one who invited them, and they know and admire the role he has played in the post-Vatican II era." Speakers have included Joan Chittister, OSB; Shawn Copeland; John Dear; Margaret Farley, RSM; Tom Fox; Elizabeth Johnson, CSJ; Teresa Kane, RSM; James Martin, SJ; Bryan Massingale; John O'Malley, SJ; Helen Prejean, CSJ; Richard Rohr, OFM; and many more. The archdiocese prohibited some of the presenters from speaking at a Catholic parish, so the venue moved to the property of an order of religious women or a union hall.[51]

Withdrawing from Archdiocesan Leadership

Gumbleton served decades in the chancery offices, including as assistant chancellor, vice-chancellor, and vicar general. His heart all the while was in parish and peace and justice work. Eventually, Archbishop Szoka reduced his administrative responsibilities and later Cardinal Maida allowed him to cease serving as regional bishop. Gumbleton's desire to reduce his administrative responsibilities demonstrates his preference for pastoral ministry over administrative leadership. While studying in Rome more than thirty years earlier he had observed priests in Rome who *fare le cariere* (make a career). This half-teasing yet sometimes à propos phrase describes priests pursuing advanced degrees who cultivate relationships with members of the curia to become known and then build their ecclesial careers. As his decades of ministry, in Detroit and beyond, demonstrate, he rejected this path.[52]

15
Ministry and the Sex Abuse Crisis in the Church

The sex abuse crisis roiling the Catholic Church throughout the world dramatically impacted Tom Gumbleton's personal life and parish ministry. His introduction to the crisis began when he tried to assist Barbara Blaine, a friend who sought his help to deal with her childhood experience of clerical sexual abuse. He met Blaine in the early 1980s, about the same time that he became pastor of St. Leo's and while he served as president of Pax Christi USA. She was working in the Chicago Pax Christi office. Their friendship developed over the years, especially when she visited her family in her hometown of Toledo, Ohio, not far south of Detroit. When she told Gumbleton about being abused, from the age of thirteen, by her parish priest, her description of this abuse shocked him. She had met with the bishop of Toledo to report the abuse, and he had assured her he would deal with it. Barbara waited, but nothing happened. "Then she told me about it. I knew that bishop very well, so I told her that I would go to see him. I did so and he told me: 'Oh yes, I have to take care of this.' He never did a thing about it. I expected that he would, that he would not brush me off. He did not do anything about it."[1]

A few years later Blaine established the Survivors Network of those Abused by Priests (SNAP) and invited Gumbleton to support SNAP efforts. He subsequently met with many survivors, thereby coming to realize that Barbara's experience of being ignored by a church minister was the norm, not the exception. In an article published at the time of Barbara's death nearly thirty years later, he wrote: "SNAP was one of the most important things that happened in bringing the sex abuse crisis to the forefront and it caused the bishops to do much more than they were doing and it helped stop the cover up."[2] Bishop Gumbleton's most notable public advocacy regarding this crisis occurred in January 2006 when he accepted Barbara's request to speak to the Ohio legislature. The House Judiciary committee was considering extending the Ohio statute of limitations for victims of child abuse. The existing law required a victim to file by the age of twenty-one.[3] The bill under consideration unanimously passed the Ohio Senate nine months earlier and was currently stalled in the House judiciary committee. It proposed giving victims a one-time, one-year lifting of the statute of limitations to allow those with claims of abuse to sue.[4]

"I told Barbara I would testify. I wrote out a brief statement about why it was important to speak out; why it was important to help the victims. I did not consult with anyone. I knew the Ohio bishops and bishops all over the country opposed this kind of legislation out of concern for the financial implications if there were judgments against a diocese."[5]

Testifying

Even though he had never told anyone about it, he decided to reveal in his testimony that he had been abused as a fifteen-year-old seminarian. A priest, a teacher at Sacred Heart Seminary, would take him with another seminarian to a cottage less than an hour away from Detroit. "At some point he would start to wrestle, he would wrestle you to the floor, like boys would do, then he starts putting his hand down the back of your pants. That's when I always made sure I extricated myself and got out. It's embarrassing, because I feel, well, I should have known better. And that's the same thing all of these victims go through."[6] He added, "I had never shared this because I was embarrassed, and it was not severe abuse. Yet I thought if I told the legislators what happened to me it would help in getting the legislation passed. But the Ohio legislature had called off the hearing without explanation, so Barbara and team called a press conference. I made the statement for the press that I would have made for the legislature."[7]

In the prepared statement to the chair of the House Judiciary Committee he quoted from the 1971 Synod of Bishops on Justice in the World, "...anyone who ventures to speak to people about justice must first be just in their eyes."[8] He was clear about his rationale for publicly advocating extending the statute of limitations. "I am not out to get the Ohio bishops, but I care about the victims. I have a deep sense of compassion for how difficult it has been for them." He argued that "full disclosure of the abuse is essential to hold perpetrators and the church accountable, heal victims and re-store the church's 'moral credibility' at a time when 'more than a few feel that church social teachings ring with hypocrisy....I am convinced that set-tlement of every case by our court system is the only way to protect chil-dren and to heal the brokenness within the church."[9]

Widespread press coverage of his testimony evoked immediate contro-versy. "The bishops of Ohio got word, of course. By the time I got home from Columbus, Ohio, that evening the apostolic nuncio had contacted Car-dinal Maida who contacted me the next day and told me all of the Ohio bishops protested to the nuncio."[10] Yet none of those bishops contacted Tom who had been their brother bishop for nearly forty years. "I know all these bishops. I've met with them many times....Not one of them called me up to talk to me about it. Now, if they were angry, they could call me up and holler at me and scream at me if they wanted. Or they could have asked, 'Why did you do it?'"[11]

Maida wrote Gumbleton the week after his trip to Ohio and informed him he would have to resign immediately from both of his roles as bishop and pastor of St. Leo's.[12] The matter of his resigning as bishop had been an issue since January 2005 when he turned seventy-five. Canon law requires a bishop to submit his resignation at seventy-five. He wrote Pope John Paul II the day before his seventy-fifth birthday requesting not to retire at that time. Noting his excellent health and the critical shortage of priests, he added, "I have prayed sincerely and often to know God's will in this regard. I truly feel I am being called to continue my active ministry as a bishop. Your own witness encourages me to make this request. You are an inspiring example of the ability of older people to share their wisdom and leadership in active ministry. I would like to do the same."[13]

This letter was the first of several letters to and from the Congregation of Bishops on the topic of his resignation in 2005. In September, Giovanni Battista Cardinal Re, Prefect of the Congregation of Bishops, informed him that the newly elected Pope Benedict XVI requested that he submit his res-ignation immediately, noting "the decision to accept, reject, or delay such an offer of resignation is left in the hands of the Successor of Peter."[14] Gumbleton had not yet submitted that letter by the time he traveled to Ohio the following January. Maida also had turned seventy-five that year, but the pope delayed his resignation for four additional years. The pope's decision regarding Tom seemed based on a critique of his actions, not the needs of the Detroit archdiocese.

Despite Maida's reference to Gumbleton's having to resign both roles, he assumed that he would continue as the parish administrator. It is common practice that once a pastor reaches retirement age, he is named administrator. This assignment continues as long as he is able to serve. Tom shared with the parish his understanding of the implications of his resignation as pastor.

> It does not change anything as far as the Sacrament of Holy Orders is concerned. I will continue to exercise my ordained ministry but will no longer serve in any administrative role as a bishop within the archdiocese. It does not change any pastoral/sacramental role as long as I am physically capable of serving. This means I will continue to teach, preach, celebrate sacraments and carry on my work for justice and peace wherever I am called. This, of course, includes as a priority, my ministry at St. Leo's.[15]

Yet as the local press publicized the official reaction to his Ohio advocacy, concern arose about his future role at St. Leo's. The *Detroit Free Press* editorialized:

> For those who've grown up in his nearly continual presence in southeast Michigan, it's sometimes easy to forget that Thomas Gumbleton's voice carries across the nation and world.... Ecclesiastical formalities aside, there is no reason Thomas Gumbleton can't keep being Thomas Gumbleton, an inspired preacher who faithfully holds up the most marginalized members of society. He has had no administrative duties for years, so where he stands in the hierarchy should make little difference. In an era when the Catholic Church can't find enough priests, it would seem odd indeed if he did not retain his pastoral duties, for as long as he desires and is able, at the near-west side parish that he calls home.[16]

It became clearer to the public that the official church would punish Tom. Catholic writer and columnist Joan Chittister, OSB, compared the public's support of Bishop Gumbleton and the hierarchy's behavior toward him to its treatment of Boston's Bernard Cardinal Law.

> You'd think a church would be giddy with glee to see such a thing (praising a bishop) happen. So, the question is not whether or not what has been done has been done legally. Of course it has. Rome has the power, we are reminded often, to do whatever it wants to do to the clerical personnel of the church. The question is only,

"Should they?"…Cardinal Law resigned for not telling the truth about pedophile priests. Rome gave him a promotion, a position on five of the curial congregations of the church, St. Mary Major, one of the four principal churches in Rome, and a luxurious Roman apartment. On the other hand, this bishop, Bishop Thomas Gumbleton, told the truth, even about his having been abused by a priest himself when he was a young seminarian. Most of all, he took the position that it is the obligation of bishops to bring transparency, accountability and justice to the plight of sex abuse victims, whatever the financial ramifications for the church itself.[17]

Maida wrote to him saying that his speaking in Ohio without informing him in advance was both a profound personal disappointment as well as inconsistent with the church's expectations of an auxiliary bishop. Maida described it as nothing less than an attack on the fraternal "*communio*" of the bishops of the United States. "It is unseemly and contrary to the apostolic *communio* of bishops and scandalizing to the faithful that a bishop of another state and diocese would publicly interfere in the disputes and discussions of a jurisdiction not their own." He cited the specific canons from the Code of Canon law which Tom had breached and issued a formal precept enjoining him "to observe the laws of the Church regarding auxiliary bishops."[18]

In response, Tom explained his conviction in choosing to speak before the Ohio legislature without informing Maida in advance. "I was going as a victim. I didn't give that up when I became a bishop. Cardinal Dearden told me when I received the letter appointing me bishop to 'Be yourself.'"[19] In addition to this private reprimand from Maida, Tom's Ohio statement evoked public rebuke from the archdiocesan spokesperson, Ned McGrath, who labeled him a hypocrite. McGrath claimed Gumbleton had authorized the archdiocesan lawyers to use the statute of limitations in his own defense when he had been named as one of the defendants in a lawsuit. Gumbleton vehemently disputed McGrath's assertion, saying there was no basis for his being listed as a defendant since he had no supervisory role over the plaintiff. He had never been involved in discussions concerning how best to defend against the allegations in the lawsuit so he had no role in the archdiocese's defense preparation. In fact, he said, the archdiocese had invoked the statute of limitations defense in that lawsuit "without my knowledge."[20] He wrote McGrath saying, "it is misleading on your part to suggest that I chose a 'statute of limitation' defense for myself in this or any lawsuit."[21] On the contrary, he explained to the *Detroit Free*

Press, decades ago when abuse was reported to him and other bishops, "I remember I was very firm in trying to encourage families to go to civil authorities, and my experience is that people didn't. People were afraid of going into court and going... against the church."[22] In addition, he acknowledged that he was unaware of previous attempts to change the Michigan statute of limitations but, now informed, he would lobby to support them. He believed "a one-time, one-year lifting of the legal deadlines to allow those with claims of abuse to sue... provides an opportunity for the church to deal directly with its past and restore its credibility on moral issues."[23]

McGrath countered that such statements ignore the "archdiocese's efforts to help victims of abuse and pay for their counseling." Instead it favors attorneys "who will benefit greatly themselves from the claims they are making."[24] The archdiocese preferred that a victim complain to the archdiocese rather than seek legal redress. The delegate for the clergy, Monsignor Ricardo Bass, invited "those who want to come forward with a complaint of clergy sexual abuse to do so" and he also affirmed the current Michigan statute of limitations saying, "it has served our society well in protecting the rights of everyone, especially after a long passage of time."[25]

Bishops throughout the country lobbied strenuously against legislation to relax the statute of limitations out of fear of embarrassment, shame, and financial risk. Mark Chopko, the general counsel for the United States Conference of Catholic Bishops (USCCB), described creating the window for litigation as "fundamentally unjust.... It won't protect one more child in the USA. The abuse has cost the church more than $1 billion in settlements with victims, care and counseling for victims and priests, and prevention programs."[26] In addition to being seen as disloyal to his brother bishops, Tom was also criticized for aligning himself with lay activists, like SNAP advocates, who were "denigrated by church officials and their surrogates for their attempts to rally the public against institutional secrecy and reluctance to co-operate with civil authorities."[27]

Gumbleton's Ohio advocacy had thrust him into the heart of the scandal dividing the church: how to deal with priests who abused minors and how to deal with bishops who covered up the priests' behavior. Four years earlier, the U.S. bishops, stirred by the 2002 Boston clerical abuse scandal, met in Dallas and developed the Charter for the Protection of Children and Young People. Yet despite their Dallas effort, the bishops did not succeed. This may explain the *New York Times* editorial: "More than three years after the American bishops resolved to set things right, that goal has not been met. Many dioceses have been less than enthusiastic in urging the victims to come forward, and some still rebuff such complaints. As Bishop Gumbleton pointed out, the continued existence of many hidden abusers and silent victims demands further action."[28]

At the time of the Dallas meeting, Catholics indicated their distrust toward the hierarchy on the topic of clerical sexual abuse. A Quinnipiac poll "reported that 87% of Catholics wanted a zero-tolerance policy for priests accused of sexually abusing young people; 69% believed Church leaders who transferred priests should resign; 89% wanted bishops to report accusations to civil authorities; and 70% wanted to have a say in deciding how to deal with such priests, while only 23% percent actually believed that the bishops would be able to accomplish something worthwhile and help alleviate the scandal."[29] Yet official church representatives adopted the minority view that the bishops had or would soon have the clerical sex abuse crisis under control. USCCB's Chopko challenged Gumbleton, saying: "Most Catholic leaders would strongly disagree with Gumbleton's claim that a significant number of abusers are lingering in the priesthood. Most bishops have done all they can to remove abusers." Paul Long of the Michigan Catholic Conference stated on behalf of the Michigan bishops: "It is our belief that Michigan's statute of limitations is in the mainstream of national law and serves well its intention of fairness."[30] Yet Tom remained unconvinced. "I figure whatever the price, you have to speak the truth....If it costs us in material goods, the spiritual purification is worth it. The more I hear from these survivors, the more widespread I think this is."[31] Events in the subsequent years confirmed his assessment. In 2018, sixteen years after the Dallas Charter, the Pennsylvania attorney general concluded a two-year investigation into child sex abuse by Catholic priests in six dioceses. "The investigation has helped renew a crisis that many in the church thought and hoped had ended nearly twenty years ago after a church scandal erupted in Boston. Recent abuse-related scandals, including in Australia and Chile, have reopened questions about accountability and whether church officials at the highest levels are still covering up crimes."[32]

In 2020, Pope Francis pledged to rid the church of sexual abuse after he received a report blaming "a host of bishops, cardinals and popes for downplaying and dismissing mountains of evidence of [Cardinal Theodore] McCarrick's misconduct...."[33] Tom's unyielding advocacy for clerical sex abuse victims, though widely resisted by church leaders, brought comfort and healing to many survivors of clerical abuse.

Repercussions for St. Leo Parish

In light of the official church's stance, Tom's dissenting views on the scope of and the remedies for dealing with clerical sexual abuse unavoidably impacted St. Leo's parishioners. In fact, they experienced twelve months of confusion, frustration, and anxiety. Once he submitted his letter of resignation as bishop, Maida informed him he could serve only as a temporary administrator at St. Leo's until another pastor was appointed.[34] He contacted the cardinal to clarify this limitation and reiterated his "expectation that my resignation would be handled like that of any priest of the archdiocese, and that I would be appointed as administrator of St. Leo's on a year-to-year basis."[35]

He soon learned from Maida that the Vatican Office of the Congregation of Bishops had directed that he be precluded from serving even as administrator. Instead, the cardinal instructed that since the archdiocese was engaged in a "Together in Faith" (TIF) restructuring process, St. Leo's would be served in a cluster with another parish.[36] Tom and the parish council began participating in the TIF process by developing criteria for a cluster parish. In July, he reported to the parish that the council agreed on the following criteria: the cluster parish would have "some of the same characteristics that mark our community, such as leadership style (with strong emphasis on lay involvement), African American spirituality and liturgical expression and commitment to education, faith formation and service."[37] By October, the council was ready to propose the names of three parishes for the cluster relationship. Yet almost immediately after submitting the parish names to the archdiocese, the parish council learned that the archdiocese had unilaterally intervened by contacting a pastor seeking to cluster his parish with St. Leo's. The council had already excluded this pastor's parish because the worship in each parish differed in cultural expression. The other parish emphasized Hispanic music and liturgical celebrations. Combining it with St. Leo's African American spirituality would not promote meaningful worship in either parish.[38]

When he reported this archdiocesan interference to the parish, Gumbleton added: "These are all examples that the TIF process and the credibility of the archdiocese are endangered." He noted that the members of the vicariate also objected to this bypassing of the published process. They wrote the archdiocese asking the officials not to subvert parish participation in the TIF program.[39] He also contacted Maida to object to this clustering and the cardinal agreed not to create this cluster. He learned, though, that the TIF process would be concluding soon and that Detroit Auxiliary Bishop John

Quinn would communicate to the parish the archdiocese's decision on pastoral leadership succession. Apparently, the TIF process was not going to apply to Tom and St. Leo's after all. He wrote Bishop Quinn to inform him of some parishioners' questions, including: "Why was our original proposal totally disregarded and why did we not receive any official response? Why am I forbidden to live at St. Leo's? Why cannot the usual diocesan policy be followed for St. Leo's as it has been at other parishes with the retired pastor being allowed to minister on a year-to-year basis?"[40]

In the midst of this frustrating, contradictory process Bishop Gumbleton remained focused on reassuring the parish.

> For me, and I am confident for all of us, our most important concern is that we stay together as a parish community with the very strong bonds that we have developed over the past couple of decades. The love and caring that marks this parish is experienced immediately by anyone who joins us at a Sunday liturgy celebration, or who experiences the loving outreach that emanates from the multiple services we are able to give to all who come to us in need. None of us wants to lose this spirit of life and love....I plead with all who care about St. Leo's—our parish members and all our friends—pray for the successful transition to new pastoral leadership and pray for the grace for all of us to trust in God's loving care for us. God will show us the way. We must have the courage to follow.[41]

He wanted his final days at the parish not to become a "media circus."

> I don't see any point in people coming to demonstrate or anything of the sort. It's not like it's my funeral Mass or something like that. I just want everything to continue to be as much for the parish as possible and not be flooded with outsiders. Christmas celebrations and Sunday liturgies should continue to be parish liturgies and not liturgies that are all about me. We have a very vibrant parish community and I want it to be that way.[42]

The story drew national attention. The *New York Times,* upon consulting three canon lawyers, reported there was nothing in canon law that "would prohibit an archbishop from permitting a retired auxiliary bishop from serving as a pastor after 75."[43] Clearly, the ecclesial directive that he not serve as a leader of a parish had supplanted canon law.

Early in 2007 the archdiocese terminated his assignment as temporary administrator of St. Leo's effective January 22, 2007.[44] The day before Tom's final Mass, Bishop Quinn and another archdiocesan staffer met with concerned parishioners. The two-hour session was intense, sad, and heart-breaking, yet very affirming of Tom. The parishioners were well aware that they were suffering because of his being sanctioned for his Ohio advocacy on behalf of clerical sexual abuse victims.[45]

At his final Mass many parishioners wept. He told them that he had been forced to step down as pastor because of his advocacy on behalf of clerical sexual abuse victims, a stance that put him in conflict with his fellow bishops. "I'm sure it's because of the openness with which I spoke out last January concerning victims of sex abuse in the church. So, we're all suffering the consequences of that, and yet, I don't regret doing what I did because I still think it was the right thing to do." The tearful congregation rose and erupted in applause.[46]

As the parishioners entered Mass, they had been handed a letter from Maida naming Fr. Gerald Battersby as parish administrator. The letter omitted any reference to a cluster parish. It confirmed that the archdiocese, unable to identify a cluster parish, decided to ignore the TIF process so they could move ahead without Tom. The cardinal's letter described the new administrator as coming "with experience of ministry in the city."[47] Yet he had not previously ministered at a parish with African American spirituality.

Parishioner Maryfran Barber, IHM, characterized Bishop Gumbleton's removal from St. Leo's: "I think of us as collateral damage. . . . That was really, really hard for the parish. . . . I think that was hard for him. I'm sure it was hard for him to see the suffering of the parish."[48] Once he was replaced, the archdiocese offered a different removal rationale. Archdiocesan spokesperson McGrath released a statement saying that 'Bishop Gumbleton's removal from St. Leo Parish had nothing to do with his lobbying on sexual abuse or his political stands.'"[49] This is inconsistent with Cardinal Maida's January 14, 2006 letter to Tom, quoted above, in which Maida said that going to Ohio without consulting with him was "a serious lapse in your duty as an Auxiliary Bishop of the Archdiocese of Detroit (cfr can. 407 sec. 1 and 2)."

In late January the ousted bishop-pastor gave a character-revealing interview on his removal. "This is an instance where my choice would be different, but I can follow this decision. I expect it will open up new avenues for God's blessing and God's grace."[50] The parish and the Detroit Catholic Pastoral Alliance were unwilling to accept his fate. They picketed the chancery and took out an ad in the *Detroit Free Press* with more than a thousand signatures: "Bishop Thomas Gumbleton...Life-long Detroiter, Priest, Pastor, Bishop, Elder, Global Peacemaker, Visionary, Prophet, Spiritual Leader and Friend...We honor, respect and love you...We are opposed to the decision to remove you as Pastor of St. Leo the Great Parish, Detroit."[51]

The parish tried to overturn the decision, filing an unsuccessful formal appeal. They then requested a meeting with Cardinal Maida, but never received a response.[52] Soon the parish began to decline. The priest who succeeded Gumbleton served one year until the parish became clustered with St. Cecilia's under a different pastor. The two clustered parishes eventually merged, were renamed, and St. Leo's Church was closed in 2017.[53] Ecclesial defenders of mergers have described them as offering "the promise of more robust parishes and a sounder financial footing as the archdiocese seeks to recruit new clergy and implement more growth plans."[54] Such words echo Cardinal Szoka's rationale for closures more than twenty years earlier—words that Tom disputed then, saying in 1988, "My judgment is that we will not end up with these larger parishes. I could be totally wrong."[55] He was not wrong; the intervening years witnessed the continuing closure of city parishes, not the growth of vibrant parishes.

Soon after being displaced from St. Leo's he began serving at other parishes. The parishioners at one of these parishes asked if he would serve as their pastor. He was willing but doubted the archdiocese would appoint him pastor or pastoral administrator. The parish asked and learned he was correct. Yet his pastoral service persisted, and he celebrated Sunday liturgy and ministered the sacraments at least until the Covid-19 pandemic. The *National Catholic Reporter* has many years of his weekly homilies online (and available for listening) as *The Peace Pulpit*. In this way and in other ways, Bishop Gumbleton's prophetic voice continues to challenge and inspire.[56]

PART THREE

16

Character

Media coverage over the decades has depicted Bishop Gumbleton as a steadfast voice against war and as a determined, vocal, even stubborn advocate for the rights of those discounted by society and church. But to get to know him personally is to observe a quiet, introverted man happy to be at home praying and reading. Though he treasures family and friends, praying alone in the first hours each morning has always been special to him. In a walk through his four-hundred-square-foot apartment in Corktown, Detroit's oldest neighborhood, one sees what has inspired the public and private man. Every wall holds images—among them Thomas Merton, the four U.S. churchwomen martyred in El Salvador, Martin Luther King, Jr., Cesar Chavez, and Dorothy Day. Pictures of many deceased friends, especially John Dearden and Ken Untener, hang on the bedroom wall. His kitchen wall and refrigerator are covered with photos of family, friends, and former parishioners. On the top of the small desk in his bedroom is an image of a "small, starving girl, crouched over in the bush, her forehead almost touching the ground. She might be praying. Behind her stands a vulture, watching and waiting." This Pulitzer Prize-winning photograph, taken in Sudan in 1993 by South African journalist Kevin Carter, appeared in the March 26, 1993 issue of the *New York Times*[1] and other publications around the world.

A reporter once asked, what experiences most shaped him? "The true conversion I underwent came about because of two things. One was a trip to Cairo, Egypt, in the early 1960s. And the other was the Vatican Council."[2] That trip to Cairo introduced him to absolute destitution, where he saw thousands of people dressed in dirty rags, hungry and without water.

"Deep in my interior somewhere, I made a commitment to find out about why this is, where else it is, and what can be done about it. This was the first opening I had to the idea of trying to do justice in the world."[3] His canon law studies in Rome coincided with Vatican II. Yet prior to the Council, on the cruise en route to Italy, he learned a key lesson about the limits of his seminary education. That's when he met the couple who engaged him in a long conversation about birth control and church teaching on contraception. Despite putting forth all the moral arguments he had learned at St. John's Seminary, he could not persuade the couple to accept them. His seminary bubble had never been challenged by independent thought. "I realized I wasn't prepared to deal with people in the real world." Not having all the answers opened him to the spirit of Vatican II as it took up the call of Pope John XXIII for "aggiornamento"—"updating" the Church.

The Council proclaimed in the *Pastoral Constitution on the Church in the Modern World*, "The joys and hopes, the griefs and the anxieties of the people of this age, especially those who are poor or in any way afflicted, these are the joys and hopes, the griefs and anxieties of the followers of Christ. Indeed, nothing genuinely human fails to raise an echo in their hearts."[4] Tom realized "that's where the church is supposed to be, to insert itself into the world around us, which means the people, and to bring about a transformation of the world so that it begins to look like the reign of God. So this gave a whole different thrust to my understanding of the priesthood. That was a huge shift. You're not trying to convert every person; you're trying to transform the world."[5]

A disciplined person from his youth, he regularly set goals and accomplished them. An early example of this was his desire to become an Eagle Scout. Knowing he could not achieve this once in the seminary, he drove himself to gain the necessary badges and earned Eagle Scout status before finishing the eighth grade. In Rome he completed most of his canon law classes early so that he could travel in Europe with his parents for several weeks during his final semester. Even in retirement, he responds to every phone call, email, text and letter. When asked to what he attributes his sense of responsibility and determination, he has explained, "I learned from the example of my parents who carried out their responsibilities daily without complaining, making life very pleasant for the rest of the family."[6] He also credits Monsignor Frank McPhillips who encouraged the seminarians to always respond affirmatively to invitations from parishioners asking the priest to speak at Communion breakfasts or school graduations. McPhillips could not have imagined that his guidance would lead to Gumbleton's agreeing to meet with the hostages in Iran or to set up a health care clinic for Haitians. "I got involved in so many issues of social justice by accepting the invitations. I never regretted it. After I traveled to places (like Central America, Haiti, Iraq) I usually ended up with many speaking engagements about my experience. I used to wonder sometimes what I was going to say, but I always came up with something. I just said 'yes' if I could do it and if I couldn't do it, I would say so."[7]

He has likewise so often responded in the affirmative to personal requests. The day his grandniece Sarah was to be baptized, he was returning from Amman, Jordan. On arrival at the Detroit airport, after the six-thousand-mile trip, he headed straight to celebrate her baptism. And Daniel Tillas, his translator and driver in Haiti, remembered with great joy that "Bishop Gumbleton came all the way to my house to do the baptism of my son, Younme."[8] Good friend Therese Terns observes, "His love is big. He will go above and beyond for people. What nobody else will do, he will do."[9]

Rising early every day allows him more time to do what he thinks valuable. A sound sleeper, he falls asleep almost as soon as his head hits the pillow. In his active years in ministry, he now admits, he was sleep-deprived and once even started to doze while celebrating Sunday Mass. He had just begun the "Our Father" with the congregation joining in, when he caught himself inclining against the altar. He used to get about five hours each night.[10] Until he began to slow down nearing age ninety, he was ever on the move, lightning fast, rushing down the hall or to the airport to catch the next flight. For years he arrived at scheduled activities, from airports to confirmations, at the last minute. Eventually, he revised this practice and arranged to arrive early, at last realizing that last-minute arrivals were disrespectful to his hosts, the parish congregations, or the persons driving him to the airport.

He generously gives money to those with tuition expenses, utility bills, rent, and so forth. During the Covid crisis he used his federal pandemic relief money to aid others. He keeps cash in his car visor so he can easily offer assistance to people on street corners seeking help. He tips generously, noting that many workers, such as those at car washes, are living on the edge and working in harsh conditions. He has been known to tip several times the cost of the car wash itself. Despite his reticence and humility, he has allowed many nonprofit organizations to honor him to help them fundraise. He takes to heart the words of Pope Paul VI, "No one may appropriate surplus goods solely for his (sic) own private use when others lack the bare necessities of life...."[11] His ability to concentrate conserves energy and his tendency to focus, especially when reading, enables him to ignore other activities around him. Of late his hearing loss increases his ability "to tune out" his environment. Sometimes he even does this deliberately, removing his hearing aids.

This book has depicted him as a studious child who loved to read, even if this love was stimulated in part by a teacher's rejection of his musical ability. Years later in Rome he developed a practice of summarizing the text in the margins of the translated lecture notes he purchased, and this led to a life-long habit of annotating books, magazines, and newspapers. He often passes them on to friends, saying, "I don't have time to discuss these interesting items, so this is a substitute way to share, and it helps justify the money I spend on subscriptions."

He admits he has become dependent on having something available to read at all times. If he has to wait for an appointment, he remarks, "as long as I have a book, my security blanket, I will happily wait." On the other hand, he claims to only procrastinate when he is reading a very good book.[12] Voices in the Wilderness leader Kathy Kelly says he brings his love of reading with him wherever he is. "Tom, on any travels I have done with him, whether on a plane or bus or whatever, once he gets his seat, he pulls out the *New York Review of Books* or something else and uses the travel time to read and study. He needs to be on top of so many different issues, and he would faithfully read the *NY Review* to help him."[13]

His habit of focusing and his love of reading the daily newspaper collided with reality during Super Bowl XL weekend in Detroit. He was enjoying the *New York Times* during breakfast on Saturday at a downtown diner. Street parking had been restricted in advance of the game. While he was engrossed in reading, a parking officer entered the diner warning that all illegally parked cars would be towed. After breakfast he left and discovered his car was missing. When he then returned to the diner everyone told him he must have ignored the warning. Laughing, but slightly annoyed at himself, he called a friend to pick him up and take him to where his car had been towed.

His intense competitive side extends to when he is off the playing field or court, even to watching Tigers baseball on TV. He admires the championship ability of Miguel Cabrera but objects to his "fraternizing with the enemy" when, as first baseman, "Miggy" chats with the runner from the opposing team. This attitude matches his extremely competitive approach to sports. It's one reason he does not like playing golf because "you only compete with yourself." In a rare fondness for "things as they were," he prefers sports as they were during his youth, so the expansion of baseball and hockey teams and the introduction of interleague baseball annoy him. He is no less irritated by the Stanley Cup play-offs ending in June and the World Series ending in November.[14]

He does not get angry easily. On a couple of occasions, his secretary, Nancy Driscoll, in the days before e-tickets and cell phones, ordered a plane ticket sending him to the wrong city for a speaking engagement. In both cases, Nancy recalls, "Tom called me from the wrong location and calmly said, 'Nance, I think I'm in the wrong place.' He didn't blow up; he didn't cuss me out, and—most importantly—he didn't fire me! In one case his response was, 'It's no big deal, Nance. I didn't want to go there anyway!!!!' But then he went above and beyond and told the folks in the correct cities that HE had screwed up his travel schedule and it was all his fault."[15]

When he has received criticism or insults over decisions he made as vicar for parishes or for his advocacy on controversial U.S. policies, he has not responded in kind. His way of dealing with these kinds of matters is to evoke the phrase *"quid hoc ad aeternitatem"*—how important is this in the light of eternity? Given this perspective, he's been able to let go of the affronts. When dealing with personal disappointments or challenging decisions, Tom processes his thoughts and feelings internally. These concerns become part of his prayer. His introverted disposition, along with his relationship with Jesus, have enabled him to be peaceful in the midst of such difficulty. In a reflection on prayer he wrote of Jesus what seems to be true for himself, "Prayer was fully integrated in the life of Jesus—part of it—his life cannot be described without including prayer as an essential part of it."[16]

In some ways, the man has been a loner. He long lived in rectories where community living is not generally an expectation. Since 2007, he has resided alone in his Corktown studio apartment except for breaks at the family condo in northern Michigan. This history does not lead to habits of shared decision-making. When he is in a situation that calls for participatory decision-making, he can seem oblivious to a topic's being appropriate for conversation and instead communicates a decision as if his conclusion is obvious and there was nothing to discuss.

Yet he does recognize and affirm the pull of community. Johanna Berrigan has described what occurred on a bus trip with him while in Iraq. "At a certain point in this long ride someone recommended that we all do prayer together. Tom was way in the back by himself, typical, and I think initially he said, 'no,' since he was doing his own late afternoon prayer. Then in a fraction of a second, he realized, 'wait a minute, there is a community, and I should be part of it,' or at least this is what I imagined him thinking. Eventually he came up and everyone was happy that he joined us."[17] He has what might seem to be contradictory behaviors in his interactions with others. Usually, he is interested and friendly. He seeks to learn the names of wait-staff at local diners. If he saw a neighbor in need, he would immediately try to help, yet he has not gotten acquainted with most of his neighbors in Detroit or Frankfort. When home he is "off duty" and can just be his comfortable, private self.

And yet, in all sorts of situations, he has been a fearless (nonviolent) fighter. And this bold tenacity, no doubt tied to his competitive nature, is manifest not only in the many causes he has championed over the years. In Northern Michigan, he still relishes, even into his ninth decade, unhesitatingly jumping into the cold water of Lake Michigan in the spring. In El Salvador, days after a bombing, he elected to join with peasants who chose to confront the military barricade so they could return to their bombed village. "I didn't think about what might happen; I just decided the right thing to do and did it."[18]

He does not worry, and he lives in the present moment, not focusing on the past or fretting about the future. Asked about what might be ahead with aging and health issues, he says he does not really think about this since there's nothing he could do about it anyway. Nor does he hold grudges. Eileen Burns, a good friend and his assistant, says, "He can be stubborn, and dig in his heels with the best of us. But what I love is that no matter how he may screw up, the next day is a clean slate. Start again. He often says, 'All's well that ends.' God loves us today just as much as God loved us yesterday."[19] He can be a tender, thoughtful person, even in times of stress. Two days after his older brother Vinnie was killed in a work accident in January 1973, he stopped by the home of some friends, IHM sisters, for a bite to eat prior to going to the funeral home. Asked how they could help him, such as by picking up family members arriving at the airport for the funeral, or typing up the funeral program, he responded with a specific request: would they please visit his parents after all of the funeral activity quieted down? Up to this point, the sisters had not even met his parents. Yet soon they were regular visitors to the Gumbleton home—including while he was off to Vietnam three months later—helping distract them from their anxiety over the dangers inherent in his trip.[20]

Every Day Is Gift

When he lifts a glass in a toast with others, Tom's favorite phrase is "Happy New Year!" to express his conviction of each day's preciousness. He prefers not to celebrate his birthdays or anniversaries, and always tries to escape on his birthday as he finds all of the attention too much. One year he chose to travel to New York to visit a friend dying of cancer. Other years he scheduled international travel, Haiti, in 2010, shortly after the earthquake, and Vietnam, in 2013 for the fortieth anniversary of the Peace Treaty. In recent years he has escaped to Frankfort (where the family condo is, a wise investment made by his brother Jack) with his sister Irene and a friend. Even so, he enjoys remembering the special occasions of family and friends, and writes the birthday dates of many of them in the Calendar of the Saints in his breviary, a prayer book containing the liturgy of the hours. He reaches out to that person during that day. And, as his schedule allows, he happily attends celebrations for family and friends.

In sum, he is a private man who has good friends throughout the world, yet he hardly knows many of his neighbors. He is a self-described pacifist, yet fiercely competitive. He has received a litany of awards across five decades yet does not focus on his achievements or recognition. He is a peripatetic global traveler in solidarity with suffering people almost everywhere, it seems, yet finds great joy in being alone at home. Those who know him well might say that in a way part of his character evokes something of the Jesus described in the first chapter of Mark's Gospel, "Rising early before dawn, he left and went off to a deserted place, where he prayed."

Tom Gumbleton has nurtured and continues to cherish enduring friendships which often give him insight into life's joys and sorrows. The orbit of friends widened as he journeyed through life from his years with seminary buddies, Norm Thomas and Dan Walsh especially, to his relations with former parishioners and students at his first parish, St. Alphonsus, to his bonds with parishioners throughout the archdiocese he met while vicar for parishes, to his friendships and solidarity with so many people he met through his peace and justice ministry in Detroit, across the nation, and around the globe. Chancery work introduced him to Ken Untener and, together with Joe Imesch whom he knew from seminary days, the three became the best of friends. They often traveled on "mystery trips"—which each would take turns planning. Nancy Driscoll, Tom's longtime secretary who often worked with Ken Untener to organize the trips, recalled a November outing: "Ken sent out precise instructions to meet at St. Aloysius

Church next to the chancery at 3:27 p.m., to bring three days' worth of warm clothes—boots, jackets, gloves—and plan on a long ride 'with no complaining allowed.' The instructions were not followed, as Joe and Tom arrived late, didn't bring extra clothing, and complained. As for the 'long ride,' that turned out to be 20 minutes through the Windsor Tunnel into Canada. They stayed at a nearby hotel where they played cards, watched hockey, and played more cards (except for Tom who read!!)." One hilarious episode happened when Ken, while studying in Rome, sent Tom and Joe some cassette tapes. In one he sang. They requested he do anything but sing on future tapes. So, in the next tape he sent he started out counting "1, 2, 3..." and continued counting for the duration of the tape! Their friendship thrived on each one's delightful sense of humor.[21]

Fr. Gumbleton's first parish assignment, St. Alphonsus in Dearborn, as described in the third chapter, initiated him to pastoral ministry. To this day when the phone rings, it is not surprising for Tom to hear the voice of a 1950s St. Alphonsus parishioner. The members of one family mentioned in that chapter, the Hunts, have been cherished friends from his earliest days at the parish. He cried with them over their loss of their father. Reflecting on the years since then, Jan Hunt shared, "He has been a part of almost everything important in our lives. We rented this summer cottage in Wheatley, Ontario, for many, many, years, and Tom would come and visit when the family was there. Shortly after my sister Ann got married and discovered she was pregnant, she said to him as he got out of his car, 'Uncle Bishop, Uncle Bishop, you're gonna be an uncle!'"[22]

Serving as vicar for parishes introduced him to conflict situations between parishioners and pastors. Several of these difficult situations also evolved into enduring friendships. At St. Genevieve Parish in Livonia in the late 1970s, the pastor asked that a newly ordained priest, Fr. Joe Dailey, be appointed to his parish to help attract young people. But as Dailey began to connect with the people and began to implement the spirit of Vatican II, his presence threatened the pastor. As the regional bishop, Tom tried to help improve this situation. Cardinal Dearden also met with both priests. Despite efforts at conflict resolution, the situation grew unworkable and the young priest left the parish before a year passed.[23]

The pastor remained, and many parishioners, extremely frustrated with this outcome, wrote a letter to the whole parish informing them of their decision to leave and form what they called Spirit of Hope Community, a home church. They would attend various parishes on the weekends, but the members would direct their children's religious formation. Bishop Gumbleton agreed to come to one of their homes each month to celebrate Mass for the community and administer the sacraments. This continued for more than thirty years as he joined in their joys and sorrows.

Over the decades of travel for talks and workshops, he usually chose to stay with a family to save the local sponsors the expense of paying for a hotel. In doing this, he made new friends and often had repeat stays on future visits. Soon he would be invited to return for significant family celebrations. He seems to have a family in almost every town. Since 1986 he has set aside an afternoon and evening to get together with Mary and Bill Carry and Sue Sattler (co-author of this book) every four to six weeks to share friendship, prayer, and solidarity work. They begin with personal prayer reflecting on the Scriptures for the following Sunday and then share their reflections. Later they celebrate Mass and enjoy dinner. These friends began calling themselves "El Grupo" once they started traveling together to Nicaragua in 1986 and then to El Salvador on many delegations from 1987 to 2015.[24]

When close friends Joe Imesch and Ken Untener were named bishops of their own dioceses, Ordinaries (Joe in 1979 and Ken in 1980), Tom celebrated their new posts, and yet these appointments made it clear he would likely never become an Ordinary (as it were, some might say he was destined to become extraordinary!). Auxiliary Bishop Gumbleton since 1968, he was overdue to be appointed an Ordinary. Another friend, Bishop Peter Rosazza, asked Imesch why Tom had not become an Ordinary. "Joe said he had talked with Cardinal Ed Szoka, and asked him, 'Why don't you give Tom a diocese?' Szoka said, 'Don't you think I've tried? I do not know where the opposition came from, the papal nuncio, other prelates who did not want to see him become an Ordinary?'"[25]

Jesuit political scientist Thomas Reese has provided an apt explanation, when describing the priorities of Pope John Paul II who became pope ten years after Gumbleton was named Auxiliary Bishop.

It was very clear that he wanted loyalists. He wanted people who would never question Vatican teaching. Frankly, I think they were afraid if they appointed Tom a diocesan bishop it would give him a higher profile, a better position from which to express his views, and these views would not always be in sync with those of the Vatican. And as a result, as far as they were concerned, it had been a mistake to make him an auxiliary bishop and they were not going to compound the mistake by making him a diocesan bishop.[26]

Not being appointed an Ordinary was a difficult realization for him at first. He worked through this in the way he almost always handled difficult matters, with prayer. Yet in conversations with friends over the years Tom has affirmed that he is genuinely grateful he remained in Detroit as an Auxiliary for over fifty years. It allowed him to focus on his social justice ministry in ways that he never could have if he had the responsibilities of an Ordinary.[27] Longtime *NCR* journalist Tom Fox has confirmed this, observing of Gumbleton: "He never made a big thing about being a bishop. He always saw himself as a priest and as a witness."[28]

Celibacy

Many, but certainly not all, of Tom's closest friends are women. It would be a generalization to describe them all as strong, assertive women, but these are common characteristics of many. His formative years in a male, thoroughly clerical culture make it obvious that healthy, mutual friendships with women did not come readily. The seminary warned against becoming friends with women, in order to protect celibacy. Yet as Tom Gumbleton grew in confirmation of his call to a life of celibacy, he matured in an awareness of the importance of healthy, mutual friendships with women.

And he has consciously worked over the years to try to understand how clericalism and patriarchy have infected him and the Church, and he has endeavored to counteract these attitudes and behaviors in himself. True to his nature, he turned to prayer and introspection in order to become a relatively healthy celibate priest. At one point he arranged to make a directed retreat centering on Jesus and his friendships, especially with women. He prayed over several themes: Jesus' relationships with Martha, Mary, and Mary Magdalene, how Jesus was a friend to people, how Jesus became emotionally attached to people, was affectionate and had all the emotions we have. Tom's prayer life, together with probing conversations, misunderstandings, and sustained interactions with close female friends, helped him gradually foster mutual friendships, relational and affectionate.[29]

He has fully embraced celibacy for himself though he does not consider that it should be a precondition for the ordained priesthood. Michael Crosby, OFM Cap, who has written extensively on celibacy, has offered perspective on the essential aspects of a healthy celibate life. "Intimacy for the celibate involves three interrelated dynamics: de-centering oneself, centering on God as the 'other' through contemplation, and becoming centered on 'others' through compassion."[30] Such an understanding of celibacy is captured in a phrase attached to the top of Tom's iPad, "God is the strength of my heart."[31]

Spirituality

One might ask, how did the subject of *No Guilty Bystander* become someone of whom Tom Fox said, "the richness and the integrity of his personality, the humility of his ways, the quietness of his voice, just scream out at
you, it's an overwhelming human experience to be near him. He's got that
sort of sheepish smile. Even in his demeanor he is not gregarious, he's
more of a shy person, shy and humble."[32] Readers of this book are familiar
with some of ways that Tom Gumbleton altered his perceptions and then
took actions consistent with the new insights gained. He acknowledged his
obliviousness to racism in the segregated community of Dearborn where he
served after ordination. He entered into a transforming consciousness on
matters of war and peace, a true personal turning point, when he learned the
facts about the war in Vietnam and especially when he listened to the personal appeals of conscientious objectors. He accepted the just war theory
before he began to really examine its implications in a nuclear age. He became angry at first when his brother Dan revealed his homosexuality, but
then Tom underwent a genuine transformation and discovered a whole new
field of ministry—New Ways Ministry. Many other examples of how he
has been a transformed transformer have shaped the chapters of this book.

The urge to attend to the lessons from his experience and to shift his
perceptions and actions seems to constitute the core of his character. Prayer
has been a key to these transformations. His daily prayer regimen always
begins in the early morning when, with a cup of coffee, he prays for an
hour or two. Like Elijah, he has found God not in the wind, the earthquake
or fire, but in a quiet whisper (1 Kings 9:12). In addition, he prays the Divine Office (breviary) throughout the day, regardless of his travels. He also
prays twenty decades of the Rosary daily. Tom summarizes his approach
saying, "When your relationship with God is good, that is what matters."
His personal prayer dramatically altered after Vatican II when he began to
make directed retreats that opened him in a way he had not previously
known.

I came to *know* Jesus. I had always accepted readily, and almost
exclusively, the idea that Jesus is the Son of God, and I prayed to
Jesus as God. But during this time, I began to pray with Jesus.
Through the Scripture passages, I found a way to enter into the
humanness of Jesus, the Jesus who had doubts, the Jesus who
was afraid at times, the Jesus who was discouraged, the Jesus

who rejoiced and celebrated. So now when I pray, I can pray in union with Jesus, in communion with Jesus. As I experience discouragement or sadness at what is happening in my life, or struggle with the failures of the Church, it's all shared with Jesus, who experienced the same kind of things. I find that by continuing this type of prayer every day for a period of time, taking the Sunday Scriptures for that week and entering into them, discovering Jesus in them and bringing my situation into that prayer and then drawing from the experience of Jesus, I find myself grounded in the struggle to remain faithful to his gospel and his call to live that gospel. [33]

These words call to mind the spiritual master, Thomas Merton, who wrote "One's solitude belongs to the world and to God." Thomas Merton and Thomas Gumbleton (the first Tom having deeply inspired the formative spirituality of the second Tom) have been rooted in prayer which led them to follow the Gospel's call. Merton expressed his concern that "The greatest temptation that assails Christians is that in effect, for most of us, the Gospel has ceased to be news. And if it is not news, it is not Gospel." For both men the Gospel has been a Living Word.[34]

In fact, Scripture is the daily bread that has nourished Tom Gumbleton in his ministry. As people in need have sought him out, he has responded without judgment, entering into their trying situations with understanding, respect and empathy, trusting in God's work in their lives. The words of Isaiah 49:4 guide him. "The Lord Yahweh has taught me so I speak as his disciple and I know how to sustain the weary. Morning after morning he wakes me up to hear, to listen like a disciple." Each day of Tom's life has been an opportunity to do Jesus's work. "Jesus is in our midst to bring about the reign of God. Our task is to enter into the work of Jesus. It is not really our work; it is God's work."[35] Writer and friend Donald Spoto confirms this in observing of Tom, "It's impossible to find any of his speeches, interviews, or homilies that doesn't include an invitation to listen to Jesus, to respond, to follow, to be his emissaries in the world.[36] His impact on people can be poignant and powerful. Cindy Estrada, a labor organizer with the United Auto Workers, who got to know Bishop Gumbleton when she reached out for his support during a strike, described it this way: "It was not anything he said, it was his ability to listen and to be present. He gives the most amazing hugs, just pure love and comfort."[37] It might be said that Tom Gumbleton throughout his ministry has tried to live up to the aspirations recently voiced by Pope Francis in *Let Us Dream*, "Our greatest power is not in the respect that others have for us, but the service we can offer others."[38]

As a bishop, Tom found inspiration in the lives of several Latin American colleagues and theologians he saw as being "faced with the evil of oppressive and widespread poverty in their society. Once they began to hear the Gospel as a truly living word, they knew that it was necessary to make a 'preferential option for the poor.'"[39] He particularly looked to the writings of Fr. Gustavo Gutiérrez, OP, who called on the Church to live Jesus's message of liberation. "The challenge of liberation is to understand Jesus as God-made-flesh and then to ask how the church can be more like Jesus and incarnate itself in the world. No, not in the centers of power and wealth but in the peripheries that long to hear good news."[40] Many people see Bishop Gumbleton embodying this call to liberate. Activist Jean Stokan says he has "a laser-like focus on peace and justice issues, speaking truth, fearless in going after the issues. Yet he is gentle and soft-spoken. I would just notice him praying in a corner before a meeting. And he has a capacity to listen to the story of another person and to be transformed by it...to allow himself to be transformed, and to travel on an inner journey as well as many an outer journey."[41]

Of Late

The Covid-19 pandemic became manifest in the United States starting in March 2020, as no one can forget. This was about six weeks after Tom Gumbleton turned ninety years old. He headed to Frankfort with his sister Irene and a friend, spending long stretches of time there and returning to Detroit primarily for medical appointments. He kept up with emails and correspondence with the invaluable support of his assistants, especially Eileen Burns. Yet he was relieved to be away from interacting with people and to avoid exposing himself to the virus. In some ways, the pandemic favored an introvert. In Frankfort, he enjoyed his sister's cooking, especially her short-order-prepared breakfasts. Yet when back in Detroit, he adjusted easily to taking home, after dinner at a neighbor's each evening, the makings of a simple breakfast, a banana and piece of whole wheat bread. In the morning he added peanut butter and created a banana rollover for breakfast.

After being diagnosed with bladder cancer in 2019, he underwent quarterly surveillance procedures to monitor the potential progression of the cancer. In November 2020 he was diagnosed with a second type of bladder cancer requiring radiation and then quarterly CT scans. He dealt with all of this with equilibrium relying on his life-long approach to looking at problems through the lens of "*quid hoc ad aeternitatem*"—view this in the light of eternity.[42] Though not inclined to focus on diminishment and death, he did answer a question about these realities by simply saying, "I depend on one of the most fundamental teachings of Christianity, that new life comes through death. The resurrection of Jesus is really the model that we trust will happen for all of us, for the world, and even for the universe."[43]

17

Significance

I n their conversation about whether Gumbleton should accept the Vatican's appointment to be a bishop, Dearden told him, "Just be yourself." Encouraged by this simple advice, Gumbleton dedicated his episcopal ministry to working "to try to transform our world into as close an image of the reign of God as possible, which means that everyone has the opportunity to share in the gifts that God's given for all."[1] Determined to be a "Doer of the Word," he became a transformational leader, open to being continually transformed.

Even in his habits of solitude Thomas Gumbleton has drawn strength both for and from communal solidarity. The great twentieth-century mystic, Thomas Merton, famously described in *Conjectures of a Guilty Bystander* his overpowering realization that all are related. "At the corner of Fourth and Walnut, in the center of the shopping district, I was suddenly overwhelmed with the realization that I loved all those people, they were mine and I theirs, that we could not be alien to one another even though we were total strangers."[2] Thomas Gumbleton, in a similar spirit, conceived of his calling as a bishop differently from what seems to be the norm.

> As I began to try to visualize what my job as a bishop really was, it became clear that it was not in being some remote, powerful, authoritarian figure, but more like being a pastor in a parish, preaching and teaching the gospel and applying it to things that are happening today. As a bishop it seems that the responsibility is simply a bit broader, to speak to bigger audiences about larger issues, although they are essentially the same issues that should be handled in every parish.[3]

Standing for Peace

In May 1968, Thomas Gumbleton had his first opportunity to take an active role in the NCCB. In July that year Pope Paul VI issued *Humanae
Vitae*,[4] the encyclical which included teaching on contraception, steriliza-
tion, and abortion. The teaching on contraception in particular evoked intense controversy. Many bishops knew the encyclical was not being well-
received and wanted to put it within the broader context of their teaching
on other issues concerning human life. Conference President Archbishop
Dearden wanted to communicate with the public soon after its publication.
In consultation with the NCCB administrative committee and with the
help of Gumbleton, and also Ken Untener, Archbishop Dearden issued an
interim statement with the understanding that a document would be prepared for the country's bishops to review and act on at their November
1968 meeting. He appointed Bishop John Wright to chair a committee to
draft the document. Wright's committee met before and during the November assembly. Bishop Gumbleton was invited to present an amendment in which he advocated broadening the scope of life issues to include
war, also as a matter of conscience. His amendment was incorporated into
chapter 2, The Family of Nations, and the bishops approved and promulgated *Human Life in Our Day*.[5]
    Although the November 1968 NCCB encounter was his first, Gumble-
ton urged his colleagues to pass a resolution condemning the Vietnam War.
A number of bishops supported him, but he was unsuccessful in persuading
the majority. After all, the NCCB had previously issued statements supporting the war. He persisted, together with some others, and three years later
the Conference finally if belatedly declared, "Whatever good we hoped to
achieve in Vietnam has been surpassed by the evil we have done."[6]
    During his decades as an active member of the Conference arguably
the zenith of his influence in the episcopacy was his role in helping to
foster and shape *The Challenge of Peace: God's Promise and Our Response*. Detroit journalist Harry Cook wrote in May 1983, "Passage is a
personal triumph for the Most Rev. Thomas Gumbleton of Detroit, who
for years was a solitary voice among U.S. Catholic prelates for non-violence and pacifism.... After the vote late Tuesday afternoon, Bishop
Gumbleton smiled broadly as he was greeted with hearty handshakes and
embraces by some of the bishops who not so many years ago shunned
him as a radical."[7]
    The favorable attitude of his colleagues toward him did not last. The
selection and appointment of bishops affected their focus, as he later ob-

served. "Soon after John Paul II became pope...what got really sticky were questions about orthodoxy. Birth control became the number one issue. If a priest had spoken out against *Humanae Vitae* or expressed any doubt whatsoever, his name was not sent forward. The same on abortion, and more recently, on the role of women in the church. Anyone who has spoken out about women's ordination is immediately ruled out."[8] And Tom had spoken out on this issue early on. The Conference began to toe Pope John Paul II's line. "We have reverted to a church where bishops consider themselves delegates of the pope. The pope makes a decision, the bishop carries it out, he expects his priests to do the same thing, and it finally gets down to the lay people."[9]

Accompaniment

He nonetheless continued to press his colleagues to exercise their teaching authority on issues of peace and justice, and he proposed resolutions on a range of concerns, including U.S. policy in Iran, Afghanistan, and Iraq. His proposals were all too often rejected by a majority of his brother bishops. Tom Fox put the matter candidly: "The bishops' conference absolutely did not want to hear the matters Tom was bringing up. They much preferred that he would disappear and go away."[10] After many years Gumbleton stopped attending NCCB meetings, though he continued through his public statements, and perhaps even more so through his activism and ministry, to challenge the hierarchy to step up for justice and peace. Despite his frustration with the insular and rightward drift of the Conference, he remained a person of hope, as in Hebrews 11:1: "Now faith is the assurance of things hoped for, the conviction of things not seen."[11]

Gumbleton carried the Gospel of justice, peace, and reconciliation to the far reaches of the globe and into the streets and parishes of his native Detroit. Freed up from many of the management duties normally required of a bishop, he traveled to nearly thirty countries, some of them multiple times, to be with vulnerable people. "You can't know the situation of the poor and their suffering from the violence...unless you see some of it firsthand, experience it, and come to understand their life from their perspective. Otherwise, if there aren't people doing this, getting the firsthand experience and trying to share it with others, we will never be successful in changing those structures of violence that need to be changed, and ultimately that's the main goal."[12]

Back home he regularly spoke of the people he met on his trips. After one of his many visits to Iraq witnessing the painful impact of sanctions on civilians, he entreated President Clinton, "If you saw what we saw, you would be outraged. People just don't know that. Put yourself in their shoes. Imagine watching your child dying of hunger, or if there are not medical supplies to take care of your child, imagine if you were suffering that way, your outrage, your pain. If only we could put ourselves in their shoes."[13] On numerous occasions when he criticized U.S. foreign policy, he—as might be expected—provoked considerable public controversy. Cardinal Dearden, commenting on criticism of Gumbleton's trip to visit the hostages in Iran, said, "I think a careful line should be drawn between activities that are truly 'pastoral' and those that are clearly 'political.' The thrust of Bishop Gumbleton's effort, as was evident from his interviews after the visit to Iran, was consistently pastoral. We all have reason to be proud of what he accomplished."[14]

It was a diplomatically astute Gumbleton (and Dearden) who cast his trip to Tehran as a pastoral voyage, but in his ministry anywhere and everywhere he necessarily had to engage the realm of politics to the degree that it impacted issues of justice and peace he cared about so much. Archbishop Maida came to his defense a decade later, on an anti-war controversy, saying that although he and Gumbleton might not see things the same way, people should not fail to recognize the auxiliary's integrity.[15]

Despite amassing a legion of detractors, some of them quite vocal, there can be no doubt that Tom Gumbleton has had a positive impact on countless people. As noted in chapter 11, Colleen Kelly, whose brother died in the 9/11 attacks, wrote to Bishop Gumbleton urging him to advocate with the bishops to oppose retaliatory bombing. Later she shared how "it was this massive weight off my shoulders to know that there was this Catholic bishop who felt as strongly as I did about the fact that there was sure to be civilian harm in Afghanistan and who was worried about that and was willing to speak out against that. It was definitely a minority opinion, and it meant the world to me to have that support. It propped me up for what was to come."[16]

El Salvador's Oscar Chacón has described his perception of this bishop:

Tom belongs to a very exclusive group of human beings who have risen above the ordinary. How many bishops have really given a good percentage of their lives actively engaged in questioning why people around the world endure the consequences of what Archbishop Romero called institutional sin? By being willing to go into war zones he helped neutralize the chance for more massacres because he was willing to bring light to what the Salvadoran government was doing with the support of the U.S. government.[17]

Though he was never made an Ordinary (put in charge of a diocese), in the eyes of many he rose "above the ordinary" mode of a bishop. Daniel Tillas of Haiti urges: "We need more bishops like Bishop Gumbleton, who has the ears of so many people, to open their hearts, to try to push the elected officials in the U.S., to have a new way of relating to the people of Haiti, that the people are respected, that they have dignity, just as Bishop Gumbleton always tried to show the people on every single trip that he made to Haiti." He was a role model. "Gumbleton's humility was such a shock to me, we don't expect a bishop to be humble. We do not expect a bishop to be driven in a junk car. I remember how he would get out of the car and wait for me when the car gave us trouble. When I am old, if there is one person I would like to be, it is Bishop Gumbleton because of his humility and his care and knowledge."[18]

Bishop Gumbleton has been active in more than fifty organizations, coalitions, institutes, steering committees, commissions and more. He has shared his leadership skills within Catholic groups and actively engaged in interfaith advocacy. In December 1980, he joined Episcopal Bishop H. Coleman McGehee Jr. and Rabbi Richard Hertz to launch the Michigan Coalition for Human Rights in response to growing divisive elements in religion and politics and he continues to serve on its advisory board to help further MCHR's education and advocacy mission.

Justice in the World, promulgated by the Synod of Bishops in 1971, has long been a guide for his work, especially a key passage he often cites: "Action on behalf of justice and participation in the transformation of the world fully appear to us as a constitutive dimension of the preaching of the Gospel, or, in other words, of the Church's mission for the redemption of the human race and its liberation from every oppressive situation."[19] He interprets this as "not just saying things, not just reading about poverty. Do something. Get involved on behalf of justice and then get involved in the transformation of the world."[20] Jesuit moral theologian Richard McCormick, in discussing authority and power in the Catholic Church, could have been describing Gumbleton when he wrote, "True leadership therefore, if it would build on the example of Christ, does not control. It liberates."[21]

A Liberative Spirit

The liberative, reformative, and compassionate spirit of Vatican II has long undergirded Bishop Gumbleton's pastoral work. He has reached out to suffering and marginalized people, and although this has led to conflict with other bishops at times, he has not sought conflict. His focus: serving the people. Long-time peace advocate Marie Dennis has said of him: "He is one of the figures in the Catholic hierarchy that has given many people hope for a more just church, mostly in the years before Pope Francis was elected and since then as well. Throughout all of his ministry his compass was: how will this affect the people who are in the most difficult circumstance in a given situation?"[22]

He listened to the pain voiced by Barbara Blaine when she shared with him her story of sexual abuse. Soon he was meeting more survivors and attending meetings of the Survivors Network of those Abused by Priests (SNAP). As he listened to the experiences of the survivors, he began to advocate for them to have their day in court. He went to Ohio in 2006 to support extending the statute of limitations, for which he was sanctioned by Rome.

> I was doing nothing illegal, nothing contrary to Church law, I was trying to support people who were victims of abuse by church leaders, and I understand how it happened and I regret that it happened. But it still shows the different ways that the official Church responded to situations involving sex abuse, and I've continued to work ever since on behalf of survivors and will continue to work for survivors in any way I can, within the Church and within organizations that are trying to bring change within the Church. I continue to feel the sex abuse crisis is far from over. We have to do a lot more to bring about change within the Church, and I'm committed to continue to make that happen.[23]

Canon lawyer Thomas Doyle has captured the prophetic meaning of Gumbleton's stance:

> If a bishop stands up for what is right and has the courage to express his stand, he will quickly find himself cast out of the sacred club and into the real church with the rest of us. Tom Gumbleton, probably the only *real* bishop in the U.S., publicly has stood with victims. The Vatican acted quickly. He was fired on orders from the top because he 'broke *communio* with the bishops.' Bravo for Tom. He did what Jesus would have done.[24]

Bishop Gumbleton has reached out to others treated poorly by the Catholic Church. After learning that one of his brothers was gay, gradually Tom grew in consciousness and came to embrace the LGBTQ community. In a 1995 interview he described a folder he kept of letters from grateful gay Catholics and their relatives. A New Yorker had recently learned his daughter was gay and wrote, "I realized there was nothing I could say which would change her lifestyle and anger would only alienate her. My sincere thanks to you for helping. Jesus was not a legal technician, and you are not either. Jesus was full of compassion and so are you."[25]

A Genuine Leader

This is a Catholic bishop well known for his ministry to the victims of injustice and the most vulnerable. He first came to prominence speaking out against the war in Vietnam. He challenged the status quo, emphasized the primacy of conscience, and gave voice to legitimate dissent within church and nation. He moved deeply into nonviolence but never neglected justice. He resonated with the springtime of Vatican II but by the 1980s he was not alone in facing a long winter of discontent—the often cold, legalistic, and restrictive orthodoxy of the two papacies prior to Pope Francis.

Thinking about the archetypal notion of "the rise and fall" it is interesting to contrast the descending curve of Bishop Gumbleton's influence within the Roman Catholic hierarchy with the ascending and enduring curve of his authority with people in Latin America, with Pax Christi, with New Ways Ministry, with Kay Lasante and the people of Haiti, with Voices in the Wilderness, with so many conscientious objectors and with Franziska Jägerstätter, and in all the other journeys of accompaniment chronicled in this book. Ironically, his episcopal authority and influence as an agent of transformation in the church and the world grew because of his *way* of being a bishop. Simply by being himself he challenged the top-down authority model and the "trappings" prevalent in too many prelates. The political scientist Thomas Reese, SJ, has explained how the model of church embraced by bishops such as Gumbleton faced mounting opposition from bishops appointed by the two papacies prior to Francis: "That just goes directly against the model of the church... imposed by John Paul II after the Second Vatican Council. He saw the church in chaos after Vatican II, and he was going to restore order."[26]

John Carr, co-director of Georgetown's Initiative on Catholic Social Thought and Public Life, staffed the Conference of Bishops for a quarter century, coming to know bishops all over the nation. Of Bishop Gumbleton, Carr has commented:

He saw the world from the bottom up, from the most vulnerable. While he was a bishop which was a position of power, he never saw himself as a powerful person. He identified with people who were pushed to the side, who were left behind. And so that was the poor; that was the victims of violence; that was the survivors of sex abuse; and that was the LGBTQ community. So he always found himself in some ways on the outside with those who were kept on the margins. Tom was a Francis bishop before there was a Francis. And you can ask, who was more consequential, some of the "get along go along" guys or Tom, who did not get along and who did not go along?[27]

A few years ago, Tom Gumbleton was asked what he believed to be the three most valuable qualities for a bishop. He replied, "learning how to be a servant in a community of disciples of Jesus, which includes learning how to listen; developing a spirit of compassion by sharing the emotional burden of other people; and developing an intellect that keeps reading to learn what is going on in the world."[28]

In 2021 Pope Francis distributed a card to the Italian bishops entitled "The Beatitudes for Bishops":

Blessed is the bishop who makes poverty and sharing his lifestyle because with his witness he is building the kingdom of heaven.

Blessed is the bishop who does not fear to water his face with tears, so that in them can be mirrored the sorrows of the people, the labors [fatigue] of the priests, [and] who finds in the embrace of the one who suffers the consolation of God.

Blessed is the bishop who considers his ministry a service and not a power, making meekness his strength, giving to all the right of citizenship in his own heart, so as to inhabit the land promised to the meek.

Blessed is the bishop who does not close himself in the palaces of government, who does not become a bureaucrat more attentive to statistics than to faces, to procedures than to [people's] stories, who seeks to fight at the side of people for the dream of the justice of God because the Lord, encountered in the silence of daily prayer, will be his nourishment.

Blessed is the bishop who has a heart for the misery of the world, who does not fear dirtying his hands with the mud of the human soul in order to find there the gold of God, who is not scandalized by the sin and fragility of the other because he is conscious of his own misery, because the look of the Risen Crucified One will be for him the seal of infinite pardon.

Blessed is the bishop who wards off duplicity of heart, who avoids every ambiguous dynamic, who dreams good even in the midst of evil, because he will be able to enjoy the face of God, tracking it down in every puddle of the city of people.

Blessed is the bishop that works for peace, who accompanies the paths of reconciliation, who sows in the heart of the presbyterate the seed of communion, who accompanies a divided society on the pathway of reconciliation, who takes by hand every man and every woman of good will in order to build fraternity: God will recognize him as his son.

Blessed is the bishop who for the Gospel does not fear to go against the tide, making his face "hard" like that of Christ heading to Jerusalem, without letting himself be held back by misunderstandings and by obstacles because he knows that the Kingdom of God advances in contradiction to the world.[29]

Over the decades, Gumbleton grew in compassion, empathy, and courage, fighting for justice. He may have been in some ways more of a stream than a mighty river, yet let us not forget the competitive spirit described by his good friend Fr. Norm Thomas. "Gump" would eventually have to take off the hockey ice skates, but even in his nineties he still holds his own in debates on the issues that matter to him. The historical record makes a strong case that he is one of the most significant American Catholic leaders in the post-Vatican II church. He is certainly one of the most marginalized members of the hierarchy. Perhaps one key to his enduring significance can be found precisely in his marginalization. The higher powers of his church pushed this bishop to the margins of their logic of maintenance. Another kind of power, a logic of mission, called him to accompany individuals and communities who know all too well what it means to be marginalized.

Some of his many admirers view him as nothing short of a saint. Other people see him as a conscientious work in progress. Some of his critics have had plausible disagreements with him. Some detractors have just been mean-spirited. Whatever one might conclude about Bishop

Gumbleton and his legacy, the record illustrates that he has not been a guilty bystander.

Sr. Christine Schenk CSJ, advocate and writer, has noted that "Tom ministers to the rejected of this world. He loves his people and knows what it is to share their rejection. There can be no higher calling for a bishop."[30] Joan Chittister OSB, has described him as a special kind of leader. "There are leaders and there are leaders. Leadership is transforming, but sometimes you'll find a leader who is not just transforming but is transformed themselves. That's who he is to me. Is this mild, gentle, quiet man, a leader? *Yes*, he is."[31] He is an effective leader because he has led with courage and integrity derived from seeing the world through the eyes of others. Sr. Simone Campbell SSS, former executive director of NETWORK, the Catholic social justice lobby, has said that "Tom Gumbleton was never seduced by hierarchy, and at least to this day never stood on hierarchy, and I think that is part of the reason he does not like his birthday celebrated because that would get everyone focused on him. Tom, like Pope Francis, wants to be among the sheep. Francis says we have to smell like the sheep. That has been the way that Tom has ministered all these years, being one among."[32]

Here the metaphor of sheep is certainly not about timidity. Rather, it is about truly caring, it is about experiencing communion and sharing courage, being transformed together. One of Tom's steadfast companions on that long road to justice and peace, Erie, Pennsylvania's Benedictine Sr. Mary Lou Kownacki, spoke for many people when she said:

> He was the heartbeat. He was the most important presence, the official blessing of Pax Christi, and he was such a stalwart representative, and I just admire the man. He is courageous, loyal, you can count on him. You can trust him. He has no fear when it comes to peace and justice, on multiple levels, within the church and outside the church. You are going to have a hard time finding another bishop who matches his credentials as far as being imbued with the Gospel.[33]

Final Questions for the Road Ahead

In your heart of hearts, Bishop Gumbleton, what might you say to the readers of this book about your life and the issues you have cared about? What might you say that could help each reader to be inspired to work for justice and peace going forward?

Well, I just hope that somehow my life has been a living out of the Gospel, especially the Gospel of justice and peace, and that readers of this book might be inspired to try to follow the same path.

What would you say to people looking around at all the discord, the economic injustices, the wars, the climate crisis? Is there anything specifically you might wish to speak to at this moment about the social realities we are facing right now and which we may face in the future?

Well, I am convinced that absolutely the most important question is the overcoming of our constant use of violence to try to achieve our goals, politically and socially and so on. And that becomes much more apparent right now when President Putin reminds the world that he has nuclear weapons. It's the implied threat, he could use them. That's terrifying! And we have not made much progress in getting rid of nuclear weapons and getting rid of our determination to use them. This is clearly our (the United States) national policy, that we will use them when we have to. As Defense Secretary Caspar Weinberger said (in response to a question put to him by Gumbleton at the Pentagon, see chapter 7), "When we have to, we will use them." That is the most important threat facing our world right now.

As a person who has spent a lifetime calling for an end to war, what would you say about threats of aggression and the very real wars of aggression?

What about security and freedom, defense of the common good? Could there ever be a good reason to take up arms?

First of all you don't have to be a pacifist. It just takes common sense to see that to have nuclear weapons on submarines on hair-trigger alert, that's a crime in itself! And we do not have to take up arms. There are other ways to secure our defense. Nonviolence is capable of civilian-based defense (he recommends the work of the late Gene Sharp on all the methods of nonviolent civil defense), but you have to teach people. You have to prepare ahead of time. You can't just take a nation that is being attacked (such as Ukraine) and say, lay down your arms and be nonviolent. You've got to prepare for that, and that is what we refuse to do. We have those nuclear weapons, and we say, when we have to use them, we will use them, instead of preparing nonviolent defense. Civilian-based defense takes time, and it takes training, and you can't just do it by signing a decree of some sort.

Do you think that we in the United States still glorify in violence and war?

Absolutely, we have this commitment to use military means.

So, to really understand your vision and what you've tried to work for in this area of your wide-ranging ministry, especially during the time of the pastoral letter The Challenge of Peace *but also before that, with the Vietnam war, and ever since, one theme among many that's developed in your life has been your call to transform swords into plowshares, to transition from weaponry and war to nonviolent civil defense, correct?*

Yes, and preaching the Gospel at a military base, which is what we (the church) should be doing. Preaching the Gospel on nuclear submarines, but they won't let us. We have chaplains on those submarines, we have chaplains on military bases. If they were preaching the Gospel of Jesus they would not be allowed or they would not be paid for by the government, but we buy into the whole system by having our priests preaching the government's line rather than the line of Jesus.

Sometimes religious communities seem tempted to focus on simply being witness communities, not really trying to transform the social order as much as just trying to be true to their faith. What do you say about this, Bishop Gumbleton?

You have to do action for justice, you have to participate in the transformation of the world. You can't just do your personal thing. It's got to be societal. That's living the Gospel message.[1]

ACKNOWLEDGMENTS

We co-authors wish to express our gratitude to all whose knowledge, wisdom, and enthusiasm have contributed to the creation of this book. There is not enough space to mention every person by name here, but we are grateful to each one of you for your generosity of spirit.

Bishop Thomas Gumbleton: It is your inspiring life that has drawn us to this project. Thank you, Tom, for generously making yourself available for countless interviews and conversations.

Gumbleton's assistants: Eileen Burns, Nancy Driscoll, Juleen Henry, Rita Mary Olszewski, RSM (dec.), and Mary Beth Seymour, we are most grateful for your unstinting help and creativity in many crucial ways throughout the four years of this endeavor.

Gumbleton Family: Tom's sister Irene and nephews and nieces, thank you for sharing your deep love and special stories and insights regarding your brother, uncle, and great-uncle.

Interviewees: Thank you. Your years of friendship and ministry with Tom have helped to shape the narrative. Many of you are quoted in this book and are cited in the endnotes, and many more of you shared stories and other information we would have included had there been more space.

Staff at archives and libraries: You have offered indispensable research support. University of Notre Dame archivists Joseph Smith and Patrick Milhoan; Archdiocese of Detroit archivist Steve Wejrock; IHM archivist Jennifer Meacham and IHM librarian Anne Marie Murphy, IHM; Megan Judd of the National Catholic Reporter; Tony Gallucci, videographer; and staff at the Walter P. Reuther Library, Wayne State University. Thank you.

Readers of draft chapters: You have provided eagle-eyed clarification and timely encouragement. José Artiga, Johanna Berrigan, William and Mary Carry, Dennis Coday, Marie Dennis, Cathey DeSantis, CSJ, Joe Fahey, Jim Forest (dec.), Tom Fox, Jeannine Gramick, SL, Jerry Gumbleton, Rev. John Heagle, Tom Hinsberg (dec.), Michael Hovey, Colleen Kelly, Kathy Kelly, James Martin, SJ, Brian McNaught, Joseph Mulligan, SJ, Rev. Thomas Lumpkin, Rudy Simons, Therese Terns, Rev. Norm Thomas, Mary Lou VanAntwerp, Paul Wilkes, and Johnny Zokovitch. Thank you.

Our own families and friends (living and deceased): We are forever grateful for your love and support. Your spirits have encouraged and guided our steadfast commitment to this work.

Publisher: Robert Ellsberg, a superb editor with whom to work, we thank you and your team at Orbis Books.

NOTES

Abbreviations

AAD   Archives of the Archdiocese of Detroit
AUND, CGUM   Archives of the University of Notre Dame, Gumbleton Collection
NWM   New Ways Ministry
Nps   Newspapers.com
TBAPEC   Talks: The Bishop in the American Political and Economic Context
TJG   Thomas J. Gumbleton

Chapter 1: Personal Turning Point: America's War in Vietnam

1. Thomas J. Gumbleton, (hereafter abbreviated as TJG), from pp. 7–8 of "The Bishop in the American Political and Economic Context," June 1982, Gumbleton Collection (hereafter abbreviated as AUND, CGUM), box 45, folder title: Talks: The Bishop in the American Political and Economic Context (hereafter abbreviated as TBAPEC).

2. "Waist Deep in the Big Muddy" was written by Pete Seeger in 1967 and made famous when censored from The Smothers Brothers Comedy Hour.

3. TJG, personal interview, Portland, OR, Sept. 24–25, 2018, and follow-up phone interview, Frankfort, MI, May 9, 2020.

4. TJG, personal interview, Portland, OR, Sept. 24–25, 2018, and follow-up phone interview, Frankfort, Michigan, May 9, 2020.

5. Jim Wallis, ed., *Peacemakers: Christian Voices from the New Abolitionist Movement* (New York: Harper & Row, 1983), 29–30.

6. See "In Context: The Bishops and the War," *Origins*, Sept. 16, 1971, pp. 213–15.

7. "Bans Vietnam Talk in Pulpit," *National Catholic Reporter*, Oct. 12, 1966, p. 1.

8. "Lucey Praises, King Condemns Vietnam policy," *National Catholic Reporter*, April 12, 1967, pp. 1, 6.

9. TJG, from pp. 7–8 of "TBAPEC," June 1982, AUND, CGUM, box 45, folder title: Talks: TBAPEC.

10. TJG, from pp. 7–8 of "TBAPEC," June 1982, AUND, CGUM, box 45, folder title: Talks: TBAPEC.

11. Nancy Driscoll, personal interview, Dearborn, MI, Sept. 6, 2019.

12. TJG, correspondence, Nov. 13, 1974, AUND, CGUM, box 4, folder title: Need to Make Conscientious Decisions.

13. TJG, from pp. 7–8 of "TBAPEC," June 1982, AUND, CGUM, box 45, folder title: Talks: TBAPEC.

14. Thomas Lumpkin, personal interview, Dearborn, MI, Sept. 14, 2019. Correspondence between Lumpkin and Gumbleton, and between Gumbleton and Rembelski, shared by Lumpkin from personal files.

15. United Press International news release, "Draft Director May Quit If 'CO' Law Broadened," *The Press Democrat*, Nov. 23, 1970 (via Newspapers.com, hereafter abbreviated as Nps), 15.

16. TJG, "On the Morality of War," July 2, 1971. Digital archives, *The New York Times*, www.nytimes.com/1971/07/02/archives/on-the-morality-of-the-war.html.

17. Eleanor Blau, "U.S. Catholic Bishops Call for End to Indochina War," Nov. 20, 1971. Digital archives, *The New York Times*, www.nytimes.com/1971/11/20/archives/us-catholic-bishops-call-for-end-to-indochina-war-a-halt-with-no.html.

18. Michael Maidenberg, "Bishop Denounces War in Vietnam," *Detroit Free Press*, Dec. 6 , 1971 (via Nps), 21.

19. Correspondence. AUND, CGUM, box 24, folder title: Correspondence re: Phil Donahue Show.

20. Correspondence. AUND, CGUM, box 24, folder title: Correspondence re: Phil Donahue Show.

21. Correspondence. AUND, CGUM, box 24, folder title: Correspondence re: Phil Donahue Show.

22. TJG, "Courage in Abundance," in *Apostle of Peace: Essays in Honor of Daniel Berrigan*, ed. John Dear (Maryknoll, NY: Orbis Books, 1996), 33–35.

23. Hiley Ward, "Catholic Bishops Rap Birth Control Report," *Detroit Free Press*, April 14, 1972 (via Nps), 26; Ben Kaufman, "Bishops Fire Blast at Abortion, But Don't Renew War Stance," *The Cincinnati Enquirer* (via Nps), 14.

24. See Tom Fox, *Iraq: Military Victory, Moral Defeat* (Kansas City: Sheed & Ward [National Catholic Reporter Publishing], 1991), 21.

25. Eleanor Blau, "Catholic Bishops Ask End of Bombing in Vietnam," Nov. 17, 1972. Digital archives, *The New York Times*, www.nytimes.com/1972/11/17/archives/catholic-bishops-ask-end-of-bombing-in-vietnam.html.

26. Edward Rohrbach, "Bishops Clash on War, Amnesty," *Chicago Tribune*,

Nov. 15, 1972 (via Nps), 37; Glen Elsasser, "Nation's Bishops Urge Bomb End," *Chicago Tribune*, Nov. 17, 1972 (via Nps), 85.

27. TJG, "Bishop Reports on South Vietnam Visit," *National Catholic Reporter*, May 11, 1973.

28. Religion News Service, "Bishop Says Saigon Holds Many Political Prisoners," May 9, 1973 (copy of RNS release provided by the *National Catholic Reporter* in response to request by this book's authors).

29. Correspondence, AUND, CGUM, box 41, folder 5, folder title: Vietnam: Letter to the Vietnamese Government 1973–1977.

30. "Bp. Gumbleton Joins Protest of Viet Policy," *The Michigan Catholic*, Jan. 14, 1977, p. 3.

2: Competitive Gump

1. Irene Therese Gumbleton, personal interview, Clinton Township, MI, Sept. 7, 2019.

2. TJG, personal interview, Portland, OR, Sept. 24–25, 2018; personal interview, Detroit, MI, March 17, 2019; see also "Vocation to Justice" (an interview with Bishop Thomas J. Gumbleton) Education for Justice (via Educationforjustice.org), 2014.

3. TJG, personal interview, Portland, OR, Sept. 24–25, 2018. Irene Therese Gumbleton, personal interview, Clinton Township, MI, Sept. 7, 2019.

4. TJG, personal interview, Portland, OR, Sept. 24–25, 2018.

5. TJG, personal interview, Portland, OR, Sept. 24–25, 2018; personal interview, Clinton Township, MI, Sept. 7, 2019. Untitled article, *Detroit Free Press*, June 12, 1932 (via Nps), 7.

6. TJG, personal interview, Portland, OR, Sept. 24–25, 2018; personal interview. Detroit, MI, March 17, 2019.

7. TJG, personal interview, Portland, OR, Sept. 24–25, 2018.

8. TJG, personal interview, Detroit, MI, March 17, 2019.

9. TJG, personal interview, Detroit, MI, March 17, 2019. Irene Therese Gumbleton, IHM, personal interview, Clinton Township, MI, Sept. 7, 2019.

10. TJG, personal interview, Portland, OR, Sept. 24–25, 2018.

11. TJG, personal interview, Portland, OR, Sept. 24–25, 2018; personal interview. Detroit, MI, March 17, 2019.

12. TJG, personal interview, Portland, OR, Sept. 24–25, 2018.

13. TJG, personal interview, Portland, OR, Sept. 24–25, 2018; Irene Therese Gumbleton, IHM, personal interview, Clinton Township, MI, Sept. 7, 2019.

14. TJG, personal interview, Portland, OR, Sept. 24–25, 2018.

15. TJG, personal interview, Portland, OR, Sept. 24–25, 2018.

16. TJG, personal interview, Portland, OR, Sept. 24–25, 2018; personal interview. Detroit, MI, March 17, 2019.

17. TJG, personal interview, Portland, OR, Sept. 24–25, 2018.

18. Norm Thomas, personal interview. Dearborn, MI, Sept. 10, 2019.

19. TJG, personal interview, Detroit, MI, March 17, 2019.

20. Norm Thomas, personal interview, Dearborn, MI, Sept. 10, 2019.

Chapter 3: Doer of the Word

1. TJG, personal interview, Portland, OR, Sept. 24–25, 2018.

2. TJG, from pp. 7–8 of draft of chapter for a manuscript, March 1973, AUND, CGUM, box 16, folder title: Chapter on Bishop Gumbleton—Paul Wilkes Book.

3. TJG, personal interview, Portland, OR, Sept. 24–25, 2018.

4. TJG, personal interview, Dearborn, MI, Sept. 8, 2019.

5. Janet Hunt, personal interview, Dearborn, MI, Sept. 1, 2019.

6. Judy Beyersdorf, personal interview, Dearborn, MI, Sept. 4, 2019.

7. Carmen and Eugene Hrynewich, personal interview, Dearborn, MI, Sept. 15, 2019.

8. TJG, personal interview, Detroit, MI, March 17, 2019.

9. TJG, from p. 2–3 of "TBAPEC," June 1982, AUND, CGUM, box 45, folder title: Talks: TBAPEC.

10. See report of this in "Racism Charges Return to Dearborn," *New York Times* Jan. 5, 1997, https://www.nytimes.com/1997/01/05/us/racism-charges-return-to-dearborn.html.

11. TJG, from p. 3 of "TBAPEC," June 1982, AUND, CGUM, box 45, folder title: Talks: TBAPEC.

12. TJG, personal interview, Portland, OR, Sept. 24–25, 2018.

13. TJG, personal interview, on road trip between Erie, PA, and Detroit, MI, Sept. 19, 2019.

14. TJG, personal interview, on road trip between Erie, PA, and Detroit, MI, Sept. 19, 2019.

15. TJG, personal interview, Portland, OR, Sept. 24–25, 2018; TJG, *Separation and Divorce* (dissertation), 1964, Rome. Papers of Thomas Gumbleton, Gumbleton Office, Bagley Street, Detroit.

16. TJG, personal interview, Portland, OR, Sept. 24–25, 2018.

17. TJG, personal interview, Detroit, MI, March 17, 2019.

18. TJG, personal interview, Portland, OR, Sept. 24–25, 2018.

19. TJG, notes from a talk on the Inter-Parish Sharing Program, Feb. 1, 1965, AUND, CGUM, box 44, folder title: Talks: Archdiocesan Opportunity Program. Teacher's Institute, Univ. of Detroit.

20. Hiley Ward, "Catholics Eye 'Teams' for City Parishes," *Detroit Free Press,* July 17, 1965 (via Nps), 6.

21. Hiley Ward, "Catholics Eye 'Teams' For City Parishes," *Detroit Free Press,* July 17, 1965 (via Nps), 6.

22. Hiley Ward, "Pope's Synod: Part of Quest for Youthfulness," *Detroit Free Press,* Sept. 18, 1965 (via Nps), 7.

23. TJG, from p. 14–15 of draft of chapter for a manuscript, March 1973, AUND, CGUM, box 16, folder title: Chapter on Bishop Gumbleton—Paul Wilkes Book. See also Paul Wilkes, *These Priests Stay: The American Catholic Clergy in Crisis* (New York: Simon & Schuster, 1974).

24. TJG, personal interview, Portland, OR, Sept. 24–25, 2018.

25. TJG, personal interview, Portland, OR, Sept. 24–25, 2018.

26. Jerry, Pete, Tom, and Bill Gumbleton, group interview, Detroit, MI, Sept. 20, 2019.

27. Norm Thomas, personal interview, Dearborn, MI, Sept. 10, 2019.

28. TJG, personal interview, Portland, OR, Sept. 24–25, 2018.

29. Thomas, Norm. personal interview, Dearborn, MI, Sept. 10, 2019.

30. TJG, personal interview, Detroit, MI, March 17, 2019.

31. TJG, personal interview, Portland, OR, Sept. 24–25, 2018.

32. Norm Thomas, personal interview, Dearborn, MI, Sept. 10, 2019.

33. TJG, personal interview, Portland, OR, Sept. 24–25, 2018.

34. TJG, personal interview, Portland, OR, Sept. 24–25, 2018.

35. TJG, personal interview, Helena, MT, July 27, 2018.

36. Irene Therese Gumbleton, IHM, personal interview, Clinton Township, MI, Sept. 7, 2019.

Chapter 4: Call to Action in Church and World

1. TJG, AUND, CGUM, box 45, folder title: Talks, "The Bishop in the American Political and Economic Context," St. John's University, June 1982.

2. Justice in the World (Synod of Bishops, 1971); see David J. O'Brien and Thomas Shannon, eds., *Catholic Social Thought: The Documentary Heritage* (Maryknoll, NY: Orbis Books, 1992), 289.

3. TJG, AUND, CGUM, box 45, folder title: Talks, "The Bishop in the American Political and Economic Context," St. John's University, June 1982.

4. TJG, personal interview, Portland, OR, Sept. 24–25, 2018.

5. TJG, personal interview, on road trip between Erie, PA, and Detroit, MI, Sept. 19, 2019.

6. TJG, "Changing Values in the Community," Jan. 15, 1970, AUND, CGUM, box 44, folder title: Talks: Supermarket Institute Presidents Conference.

7. See various items related to Synod '69 implementation, including letter from Cardinal Dearden to Bishop Gumbleton (May 23, 1969), AUND, CGUM, box 13, folders: Synod Implementation Committee (early communication, priorities).

8. See set of pertinent documents, including the letter from Woodcock to Gumbleton (Dec. 1, 1970), AUND, CGUM, box 25, folder title: GM Strike.

9. See the July 13, 1972 letter from NAACP Alabama Field Director Rev. K. L. Buford, plus a copy of Gumbleton's July 4, 1972 address to the NAACP, in AUND, CGUM, box 17, folder title: NAACP Convention Talk.

10. Janet Hunt, personal interview, Dearborn, MI, Sept. 1, 2019.

11. See "Nuns Quit School in Race Dispute," *New York Times*, Feb. 14, 1971 (via www.nytimes.com/archives).

12. See a collection of correspondence as well as Gumbleton's own copy of the Farley Clinton series (from Oct. 1972), with Gumbleton's handwritten comments, AUND, CGUM, box 23, folder title: F. Clinton—Wanderer.

13. TJG, Keynote Address: General Chapter Meeting of the Adrian Dominicans, Adrian, MI, Aug. 12, 1974, AUND, CGUM, box 45, folder title: Talks: Priests, Three Talks.

14. See pertinent documents, including the text of the resolution, Nov. 10, 1972, in the Archives of the Archdiocese of Detroit (hereafter abbrev. AAD), Dearden Collection, box 8, folder 35.

15. TJG, personal interview, on road trip between Detroit, MI, and Erie, PA, Sept. 19, 2019.

16. Nick Lamberto, "Group Asks Public to Abstain from Meat 3 Days a Week," *The Des Moines Register*, June 2, 1974 (via Nps), 6.

17. Editorial department. "Meatless Days?" *Des Moines Tribune*, June 6, 1974 (via Nps), 22.

18. Art Toalston, "Bread for the World: Fighting Hunger with Pens and Typewriters," *Clarion-Ledger*, Sept. 12, 1981 (via Nps), 14.

19. "'Call to Action' Opens in Detroit," *The Michigan Catholic*, Oct. 22, 1976, p. 1.

20. John Dearden, Opening Address, Call to Action Conference, Detroit, MI, Oct. 21, 1976, AAD, Dearden Collection, box 40, folder 43.

21. Correspondence, Keating to Gumbleton, Oct. 29, 1976, AAD, Gumbleton Collection, box 1, folder 27.

22. Correspondence between Teipen and Gumbleton, Nov. 8, 1976, and Nov. 22, 1976, AAD, Gumbleton Collection, box 1, folder 27.

23. Correspondence, Gumbleton to Mrs. Jendrzyewski, Oct. 30, 1976, AUND, CGUM, box 40, folder title: General (Misc.) Correspondence, #1. See, in same archive folder, many other examples of correspondence between Gumbleton and critics of the conference (as well as supporters).

24. TJG, personal interview, on road trip between Detroit, MI, and Erie, PA, Sept. 19, 2019.

25. "America Hears: 'A Call to Action,'" *The Michigan Catholic*, Oct. 29, 1976, p. 1.

26. TJG, personal interview, on road trip between Erie, PA, and Detroit, MI, Sept. 19, 2019.

27. Correspondence, Dearden to Kelly, March 29, 1977, AAD, Dearden Collection, box 5, folder 15.

28. Correspondence between Baranyk and Gumbleton, May 16, 1980, and June 16, 1980, as well as May 16, 1980 letter from Baranyk to Dearden, AUND, CGUM, box 49, folder title: Correspondence, General 1979.

29. Correspondence between Murphy and Gumbleton, Dec. 21, 1979, and Feb. 18, 1980, AAD, Gumbleton Collection, box 4, folder 3. See also documents related to Big Business Day, in same folder.

Chapter 5: Pax Christi and Gospel Nonviolence

1. TJG, personal interview. Portland, OR, Sept. 24–25, 2018.

2. TJG, personal interview. Dearborn, MI, Sept. 8, 2019.

3. Gerard Vanderhaar, "A History Worth Celebrating," *Pax Christi USA* Spring/Summer 1992, 20th Anniversary Issue, pp. 4–5

4. Vanderhaar, "A History Worth Celebrating," 5–7.

5. See pertinent documents, including correspondence among several of the early organizers of Pax Christi USA, AUND, CGUM, box 28, folder title: Pax Christi, #3 and #4.

6. Gordon Zahn, "Carrying Our Weight in the Catholic Peace Movement," *America*, Sept. 20, 1975, AUND, CGUM, box 28, folder title: Pax Christi, #3.

7. See "Catholics Look at War," by Carrie LaBriola, *The Journal Herald*, Nov. 9, 1975 (via Nps), 10.

8. Vanderhaar, "A History Worth Celebrating," 7–8.

9. See pertinent documents, including letter from Mary Evelyn Jegen to Gumbleton, Dec. 2, 1975, and NC News Service report of Nov. 26, 1975 on Pax Christi/USA meeting in Dayton, OH, AUND, CGUM, box 22, folder title: Catholic Relief Services USCC.

10. See "Bicentennial America: Thou Shalt Not Overkill" and related documents from Pax Christi/USA, Jan. 1976, AUND, CGUM, box 28, folder title: Pax Christi, #3.

11. Correspondence from Dozier to Gumbleton, Oct. 26, 1976, AUND, CGUM, box 28, folder title: Pax Christi, #5.

12. TJG, "Christian Nonviolence," *Gamaliel* magazine, Winter 1976. AUND, CGUM, box 17, folder title: Article on Non-violence.

13. See AUND, CGUM, box 7, folder title: Vietnam Text. One of the best collections of Merton's writings on such matters was edited by William Shannon, *Thomas Merton, Passion for Peace: The Social Essays* (New York: Crossroad Publishing, 1986).

14. TJG, personal interview. Dearborn, MI, Sept. 8, 2019.

15. Correspondence between Dickman and Gumbleton, Dec. 11, 1978, and Dec. 18, 1978, AUND, CGUM, box 47, folder title: Nuclear Arms, 1980.

16. TJG, "A Change of Heart," March 1980, *The Worker,* AAD, Gumbleton Collection, box 4, folder 16.

17. Vanderhaar, "A History Worth Celebrating," 9-10.

18. "U.S. Catholic Bishops Agree to Support Salt II," *The Catholic Advance,* March 1, 1979 (via Nps), 3.

19. "SALT II Draws Qualified Religious Support" (Religious News Service), *The Pantagraph* 4 March 1979 (via Nps), 27.

20. "Bishop Blasts SALT II, Urges Disarmament," *The Dispatch,* April 6, 1979 (via Nps), 6.

21. TJG, personal interview, Portland, OR, Sept. 24–25, 2018.

22. Gregg Hoffmann, "Speaker Blasts Buildup of Nuclear Arms Race," *The Journal Times,* Aug. 6, 1981 (via Nps), 15.

Chapter 6: With the Hostages in Iran

1. TJG, "Bishop Thomas J. Gumbleton Remarks on the American Hostage Crisis in Iran" (TJG Remarks), Jan. 14, 1980, AAD, Gumbleton Collection, box 3, folder 14. This almost "real time" chronicle by Gumbleton has provided the narrative line of most of this chapter.

2. TJG, "TJG Remarks," Jan. 14, 1980, AAD, Gumbleton Collection, box 3, folder 14. See also regarding the Lawrence, KS, "Committee for American-Iranian Crisis Resolution" pertinent documents in AUND, CGUM, box 46, folder title: Iran Correspondence and Clippings re: visit 1979.

3. TJG, "TJG Remarks," Jan. 14, 1980.

4. TJG, "TJG Remarks," Jan. 14, 1980.

5. TJG, "TJG Remarks," Jan. 14, 1980.

6. TJG, "TJG Remarks," Jan. 14, 1980.

7. TJG, "TJG Remarks," Jan. 14, 1980.

8. TJG, "TJG Remarks," Jan. 14, 1980.

9. TJG, "TJG Remarks," Jan. 14, 1980.

10. Associated Press, "4 American Hostages Read Statements Critical of U.S.," *The Ithaca Journal,* Dec. 31, 1979 (via Nps), 12.

11. Kathryn Koob, correspondence with her family, Jan. 4, 1980, AUND, CGUM, box 46, folders 19 and 20: Iran Correspondence and Clippings.

12. Allen Harris, "Bishop Calls for U.S. Apology to Iran," *Pittsburgh Post-Gazette*, March 12, 1980 (via Nps), 17.

13. Richard Carreno, "Bishop Who Visited Iran Condemns Carter Sanctions," *The Boston Globe*, April 13, 1980 (via Nps), 17.

14. See "Bishop Gumbleton Fears Reprisal against Hostages" and "Imam Condemns the Violence," *Detroit Free Press*, April 26, 1980 (via Nps), 11.

15. Harry Cook, "Catholic Bishops Oppose any Show of Force in Iran," *Detroit Free Press*, May 2, 1980 (via Nps), 12.

16. Stephen Franklin, "Bishop Thomas Gumbleton on Shah's Death," *Detroit Free Press*, July 28, 1980 (via Nps), 1.

17. No author noted, "Michigan Sighs in Relief over Hostage Freedom," *Detroit Free Press*, Jan. 19, 1981 (via Nps), 1.

18. TJG, untitled piece, Feb. 8, 1981, AAD, Gumbleton Collection, box 3, folder 6.

Chapter 7: Taking Up *The Challenge of Peace*

1. Jim Castelli, *The Bishops and the Bomb: Waging Peace in a Nuclear Age* (Garden City, New York: Image Books, 1983), 17–18.

2. Correspondence between Bernardin and Gumbleton, Feb. 24, 1981, and March 3, 1981, AUND, CGUM, box 41, folder title: WPP: Committee Minutes, Notes, Correspondence, Sept.–Dec. 1981.

3. Castelli, *The Bishops and the Bomb*, 26–27.

4. See Gumbleton's notes, etc., July 28, 1981, AUND, CGUM, box 41, folder title: WPP: Committee Minutes, Notes, Correspondence.

5. See the "Faith and Disarmament" speech, in Frank Fromherz, *A Disarming Spirit: The Life of Archbishop Raymond Hunthausen* (Los Angeles: Marymount Institute Press/Tsehai Publishers, 2018), 4–9.

6. TJG, see piece (title unavailable) by James Shannon in *Star Tribune*, July 12, 1981 (via Nps), 13.

7. Correspondence—letter from Benedictines for Peace to Bernardin and ad hoc committee, letter to all the U.S. bishops, both sent in Oct. 1981, AUND, CGUM, box 44, folder title: WPP Correspondence re Unsolicited Responses 1981.

8. TJG, talk delivered at retreat in Santa Barbara, Aug. 1982, AUND, CGUM, box 45, folder title: Talks: Draft of Pastoral: Santa Barbara, Aug. 1982.

9. J. Bryan Hehir, phone interview, Boston, MA, Sept. 20, 2020.

10. TJG, phone interview, Frankfort, MI, May 23, 2020.

11. Robert Aldridge, background paper prepared for the NCCB ad hoc Committee on War and Peace, March 16, 1982, AUND, CGUM, box 41, folder title: WPP Committee Minutes, Notes, Correspondence, March–April 1982.

12. Gumbleton's handwritten notes of presentation by Casper Weinberger and to ad hoc committee, May 13, 1982, AUND, CGUM, box 41, folder title: WPP Committee Minutes, Notes, Correspondence, May–July 1982. Also from phone interview with Gumbleton, Sept. 10, 2021.

13. Correspondence between Gumbleton and Zahn, June 14, 1982, and June 23, 1982, AUND, CGUM, box 44, folder title: WPP Correspondence Re Unsolicited Responses, Jan–June 1982.

14. Correspondence between Zahn and Gumbleton, July 8, 1982, and July 29, 1982, AUND, CGUM, box 44, folder title: WPP Correspondence Re Unsolicited Responses, July–Oct. 1982.

15. Correspondence from Quinn to Bernardin, July 12, 1982, UND, CGUM, box 42, folder 15.

16. Correspondence from Hunthausen to Gumbleton, July 15, 1982, AUND, CGUM, box 42, folder 9.

17. See *The Challenge of Peace: God's Promise and Our Response: A Pastoral Letter on War and Peace*, National Conference of Catholic Bishops, May 3, 1983, paragraphs 172–73, citing from John Paul II "Message U.N. Special Session 1982."

18. Correspondence from Gumbleton to Hehir, Aug. 14, 1982, AUND, CGUM, box 43, folder title: WPP Committee Minutes, Notes, Correspondence, June–Oct. 1982.

19. Correspondence from Weinberger to Bernardin, Sept. 13, 1982, AUND, CGUM, box 44, folder title: WPP Correspondence from US Govt. Officials, June–Dec. 1982.

20. Correspondence from Benedictines for Peace Steering Committee members to Archbishop Bernardin, July 20, 1982, AUND, CGUM, box 42, folder 3.

21. Correspondence from Chittister and Kownacki to Gumbleton, Aug. 8, 1982, AUND, CGUM, box 42, folder 3.

22. Correspondence from Cooke to Bernardin, July 15, 1982, AUND, CGUM, box 42, folder 4.

23. William Ringle (Gannet News Service), "Deterrence Snags Bishops' Letter," *The Courier-News*, Nov. 18, 1982 (via Nps), 3.

24. Castelli, *The Bishops and the Bomb*, 105.

25. Castelli, *The Bishops and the Bomb*, 105.

26. Harry Cook, "Bishops Speak Out Strongly on War and Peace," *Detroit Free Press*, Nov. 21, 1982 (via Nps), 17.

27. Harry Cook, "Bishops Resist Softening Nuclear Stand," *Detroit Free Press*, Nov. 19, 1982 (via Nps), 58.

28. Kevin Phillips, "Mayer Undercuts Disarmament Cause" (syndicated column), *South Florida Sun Sentinel*, Dec. 13, 1982 (via Nps), 19.

29. See "Battle of the Bishops: Should Church Oppose Nuclear Arms?" interview with Philip Hannan and interview with Thomas Gumbleton, *U.S. News & World Report*, Dec. 1982, 47–48, AAD, Gumbleton Collection, box 4, folder 16.

30. See "Battle of the Bishops: Should Church Oppose Nuclear Arms?" interview with Philip Hannan and interview with Thomas Gumbleton. *U.S. News & World Report*, Dec. 1982, 47–48, AAD, Gumbleton Collection, box 4, folder 16.

31. Correspondence from Gumbleton to Hehir, Jan. 10, 1983, AUND, CGUM, box 43, folder title: WPP Committee Minutes, Notes, Correspondence, Jan. 1983.

32. Remarks of Archbishop John Roach at the Informal Consultation of Episcopal Conferences on War and Peace, at the Vatican, Jan. 18, 1983, AUND, CGUM, box 43, folder 7.

33. Remarks of Archbishop Joseph Bernardin at the Informal Consultation of Episcopal Conferences on War and Peace, at the Vatican, Jan. 18, 1983, AUND, CGUM, box 43, folder 7.

34. Jan Schotte, Report on Informal Consultation on Peace and Disarmament, Old Synod Hall, the Vatican, Jan. 18–19, 1983. AUND, CGUM, box 43, folder 7.

35. See the evidence summarized in chapter 7 of *A Disarming Spirit: The Life of Archbishop Raymond Hunthausen* (Los Angeles: Tsehai Publishers, 2019).

36. Correspondence from Clark to Bernardin, Jan. 15, 1983, AUND, CGUM, box 43, folder title: WPP Committee Minutes, Notes, Correspondence, Feb. 1983.

37. Confidential Memorandum from Cardinal Bernardin to Roach et al., Talks with Pope John Paul II, Cardinal Casaroli, and Cardinal Ratzinger, Feb. 3–4 1983, AUND, CGUM, box 43, folder 7.

38. LCWR—Region VII—Michigan Unit, Memo to Gumbleton re: "The Challenge of Peace: God's Promise and Our Response" (second draft), AUND, CGUM, box 43, folder title: WPP Committee Minutes, Notes, Correspondence, Feb. 1983.

39. Castelli, *The Bishops and the Bomb*, 151.

40. Associated Press, "Bishops Reviving Nuclear Dispute," found in *Lubbock Evening Journal*, AP story, April 15, 1983 (via Nps), 32.

41. See reference to NCR editorial in AP story by George Cornell, "Reaction Mixed to New Draft of Bishops' Letter," *Pensacola News Journal*, April 22, 1983 (via Nps), 36.

42. Correspondence from Link to Gumbleton, April 19, 1983, AUND, CGUM, box 43, folder title: WPP Correspondence.

43. Harry Cook, "Bishops' Peace Letter Will Be Basis of Sermons," *Detroit Free Press*, April 19, 1983 (via Nps), 13.

44. Harry Cook, "Bishops Toughen Wording of Anti-Nuke Letter," *Detroit Free Press*, May 3, 1983 (via Nps), 11.

45. Harry Cook, "U.S. Catholic Bishops Vote 238–9 to Condemn Nuclear Arms Race," *Detroit Free Press*, May 5, 1983 (via Nps), 36.

46. Harry Cook, "Collision of Clerics," *Detroit Free Press*, May 6, 1983 (via Nps), 1.

47. TJG, personal interview, Frankfort, MI, May 23, 2020.

Chapter 8: Moving Beyond *The Challenge of Peace*

1. Michael Novak, "The Church and Politics," *The Baltimore Sun*, Aug. 3, 1983 (via Nps), 11.

2. Walter Naedele, "Catholic Veterans Dispute Bishops," *The Philadelphia Inquirer*, Aug. 5, 1983 (via Nps), 19.

3. Editorial, "Protestors: The Court Shouldn't Try to Mandate a Matter of Conscience," *Detroit Free Press*, Sept. 1, 1983 (via Nps), 8.

4. Edsel Ammons and Thomas Gumbleton, letter to Thorburn, Aug. 29, 1983, AAD, Gumbleton Collection, box 5, folder 63.

5. Lona O'Connor, "5 Fasting Protesters Are Released from Jail," *Detroit Free Press*, July 17, 1984 (via Nps), 2.

6. For Immediate Release (statement by religious leaders), July 11, 1984, AAD, Gumbleton Collection, box 5, folder 63.

7. Correspondence between Bourgeois and Gumbleton, Aug. 16, 1984, and Sept. 17, 1984, AAD, Gumbleton Collection, box 2, folder 38.

8. William Simbro, "Activist Priest Adjusts to Role in Rural Parish," *The Des Moines Register*, Dec. 1, 1985 (via Nps), 19, 24.

9. United Press International, "Catholic Bishops Review Arms Deterrence Approval," *The Daily Review*, Jan. 31, 1986 (via Nps), 14.

10. Editorial, "Prelates Throw a Tantrum," *Arizona Republic*, Feb. 1, 1986 (via Nps), 24.

11. J. Bryan Hehir, phone interview, Boston, MA, Sept. 20, 2020.

12. Associated Press, "Bishop: Brethren Will Change Nuclear Stand," *El Paso Times*, June 27, 1986 (via Nps), 21; see also New York Times News Service, "Catholic Panel Again Studies Morality of Nuclear Strategy," *Daily Press*, May 5, 1986 (via Nps), 10.

13. Roddy Ray, "Anti-Nuclear Protesters Trespass at Air Base," *Detroit Free Press*, Aug. 7, 1986 (via Nps), 65.

14. Interview with Gumbleton by national staff of Pax Christi USA, "Bishop Thomas Gumbleton: Speak Truth with Love," *Pax Christi USA*, Winter 1986, pp. 16–17.

15. Vincent Wilmore and Alice Moynihan, "High-Profile Activists Add Voices to Rally," *Florida Today*, Jan. 17, 1987 (via Nps), 1; see also Laurin Sellers and Lynne Bumpus-Hooper, "Spock Tells Rally: Do More Than Before in Nuclear Protests," *The Orlando Sentinel*, Jan. 18, 1987 (via Nps), 8.

16. Larry King, "Pacifists at Cape Make Point—Peacefully," *Tampa Bay Times*, Jan. 18, 1987 (via Nps), 2.

17. Kimberly Lord, "Bishop Seeks End to Nuclear Arms Testing," *Press and Sun-Bulletin*, Feb. 27, 1987 (via Nps), 15.

18. Patricia Edmonds, "Paper Presses for FBI's File on Catholic Auxiliary Bishop," *Detroit Free Press*, Feb. 13, 1987 (via Nps), 1, 19.

19. Editorial, "The FBI Kneels at Altar of Politics," *The Miami News*, Feb. 16, 1987 (via Nps), 8.

20. See the Spring 1987 edition of the quarterly newsletter/magazine, *Pax Christi USA*, p. 3.

21. United Press International, "Auxiliary Bishop among Protesters Held at A-Test Site," *The Los Angeles Times*, May 6, 1987 (via Nps), 41.

22. See brief note in *The Catholic Advance*, May 14, 1987 (via Nps), 3.

23. Deborah Kaplan, "Crossing the Line: Each Protester Takes a Path of Conscience," *Detroit Free Press*, May 10, 1987 (via Nps), 105, 108.

24. Press release by Pax Christi USA and Nevada Desert Experience, "Catholic Bishops Arrested at Nevada Test Site," May 5, 1987. Papers of Suzanne Sattler, Detroit, MI.

25. Mary Jo Leddy, "The Church is Crossing the Line," *Pax Christi USA*, Summer 1987, pp. 4–6.

26. "Religious Leader: Nuclear Race Evil," *Lansing State Journal*, Nov. 22, 1987 (via Nps), 16.

27. No author indicated, "Bus Will Go to New York Peace Rally," *Lansing State Journal*, June 2, 1988 (via Nps), 20.

28. Mary Lou Kownacki, personal interview, Erie, Pennsylvania, Sept. 18, 2019.

29. Associated Press, "Catholic Bishops OK Nuclear Policy Report," *Victoria Advocate*, June 26, 1988 (via Nps), 12.

30. Gerard Powers, phone interview, Notre Dame University, South Bend, IN, Sept. 4, 2020.

31. Jingle Davis, "80 Activists Detained at Kings Bay," *The Atlanta Constitution*, May 7, 1989 (via Nps), 44.

32. See story marking the 6th anniversary of *The Challenge of Peace*, in *Pax Christi USA*, Summer 1989, pp. 24–25.

33. William Simbro, "Bishop Recalls 'Faith Journey' to 'Pacifism,'" *The Des Moines Register*, May 13, 1989 (via Nps), 12.

34. Patricia Chargot, "King Is Honored in Michigan, Across the Nation," *Detroit Free Press*, Jan. 16, 1990 (via Nps), 1, 12.

35. TJG, "International Citizens Congress in the Soviet Union," *Pax Christi USA*, Winter 1990, p. 25.

36. David Briggs, "Bishops Note a Just War May Be Means to Peace," *The News Journal*, Dec. 4, 1993 (via Nps), 21.

37. TJG, "Peace Pastoral and Structural Violence," *Pax Christi USA*, Summer 1993, p. 23.

38. Dorothy Vidulich, "'Peace' Now Not Quite Like It Was in '83" *National Catholic Reporter*, Jan. 7, 1994.

39. David Crumm, "Bishop's Fast against Nukes Takes Its Toll," *Detroit Free Press*, May 4, 1995 (via Nps), 17.

40. James Carroll, "US Position on Nuclear Arms Ironically Encourages Their Spread," *The Boston Globe*, May 9, 1995 (via Nps), 19.

41. Kathleen Laufenberg, "Bishop Visits Jailed Activist for Peace," *Tallahassee Democrat*, June 17, 1997 (via Nps), 23.

42. Correspondence from Gumbleton to Johnson, Dec. 18, 1997. Papers of Thomas Gumbleton, Gumbleton Office, Bagley Street, Detroit, MI.

43. Pax Christi USA press release, Oct. 9, 1997. Papers of Thomas Gumbleton, Gumbleton Office, Bagley Street, Detroit, MI.

44. Magdalene House Catholic Worker press release, July 29, 1998. Papers of Thomas Gumbleton, Gumbleton Office, Bagley Street, Detroit, MI.

45. Associated Press, "Activists Demand Access to Nuclear Weapons Arsenal," *Carlsbad Current-Argus*, March 27, 1998 (via Nps), 3.

46. TJG, "A Spiritual, Ethical, and Humanitarian Perspective on Nuclear Weapons," presentation to the NPT Preparatory Committee, April 28, 1998 Geneva, Switzerland. Papers of Thomas Gumbleton, Gumbleton Office, Bagley Street, Detroit, MI.

47. Pax Christi USA Bishops, "The Morality of Nuclear Deterrence: An Evaluation," Oct. 1998, Pax Christi USA.

48. TJG, phone interview, Detroit, MI, Feb. 19, 2021.

49. TJG, phone interview, Detroit, MI, March 26, 2021.

50. TJG, phone interview, Frankfort, MI, Oct. 16, 2020.

Chapter 9: My Brother Came Out

1. Brian McNaught, phone interview, Wilton Manor, FL, Jan. 11, 2021.

2. Jeannine Gramick, phone interview, Mt. Rainier, MD, Nov. 9, 2020.

3. Michael Graham, "Hunger Striker Out of Job," *Detroit Free Press*, Oct. 11, 1974 (via Nps), 4; see also Dignity Detroit history piece. Papers of Thomas Gumbleton, Gumbleton Office, Bagley Street, Detroit, MI.

4. Brian McNaught, phone interview, Wilton Manor, FL, Jan. 11, 2021.

5. Correspondence between Diederich and Gumbleton, Aug. 16, 1974, and Aug. 26, 1974; see also letter from Gumbleton and Imesch to McNaught, Oct. 1974. See also Letter from Cardinal Dearden to Priests of the Archdiocese, Aug. 20, 1974, AUND, CGUM, box 25, folder title: Homosexuality.

6. Letter from Paul Diederich et al. to Bishops Gumbleton and Imesch, Oct. 7, 1974, AUND, CGUM, box 25, folder title: Homosexuality.

7. Cronyn and others claimed that McNaught had not fulfilled his contract obligations, since during his hunger strike he was not at work—ergo, unexcused absence from work. But in fact McNaught had a doctor's office call daily to say that he was too weak to be at work. Nevertheless, the business manager, John Howell, told McNaught not to come to work on Monday. Brian later sued the paper for wrongful

discharge and settled out of court for $2,500. He had no money and no options at the time. The real reason for the firing: pressures on the archdiocese and its newspaper from all who saw the presence of an "out" gay person as a scandal for the Catholic Church.

8. Book of Memory and Thanksgiving: Celebrating the 25th Anniversary of the Foundation of New Ways Ministry in 1977. See narrative and chronology, by Francis DeBernardo, "Ministering in New Ways to Gay and Lesbian Catholics and the Church," NewWaysMinistry.org. (abbrev. hereafter as NWM.org).

9. Michael Hovey, phone interview, Detroit, MI, Oct. 27, 2020.

10. Pax Christi National Council, "Statement on Protection of Human Rights for Persons of Homosexual Orientation," adopted Aug. 15, 1986. *Pax Christi USA*, Winter 1986, p. 21.

11. TJG, "My Brother Dan: A Talk with Parents," address delivered at Villa Maria Retreat Center, Stamford, CT, Oct. 7, 1995 (via NWM.org).

12. TJG, "Parish-Based Ministry to Gay and Lesbian People and Persons with AIDS," address delivered at a New Ways Ministry Symposium, Chicago, IL, 28 March 1992.

13. TJG, "Parish-Based Ministry to Gay and Lesbian People and Persons with AIDS."

14. TJG. "Parish-Based Ministry to Gay and Lesbian People and Persons with AIDS."

15. TJG, "My Brother Dan: A Talk with Parents."

16. Robert McClory, "Bishops Buck Criticism, Attend Gay Symposium in Chicago," *National Catholic Reporter*, April 10, 1992. David Crum and Frank Bruni, "Gays Inspire Soul-searching," *Detroit Free Press,* April 11, 1992 (via Nps), front page story. Also by Crum and Bruni, "Revolution in Religion, for Faiths and Gays: A Painful Reckoning," *Detroit Free Press,* April 12, 1992 (via Nps), feature story; see also Associated Press, "Catholic Leaders Look at Gay Issues," *The Herald-Palladium,* March 30, 1992 (via Nps), 4.

17. TJG, phone interview, Detroit, MI, Dec. 18, 2020.

18. Correspondence between McNaught and Gumbleton, Oct. 24, 1991, Stonewall National Museum and Archives, Fort Lauderdale, FL. See Brian McNaught, *Now That I'm Out, What Do I Do? Thoughts on Living Deliberately* (New York: St. Martin's Press 1997), 171.

19. McNaught, *Now That I'm Out, What Do I Do?* 172–73.

20. McNaught, *Now That I'm Out, What Do I Do?* 174.

21. Andrew Sullivan, "'I'm Here': An Interview with Andrew Sullivan," *America*, May 8, 1993.

22. TJG, "A Call to Listen: The Church's Pastoral and Theological Response to Gays and Lesbians," in Patricia Beattie Jung et al., *Sexual Diversity and Catholicism: Toward the Development of Moral Theology* (Collegeville, MN: Liturgical Press, 2001). See also Andrew Sullivan, "'I'm Here.'"

23. Dawn Gibeau, "Gumbleton Hears Gay Stories, Some Angry," *National Catholic Reporter*, Nov. 11, 1994.

24. David Crumm, "Detroit's Gumbleton Honored by National Gay Catholic Group," *Detroit Free Press*, Nov. 15, 1995 (via Nps), 15. See also "Bishop Receives New Ways Award," *National Catholic Reporter*, Dec. 1, 1995.

25. Dan Gumbleton, interviewed by Tony Gallucci, Detroit, MI, July 2006.

26. TJG, "My Brother Dan: A Talk with Parents."

27. Correspondence from Bishop Thomas Gumbleton (with Bishops Charles Buswell, Mathew Clark, Thomas Costello, Joseph Delaney, John Fitzpatrick, William Hughes, Michael Kenny, Leroy Matthiesen, Peter Rosazza, John Snyder, Joseph Sullivan, Walter Sullivan, Kenneth Untener) to Joseph Cardinal Bernardin, July 14, 1993. Papers of Thomas Gumbleton, Gumbleton Office, Bagley Street, Detroit, MI.

28. Thomas Fox, *Sexuality and Catholicism* (New York: George Braziller, Inc. 1995), 148–49, including the quoted citation from the 1986 Vatican document, *Letter to the Bishops of the Catholic Church on the Pastoral Care of Homosexual Persons.*

29. Fox, *Sexuality and Catholicism*, 152–53,

30. Leslie Scanlon, "Catholics Split on Vatican's Document on Gay Rights," *The Courier-Journal*, Aug. 1, 1992 (via Nps), 1–3.

31. Peter Steinfels, "Bishops Protest Vatican Advisory Condoning Anti-Homosexual Bias," *New York Times*, Nov. 2, 1992, p. 11.

32. Correspondence from Bernardin to Gumbleton, Aug. 16, 1993. Papers of Thomas Gumbleton, Gumbleton Office, Bagley Street, Detroit, MI.

33. National Conference of Catholic Bishops, Committee on Marriage and Family. *Always Our Children: A Pastoral Message to Parents of Homosexual Children* 10 Sept. 1997 United States Catholic Conference.

34. Chuck Colbert, "The Conscience of a Gay Catholic," Dec. 22, 1997, *The Boston Globe* (via Nps), 21.

35. Reuters, "Bishop Commends Respect for Gays," *Detroit Free Press*, Aug. 7, 1999 (via Nps) 7.

36. Correspondence from Vaughn to Gumbleton, Aug. 12, 1999. Papers of Thomas Gumbleton, Gumbleton Office, Bagley Street, Detroit, MI.

37. Correspondence from Gumbleton to Vaughn, Aug. 30, 1999. Papers of Thomas Gumbleton, Gumbleton Office, Bagley Street, Detroit, MI.

38. Correspondence from Chaput to Gumbleton, Aug. 13, 1999. Papers of Thomas Gumbleton, Gumbleton Office, Bagley Street, Detroit, MI.

39. Correspondence from Chaput to Maida, Aug. 13, 1999. Papers of Thomas Gumbleton, Gumbleton Office, Bagley Street, Detroit, MI.

40. Correspondence from Gumbleton to Chaput, Aug. 30, 1999. Papers of Thomas Gumbleton, Gumbleton Office, Bagley Street, Detroit, MI.

41. See "Largest U.S. Catholic Statement Critical of the Vatican Is Published as American Bishops Meet," *National Catholic Reporter*, Nov. 19, 1999.

42. David Crumm, "Maida to Head Inquiry on Gays, Groups Influence Concerns Vatican," *Detroit Free Press*, June 20, 1992 (via Nps), 1. See also Fox, *Sexuality and Catholicism*, 156–57. See also "NCCB President Calls for Acceptance of Church Teaching on Homosexuality/Detroit's Cardinal Maida Reacts on Behalf of Vatican-Appointed Commission," July 13, 1999. Papers of Thomas Gumbleton, Gumbleton Office, Bagley Street, Detroit, MI.

43. Correspondence from Gumbleton to fellow members of NCCB, Aug. 6, 1999. Papers of Thomas Gumbleton, Gumbleton Office, Bagley Street, Detroit, MI.

44. See correspondence between Gumbleton and some colleagues, Aug./ Sept., 1999. Papers of Thomas Gumbleton, Gumbleton Office, Bagley Street, Detroit, MI.

45. David Crumm, "Gumbleton Backs Gay Ministry," *Detroit Free Press*, Nov. 16, 1999 (via Nps), 4.

46. Jeannine Gramick, Statement of May 25, 2000. See also other related documents and email correspondence from New Ways Ministry. Papers of Thomas Gumbleton, Gumbleton Office, Bagley Street, Detroit, MI.

47. Correspondence from Gumbleton to Sr. Rosemary Howarth, SSND, Aug. 26, 2000. Papers of Thomas Gumbleton, Gumbleton Office, Bagley Street, Detroit, MI.

48. Jeannine Gramick, phone interview, Mt. Rainer, MD, Nov. 9, 2020.

49. Chuck Colbert, "The Spectrum of Belief," *The Boston Globe*, 31 March 2002 (via Nps), 74.

50. Chuck Colbert, "Rome's No Doesn't Stop Mass at New Ways Conference," *National Catholic Reporter*, March 22, 2002, p. 3.

51. Correspondence from Re to Gumbleton, May 21, 2002. Papers of Thomas Gumbleton, Gumbleton Office, Bagley Street, Detroit, MI.

52. Correspondence from Gumbleton to NWM Board of Directors, Oct. 22, 2002. Papers of Thomas Gumbleton, Gumbleton Office, Bagley Street, Detroit, MI.

53. TJG, phone interview, Detroit, MI, Dec. 18, 2020.

54. David Crum and Patricia Montemurri, "3 Gays Are Refused Communion with Nation's Bishops," *Detroit Free Press*, Nov. 13, 2002, p. 5A.

55. Correspondence from Edwards to Gumbleton, Jan. 31, 2003. Papers of Thomas Gumbleton, Gumbleton Office, Bagley Street, Detroit, MI.

56. "Catholics Disagree on Proposal 2," *Detroit Free Press*, Oct. 29, 2004.

57. Correspondence from Gumbleton to Montalvo, Feb. 12, 2005. Papers of Thomas Gumbleton, Gumbleton Office, Bagley Street, Detroit, MI. Also TJG, personal interview, Detroit, MI, March 17, 2019.

58. Correspondence from Gumbleton to Niederauer, May 8, 2009. Papers of Thomas Gumbleton, Gumbleton Office, Bagley Street, Detroit, MI.

59. Email correspondence from Niederauer to Gumbleton, June 23, 2009. Papers of Thomas Gumbleton, Gumbleton Office, Bagley Street, Detroit, MI.

60. Patricia Montemurri, "Catholics Protest Archbishop's Gay Dictum," *Detroit Free Press*, May 3, 2013 (via Nps *Arizona Daily Star*), A20. Also personal interview with Linda Karle Nelson and Tom Nelson, Dearborn, MI, Sept. 12, 2019.

61. Patricia Montemurri, "Catholics Say Ruling Creates Conflicts," *Detroit Free Press*, June 27, 2015 (via Nps *Times-Herald*), A9.

62. Robert Shine, "Bishop Gumbleton: 'No Parent Should Ever Tell a Child That He or She Is Intrinsically Disordered'" (via NWM.org).

63. Brian McNaught, phone interview, Wilton Manor, FL, Jan. 11, 2021.

Chapter 10: Accompaniment and Solidarity in Central America

1. Carolyn Forché, *What You Have Heard Is True: A Memoir of Witness and Resistance* (New York: Penguin Press, 2019), 335.

2. TJG, personal interview, Portland, OR, Sept. 24–25, 2018.

3. TJG, personal interview, Dearborn, MI, March 20, 2019.

4. Forché, *What You Have Heard Is True,* 328.

5. TJG, personal interview, Dearborn, MI, March 20, 2019.

6. Michael S. Serrill, "A Nation at War with Itself," *ReVista: Harvard Review of Latin America*, Spring 2016.

7. TJG, personal correspondence, Dec. 18, 1980, AAD, Gumbleton Collection, box 3, folder 19.

8. Robert Lindsey, "A Flood of Refugees from El Salvador Tries to Get Legal Status," *New York Times*, July 4, 1983.

9. Eileen Purcell, phone interview, San Francisco, CA, Nov. 5, 2019.

10. Vic Compher and Betsy Morgan, *Going Home: Building Peace in El Salvador* (Lexington, KY: The Apex Press, 1991), 4.

11. Eileen Purcell, phone interview, San Francisco, CA, Nov. 5, 2019.

12. Robert McAfee Brown, "A Theological Reflection on Accompaniment," quoted in *A Call to Accompaniment: American Religious Response to Repopulation in El Salvador* (San Francisco, CA: Human Rights Desk, 1986).

13. Suzanne Sattler, personal journal, Detroit, MI, Dec. 1987.

14. Sattler, personal journal, Detroit, MI, Dec. 1987.

15. Sattler, personal journal, Detroit, MI, Dec. 1987.

16. William E. Alberts, "The Manger in Copapayo," unpublished article, Boston, MA, December 1987.

17. TJG, personal interview, Dearborn, MI, March 20, 2019.

18. William Carry, phone conversation, Aug. 8, 2020.

19. Kate DeSmet, "State Bishop Is Banned by El Salvador," *Detroit News*, Sept. 15, 1989.

20. Suzanne Sattler, personal journal, Detroit, MI, Nov. 1989.

21. Sattler, personal journal, Detroit, MI, Nov. 1989.

22. TJG, personal interview, Frankfort, MI, July 8, 2021.

23. Michael Betzold, "El Salvador Releases Gumbleton," *Detroit Free Press*, Nov. 1, 1989, 236.

24. Phil Anderson and Kirsten Helin, Memorandum to Paul Wee of The Lutheran World Federation, May 30, 1988.

25. Douglas Grant Mine, "Union Hall Bomb Blast Kills 10, Wounds 29 in El Salvador," *AP*, Oct. 31, 1989.

26. James Hodge and Linda Cooper, *Disturbing the Peace* (Maryknoll, NY: Orbis Books, 2004), 129–31.

27. Martha Doggett, "Justice Thirty Years in the Making," *Commonweal*, Nov. 2020, 16–17.

28. Hodge and Cooper, *Disturbing the Peace*, 132, 134, 146.

29. Martha Doggett, "Justice Thirty Years in the Making," *Commonweal*, Nov. 2020, 16.

30. John Dear, *Seeds of Non-Violence* (Baltimore: Fortkamp Publishing Company, 1992).

31. Jose Artiga, phone interview, San Francisco, CA, Nov. 5, 2019.

32. Jose Artiga, phone interview, San Francisco, CA, Nov. 5, 2019.

33. TJG, "U.S.-made Rockets Ravage a Tiny Village in El Salvador," *National Catholic Reporter*, March 23, 1990.

34. Hodge and Cooper, *Disturbing the Peace*, 142.

35. Jack Nelson-Pallmeyer, *School of Assassins* (Maryknoll, NY: Orbis Books, 1997), 7.

36. Eileen Purcell, phone interview, San Francisco, CA, Nov. 5, 2019.

37. Suzanne Sattler, personal journals. Detroit, MI.

38. Kate DeSmet, "Gumbleton Charges U.S. Lied about Nicaragua," *The Detroit News*, Dec. 11, 1986.

39. Correspondence between Bill O'Brien and Tom Gumbleton, Nov. 14, 1979, and Jan. 30, 1980, AAD, Gumbleton Collection, box 4, folder 19.

40. Edward Boland, *H. Amdt. 974 to H. R. 7355, 97th* Congress, Oct. 20, 1983, Congress.gov.

41. Stephen Kinzer, "U.S. Aid to the Contras: The Record Since 1981," *New York Times*, March 20, 1986, p. A8.

42. American Archive of Public Broadcasting, MacNeil-Lehrer NewsHour, March 4, 1986.

43. AAP, MacNeil-Lehrer NewsHour, March 4, 1986.

44. AAP, MacNeil-Lehrer NewsHour, March 4, 1986.

45. AAP, MacNeil-Lehrer NewsHour, March 4, 1986.

46. Hodge and Cooper, *Disturbing the Peace*, 108.

47. Thomas Ewald, "Bishop Gumbleton: 'I'm Not Alone' in Opposing Contra Aid," *The Michigan Catholic*, March 21, 1986, p. 15.

48. Joe Cortina, correspondence, Aug. 11, 1986, AAD, Gumbleton Collection, box 3, folder 38.

49. "Iran-Contra Report: Arms, Hostages and Contras: How a Secret Policy Unraveled," *New York Times*, Nov. 19, 1987.

50. Hodge and Cooper, *Disturbing the Peace*, 114.

51. "The Pardons; Bush Pardons 6 in Iran Affair, Aborting a Weinberger Trial; Prosecutor Assails 'Cover-up, '" *New York Times*, Dec. 25, 1992, p. A1.

52. Dianna Ortiz, *The Blindfold's Eye: My Journey from Torture to the Truth* (Maryknoll, NY: Orbis Books, 2002), 21.

53. Dianna Ortiz, "Notes from Talk at Auckland, NZ, Eucharistic Conference," April 2007.

54. Judith Weinraub, "Back from the Dead," *The Washington Post*, July 18 1995.

55. Ortiz, *The Blindfold's Eye*, 33.

56. Ortiz, *The Blindfold's Eye*, 33.

57. Weinraub, "Back from the Dead."

58. Ortiz, *The Blindfold's Eye*, 253.

59. Ortiz, *The Blindfold's Eye*, 231.

60. Ortiz, *The Blindfold's Eye*, 266.

61. Ortiz, *The Blindfold's Eye*, 270.

62. Ortiz, *The Blindfold's Eye*, 274.

63. Ortiz, *The Blindfold's Eye*, 270.

64. TJG, personal interview, Frankfort, MI, Sept. 28, 2020.

65. Hodge and Cooper, *Disturbing the Peace*, 158.

66. David Corn, "The Spy Who Shoved Me: The C.I.A. Got Revenge on Richard Nuccio for Telling Congress of Its Stonewalling," *The Nation* 264, no. 19 (May 19, 1997).

67. Ortiz, *The Blindfold's Eye*, 350, 379.

68. TJG, letter to Dianna Ortiz, April 2, 1996, personal correspondence in Papers of Thomas Gumbleton, Gumbleton Office, Bagley Street, Detroit, MI.

69. Patricia Zapor, "Bishop Hopes His Arrest Will Help Sister's Cause," *The Brooklyn Tablet*, May 11, 1996.

70. Ortiz, *The Blindfold's Eye*, 376–7, 386.

71. Jorge Banales, "US Victims Criticize IOB Report," UPI, July 1, 1996.

72. Dana Priest, "U.S. Instructed Latins in Executions, Torture," *The Washington Post*, Sept. 21, 1996.

73. Ortiz, *The Blindfold's Eye*, 440.

74. Hodge and Cooper, *Disturbing the Peace*, 179.

75. TJG, Letter to Office of Human Rights, May 16, 1996, personal correspondence in Papers of Thomas Gumbleton, Gumbleton Office, Bagley Street, Detroit, MI.

76. Ortiz, *The Blindfold's Eye*, 473.

77. Hodge and Cooper, *Disturbing the Peace*, 58.

78. Nelson-Pallmeyer, *School of Assassins*, 142-43.

79. Hodge and Cooper, *Disturbing the Peace*, 4, 143.

80. Hodge and Cooper, *Disturbing the Peace*, 184.

81. Hodge and Cooper, *Disturbing the Peace*, 187.

82. Louis Caldera, "No School for Scandal," *Washington Times*, July 27, 1999, A21.

83. TJG, response to letter sent by the Chaplain/Col. Weidner, Oct. 4, 2001, personal correspondence in Papers of Thomas Gumbleton, Gumbleton Office, Bagley Street, Detroit, MI.

84. Hodge and Cooper, *Disturbing the Peace*, 194.

85. TJG, letter of appeal of March 2001, personal correspondence in Papers of Thomas Gumbleton, Gumbleton Office, Bagley Street, Detroit, MI.

86. Nelson-Pallmeyer, *School of Assassins*, 104.

Chapter 11: Cries of Iraq, 9/11, and Afghanistan

1. Michael McManus, "On the Brink of War, Where Are the Voices of the Church?" *The Paducah Sun*, Sept. 28, 1990 (via Nps), 11.

2. "Pax Christi Statement on Iraq," Aug. 22, 1990, *Pax Christi USA*, Fall 1990, pp. 20–21.

3. Kate DeSmet, "Anti-War Stand: Gumbleton Says Catholics Should Object to Combat Duty in Middle East" (*The Detroit News*) as found via *Detroit Free Press*, Nov. 11, 1990 (via Nps), 1, 5.

4. David Crumm, "Bishops Admonish Bush," *Detroit Free Press*, Nov. 13, 1990 (via Nps), 1, 6.

5. David Crumm, "Bishops' Letter Urges Bush to be Cautious," *Detroit Free Press*, Nov. 16, 1990 (via Nps), 3.

6. Robert Musial, "Bishop, Families to Visit Iraq to Seek Release of Hostages," *Detroit Free Press*, Nov. 30, 1990 (via Nps), 1, 14.

7. Associated Press, "Selfridge Guard Unit Sends 12 to Mideast," *The Times Herald*, Dec. 7, 1990 (via Nps), 2. See also Jocelyne Zablit. "Families Party with Hostages," *Detroit Free Press*, Dec. 7, 1990 (via Nps) 1, 9.

8. Jocelyne Zablit, "Scores of U.S. Hostages Set Free," *Detroit Free Press*, Dec. 10, 1990 (via Nps). 1.

9. "Area Clergy Try Prayers of Solace," *Detroit Free Press*, Jan. 17, 1991 (via Nps), 9.

10. Rochelle Sharpe, "Religious Leaders Head War Protest" (Gannet News Service), *The Daily Journal*, Jan. 23, 1991 (via Nps), 4. See also "Non-Violent Action Opposing Persian Gulf War," Washington, DC, Jan. 22, 1991 (via C-SPAN videos).

11. TJG, personal interview, on road trip between Detroit, MI, and Erie, PA, Sept. 17, 2019.

12. See the letter from Ramsey Clark to the ambassadors and foreign ministers of each member of the UN Security Council and the UN General Assembly, Dec. 11, 2001. Papers of Thomas Gumbleton, Gumbleton Office, Bagley Street, Detroit, MI. See also Ramsey Clark, *The Fire This Time: U.S. War Crimes in the Gulf* (New York, International Action Center, 2005), a key reference for studying the 1991 Gulf War.

13. William Mitchell, "Gumbleton Participates in Offering Peace Plan," *Detroit Free Press,* Feb. 16, 1991 (via Nps), 5. See also Kate DeSmet (*The Detroit News*), "Maida Backs Gumbleton in Anti-War Controversy," found in *Detroit Free Press,* Feb. 17, 1991 (via Nps), 3.

14. Associated Press, "Religious Leaders United in Praying for Swift Peace," *The Times* (Munster, IN), Feb. 25, 1991 (via Nps), 2.

15. Maryanne George, "Peace Activists Say Body Counts Will Sway Opinion," *Detroit Free Press,* Feb. 25, 1991 (via Nps), 7.

16. Rick Barret, "Bishop Pleads for Peace," *The Times Herald,* Feb. 27, 1991 (via Nps), 1.

17. TJG, personal interview, on road trip between Detroit, MI, and Erie, PA, Sept. 17, 2019.

18. Lynn Dickey, letter to the editor, "Sanctions Kill Half a Million Kids," *Caspar Star-Tribune,* Nov. 10, 1997 (via Nps), 9.

19. TJG, letter to McCarrick, Oct. 2, 1997. Papers of Thomas Gumbleton, Gumbleton Office, Bagley Street, Detroit, MI.

20. Patricia Lefevere, "Iraq, Global Solidarity Debated by Bishops," *National Catholic Reporter*, Nov. 21, 1997.

21. Lefevere, "Iraq, Global Solidarity Debated by Bishops."

22. Glen Elsasser (*Chicago Tribune*), "Bishops Fast to Draw Attention to Iraq," *Detroit Free Press,* Jan. 21, 1998 (via Nps), 7. See also from Associated Press, "54 U.S. Bishops Urge Clinton to Work for End to Iraq Embargo," *The Los Angeles Times,* Jan. 21, 1998 (via Nps), 4.

23. TJG, "54 Catholic Bishops Delivering their Letter to President Clinton Today," statement at press conference, Jan. 20, 1998, Washington, DC (via C-SPAN videos).

24. Connie Nogan, "Bishop: End Iraq Embargo," *Press and Sun-Bulletin,* Feb. 4, 1998 (via Nps), 9.

25. Richard Black, "Catholic Leader Disapproves of Iraq Sanctions; Detroit Bishop Speaks at CU," *The Ithaca Journal,* Feb. 5, 1998 (via Nps), 2.

26. TJG, Statement on Archdiocese of Detroit letterhead. No date indicated, but evidently prepared shortly before the Feb. 12, 1988 action at the White House. Papers of Thomas Gumbleton, Gumbleton Office, Bagley Street, Detroit, MI.

27. Mark Pattison, "Bishop and 25 Others Arrested in Protests," *The Catholic Free Press,* Feb. 20, 1998.

28. "Across The Nation: Humanitarians to Deliver Medical Supplies to Iraq," *Detroit Free Press,* May 8, 1998 (via Nps), 4.

29. Associated Press, "Ex-US Attorney, Bishop Rap Iraq Sanctions," *The Boston Globe,* May 10, 1988 (via Nps), 12. See also "Initial Report about the National Planning Conference on Iraq," New York City, March 21, 1998. Papers of Thomas Gumbleton, Gumbleton Office, Bagley Street, Detroit, MI.

30. David Bruce, "Bishop Calls for Change," *The Michigan Catholic,* Nov. 13, 1998, 5, p. 18.

31. TJG, handwritten notes, inside of file folder, on May 1998 trip to Iraq. Papers of Thomas Gumbleton, Gumbleton Office, Bagley Street, Detroit, MI.

32. TJG, homily delivered at St. Leo's, Sept. 16, 2001, Detroit, MI. Papers of Thomas Gumbleton, Gumbleton Office, Bagley Street, Detroit, MI.

33. Arthur Jones, "'We Have Built up This Anger,' Bishop Says," *National Catholic Reporter,* Sept. 28, 2001, p. 8.

34. Associated Press, "Catholic Bishops Review Position on War," *The Baltimore Sun,* Nov. 13, 2001 (via Nps), 91.

35. Rachel Zoll, "Roman Catholic Bishops Back U.S. War," *The Philadelphia Inquirer,* Nov. 16, 2001 (via Nps), 3. See also "Speaking Out on the Manhunt," *Detroit Free Press,* Nov. 16, 2001 (via Nps), 4. See also Patricia Rice, "Catholic Bishops Cautiously Back Afghan War," *St. Louis Post-Dispatch,* Nov. 16, 2001 (via Nps), 10.

36. Gustav Niebuhr, "A Nation Challenged: Peace Activists; Groups Plan Vigils and Rallies to Urge Alternatives to War," Oct. 5, 2001, Digital Archives, *The New York Times,* www.nytimes.com/2001/10/05/us/nation-challenged-peace-activists-groups-plan-vigils-rallies-urge-alternatives.html.

37. Colleen Kelly, letter to Bishop Gumbleton, Nov. 10, 2001, personal records of Colleen Kelly.

38. TJG, phone interview, Frankfort, MI, Dec. 4, 2020.

39. Jean Stokan, phone interview, Washington, DC, Nov. 16, 2020.

40. Colleen Kelly, phone interview, Bronx, NY, Dec. 3, 2020.

41. TJG, "Living Nonviolence in Today's Reality," keynote address at Pax Christi USA National Assembly, 26–28, 2002, University of Detroit-Mercy. Papers of Thomas Gumbleton, Gumbleton Office, Bagley Street, Detroit, MI.

42. TJG, "Living Nonviolence in Today's Reality." See also the Iraq Peace Pledge, a project of the Campaign of Conscience, with national sponsors including not only Pax Christi USA but also the American Friends Service Committee, Fellowship of Reconciliation, Voices in the Wilderness, the Episcopal Peace Fellowship, and others. Papers of Thomas Gumbleton, Gumbleton Office, Bagley Street, Detroit, MI.

43. Marie Dennis, "Afghanistan: A Fragile Peace or a Precipice," June 2002 (email correspondence with Fromherz, Feb. 9, 2021; a version of the article was published in the August 2002 issue of *Maryknoll Magazine.*

44. Marie Dennis, email correspondence with Fromherz, Feb. 9, 2021.

45. TJG, personal interview, on road trip between Detroit, MI, and Erie, PA, Sept. 17, 2019.

46. TJG, Christmas 2002 Card. Papers of Suzanne Sattler, Sattler office, Detroit, MI.

47. Michael Paulson, "Law Leads US bishops' Discussion on Iraq," *The Boston Globe,* Nov. 13, 2002 (via Nps), 1, 12.

48. Robert Delaney, "Bp. Gumbleton Is Key Force as Bishops Adopt Anti-War Stance," *The Michigan Catholic,* Nov. 22, 2002, p. 9.

49. Gerard (Jerry) Powers, phone interview, Notre Dame, South Bend, IN, Sept. 4, 2020.

50. Colleen Kelly, phone interview, Bronx, NY, Dec. 3, 2020.

51. Frank Provenzano, "Here and Around the Globe, a Plea for Peace," *Detroit Free Press,* Feb. 15, 2003 (via Nps), 1.

52. Abayomi Asikiwe, "Thousands March in Detroit against War on Iraq," Pan-African Research and Documentation Center, Wayne State University, Feb. 16, 2003. Papers of Thomas Gumbleton, Gumbleton Office, Bagley Street, Detroit, MI.

53. Erik Schwartz, "Bishop Says War Will Incite More Hatred," *Courier-Post,* March 24, 2003 (via Nps), 4.

54. Associated Press, "Daniel Ellsberg, Two Peace Laureates Arrested in Protests," *Sioux City Journal,* March 27, 2003 (via Nps), 28.

55. TJG, Address for National Press Club panel, A.N.S.W.E.R Coalition, Sept.3, 2003. Papers of Suzanne Sattler, Sattler office, Detroit, MI.

56. See C-SPAN video, "U.S. Policy toward Iraq," Sept. 3, 2003 National Press Club, Washington, DC.

57. Tina Lam, "Activist Bishop Heads to Iraq for Information," *Detroit Free Press,* Jan. 12, 2004 (via Nps), 12.

58. Robert Delaney, "Iraqis Still Suffering, Says Bp. Gumbleton," *The Michigan Catholic,* Jan. 30, 2004, pp. 1, 18.

59. TJG, "Journey to Iraq" (based on his Jan. 25, 2004 homily), *National Catholic Reporter,* Feb. 13, 2004, p. 11.

60. TJG, personal interview, on road trip between Detroit, MI, and Erie, PA, Sept. 17, 2019.

61. TJG, phone interview, Detroit, MI, Feb. 19, 2021.

Chapter 12: With the People of Haiti

1. Bill Quigley, "Haiti Human Rights Report" 2005. Papers of Thomas Gumbleton, Gumbleton Office, Bagley Street. Detroit, MI. See also "Haiti: A History of Exploitation" (by Thomas Gumbleton, synopsized from many sources), Feb. 2011. Papers of Thomas Gumbleton, Gumbleton Office, Bagley Street. Detroit, MI.

2. No author noted. "Haiti's Moment of Victory," *Pax Christi USA,* Winter 1991, p. 27.

3. Marie Dennis Grosso and Rose Gallager, SNJM, "The Rooster Crows a New Day: Free and Fair Elections in Haiti," *Pax Christi USA,* Spring 1991, pp. 12–14.

4. No author noted. See very brief pieces in *Pax Christi USA,* Summer 1991, pp. 28–29.

5. Kate DeSmet, "Aristide: Exiled by Beliefs," *The Detroit News* (found via *Detroit Free Press*), Nov. 29, 1992 (via Nps), 137, 140.

6. Morris Thompson, "An Unyielding Vision," *Detroit Free Press,* Dec. 4, 1992 (via Nps), 14.

7. Brenda Gilchrist, "Haitians in U.S. and at Home Cry Out for Help," *Detroit Free Press*, March 11, 1993 (via Nps), 18.

8. Susan Baer, "Aristide Called Psychopath, Savior of Hope," *The Baltimore Sun*, Oct. 21, 1993 (via Nps), 1.

9. TJG, "Deadly Contrast Divides Haitian Catholics," *National Catholic Reporter*, Oct. 29, 1993.

10. Mary Lou Kownacki and Mary Miller, phone interview, Erie, Pennsylvania, July 15, 2021.

11. Mary Lou Kownacki and Mary Miller, phone interview, Erie, Pennsylvania, July 15, 2021.

12. Associated Press, "Mass Marks Haiti Coup Anniversary," *Hartford Courant*, Oct. 1, 1993 (via Nps), 20.

13. Joan Connell, "Murder of Haitian Priest Breaks Taboo" (New York Times Syndicate), *Casper Star-Tribune*, Sept. 2, 1994 (via Nps), 10.

14. Pierre-Yves Glass (Associated Press), "Haitians Urged to Sue," *The Atlanta Constitution*, Dec. 14, 1994 (via Nps), 12.

15. TJG, phone interview, Detroit, MI, July 30, 2021.

16. TJG, personal interview, on road trip between Detroit, MI, and Erie, PA, Sept. 17, 2019.

17. TJG, "Statement about the Coup in Haiti," June 24, 2004. Papers of Thomas Gumbleton, Gumbleton Office, Bagley Street. Detroit, MI.

18. See "Pax Christi Haiti Task Force Takes Part in Humanitarian Delegation to Haiti," *The Catholic Peace Voice*, Nov/Dec 2004. Papers of Thomas Gumbleton, Gumbleton Office, Bagley Street. Detroit, MI.

19. Robert Delaney, "Bp. Gumbleton: Human Rights under Attack in Haiti," *The Michigan Catholic*, Dec. 3, 2004. Papers of Thomas Gumbleton, Gumbleton Office, Bagley Street. Detroit, MI.

20. TJG, "The Peace Pulpit," *National Catholic Reporter* (via NCRonline.org), Aug. 28, 2005.

21. Based on journal notes from Suzanne Sattler, who accompanied Gumbleton on trip to Rome in early March 2006.

22. Claire Schaeffer-Duffy, "Haitian Priest Released from Prison: Whisked to Miami for Treatment," *National Catholic Reporter*, Feb. 10, 2006, 8.

23. TJG, "The Peace Pulpit," *National Catholic Reporter* (via NCRonline.org), Feb. 18, 2010.

24. TJG, "The Peace Pulpit," *National Catholic Reporter* (via NCRonline.org), May 20, 2010.

25. TJG, "The Peace Pulpit," *National Catholic Reporter* (via NCRonline.org), June 24, 2010.

26. Daniel Tillas and Johanna Berrigan, Zoom conversation, Orlando, FL, and Philadelphia, PA, July 7, 2021.

27. Daniel Tillas and Johanna Berrigan, Zoom conversation, Orlando, FL, and Philadelphia, PA, July 7, 2021.

28. Johanna Berrigan, "A Transformative Journey," Berrigan personal papers, from Spring 2017.

29. Daniel Tillas and Johanna Berrigan, Zoom conversation, Orlando, FL, and Philadelphia, PA, Aug. 23, 2021.

30. Daniel Tillas and Johanna Berrigan, Zoom conversation, Orlando, FL, and Philadelphia, PA, Aug. 23, 2021.

31. Daniel Tillas and Johanna Berrigan, Zoom conversation, Orlando, FL, and Philadelphia, PA, July 7, 2021.

Chapter 13: Two Graces in a Small Village

1. Roger Bergman, *Preventing Unjust War: A Catholic Argument for Selective Conscientious Objection* (Eugene, OR: Cascade Books, 2020), 19.

2. TJG, personal interview, Detroit, MI, March 17, 2019.

3. Molly Fumia, personal recollections in May 2021, prepared as information for this chapter.

4. TJG, homily, St. Radegund, Austria, Aug. 9, 1985. Papers of Thomas Gumbleton, Gumbleton Office, Bagley Street, Detroit, MI.

5. Tom Roberts, "'A Man for the World,'" *National Catholic Reporter*, Nov. 9, 2007, 12.

6. Roberts, "'A Man for the World,'" 12.

7. TJG, "The Peace Pulpit, The Feast Day of Franz Jägerstätter," *National Catholic Reporter,* June 17, 2010 (via www.ncronline.org).

8. TJG, "The Peace Pulpit, The Feast Day of Franz Jägerstätter."

9. Donald Moore, "Franz "Jägerstätter and the Dilemma of the Austrian Church," *America*, Oct. 11, 1986, pp. 187–90. See the works of Erna Putz, especially *Franz Jägerstätter: Letters and Writings From Prison* (Maryknoll, NY: Orbis Books, 2009). Michael Hovey, who worked closely with Zahn for many years, has noted that Zahn certainly knew there were other people who objected and acted in conscience

against the Nazis, but Zahn ascertained that Franz was a "solitary witness" in the town of St. Radegund and received no support from Catholic Church authorities.

10. TJG, "The Peace Pulpit, Twenty-ninth Sunday in Ordinary Time," *National Catholic Reporter*, Oct. 25, 2007 (via www.ncronline.org).

11. Gordon Zahn, "Martyr Remembered," *Pax Christi USA*, Fall 1987, p. 9.

12. TJG, address at public commemoration of what would have been the 80th birthday of Franz Jägerstätter, Linz, Austria, May 20, 1987. Papers of Thomas Gumbleton, Gumbleton Office, Bagley Street, Detroit, MI.

13. Correspondence from Tom Gumbleton to Franziska Jägerstätter, on the occasion of her 90th birthday, shared by Molly Fumia in May 2021, who noted that Franziska had saved this letter and it was found by Franziska's daughter, Maria Dammer.

Chapter 14: Ministry in Detroit and Michigan

1. TJG, personal interview, Frankfort, MI, Feb. 4, 2021.

2. Campbell Gibson and Kay Jung, "Table 23. Michigan: Race and Hispanic Origin for Selected Large Cities and Other Places: Earliest Census to 1990," *United States Census Bureau*, Feb. 2005.

3. TJG, personal interview. Portland, OR, Sept. 24–25, 2018.

4. Tom Lumpkin, "An Interview with Tom Gumbleton," *On the Edge*, Winter, 1996, p. 1.

5. Cathey DeSantis, CSJ, personal interview, Dearborn, MI, Sept. 10, 2019.

6. Laurie Hansen, "75,000 March against Contra Aid, Apartheid," *Michigan Catholic*, May 1, 1987.

7. Keir Ward, personal interview, Dearborn, MI, Sept. 12, 2019.

8. Keir Ward, personal interview, Dearborn, MI, Sept. 12, 2019.

9. Angela Thomas-Weldon, personal interview, Dearborn, MI, Sept. 6, 2019.

10. Keir Ward, personal interview, Dearborn, MI, Sept. 12, 2019.

11. TJG, *St. Leo Bulletin*, Jan. 4, 2004.

12. Angela Thomas-Weldon, personal interview, Dearborn, MI, Sept. 6, 2019.

13. TJG, personal interview, Frankfort, MI, Feb. 2, 2021.

14. TJG, homily for Almena Jones, Jan. 22, 2005. Papers of Thomas Gumbleton, Gumbleton Office, Bagley Street, Detroit, MI.

15. *Michigan Catholic*, Oct. 24, 1889. Papers of Thomas Gumbleton, Gumbleton Office, Bagley Street, Detroit, MI.

16. Mary Lou Van Antwerp, personal interview, Dearborn, MI, Sept. 13, 2019.

17. TJG, personal interview, Detroit, MI, March 1, 2021.

18. Mary Lou Van Antwerp, personal interview, Dearborn, MI, Sept. 13, 2019.

19. Mary Lou Van Antwerp, personal interview, Dearborn, MI, Sept. 13, 2019.

20. Mary Lou Van Antwerp, personal interview, Dearborn, MI, Sept. 13, 2019.

21. Bruce Drake, "Incarceration Gap Widens between Whites and Blacks," *FAC-TANK*, Pew Research Center, Sept. 6, 2013. In 2010, Black men under local, state, and federal jurisdiction were six times as likely as white men to be incarcerated—per the Bureau of Justice Statistics.

22. TJG, Christmas 2007 correspondence. Papers of Thomas Gumbleton, Gumbleton Office, Bagley Street, Detroit, MI.

23. Core City Neighborhoods, *1998 Commemorative Souvenir Book*, Oct. 15, 1998.

24. TJG, *St. Leo Bulletin*, June 18, 2006.

25. TJG, *St. Leo Bulletin*, April 1, 1990.

26. Isabel Wilkerson, "Detroit Catholics Vow to Fight Closings," *New York Times*, Oct. 3, 1988.

27. Isabel Wilkerson, "Detroit Catholics Vow to Fight Closings," *New York Times*, Oct. 3, 1988.

28. Marjorie Hyer, "Detroit Bishop Defends Inner-City Closings," *Washington Post*, May 4, 1989.

29. Isabel Wilkerson, "Detroit Catholics Vow to Fight Closings," *New York Times*, Oct. 3, 1988.

30. Marjorie Hyer, "Detroit Bishop Defends Inner-City Closings," *Washington Post*, May 4, 1989.

31. Peter Gavrilovich, "Gumbleton: Church Plan Deplorable," *Detroit Free Press*, Dec. 1, 1988.

32. David Crumm, "City Hearing on Church Closings Spawns Legal Questions, Protests," *Detroit Free Press*, March 10, 1989.

33. David Crumm, "City Hearing on Church Closings Spawns Legal Questions, Protests," *Detroit Free Press*, March 10, 1989.

34. Marjorie Hyer, "Detroit Bishop Defends Inner-City Closings," *Washington Post*, May 4, 1989.

35. TJG, personal interview, Detroit, MI, March 11, 2021.

36. Gregg Krupa, "Lay Catholic Ministers Aid City's Poor," *Detroit News*, Nov. 26, 2007.

37. Hilary Herbold, "Never a Level Playing Field: Blacks and the GI Bill," *The Journal of Blacks in Higher Education*, no. 6 (1994): 104–8.

38. Tom Lumpkin, "An Interview with Tom Gumbleton."

39. *Catholic Caucus of SE Michigan Tenth Anniversary Booklet*, Sept. 10, 2001. Papers of Thomas Gumbleton, Gumbleton Office, Bagley Street, Detroit, MI.

40. TJG, Letter to Pastors, Oct. 4, 1996. Papers of Thomas Gumbleton, Gumbleton Office, Bagley Street, Detroit, MI.

41. TJG, letter to Adam Maida, Oct. 17, 1998. Papers of Thomas Gumbleton, Gumbleton Office, Bagley Street, Detroit, MI.

42. TJG, letter to Adam Maida, Oct. 22, 1998. Papers of Thomas Gumbleton, Gumbleton Office, Bagley Street, Detroit, MI.

43. "Seminary Meeting Features Advocate of Abortion, Euthanasia, and Gay Rights," *The Wanderer*, Sept. 10, 1998.

44. Marguerite Kowaleski, letter to Cardinal Adam Maida, Oct. 25, 1998. Papers of Thomas Gumbleton, Gumbleton Office, Bagley Street, Detroit, MI.

45. Adam Cardinal Maida, letter to Ms. Marguerite Kowaleski, Nov. 5, 1998. Papers of Thomas Gumbleton, Gumbleton Office, Bagley Street, Detroit, MI.

46. Adam Cardinal Maida, letter to Most Reverend Thomas J. Gumbleton, Dec. 2, 1998. Papers of Thomas Gumbleton, Gumbleton Office, Bagley Street, Detroit, MI.

47. Tom Lumpkin, personal interview. Dearborn, MI, Sept. 14, 2019.

48. Tom Lumpkin, personal interview. Dearborn, MI, Sept. 14, 2019.

49. Tom Lumpkin and Thomas Gumbleton, letter of May 26, 2004. Papers of Thomas Gumbleton, Gumbleton Office, Bagley Street, Detroit, MI.

50. Tom Lumpkin, personal interview. Dearborn, MI, Sept. 14, 2019.

51. TJG, correspondence 2004–present. Papers of Thomas Gumbleton, Gumbleton Office, Bagley Street, Detroit, MI.

52. TJG, personal interview, Frankfort, MI, May 14, 2021.

Chapter 15: Ministry and the Sex Abuse Crisis in the Church

1. TJG, personal interview, Portland, OR, Sept. 24–25, 2018.

2. Bill Frogameni, "Barbara Blaine, Founder of Sex Abuse Survivor Group SNAP, Dies," *National Catholic Reporter*, Sept. 25, 2017.

3. Jim Siegal and Dennis Mahoney, "Silence Shattered on Sex Abuse," *The Columbus Dispatch*, Jan. 12, 2006.

4. "The Bishop as Victim," *Toledo Blade*, Jan. 19, 2006.

5. TJG, personal interview, Portland, OR, Sept. 24–25, 2018.

6. Jodi Wilgoren, "Bishop Backs Bills Allowing Old Abuse Cases," *New York Times*, Jan. 12, 2006.

7. TJG, personal interview, Portland, OR, Sept. 24–25, 2018.

8. TJG, correspondence with Chair of Ohio House Judiciary Committee, Jan. 12, 2006. Papers of Thomas Gumbleton, Gumbleton Office, Bagley Street, Detroit, MI.

9. Cathy Lynn Grossman, "Bishop Declares He Was Abused," *USA Today*, Jan. 12, 2006.

10. TJG, personal interview, Portland, OR, Sept. 24–25, 2018.

11. Zoe Ryan, "Bishop Tells of Being Forced from Parish," *National Catholic Reporter*, Nov. 25–Dec. 8, 2011.

12. Adam Cardinal Maida, correspondence with Thomas Gumbleton, Jan. 14, 2006. Papers of Thomas Gumbleton, Gumbleton Office, Bagley Street, Detroit, MI.

13. TJG, correspondence with His Holiness Pope John Paul II, Jan. 25, 2005. Papers of Thomas Gumbleton, Gumbleton Office, Bagley Street, Detroit, MI.

14. Cardinal Giovanni Re, correspondence with Bishop Thomas Gumbleton, Sept. 17, 2005. Papers of Thomas Gumbleton, Gumbleton Office, Bagley Street, Detroit, MI.

15. TJG, "Statement to the Community at St. Leo's, Jan. 26, 2006." Papers of Thomas Gumbleton, Gumbleton Office, Bagley Street, Detroit, MI.

16. Editorial, "People's Pastor: May Bishop Gumbleton's Voice of Justice Carry On," *Detroit Free Press*, Jan. 27, 2006.

17. Joan Chittister, "Gumbleton: Nothing but the Truth," *National Catholic Reporter*, Feb. 1, 2007.

18. Adam Cardinal Maida, correspondence with Thomas Gumbleton, Jan. 14, 2006. Papers of Thomas Gumbleton, Gumbleton Office, Bagley Street, Detroit, MI.

19. TJG, personal interview, Frankfort, MI, April 23, 2021.

20. Patricia Montemurri, "Bishop, Diocese Dispute Efforts," *Detroit Free Press*, Jan. 16, 2006.

21. TJG, correspondence with Ned McGrath, April 3, 2006. Papers of Thomas Gumbleton, Gumbleton Office, Bagley Street, Detroit, MI.

22. Patricia Montemurri, Jim Schaefer, and David Crum, "Bishop Tells of His Abuse as He Fights for Victims," *Detroit Free Press*, Jan. 12, 2006.

23. Editorial, *Toledo Blade*, Jan. 19, 2006.

24. Montemurri, "Bishop, Diocese Dispute Efforts."

25. Ned McGrath, "Detroit Archdiocese on Abuse Claim by Bishop Thomas Gumbleton," Jan. 11, 2006. Papers of Thomas Gumbleton, Gumbleton Office, Bagley Street, Detroit, MI.

26. Cathy Lynn Grossman, "Bishop Declares He Was Abused."

27. Jo Renee Formicola, "The Politics of Clerical Sexual Abuse," *MDPI*, Jan. 8, 2016, p. 9.

28. Editorial. "A Path to Justice," *New York Times*, Jan. 18, 2006.

29. The Quinnipiac Polling Institute, "Sex Abuse Priests and the Bishops Who Hid Them Should Go, American Catholics Tell Quinnipiac University Poll; Catholics 3-1 Want Equal Say in Dealing with Issue," Quinnipiac University, June 12, 2002. Cited in Formicola, "The Politics of Clerical Sexual Abuse," 6.

30. Montemurri, Schaefer, and Crum, "Bishop Tells of His Abuse as He Fights for Victims."

31. Montemurri, "Bishop, Diocese Dispute Efforts."

32. Michelle Boorstein and Gary Gately, "More than 300 Accused Priests Listed in Pennsylvania Report on Catholic Church Sex Abuse," *Washington Post*, Aug. 14, 2018.

33. Nicole Winfield, "Pope Francis Vows to End Sexual Abuse after McCarrick Report," *Associated Press*, Nov. 11, 2020.

34. Adam Cardinal Maida, correspondence with Thomas Gumbleton, Feb. 14, 2006. Papers of Thomas Gumbleton, Gumbleton Office, Bagley Street, Detroit, MI.

35. TJG, correspondence with Cardinal Adam Maida, Feb. 18, 2006. Papers of Thomas Gumbleton, Gumbleton Office, Bagley Street, Detroit, MI.

36. Adam Cardinal Maida, correspondence with Thomas Gumbleton, March 3, 2006. Papers of Thomas Gumbleton, Gumbleton Office, Bagley Street, Detroit, MI.

37. TJG, *St. Leo Bulletin,* July 2, 2006. Papers of Thomas Gumbleton, Gumbleton Office, Bagley Street, Detroit, MI.

38. Maria Davis, Report from Vicariate Meeting, Oct. 20, 2002. Papers of Thomas Gumbleton, Gumbleton Office, Bagley Street, Detroit, MI.

39. TJG, *St. Leo Bulletin,* Oct. 29, 2006. Papers of Thomas Gumbleton, Gumbleton Office, Bagley Street, Detroit, MI.

40. TJG, correspondence with John Quinn, Dec. 1, 2006. Papers of Thomas Gumbleton, Gumbleton Office, Bagley Street, Detroit, MI.

41. TJG, *St. Leo Bulletin,* Dec. 24, 2006. Papers of Thomas Gumbleton, Gumbleton Office, Bagley Street, Detroit, MI.

42. Dennis Coday, "Gumbleton Removed from Parish," *National Catholic Reporter*, Dec. 19, 2006.

43. Laurie Goodstein, "Outspoken Catholic Pastor Replaced; He Says It's Retaliation," *New York Times*, Jan. 26, 2007.

44. Adam Cardinal Maida, correspondence with Bishop Thomas Gumbleton, Jan. 17, 2007. Papers of Thomas Gumbleton, Gumbleton Office, Bagley Street, Detroit, MI.

45. Suzanne Sattler, personal journal, Detroit, MI, Jan. 2007.

46. TJG, "The Peace Pulpit," *National Catholic Reporter*, Jan. 25, 2007. Papers of Thomas Gumbleton, Gumbleton Office, Bagley Street, Detroit, MI.

47. Adam Cardinal Maida, "Correspondence with Bishop Gumbleton and Dear Parishioners of St. Leo's," Jan. 21, 2021. Papers of Thomas Gumbleton, Gumbleton Office, Bagley Street, Detroit, MI.

48. Maryfran Barber, IHM, phone interview, Detroit, MI, Oct. 17, 2019.

49. Goodstein, "Outspoken Catholic Pastor Replaced; He Says It's Retaliation."

50. Patricia Mish, "Detroit Auxiliary Bishop Won't Fight His Removal," *The Grand Rapids Press*, Jan. 31, 2007.

51. The Detroit Catholic Pastoral Alliance, Jan. 29, 2007. *Detroit Free Press* and *The Detroit News*. Bagley Office Files, Detroit, MI.

52. *St. Leo Bulletin,* May 13, 2007. Papers of Thomas Gumbleton, Gumbleton Office, Bagley Street, Detroit, MI.

53. Daniel Melody, "Despite Church Closure, St. Leo's Soup Kitchen Still Strives to Serve," *Detroit Catholic*, Nov. 30, 2017.

54. John D. Stoll, "Insight: Dark Holiday in Detroit as Church Downsizes," *U.S. News*, Dec. 30, 2011.

55. Peter Gavrilovich, "Gumbleton: Church Plan Deplorable," *Detroit Free Press*, Dec. 1, 1988.

56. TJG, *The Peace Pulpit*, National Catholic Reporter, Injstar.com.

Chapter 16: Character

1. Roberta Smith, "One Image of Agony Resonates in Two Lives," *New York Times*, April 4, 2009. The photo won a Pulitzer Prize for the photographer, but the publication of it aroused intense outrage. Hundreds of readers called or wrote editors wanting to know what had happened to the little girl and asking why the photographer had not helped her instead of taking her picture. Overwhelmed, the photographer committed suicide.

2. Laura Berman, "Sexual Abuse Isn't What Shaped Detroit Bishop's Life," *The Detroit News*, Jan. 19, 2006.

3. TJG, personal interview, Portland, OR, Sept. 24–25, 2018.

4. "Pastoral Constitution on the Church in the Modern World," *The Sixteen Documents of Vatican II* (Boston, MA: Daughters of St. Paul, 1966).

5. TJG, personal interview, on road trip between Erie, PA, and Detroit, MI, Sept. 19, 2019.

6. TJG, personal interview, Frankfort, MI, Jan. 15, 2022.

7. TJG, personal interview, Detroit, MI, Nov. 19, 2020.

8. Daniel Tillas and Johanna Berrigan, Zoom conversation, Orlando, FL, and Philadelphia, PA, Aug. 23, 2021.

9. Therese Terns, personal interview, Dearborn, MI, Sept. 10, 2019.

10. TJG, personal interview, Frankfort, MI, May 5, 2021.

11. Pope Paul VI, *Populorum Progressio*, 21.

12. TJG, personal interview, Frankfort, MI, June 8, 2021.

13. Kathy Kelly, phone interview, Chicago, IL, Oct. 1, 2020.

14. Suzanne Sattler, Papers of Suzanne Sattler, Sattler Office Files, Detroit, MI.

15. Nancy Driscoll, correspondence with Sue Sattler, Nov. 15, 2021.

16. TJG, Notes on Prayer, AUND, CGUM, box 47, folder title: Prayer 1970.

17. Johanna Berrigan, phone interview, Philadelphia, PA, Nov. 30, 2020.

18. TJG, personal interview, Frankfort, MI, Jan. 15, 2022.

19. Eileen Burns, personal correspondence with Sue Sattler, Nov. 15, 2021.

20. Suzanne Sattler, personal papers. Papers of Suzanne Sattler, Sattler Office Files, Detroit, MI.

21. Nancy Driscoll, personal interview, Dearborn, MI, Sept. 6, 2019.

22. Janet Hunt, personal interview, Dearborn, MI, Sept. 1, 2019.

23. Joe Dailey, personal interview, Oct. 28, 2020.

24. Suzanne Sattler, personal papers. Papers of Suzanne Sattler, Sattler Office Files, Detroit, MI.

25. Peter Rosazza, phone interview, Bloomfield, CT, Oct. 26, 2020.

26. Thomas Reese, phone interview, Washington, DC, Nov. 5, 2020.

27. Suzanne Sattler, personal papers. Papers of Suzanne Sattler, Sattler Office Files, Detroit, MI.

28. Tom Fox, phone interview, Kansas City, MO, Nov. 10, 2020.

29. TJG, personal interview, Detroit, MI, Sept. 13, 2020.

30. Michael H. Crosby, OFM Cap., *Celibacy: Means of Control or Mandate of the Heart?* (Notre Dame, IN: Ave Maria Press, 1996).

31. TJG, personal interview, Detroit, MI, Aug. 1, 2021.

32. Tom Fox, phone interview, Kansas City, MO, Nov. 10, 2020.

33. Communication with JustFaith Ministries, Sept. 14, 2010, p. 6.

34. Thomas Merton, *Conjectures of a Guilty Bystander* (New York: Doubleday Image Books, 1968).

35. *Vocation to Justice: An Interview with Bishop Thomas J. Gumbleton,* Center for Concern, 2014, p.4.

36. Donald Spoto, correspondence with Frank Fromherz, Jan. 19, 2021.

37. Cindy Estrada, personal interview, Detroit, MI, Sept. 20, 2019.

38. Austen Ivereigh and Pope Francis, *Let Us Dream* (New York: Simon and Shuster, 2020), 127.

39. TJG, "The Bishop in the American Political and Economic Context," talk given at St. John's University, June 1982, AUND, CGUM, box 45, folder title: "Talks."

40. Michael E. Lee, "After 50 Years, Gutierrez's 'A Theology of Liberation' Still 'What's Going On,'" *National Catholic Reporter,* Dec. 20, 2021.

41. Jean Stokan, phone interview, Nov. 16, 2020, Washington, DC.

42. Suzanne Sattler, Papers of Suzanne Sattler, Sattler Office Files, Detroit, MI.

43. *Vocation to Justice: An Interview with Bishop Thomas J. Gumbleton,* Center for Concern, 2014, p.4.

Chapter 17: Significance

1. TJG, personal interview, Dearborn, MI, March 20, 2019.

2. Thomas Merton, *Conjectures of a Guilty Bystander* (New York: Doubleday Image Books, 1968), 156.

3. Paul Wilkes, "Bishop Gumbleton," *The Critic,* Jan.-Feb. 1974.

4. Pope Paul VI, *Humanae Vitae,* 50th Anniversary Edition (Huntington, IN: Our Sunday Visitor, 2018).

5. TJG, personal interview. Frankfort, MI, Jan. 19, 2022. See also, *U.S. Bishops Pastoral Letter on Human Life in Our Day* (New York: Paulist Press, 1969).

6. Jeanie Wylie-Kellermann, "Keeping the Faith," *Metro Times,* Dec. 5–11, 1990, p. 10.

7. Harry Cook, "U.S. Catholic Bishops Vote 238–9 to Condemn Nuclear Arms Race." *Detroit Free Press*, May 5, 1983 (via Nps), 36.

8. "Tom Gumbleton Is Passionate for the People's Voice in Selecting Bishops," Southern Illinois Synod of the Laity, June 19, 2004. Papers of Thomas Gumbleton, Gumbleton Office, Bagley Street, Detroit, MI.

9. Peter Feuerherd, "Gumbleton Decries Lack of Leaders," *National Catholic Reporter*, March 16, 2007.

10. Tom Fox, phone interview, Kansas City, MO, Nov. 10, 2020.

11. TJG, personal interview, Detroit, MI, Feb. 10, 2022.

12. TJG, personal interview, Dearborn, MI, March 20, 2019.

13. TJG, "54 Catholic Bishops Delivering Their Letter to President Clinton Today," statement at press conference, Washington, DC, Jan. 20, 1998 (via C-SPAN videos).

14. Correspondence between Perry and Dearden, April 27, 1980, and May 12, 1980, AAD, Dearden Collection, box 4, folder 7.

15. Kate DeSmet (*The Detroit News*), "Maida Backs Gumbleton in Anti-War Controversy" found in *Detroit Free Press*, Feb. 17, 1991 (via Nps), 3.

16. Colleen Kelly, phone interview, Dec. 3, 2020, Bronx, NY.

17. Oscar Chacón, personal interview, Detroit, MI, Dec. 8, 2021.

18. Daniel Tillas and Johanna Berrigan, Zoom conversation, Orlando, FL, and Philadelphia, PA, July 7, 2021.

19. "Justice in the World" by the 1971 Synod of Bishops, (#6) Second General Assembly," in *The Gospel of Peace and Justice: Catholic Social Teaching Since Pope John*, ed. Joseph Gremillion (Maryknoll, NY: Orbis Books, 1976).

20. TJG, Keynote Address, General Chapter Meeting of the Adrian Dominicans, Adrian, MI, Aug. 12, 1974, AUND, CGUM, box 45, folder title: Talks: Priests, Three Talks . . . .

21. Richard A. McCormick, SJ, "Authority and Leadership: The Moral Challenge," *America,* July 20–27, 1996, p.14.

22. Marie Dennis, phone interview, Washington, DC, 18, 2019.

23. TJG, personal interview, Portland, OR, Sept. 24–25, 2018.

24. Thomas Doyle, "VOTF and the Reform of the Governmental Structure of the Catholic Church," Jan. 2008. Papers of Thomas Gumbleton, Gumbleton Office, Bagley Street, Detroit, MI.

25. Patricia Montemurri, correspondence with Sue Sattler, Jan. 7, 2022.

26. Thomas Reese, phone interview, Washington, DC, Nov. 5, 2020.

27. John Carr, phone interview, Washington, DC, Nov. 11, 2020.

28. TJG, "An Interview with Bishop Thomas J. Gumbleton," *Education for Justice* (Des Plains, IL: Center for Justice, 2014) 16–17.

29. Gerard O'Connell, "Pope Francis Shared 8 Beatitudes for Bishops, Giving a Model for the 21st Century Pastor," *America*, Nov. 22, 2021.

30. Christine Scheck, CSJ, correspondence with Sue Sattler, Jan. 18, 2022.

31. Joan Chittister, OSB, personal interview, Erie, PA, Sept. 19, 2019.

32. Simone Campbell, SSS, phone interview, Washington, DC, 2020.

33. Mary Lou Kownacki, phone interview, Erie, PA, July 15, 2021.

Chapter 18: Final Questions for the Road Ahead

1. TJG, phone interview, Frankfort, MI, May 7, 2022.

INDEX

"Called to Global Solidarity" statement, 176

Call to Action, 50, 138, 219
Bicentennial Call to Action, 49–54, 60–61, 127
gay discrimination, resolutions against, 52, 127
Campbell, Simone, 266
Carr, John, 263
Carry, Mary and William (Bill), 127–28, 151, 213, 251
Carter, Jimmy, 49, 66, 68, 73, 78, 80
Carter, Kevin, 243
Casaroli, Agostino, 97, 101
Casey, Juliana (Julie), 83, 101, 103
Cassidy, Sally, 37
Catholic Caucus, 225–26
Catholic Laity United, 159
Catholic Peace Fellowship, 57, 59
Catholic social teaching, 225, 226, 266
Catholic War Veterans (CWV), 106
Catonsville Nine trial, 11
Cavanah, Jerome, 36
celibacy, 35, 39–40, 252
Chablani, Raj, 226
Chacón, Guillermo, 151
Chacón, Oscar, 151, 152, 260–61
Challenge of Peace pastoral letter, 105, 106, 117, 270
church teaching on war, plenary examination of, 82–83
defense officials' testimonies, considering, 86–87
Gumbleton commitment to, 88–89, 113, 122, 258
Hannan suggestion to drop project, 95–96
Hunthausen's call to conscience, 90–91
just war theology, exploring, 84–85
on nuclear deterrence, 91–92, 93–94, 97, 109–10, 115
press coverage of, 103–4
promotion of letter, 106–7
Ratzinger messages to draft committee, 98–99
as a teaching tool, 121–22, 174
women's voices regarding, 101–2
Chamorro, Edgar, 159
Chaput, Charles, 139, 140

Charter for the Protection of Children and Young People, 234
Cheney, Dick, 187
Chittister, Joan, 93–94, 171, 172, 227, 232, 266
Chopko, Mark, 234, 235
The Church and the Arms Race (Pax Christi), 63, 64
The Church and the Homosexual (McNeill), 131
Church of the Madonna, 33, 36
civil disobedience, 4, 107, 121, 174, 176
Bourgeous as jailed for, 108
of the Cantonsville Nine, 11
Gumbleton and, 12, 109, 112–18
Latin American injustices as inspiring, 164–65, 167
nonviolence as an aspect of, 113, 185
Clark, Ramsey, 178
Clark, William, 95, 100
Clarke, Maura, 149
Clinton, Bill, 165, 166, 168, 174, 175, 176, 197, 260
Clinton, Farley, 46–47
Cochrane, Mickey, 24
Cockrel, Sheila Murphy, 37
Coffin, William Sloane, 70–72, 75, 76, 77, 118
Colbert, Chuck, 138
Community for Creative Nonviolence (CCNV), 58
Conference of Major Superiors of Religious Men, 83
Congregation for the Doctrine of the Faith, 97, 136, 141, 143, 144
Conjectures of a Guilty Bystander (Merton), 257
Connolly, Thomas, 13
conscience, 8, 87, 98, 138, 188, 258
of Catholics, 99, 103, 105, 172, 176
civil disobedience as an act of, 107–8, 109, 121
Communists' violation of conscience, 95–96
of Gumbleton, 22, 55, 63–66, 156
Hunthausen's call to conscience, 90–91
personal conscience, 6, 52, 105, 117, 139, 143, 144